CONTENTS

Introduction   i

1861

October, November & December:
"I am as yet but very slightly acquainted with military matters"   1

1862

January: "We live a jolly, free and easy life"   10

February: "If the war goes on at this rate, we may as well all come home in a week"   34

March: "If the Rebels fight at all, they will fight near Richmond"   56

April: "We are on the eve of a great contest"   73

May: "The Rebellion seems now to be collapsing"   94

June: "The men were now falling every few moments"   117

July: "A great deal of faith in McClellan is gone"   151

August: "Let the Rebels see that we are alive still"   187

September: "The slaughter was worse than anything I have ever seen"   205

October: "The usual amount of hard marching and exposure"   224

November: "No General in his senses would undertake a winter campaign"   236

December: "A senseless butchery of men"   252

1863

January: "Stuck fast in the mud"   278

February: "At last at rest and granting furloughs"   308

March: "Where is the enthusiasm of this time last year?" 320

April: "We shall meet with nothing but disaster" 337

May: "The Army won't bear useless slaughtering much longer" 356

June: "Led to destruction by ignorant and incompetent men" 370

July, October & November:
"An unusual bereavement has befallen us" 382

Appendices

Appendix A: Biographical sketch of Henry Ropes 386

Appendix B: Historical sketch of the Twentieth Regiment Massachusetts
Volunteer Infantry 392

Appendix C: Detailed combat losses of the Twentieth Massachusetts
Volunteer Infantry 394

RIGHT UP INTO THE FIRE

—

The Civil War Letters of
Lieutenant Henry Ropes,
20th Massachusetts Volunteer Infantry

—

Edited by
John Codman Ropes & Florian Dexheimer

Copyright © 2017 Florian Dexheimer

Konrad-Adenauer-Ring 41B
67292 Kirchheimbolanden
Germany

Source manuscripts: Rare Books Department, Boston Public Library

All rights reserved.

ISBN: 1981585192
ISBN-13: 978-1981585199

Introduction

"He was in battle absolutely cool and collected, apparently unconscious of the existence of such a feeling as personal danger, the slight impetuosity and excitability natural to him at ordinary times being sobered down into the utmost self-possession, giving him an eye that noticed every circumstance, no matter how thick the shot and shell; a judgment that suggested in every case the proper measures, and a decision that made the application instantaneous. It is impossible for me to conceive of a man more perfectly master of himself; more completely noting and remembering every circumstance in times when the ordinary brave man sees nothing but a tumult and remembers after it is over nothing but a whirl of events which he is unable to separate."

Captain Henry Livermore Abbott, 20th Massachusetts Infantry

At the outbreak of the Civil War, 21-year-old Henry Ropes, son of a wealthy Boston merchant, is a student at Harvard College (Class of '62). The patriotic young man immediately takes a keen interest in military matters, and in November of 1861, with the help of influential friends he obtains a commission for a Lieutenancy in the prestigious 20th Massachusetts Volunteer Infantry. Called the "Harvard Regiment" for its officer cadre of upper class Harvard graduates, among them the future Supreme Court Justice Oliver Wendell Holmes Jr., the grandsons of Paul Revere and the great-grandson of Robert Treat Paine, the regiment soon earns a reputation for dependability and steadfastness under fire. Seeing hard service in the Army of the Potomac and fighting in most of the army's battles from the siege of Yorktown to Hatcher's Run, the regiment is bestowed with the sobriquet of "the Bloody Twentieth". The honorific is dearly paid for with staggering losses of soldiers and officers alike in the battles of Antietam, Fredericksburg and General Grant's Overland Campaign. In August of 1864, at Ream's Station, the already worn-out regiment meets with disaster and ceases to exist in all but name when its position is outflanked and overrun, though a skeleton organization of convalescents and recruits keeps its proud name alive till the end of the war.

A prolific letter-writer, Ropes keeps a constant correspondence with his parents and especially his beloved brother John. In his letters, the young lieutenant talks freely about all facets of military life, be it his opinions on the generals, the government in Washington and the conduct of the war, or the rivalries and infighting among his fellow officers, the martial abilities of the Union soldier, everyday life in camp and on the march, the horrors of battle and morale among the men, from the unswerving confidence during McClellan's Peninsula Campaign to the darkest days of despondency during the disastrous winter of 1862. All the while, Ropes serves his regiment and his country bravely and faithfully, at times losing confidence in the generals and politicians, but never in the cause of the Union. Being a product of his time and upbringing, Ropes shares the prejudices and attitudes of his class, which reveal themselves most markedly in his opinions on officers he does not consider to be "Gentlemen" and the less than enlightened convictions he holds regarding the formation of "Negro Regiments". At first, he also shows little appreciation of the "less gentlemanly" qualities of the lowly soldiers, but as the regiment's casualties are mounting and he sees the men fight and die around him, he begins to develop a genuine affection for " these poor people who have risked and endured so much".

Ropes' extensive correspondence paints a complete and vivid picture of his Civil War experiences from his first letters trying to obtain his commission to his last hurriedly jotted down lines while unknowingly marching toward the greatest battle of the war, in which the promising lieutenant's life will come to a tragic end. At Gettysburg, in the morning of July 3rd, while the confederate brigades are forming for their fateful charge and the men of the 20th Massachusetts, positioned near the famous "copse of trees", are tensely awaiting the inevitable carnage of the day, a faulty shell explodes at the muzzle of a Union cannon. One of the shell fragments tears into Ropes' back and exits through his chest, smashing his watch and stopping it at the time of his death: 09.00 AM.

These well-written and frank letters of an educated, articulate and astutely observant young man offer comprehensive insight into an officer's life in the field and into the mind of a class-conscious member of the New England Establishment.

1861

Tuesday 3 P.M.
October 22nd 1861.

Dear John.

I have seen Mr. Willard, just before dinner, and have determined to join his drill Club and shall begin to come in tomorrow at 3.15. I shall pay the expense myself, unless Father seems willing to do it for me. I have not said anything to him about it today, as I have not had a good chance. Mr. Willard is to expatiate to him on the advantages of the Club, when he sees him, and I hope you will say to Father what you can in favor of the plan when the subject comes up. If you could repay me the $10.00 you borrowed, before long, it would do to pay Mr. Willard with. There is no particular hurry about it. We have an A.D. meeting a week from today, and a "stunning" play at the H.P.C. on Friday evening.

Your affectionate brother
Henry.

Boston, October 30th, 1861.

Lt. Colonel Palfrey.
My dear Sir,

I enclose a note to you from Mrs. Col. Lee, introducing me to you as an applicant for the post of second Lieutenant in your Regiment. I applied to Col. Lee for a commission when the Regiment was first formed, and he was kind enough to offer me a second Lieutenancy, which I was at last constrained to refuse. The difficulties which then stood in my way have been removed, and I now would respectfully solicit from you the same commission.

I feel, Sir, that I am as yet but very slightly acquainted with military matters, having learnt all I know at the Harvard College Drill Club, but I now daily attend the new Rifle Club here, and hope soon to fit myself for the post. I have heard that the Regiment are to retire for the present from active service to recruit its men, and have supposed that several new Officers are to be appointed.

I also enclose three letters from Mr. Geo. O. Shattuck, from Mr. Sidney Willard, and from my brother.

I remain with great respect

Your obedient servant,
Henry Ropes.

[Letter of recommendation from George Otis Shattuck]

Boston, October 30th, 1861.

Dear Palfrey,

Henry Ropes, a son of Wm. Ropes, Esq. of this city, would like to be a second Lieutenant in the twentieth Regiment.

He is a member of the Class of 1862 at Harvard, and is well known to many of the Officers of the Regiment. Henry Ropes was one of the race crew of the Harvard Boat Club and physically is all that could be desired. As to character and pluck generally, if you know anything of the family, it is only necessary to say that he is one of them.

I learn that Col. Lee offered him a commission, but he did not then accept it, in consequence of objections in the family. The fact that they are now ready to have him go to fill the place of some one of those who have fallen at the post of duty, leaves nothing to be said of their spirit. I know of no man whose personal qualities seem to me to recommend him more highly for the post he desires, than do Ropes'.

I think you will not hesitate to give him the post, if it is in your power.

Truly yours,
Geo. O. Shattuck

RIGHT UP INTO THE FIRE

[Letter of recommendation from Sidney Willard]

Boston, October 30th, 1861.

Lt. Colonel Palfrey.
20th Regiment.
Dear Sir,

Learning that Mr. Henry Ropes was desirous of making an application for a second Lieutenant in your Regiment, allow me to say a few words in his behalf and commend him to your most favorable consideration.

I have the pleasure to say, from the experience gained in drilling several hundred men since the beginning of the year, that I consider, that Mr. Ropes will be a very valuable acquisition to your command; he is fairly drilled and is rapidly becoming thoroughly so; he is young and athletic, with plenty of energy and a very great deal of common sense; he is at present a Senior at Harvard and I believe is personally known to several of your Officers. And I must say in conclusion that he is *well* fitted to keep up the repute which the Officers of the 20th have earned for cool and determined bravery.

With great respect I remain

Yours
Sidney Willard

[Letter of recommendation from John Codman Ropes]

Boston, October 30th, 1861.

Lieut. Col. Palfrey.
Dear Sir,

Will you allow me to second the application of my brother Henry Ropes for a second Lieutenancy in the 20th Regiment? He would have gone in the Regiment in that capacity, had it not been for the strenuous objections of his parents; but now that the late terrible battle[1] has so greatly thinned the ranks of the Regiment, and deprived it of the services of so many of its Officers, he has renewed his application, and our family are all very desirous that he should obtain the commission. Perhaps it may not be out of place for me to add, that he is generally thought to be fitted for the post.

Quartermaster-General Reed told me today that the Governor gave commissions to those who were recommended by the Officers in command of Regiments, if approved by the Brigadier-General, but that he thought that vacant commissions were generally given to Warrant-Officers; but, may I suggest, that among so many vacancies, one might be selected from among the old friends, and College companions, of so many of the Officers of the 20th.

With great respect I remain.

Your obed't servant.
John C. Ropes

Cambridge, November 12th, 1861.

Lt. Colonel Palfrey.
Dear Sir,

I received last evening your letter of November 4th in reply to mine applying for a commission in your Regiment.

I am very sorry that no vacancy now exists, but will feel greatly obliged to you if you will consider me among the applicants for any future vacancy that may occur.

Thanking you for your kind consideration of my application, I remain with great respect.

Yours very truly.
Henry Ropes.

---

[1] Battle of Ball's Bluff on October 21, 1861, in which the 20th Massachusetts lost 281 men killed, wounded and missing.

RIGHT UP INTO THE FIRE

Boston, November 21st, 1861.

Lt. Colonel Palfrey.
Dear Sir,

I have received this morning your letter of November 15th. On the receipt of your former letter informing me that no vacancies then existed, I wrote to you in reply, begging you to keep my application upon your list. I fear that you did not receive this letter. I feel greatly obliged to you for the interest you have kindly manifested in my case, and would be most happy to receive an appointment whenever you may see fit to offer one to me.

With great respect I remain

Your obedient servant.
Henry Ropes.

Boston, November 28th, 1861.

Lt. Colonel Palfrey.
Dear Sir,

I have received your letter of November 15th and have delayed to answer it until I could present your letters to the Governor and receive his answer. This I have done, and find that nothing has as yet been decided in regard to the 20th Regiment, but when anything is done my case will be considered on your recommendation. It would give me great pleasure to serve in any capacity at your camp. I hear that Mr. Perkins, mentioned in your last letter, is now at the seat of war.

With renewed thanks I remain with great respect,

Your obedient servant.
Henry Ropes.

RIGHT UP INTO THE FIRE

Cambridge, December 4th, 1861.

Lt. Colonel Palfrey.
Dear Sir,

I find that a great number of applications for commissions have been made at the State House, some by men who have spent money in recruiting men, and have now been waiting a long time for promised commissions. I have tried to get a promise that whenever you may nominate me I shall have the post in your Regiment, but am told that other claims are prior, and cannot wait so well as I can, and therefore I fear that in spite of your nomination I may be passed over.

I have found it impossible to get at the Governor himself, and have been obliged to present my claims through Col. H. Lee, one of the aides. He seems very unwilling to admit my claim to the next place provided I receive your nomination, and said that had he been present he would have opposed granting a commission to Mr. Mason. His reasons are that others have prior and superior claims on the Government.

Hearing that a vacancy has just occurred by the resignation of Capt. Crowninshield[2], and fearing that my claims here would be thought slight, unless your nomination was very positive, I have written to beg you, if you see fit to nominate me, to do so with as much earnestness as possible, that the wish to have me in your Regiment you have been so kind as to express, may not be disregarded, and my own hopes dashed, by the appointment of a person you do not nominate. I shall do everything in my power to secure a commission whenever I may receive your nomination.

I remain with great respect,

Your obedient servant,
Henry Ropes.

Boston, December 14th, 1861.

Lt. Colonel Palfrey,
Dear Sir,

I have been appointed a 2d Lieutenant in your Regiment, in the place of Mr. Gordon Bolles, just resigned. I had made use of your letters to prove that it was your wish to have me appointed to the next vacancy, and had presented whatever recommendations I could obtain.

---

[2] Captain Caspar Crowninshield transferred to the 1st Massachusetts Cavalry on November 25, 1861.

RIGHT UP INTO THE FIRE

I first heard of my appointment yesterday afternoon, and this morning I have been to the State House and am told that I shall receive my commission from you at the camp. I am told to report myself to the Adjutant General when I am ready to go, and that then I shall receive an order to proceed to the camp.

I do not know how long it will take me to get my uniform made and my outfit got ready, but I understand, in general, it takes a fortnight. I should therefore like to have that length of time, and start from Boston on the 28th December, arriving in camp December 31st or January 1st, but I can get ready to start at any time you may direct, and I will be at your camp on any day you may please to order me.

As I should like to pass a day in New York, if possible, I would therefore be obliged to you if you would state what day I shall appear at your camp.

Thanking you, Sir, for your kind recommendation, I remain with great respect

Your obedient servant,
Henry Ropes.

Boston, December 26th, 1861.

Lt. Colonel Palfrey.
My dear Sir,

I have just received your letter of December 21st, and desire to express my warmest thanks for the kindness you have shown me in procuring for me this appointment. It shall be my endeavor to show by a faithful discharge of my duties, that I appreciate your kindness, and that it has not been misplaced.

I am making all haste with my preparations, and shall avail myself of your kindness by remaining till Saturday, December 28th, when I expect to be fully ready to go. If nothing prevents, I shall leave New York on Sunday evening or Monday morning and arrive in the camp on Tuesday afternoon, December 31st.

I remain with great respect,

Your obedient servant,
Henry Ropes.

RIGHT UP INTO THE FIRE

Fifth Avenue Hotel New York
December 29th, 1861.

My dear Father.

I thank you very much for your kind letter which I read in the cars on my way here. I shall always endeavor to do my duty as you say, humbly. Trusting in God for strength and support under whatever circumstances I may be placed. I thank you for all the advice contained in the letter and I shall try to profit by it.

I had a safe and comfortable journey, arrived at 5 o'clk and came here. I took a chamber, washed and felt perfectly refreshed. I breakfasted at about 8 o'clk and then walked to Mr. Trasks [sic]. Saw them all, and found them all well. I have dined with Mr. Trasks and twice attended Dr. Adams' Church. I shall take tea with them and return to this house early, and expect to take the 7 o'clk train tomorrow for Washington via Baltimore, where I shall try to spend an hour. I am perfectly well.

With much love I remain

Your affectionate son
Henry Ropes

5th Avenue Hotel
Sunday, P.M. December 29th 1861.

My dear Mother.

In my letter to Father I have said that my journey here was safe and pleasant and that I expect to go on tomorrow. I have passed a very pleasant day with Mr. Trask. Martha quite lively and the children well. Please tell Lizzie I have delivered her note and parcel to Martha.

I walked after church with Mr. Trask to and about the New Central Park. It is quite cold today and we came back with fine appetites for an excellent dinner.

I think the Sleeping Cars are much the most comfortable means of transportation. I took off my boots and hat, put on my knit sleeping cap, wrapped my feet in a blanket and was perfectly comfortable. The ventilation is excellent.

I have heard two good sermons from Dr. Adams. I may not be able to write from Washington, but shall take the earliest opportunity at the Camp, where I expect to be on Tuesday evening.

With love to all

Your affectionate son
Henry Ropes.

RIGHT UP INTO THE FIRE

National Hotel
Washington, December 30th 1861.

My dear Mother.

I passed a comfortable night in New York, and got up to a 5 ½ o'cl. breakfast this morning. The Coach left the Hotel at 6, and the Ferry left at 7, the Cars starting as soon as we got well settled and comfortably in our seats. We rode till about 6 o'cl. without getting out except to change Cars or for a moment at a station. I did not have time to go and see Keighler in Baltimore. All the way from Havre de Grace there are troops guarding the railroad and bridges. Here in the city there are Cavalry patrols, and there was a guard at the station. It was dark when I arrived and I have only seen a small part of the city and that by gaslight. It is perfectly full of soldiers and Officers and the Hotels crowded. No coach goes up to Poolesville tonight, but I have engaged passage in the first one tomorrow which leaves at 8 and expects to arrive at 5 P.M. Although I rode steadily in the cars from 7 A.M. till 6 P.M., and ate nothing nor drank between ½ past 5 A.M. and 7 P.M. yet I felt perfectly well and felt neither tired nor unpleasantly hungry. I have had no trouble at all with my baggage, and expect to have none. I shall not have time to call on Mrs. Morris here. At Philadelphia I did not stop, but rode through the city with the other passengers in horse cars. Please send me one or two of my card photographs when they are done. As to distributing some among college friends, better leave it all to John, who can do it through Hazeltine or Grinnell.

Give my love to them all and believe me

Your affectionate Son
Henry Ropes.

1862

Camp Benton, 20th Regiment
at Poolesville, Md. Jany. 1st 1862.

My dear John.

Here I am sitting in Lieut. Patten's tent, wind blowing so as to shake the canvass /sic/ very much, but warm. Lieut. Patten opposite, 2 candles between us. A little stove at one end, and the time 6.30 P.M. I shall try to write to the family a full account of my doings, and hope my letters will be kept against my return for me to write out my Journal. I shall try not to repeat the same thing in 2 letters, so please tell all the news (which is not private) to the others of the family.

On the whole I am very pleasantly disappointed in the general comfort of a camp. Whittier[3] has had a splendid log hut built and most of the tents are floored and have fires. We mess in the tents with the Company Officers. So far I have dined at other tents round. I am to have a stool and table made soon by the Carpenter. These, with a few tin plates and a basin etc. constitute the furniture of the tent. All log huts, stoves and such luxuries must be left behind on a march.

I instantly found the need of a servant, and at first thought I would have you send me one down, but I have picked up a boy here ($8.00 per month and board) who I think will do. His name is Corny, and I expect to make a good servant of him. He is smart and a regular Yankee. When I get fairly settled I shall be as comfortable as a Prince. I have now the whole of the Lieutenant's tent to myself, and shall have Corny sleep in the tent too, for I can draw for him from the Quartermaster a straw Mattress and a Blanket.

You must have a boy to cook, wait, make a fire, get wood, buy things and be generally useful. Niggers are scarce here. When we march we must leave a great deal behind, for many of the Officers have made very comfortable quarters here and have stout chairs, tables etc. I have received my commission, and shall send it with my order home as soon as convenient, to be kept safely for me. Please tell

---

[3] 1st Lieutenant Charles A. Whittier.

RIGHT UP INTO THE FIRE

Mother Herbert was very much obliged for her preserve.

All the fellows here are free and easy and very hospitable. You can eat or sleep anywhere and at any time. Lieut. Patten I like very much indeed. Macy is a very fine fellow. Herbert is doing exceedingly well is everywhere liked, and is making a *most excellent* Officer. Capt. Shepard has not a very high reputation, but he is a very kind man and I think I shall have plenty to do under him.

Excuse haste etc., for the wind is blowing terribly.

Happy new year to all. I shall write to Mary Ann[4] very soon.

Your affectionate brother
Henry Ropes.

Camp Benton,
January 1st, 1862.

My dear Father.

I wrote to Mother from Washington on Monday evening, and, on Tuesday morning I left by the Stage for Poolesville, Md. where I arrived at 5 P.M. over a road the last part of which was most horrible. I rode outside all the way in company with Mr. Low[e], the baloonist [sic], a very entertaining man. He is the Chief of the Baloon Signal Department on the Potomac, and has charge of seven baloons. He lately went up with McClellan. He has seen a great deal of the world, having been with Fremont across the Rocky Mountains, twice crossed South America from Rio to Peru, and once in North America from the Hudson's Bay settlements to the Red River. He was a very entertaining man, and I had a very pleasant ride. He asked me to call on him at his Station on the river here and perhaps I shall get an opportunity to go up with him.

I had to wait a long time at Poolesville for a wagon to take me and my luggage to Camp, but at last got one, and rode to the Camp. It was very dark, the Sentinel challenged, and I explained my visit and before long was passed in. I found Col. Palfrey in a log hut about 12 feet square, and he received me very kindly, as did all the Officers. I hear today that I am to be at first in Company K. Capt. Shepard, as his 1st Lieutenant is away, but my regular Company is to be F, Capt. Cabot,

---

[4] Henry Ropes' younger sister.

RIGHT UP INTO THE FIRE

Lieut. Harry [Henry] Sturgis. This is a most excellent place. Sturgis is our neighbor's son and a very fine fellow. Cabot is an old soldier, was with the British in the Sepoy Rebellion, and is considered a first rate Officer. At present I shall act as 1st Lieutenant. I am more than satisfied with my place. All the Officers here have treated me most kindly and done everything for me. I slept soundly last night in Hallowell's[5] tent. All the tents have either iron stoves or large stone chimneys built lately by the men, which answer as an open fireplace. Most of the tents are floored and there are several log huts, which are perfectly comfortable. I find the tents much more comfortable than I expected, and the weather is warm, and very pleasant. The 7th Michigan Regiment is camped near us, and they have built a long row of log barracks, where they are as comfortable as at home. They can all use an axe skillfully. I have received no letters as yet of course.

Give my love to all and believe me

Your affectionate son
Henry Ropes.

P.S. I am perfectly well and expect to be on duty in two days. Give all a happy new year from me.

Your affectionate son Henry.

Camp Benton 20th Mass. Regiment
near Poolesville Md. January 3rd 1862.

My dear John.

Many thanks for your New Year letter, which I have just received. Happy new year to you all. I hope soon to write a long letter to you. I saw little of Washington, but a good deal in the ride up. Virginia roads I know nothing of. Maryland ones are bad enough but as far as I can judge from here there is *nothing at all* in the state of the roads or weather which would seriously, or even slightly delay the march of this Regiment or of an Army. I feel very sure of this. Our Regiment is small now, many Officers away and men detailed for various duties,

---

[5] Captain Norwood P. Hallowell.

such as guards, outposts guards, wood chopping etc. We only turn out about 250 or 300 on battalion drill. Today I was on duty. I commanded the Company at morning Company drill and at dress parade.

The Michigan 7th, an excellent Regiment, lies between us and the River, and a New York Regiment is also in sight. The Mass. 15th 2 miles off at Poolesville, and the Mass. 19th 8 miles on the Washington road. In all about 3500 or 4000 men. The country is wide and open, and 100,000 men could easily manoeuvre (how do you spell it?) in sight of our parade ground. I should think there could not be a better country for fighting in with large armies, say of 20 or 30,000 men. However, no one knows anything, or if they do they keep it to themselves, and we live a jolly, free and easy life, that is as much so as you choose.

Tell Mr. Willard and Prof. Goodwin that I was very sorry not to see them before I left, and that I send my kindest regards. The weather is not cold here. About 25° or perhaps 28° at night is the coldest yet, and it is much warmer in the daytime. I send and buy meat etc. my boy cooks very well and does everything for me, and I get along very well indeed and am contented and happy. Bartlett[6] is a splendid Officer. So is the Colonel. He and Bartlett loaf into the tents, smoke etc., like College fellows.

I shall write to you fully if there is any sign of an advance. We passed 2 or 3 earthworks mounted with very heavy guns on the way up. It looked like business. Tell Mother her Strawberry is most excellent. I shall try the chocolate soon.

It is no use to send papers. They only come once in a very long time. Letters are very regular. I have just received yours of January 1st and am greatly obliged. Please direct to me Company K, for then the sergeant brings them to my tent.

My sleeping socks are very useful and warm. My Buffalo is invaluable. Tell Mary Ann to write me a nice long letter about *everything*. Tell her she must take a great interest in my boy Corny.

I have just received Mary Ann's letter of January 1st.

Your affectionate brother
Henry Ropes.

---

[6] Captain William F. Bartlett.

RIGHT UP INTO THE FIRE

Camp Benton, Sunday
January 5th 1862.

My dear Mother.

I received last night an envelope containing your letter of January 2nd, one from Father of the same date, one from Lizzie without date, and a note directed to "Mrs. C. H. Trask." Please thank all, and say that I have sent the letter to Martha from here by mail, as I suppose it was put in by mistake. I also received last night letters from Mary Ann of the date December 30th. These should have come to hand before, as I received letters from John and Mary Ann dated January 1st, several days ago. I suppose they were delayed at Camp till it was known to what Company I was assigned. Please mention to Mary Ann that I received her letter of Jany. 1st before that of December 30th. I have received no papers. They tell me papers are much delayed when sent by mail.

It is very cold now, and we have had snow. I have written for a number of things (a knapsack etc.). Please send me down a pair of loose fur or wool lined shoes or slippers, with moderately thick soles to come up on the foot like a rather high slipper. They are made often of leather dressed like a fur skin, and can be bought at any shoe store. Take one of the boots I gave Nash for a model and get them very large. Not however that kind made to wear *over* an ordinary boot.

Do not think I am suffering for these, for I am not, but a great many have them and they are very good to put on the first thing in the morning when we go to roll call and report to the Colonel. If you would like to send my boy a warm coat or jacket, he would be very grateful, I am sure.

I get along very comfortably here and have enough good food and warm clothing. The men are well supplied with clothes.

Today we have no drills, only the regular weekly Company inspection, and the invariable dress parade. I do not know if we shall have any religious services.

I am very much obliged for your letters and for Father's and Lizzie's, and read them with great pleasure. You must not allow yourself to get anxious for we are as safe here as at home, and there are no signs of an advance.

With love to all I remain

Your affectionate Son
Henry Ropes.

Lieut. Tilden has just gone to Boston and perhaps he, or Lt. Holmes, would bring down my knapsack containing the things I have sent for when he comes. Do not trouble yourself to send them by Express, or by any expensive means. The knapsack will contain all.

Affectionately Henry Ropes.

RIGHT UP INTO THE FIRE

Camp Benton, Monday morning
January 6th, 1862.

My dear Father.

I leave this camp this morning with 55 men of my Company, who with detachments from other Companies, in all 100 men, are detailed for picket duty on the river about 8 miles from here. The Michigan Regiment who preceded us have built excellent log huts and I expect to be perfectly comfortable. The detachment is commanded by Capt. Beckwith. We shall be absent a week, and as I probably shall not be able to write while there I thought I would write you this hasty note lest the lack of letters from me should make you anxious.

We have had an inch or two of snow, and it is cold, but I do not suffer at all. Perhaps I shall be able to write from my station.

Your affectionate son
Henry Ropes

Camp Benton, Monday evening
January 13th, 1862.

My dear Father.

I have just returned from a week's picket duty and hasten to tell you of my safety and good health. My Captain (Shepard) being unable to go with us, I had the charge of a detachment of 46 men from my Company, and we had detachments from 2 other Companies, one under Lt. Patten, and the other under Capt. Beckwith, who being the Senior Officer, commanded the whole Batalion [sic]. We marched first to Edwards' [sic] Ferry, about 2 miles, and I there first saw the Rebels, picketed on the other side of the Potomac. The river here is nearly as wide as from our house to Cambridge Bridge. The Chesapeake and Ohio Canal runs close to the river on this side, and our pickets are placed on the tow path between the Canal and the river, the whole way to Washington, or as far as the situation of our troops makes it necessary. The river is generally straight, with many long low islands, and the banks are everywhere woody. The distance between the Canal and river is about 100 to 300 feet, and varies. We marched along this tow path, in sight and hearing of the rebel pickets of Cavalry and foot,

RIGHT UP INTO THE FIRE

leaving 6 or 7 men at each post. About every half mile there is a log shanty where the men live. Lt. Patten's Company began to be posted at the Ferry, and he was left in charge. Then Capt. Beckwith's and mine last. We had in all 100 men. We left 6 men of my Company to bring along the provisions on the ice of the Canal which was frozen. The river was full of floating ice. It was quite cold. The Captain only went as far as his post and then left it to me. As the men were armed and accoutered fully with 40 rounds each, and had their knapsacks and blankets, we marched slowly, and it was 4 o'clk before I had posted my last picket. This was about 10 miles from Camp. Through some mistake of the Quartermaster's department, the provision was left some 6 miles above my lower post, and the men detailed to bring it broke through the ice and lost a large part. It was not till late in the evening that I got a small supply to my posts, and this caused me a long walk nearly to the other end of the line. I took up my abode at post No. 12. They begin at Edwards' Ferry and number down nearly to Seneca Mills in all 17 posts. As the Captain did not know the exact number of posts when he left me to finish posting the men, he gave me too many for my Company, and I was obliged to leave only 3 and 4 men at some of the lower posts. It was not till dark that I got back to my hut and took my first mouthful of food since breakfast. I had there my first sergeant, an excellent man, and 3 men. At each post sentinels are put out at dark, and kept on watch all night. They rest during the day. After 12 o'clock at night I visit every post of my Company, (I had 9), challenge the sentinels and see that all is right. This gave me 8 miles more of walking, in all about 24 miles that day. At 6 o'clk every evening the "patrol" as it is called is passed up, and repeated every 2 hours during the night. The man at the last post sends the word "All well" to the next post, he to the next, and so on through the whole line. Every morning I send to the Captain a report of the occurrences of the night. Nothing of importance occurred on Monday night, and on Tuesday evening I was ordered to remove my upper post and to reenforce the others so that at least 5 men should be on each. This I did. At the same time orders came down from Headquarters to keep a particularly sharp lookout, and I therefore placed Sergeant Campion at post 14, where there was a thick wood just on the other side of the Canal, and which I considered an important post. Campion is an old regular, went through Mexico with Scott, and is a man to be depended upon. Soon word was sent to me of shouts from the woods, and signal lights to those across the river. There is a long island here not farther from our pickets than from our house to Dr. Sharp's Church. Just at dusk the Sentinel at my post saw a body of men on the island about 30 he thought. I gave orders to post double sentinels. The standing orders I gave were not to fire except in case of attack, for every picket to be under arms at the sound of a shot, for those on either side to support the one attacked, for word instantly to be sent to me, and for all to rally on me in case of a real attack, which last was of course very unlikely to happen. I kept on the alert and at 12 o'clk started on my regular rounds. It was still and starlight. Opposite the wood I found the sentinel lying down, and on my questioning him, I found that he had heard the steps of a man in the wood opposite, had called Sergeant Campion who had also heard them distinctly, and just before I came along he had heard the snap of a cap, and had laid down to get a shot at the Rebel or whoever it was. The snapping of the cap might have been the man's imagination, but there was no doubt as to the man in the woods, who certainly was there for no good purpose. This country is full of secret enemies, who are only restrained by the presence of our troops. The next night I was hastily summoned to a lower post where the sentinels had seen a boat approaching the shore. It was foggy, and I hardly believed it, but I was obliged to tramp down to the extremity of the line, double the sentinels, and keep awake and visit the exposed posts both at night and an hour before dawn.

Then we had rainy weather, but no more alarms. Signals however were often shown from the hills, and we constantly saw the enemy's pickets. For 2 days it was very cold and the river was frozen so as to bear, and then I had to keep an extra lookout. All sleep with arms loaded, capped and at half cock, and belts etc on. I do not suppose they would cross just to attack us, but they might, and we are 10 miles from Camp, between a river and a canal, and we must keep on the alert. Although it was hard work, a good deal of walking and not much sleep at night, I enjoyed the thing, and I think it was a very good experience. My post was the most distant.

I hope I have not tired you by giving so many little particulars, but I dare say some of the family will like to hear them. I am well and very comfortable.

Your affectionate son
Henry Ropes.

Camp Benton January 14th 1862.

My dear John.

Your letter of January 10th lies before me. I am very glad you enjoyed the last A.D. so much. The mails are very uncertain and all complain of delays in the arrival of letters. I like Patten very much, but he is not a very great man, nor a very good Officer, but he is a pleasant and genial companion. It is not proper to speak

RIGHT UP INTO THE FIRE

much of other Officers but to you privately I will say (what you need not repeat) that Schmidt, Lowell and Holmes were all 3 poor Officers, though good, brave men. My little experience has shown me that business ability, fairness of judgment, consistency of character, and a spirit of disregard of personal comfort, are necessary to a good Officer. Above all he must be prompt, and not make mistakes. It will not do to see your error right after and correct it. You must decide right the first time. I have had a very good share of experience of picket duty, and have written fully to Father about it. I am very glad Joseph is to appear at Washington in a public way. He will not I think attempt the dull journey here. It is tiresome, and he has seen me so lately it would not be worth while. A man here of the Regiment takes excellent card photographs, and if I dislike my cards I shall shave, and have some taken here. At present I am unshaven and very rough. One of the large ones without uniform I liked very much, when I saw it before I left.

In regard to Ball's Bluff from what I can learn, I judge that what was needed was protection for the men and especially for the guns. This could have been easily made with logs and mud, and by digging rifle pits. In such a woody place a log and mud breastwork could have been very quickly built and would have been sufficent [sic] defence. Had our troops been able to hold their own till the next day, the Rebels would have had to retreat, with Stone and Banks behind and on their flanks, and our men pursuing them. 500 more men of the 20th and 19th Mass. were so near that they could have been got across by midnight, with at least a full battery of Cannon. Baker of course should have foreseen all difficulties and provided therefore. It might have been however that a Rebel force was in reserve sufficient to overwhelm *any* force we could have brought, but I see no proof of this. Logs and mud are an excellent protection and speedily raised. The second day I was on picket a heavy boat with 6 horses came up and broke the ice before it. It was followed by a small steam tug having in tow 3 large barges fully supplied with seats, oars, thole pins etc., and each capable of carrying 100 men, and of being rowed quite rapidly thus loaded. They were wide, full, yet sharp boats, and I saw them near Edwards' ferry when I came up yesterday. As the tug past [sic] by my post (about 12 o'cl. in the day) it stopped a few moments for the ice and a Gentleman came out of the little cabin and stood a few moments looking round, and then went back to the cabin. He wore an Officers [sic] overcoat, without the cape, had on a knit worsted cap, and was smoking a cigar. One of my men recognized him and told me it was Genl. Stone. I approached and saluted, thinking he wanted to ask some question. He bowed, but said nothing and soon returned to the Cabin. He is [a] good-sized, good looking man, with full black (or nearly black) beard etc. He looks like a cool, steady man, but not like a long-headed Dr. Walker kind of man at all, and I am sorry to add, not like a man in earnest about a great thing. He looked to me like what I imagine some good

RIGHT UP INTO THE FIRE

French Officer to be, who was brave, but not foreseeing, able, but not one trustworthy. He does not look like a traitor at all, but like a man who had no very particular sense of duty in anything beyond his mere military station and duties. However, this is only a guess at first sight. Be careful how you repeat this from me for I am an Officer now.

Last night it began to snow, and this morning we had 2 or 3 inches, and it has been very cold all day. Now (3 P.M.) it is snowing again. This is regular New England weather, and in common tents without floors or fires, it would be very uncomfortable indeed, and there would be much sickness. I think now that an advance at this season would not be attempted, unless it was certain that in a week we should reach a town or a place for a permanent camp like this. Marching all day wet, and sleeping in snow is no joke. It is pretty rough now under canvass. The men, and many Officers, have log huts. You speak of other Regiments. The 7th Michigan is the one I have seen most of. It is a good Regiment. Men, real stout Americans, full of strength and earnestness. Officers middle-aged men, and good, but not attentive to little particulars of etiquette etc. I am sure it will fight well. I have not received the Newspaper you say you sent. I was greatly humiliated to see that Mason and Slidell have gone off in an English gunboat. I do not much like the landing of troops at Portland. A riot might have occurred. It would have been better to wait till the British Government asked permission.

After a small dog has given up his bone to a big one, there is no use in offering the crumbs. It is not the time for extra compliments, and there was no call for such a privilege. I am very glad you enjoyed that final A.D. I look back with feelings of pleasant remembrance I am unable to express on my college life, my club table, my societies, and especially the A Δ Φ. May it long prosper! Who are the present Officers?

I can look back now on several periods of my life and events, which I shall not ever know again. I shall never forget my college friends, and often think of them now. I do not in the least regret that I came here, on the contrary, I am very glad. I saw it my duty to come, but, if ever I return, there will be great changes at home and I shall probably be a different man. I am more than satisfied with military life. There is always something you can do to employ your time and mind, and something, too, you are better for having done. It is a good thing to learn not so set much by personal comfort and even happiness, and not make too many hopeful plans for the uncertain future.

I shall send back by Capt. Beckwith or some man your flask which leaks, and my boots, which need mending. They were put too near the fire and had the sides nearly burnt off. I also send to you a bit of wood, a part of the scow in which the troops crossed over to Ball's Bluff, and which afterwards sank with the wounded men. It was washed ashore near my picket. If you do not want it, keep it labelled against my return. Please have Rice (or some other good workman) repair the boots and send them back to me. Please send me the bottle of Cherry Cordial I left, and a bottle of best brandy and 2 dish clothes. Do not send these by Express. I will send some private on furlough to you for them by and by.

I fear this is a very long letter.

Your affectionate brother
Henry Ropes.

Camp Benton January 18th 1862.

My dear John.

I received your letter of January 15th last evening, and I am very much obliged to you for getting and sending the slippers etc. I have sent by Corporal Goodrich my torn boots and the bit of wood from the Ball's Bluff scow about which I wrote to you. Please let the boots be mended as soon as possible. I will send some man to you, if I can who will bring them back to me. Please get and send to me a flask which does not leak. Better get an India Rubber or metal one, and have it filled with the *very best* brandy. I rarely take any, but when I do it is for medicine, and I want it good. I had the slightest touch of diarrhoea the other day, and I took about ½ of my flask, in small doses. I have not drunk a wineglass of anything since I came except this. Indeed I do not care for brandy and whisky and these are all there is. Please send me a package, about 2 lbs. of the best of ground Coffee. We drink it here all the time, and as we rarely get milk it is very desirable to have it good. That from the Quartermaster is only fair. Please send a small box of solidified milk also. All these things: milk, slippers, brandy, flask etc. I wish you to keep an account of for me to pay when I receive my pay. I shall insist on this as if I do not pay, I shall not send for things, and I wish now to support myself. Do not put yourself to any trouble to send things. Men are always going home on furlough and I will send them to you. When you get anything better keep it wrapped up and directed to me, to be called for.

I have just found out that the Governor has dated my commission November 25th 1861. The others', Patten's, Herbert's, Murphy's and Riddle's are, I believe all dated the same date, on purpose that the Colonel may give us rank according to our merit, not to mere date of commission. Thus you see I am entitled to about 1 month's more pay, and had I been a few days earlier and had my name entered at a general muster which took place, I should have received about $100.00. I do not know if it is fair for me to take this pay for time I did not serve, but shall explain the whole to the Paymaster, and let him judge.

The Regiment has just been paid off by Paymaster Major King, a very pleasant man. He told me at the end of the next 2 months I should receive 3 month's pay, about $300.00. So I shall make my hundred last till then, and after that time be rich enough. Do not let them refuse to allow me to pay for what I send for, otherwise I shall deny myself many things I want. Things are very dear here, except necessaries, which you draw for from the Quartermaster and have deducted from your pay. You have to buy food for yourself here, and keep house. The Sutler has luxuries such as cakes, oysters (sealed up in tin), pickles, candy, and quantities of other things, and he lets your bill always run till pay day. I shall send back your flask soon, and perhaps some few other things I find useless. It is now raining and we have had a very great deal of bad weather, rain, snow and deep mud.

I should be delighted to see Professor Goodwin, and would be greatly pleased if he would accept of the shelter of my tent, and put up with camp fare for as long as he would like to stay. I hope you will come down here and pass a week at least. Bring warm clothes and you will have a very pleasant time. It is worth while to visit the 7 or 8 Regiments and batteries near here, and you can be my guest and have as good a place to sleep as anyone. If you can get a passage up on a canal boat it would be very pleasant and you would see lots of pickets. You can have your baggage brought up from Edwards' Ferry in one of the many trains constantly going there. Better leave everything not absolutely needed at the Hotel in Washington. I had not heard of Cameron's resignation. I occasionally see a Baltimore paper, but have got but one yet from home. Try directing them via Poolesville, Md.

Do come and pay me a visit. It will not be very expensive to you as you must be my guest here, and my boy will cook you anything, make a fire before you rise, heat water and do anything.

Nothing new in Camp.

Your affectionate brother
Henry Ropes.

RIGHT UP INTO THE FIRE

[Letter from Captain Allen Shepard to Lieutenant Colonel Francis W. Palfrey]

Camp Benton, January 18th, 1862.

Colonel,

I understand that Lieut. Ropes was attached to my company temporarily. He has made a very favorable impression upon me, seeming to be a man of character, honor, and of correct principles. The men of the company also like him much. I should be gratified by his being *permanently assigned* to Company K.

Respectfully, Sir.
A. Shepard
Capt. Comp. K.
20th Regiment Mass. Volunteers.

Lt. Col. F. W. Palfrey.
Commanding 20th Reg. Mass. Vol.

Camp Benton, January 20th 1862.

My dear Mother.

I have to acknowledge your nice letter of January 11th, and I yesterday received by Capt. Bartlett the knapsack, and the many nice and useful things it contained including your note. Please accept Cornie's thanks for the book, which he enjoys, and thank Mary Ann very much from him for the knife. Do not send him any more presents, he will be too much elated. I hope you have not bought him a coat, for I have got a stout frock for him, which answers every purpose. The Gingerbread is delicious. You expressed some anxiety about my eyes. They have not given me the slightest trouble since I came here, and this I think is owing to the fact that I am obliged to spend about all the time in the open air, and go to bed early. When I am Officer of the Guard, for which duty my turn comes about once a week, I have to be up all night in a log hut, and inspect the reliefs every 2 hours, and then I have a great deal of time to read and write letters. I have a pot of coffee and a piece of bread, and I do not mind sitting up at all. The furshoes *[sic]* are just what I want, and are I think better for being thick. I was very much astonished when I saw my photographs, to find them so good, after you had condemned them so strongly. I do not think the bad fit of the coat of much consequence, and I think the likeness excellent, and the attitude easy. I send them back, having marked "good" on the backs of the two best. I feel perfectly satisfied with them, and do not think I could get a better. As far as I am concerned, I should like to have these 2 struck off and distributed. However, if you really are dissatisfied with them, and others are too, I can have some taken here. I intend to let the man here take my tent, with me standing in front, my boy near, and perhaps one or two of the sergeants. I have quite made friends with the men. One of them recently had a box come to him from home, and sent to me a present of a good piece of ham. One of the sergeants, a very queer fellow, a German Jew by birth, a great lover of good eating, has made me a most delicious pudding. This same man got for me a pair of quails when we were on picket. I am very glad to hear that Col. Lee is better treated, and I cannot but hope he may yet be exchanged.[7] If the Government had determined not to exchange, I should think they would have appointed a new Colonel long ago.

I should like to have a good copy of my club table kept for me.

Your ever affectionate Son
Henry Ropes.

Camp Benton, January 20th, 1862.

My dear Father.

I have to acknowledge your letter of January 11th and also that of the 15th by Capt. Bartlett, together with the knapsack and its contents. We can get really no news at all here, and I am always very glad to hear through your letters what the prospects of the war are. In the knapsack are 2 papers which I shall take great pleasure in reading. We have had heavy and continued rains for 4 days now, and the mud is dreadfully deep. It would be well nigh impossible to advance through such roads except for a few days with some village to quarter in before the troops had been long exposed to the wet.

---

[7] Colonel William R. Lee was captured at Ball's Bluff.

RIGHT UP INTO THE FIRE

The men are so well supplied with stockings and mittens that I have been unable to dispose of those I brought, but they will be needed before long no doubt. I would like you to send me a package of tracts for the men. One of my Company said he should like some. As I wrote to John, it is only necessary to do up in a package anything I write for and I will notify you where to send it or have it called for, so that it may come down by something returning from furlough. Capt. Beckwith, my commander on picket, and Lieut. Whittier both of this Regiment, leave today for Boston and I dare say they would be glad to bring down everything you may have to send.

Since I have been here, there has not been any religious service in the camp, except at the burial of a poor man wounded at Ball's Bluff, which took place the Sunday before last. Col. Palfrey then read the Episcopal service in a very impressive manner. There is quite a good Episcopal Church at Poolesville, about 2 ½ miles off where I shall try to go, but the Capt. has been heretofore and when he goes I must stay with the Company. I think we ought to have a Chaplain and the Government is remiss in not appointing one.

Please to give my love to all and believe me

Your affectionate son
Henry Ropes.

Camp Benton, January 20th 1862.

My dear John.

I am writing a great many letters today because I am confined to my tent, and am just getting better from quite a little attack of fever. Please do not tell any of the family, as it would make Mother very anxious, and I have not mentioned it to anyone but you. It came on quite suddenly the day before yesterday, and I have had the Doctor and a man to sit up one night, but today I am up though confined to my tent, and quite weak. I think it must have resulted from exposure on picket. We had very warm rains and damp, foggy nights, and poor food. However I am about well now, and as soon as it is fine, shall be out again. Do not tell them at home. Capt. Beckwith and Lieut. Whittier left today on leave of absence, and if you like, you might see them, and send any little thing to me. Capt. Beckwith is a jolly, old soldier. I spoke to an intelligent sergeant about Ball's Bluff the other day, and he says the Railroad to Leesburg was running all night after the battle, and bringing any number of Rebel troops, so, had our troops stayed and hastily entrenched themselves, they must soon have been overpowered as the enemy had the power to gather troops two times faster than we. I read with great interest the passage of the river Danver*/s/*. I shall not receive pay for 2 months, and as the Quartermaster now requires Cash for food I may have to borrow 20 or 30 $, before that time. After that I shall have plenty.

Your affectionate brother
Henry Ropes.

Enclosed letter for Mary Ann.

Camp Benton, January 23rd, 1862.

My dear Father.

I received last night a large number of letters including one from you of January 18th for which I am very much obliged. I am glad my letters about picket did not tire you. If I ever get home I shall take great pleasure in looking them over. As you say, I ought constantly to feel that my life is uncertain, and to be prepared, and I hope that I do feel so. I have the same opportunity for private devotion here that I had at home, for I am alone in the tent. I generally rise some time before reveille, and have a half hour for prayer and reading. Although we may at any time be called on to face danger, it is impossible to keep up a feeling of seriousness on that account, but I am surprised to find an undercurrent of religious feeling here, in many men whom I am sure at home are rarely troubled with thoughts about death and another world. One who has always been considered wild and dissipated in Boston, told me that before the battle of Ball's Bluff he spent some time in prayer, and that it did him so much good, and so fixed his mind on religious things, that he felt during and after the battle that he was never in so fit a state to die as at that time. I think that in general the young men here (only 2 or 3 of whom are communicants) are much more seriously disposed and are better men than they were at home in Boston.

There is no immorality here at all, and no opportunity for it, and no obscenity in conversation. I was almost astonished at the *total* absence of this last vice, which is often very common among young men. I have written thus fully on these matters because you have given me so much kind advice in your letters, and I thought you would like to know how things are here. For myself, the only religious exercise I have in the least omitted is church going. Hitherto I have been unable to go, but I hope in future to attend frequently.

It has today ceased to rain, but is very cloudy and damp. Genl. Stone has been here, and estimated our strength etc., and it is said is preparing for a move. Quartermaster Folsom however told me a long march was impossible in the present state of the roads. I rejoiced to hear last night of the victory in Kentucky.[8] I hope we shall soon take Bowling Green, and then if Burnside makes a successful move, the Rebels must concentrate somewhere or be driven by superior numbers from every stronghold. I hardly think we shall attack them here till a victory is gained nearer the sea-coast. I felt very much grieved to hear of Mr. Codman's death. He was an excellent man, and a good husband and father, and very generally respected. I did not suppose I should see him again when I left. I shall add a few words to Mother on the next page. Perhaps the first part of this letter had better not be read out loud.

I remain

Your ever affectionate son
Henry Ropes.

Camp Benton January 23rd 1862.

My dear Mother.

I believe I have no letter from you to answer but as I have a few things to ask for I drop you a line. I want a common Card Almanac for 1862. Please let John get and send it to me.

You know I keep house here and have my own cooking done by my boy. Will you give me a few receipts to make some simple dishes? Tell me how to make a simple and nourishing soup. I can get rice, salt, or fresh meat, and dried vegetables, finely cut up and pressed. Tell me how much you boil the rice and meat. Tell me how to make one or two simple puddings. I cannot often bake but can always boil and fry. How is dipped toast made? How an omelet? How

---

[8] Battle of Mill Springs on January 19, 1862.

poached and scrambled Eggs? How some simple bread puddings? These will do, I think. I forgot boiled beef. Can I make this good? Do not give me too many. I should be much obliged for the above. I am well and there is no news here. Knapsack and all came safe. I am having a cooking place built opposite my tent which will be very convenient.

Good bye.

Your affectionate Son
Henry.

Camp Benton, January 24th 1862.

My dear John.

I shall send you by Capt. Shepard who soon goes home on a sick leave a parcel containing your leaking flask, the 2nd volume of the Caxtons and a parcel for Mary Ann, which please be careful of. When I send home to you some money at next pay day you can get the other volume and keep the book. You can send to me by the Captain the boots and the flask I wrote to you of. Have the latter well filled. I want now some more paper. Send some about the size of this only wider and ruled. Do not send other kinds or envelopes. Also please send some stout line about 100 feet, as strong as a stout cod line. Also a nipple wrench for my pistol, as I have lost mine. Better let Mr. Willard direct you in regard to the latter as he will remember the size. You know in this out of the way place one has to send for almost anything. The few things that are good which the Sutler has, or which are at the Stores at Poolesville are abominably dear. Hallowell's brother just joined the Regiment as 2nd Lieutenant. He has been assigned to Company F, Capt. Cabot. As both Cabot & Sturgis knew him well in the 4th battalion, I suppose they asked for him, and he will be there permanently. So I may have to remain in Company K. It is not proper for me here to express an opinion in regard to my own position, but of course you know I would very much like to feel really settled in so good a company as F. As it is I may be put in A, Capt. Tremlett, considered one of the very best places, Whittier 1st Lieutenant. Whittier spoke to me about it. The trouble is that Capt. Shepard likes me, for I do all the work, and he told me he had asked the Colonel for me, and the men like me too. This is of course private. As it is now, I manage the Company myself, the Captain being on the sick list. I do not chum or eat with the Captain, and I can get along perfectly with him in business matters. I do not know what 1st Lieutenant will be appointed here, and this is the great question with me. If there is a real good first, the Company will improve and be well drilled, and I shall have a pleasant place. Still I should like a real soldier for a Captain, and I cannot but hope I shall be put finally in A. I have now however got acquainted with these men, and I like them; and I hate to part with them. If I remain here, I shall have very much more commanding to do, and more experience. However, I must only wait and let things go on. I am rejoiced at the Kentucky victory, and hope for further success there. Since Genl. Stone's visit we have had no unusual preparations at all, and although today it was possible to walk, tonight it is raining and snowing hard.

As soon as warm weather sets in I shall send home about 20 # of warm things, including my Buffalo. Then I shall be in marching order. I find Dr. Crehore a very pleasant man. Dr. Hayward I see little of. I fear I see too little of the fellows. I am alone a great deal. It was not a fault of mine at College, and I shall make a point soon of going round more in the evening. I have seen most of Sturgis. He is a very frank, open and jolly fellow, full of kindness. I like Macy very much. Patten is not thought much of. He is a good fellow though. I have given your direction and Father's to Captain Shepard. Show him some attention if you can, for he is a kind man.

Your affectionate brother
Henry Ropes.

Enclosed letter for Mary Ann.

Camp Benton, January 28th 1862.

My dear Mother.

I am very obliged for your letter of January 21st received last night, and for the brandy etc. you have sent. I did have a *very slight* touch of diarrhoea soon after I arrived, and not long ago one of the Officers was troubled, and asked me if I had anything good for diarrhoea, and then I wished for the Cherry Cordial which is I think the very best thing. I only brought about ¾ of a pint of brandy and some of this leaked out, and the rest I took, partly as a medicine for this slight attack, and partly afterwards, as a preventive. I think that often a few spoonfuls of brandy in one's water are a very good precaution. There is nothing so apt to produce a slight diarrhoea as a sudden change of the water one drinks.

I am now in perfect health. Thank you for the boy's overcoat. I think I shall give it to him (like a livery) only to be worn while he stays with me, for I am by no means perfectly satisfied with him. He (like most boys) is careless, lets the fire go out, breaks eggs, spills milk etc., and I want to keep the hope of reward and the fear of discharge very clearly before his eyes. He means well and as he is strong and does what I tell him (when he does not forget) and is acquainted with the customs of a camp, and knows the places where to buy milk, eggs, etc., I shall keep him and try to teach him to be a really good servant.

I am very sorry Frank did not dine at the Motley's, and hope he will be re-invited. I always thought Mr. Ed. Codman one of the best of men, and am very sorry to hear of his death. How is Mrs. Codman? I suppose she expected her husband's death for several weeks, and so it was not a sudden shock. I often think of you on a Sunday, and I should value very much now one of the Bishop's sermons which we used to think so little of. I miss very much some regular service on Sunday. Any sort of church would be better than none. Had I not been detailed on Guard duty I should have gone to Poolesville to church last Sunday. It was the only really fair day we have had for almost 20 days. Love to all.

Your affectionate son
Henry Ropes.

Camp Benton January 28th 1862.

My dear John.

I received last night your long letter of January 23rd and it now lies before me, and I shall answer it (as is my custom) taking up each thing as you wrote it. First my sickness. I am sorry you and especially Mother were anxious. I have never had any fever that I remember before, and I want you to know that this attack was *not* a case of fever and ague at all. I should be sorry indeed to get that disease. It was a sudden fever attack. Hot head, cold feet, pain in the back, very great uneasiness during the night, and vomiting, were the symptoms. But in one day I was well, that is, not strong, but fever gone and able to be up. All this time it poured with rain, and the tent was constantly damp, and the wet air blowing in. The Doctor said he did not know but that I was to be really ill, and that I recovered very quickly. Had I been ill longer, I should have been taken to the Hospital, a dry and comfortable log hut, where you have everything needed. I lay my illness to these things: 1st Wet and exposure on picket; 2nd Fat and unwholesome food for a day or two there; 3rd change of water and air. This last is a much greater thing that [sic] you imagine, and affects a perfectly well man. I think it a wise precaution to put a very little brandy in your water, and I did so for a day or two, when I was sick. I am now *perfectly* well, and do not think I am in any particular danger of future illness. Next time on picket I shall be very careful. I assure you that in case of *any illness* or *injury whatever* I should be taken care of at the Hospital here in the *very best* manner. The Hospital here is about perfect and as good as home for a sick man. You speak of discouragement etc.: I have never for an instant felt discouraged or looked wistfully toward home. When I lay abed sick I was of course very uncomfortable and in pain, but I have never once wanted to go home, and shall not, until the Regiment returns, if my life is spared to return with it. Of course we have all sorts of discomfort, and perhaps I am not quite as cheerful as I used to be in Cambridge, and do not see enough of the fellows etc., but I am not in the slightest degree discouraged or disappointed with my profession, and although I long to see the war over for the sake of the country and humanity, and would very well like to come back as one member, however humble, of a conquering army, and lay aside the sword, yet personally I am willing to stay for any length of time. I find here an opportunity to do as much good as I shall find in any profession. My time is occupied very fully, my pay is sufficient, my trade honorable, and one which calls out all the ability a man can possess. I have enough of pleasant companions, and I can see nothing better to look forward to in life.

As to the danger, somebody must endure it, and why not I? Above all I feel now it is my duty. If I live till the war is over, I shall probably find some other path open. So do not think I am discouraged, or hankering for home, for comforts and for society. I do want to see you all though very much, and being away from you, and Mary Ann, and Mother, and all, is the greatest trial I have. But this is not discouraging, only a trial every young man must bear. I long very much for letters, especially yours and Mary Ann's, and it is these letters that keep me constantly reminded of home, and seem to bring me back again.

I am glad you have got me some boots, but I really think the old might have been repaired, and a shoemaker in my Company was to have done it, had he been able to get leather. I do not care how it looks, provided it is strong. Thank you for the Professor and the brandy etc., which I shall probably soon get. Adams' Express often brings things here.

I really think you would enjoy a visit of a week here. It would only cost you about $40.00 to go and come, stay a week with me, and spend 2 days in

RIGHT UP INTO THE FIRE

Washington and Philadelphia. I have now arranged to get milk daily, and my boy often gets eggs. Yesterday I made a pretty good omelet. I will make you really comfortable, and you will see at least 7 camps and have a jolly time here with the Officers. I want you to think seriously of it. I should be delighted to see Professor Goodwin, and Hallowell desired me to add his invitation to mine. Herbert, with Curtis and Abbott have gone on picket. I see more of him than anyone else of the Officers, but not over much of any. I am delighted you are getting practice. As to the date of my Commission, you see I am entitled to one month and 6 days pay, before January 1st, and had I been 10 hours earlier at the Camp, I should have been in time for the Muster, and should have received about $90.00 when the others were paid 2 weeks ago. As it is I shall get $300.00 next pay day (about March 10th). The men of the 20th average good size, and are about ½ Irish and German. They are on the whole good soldiers, and we are specially fortunate in our non-commissioned Officers. In my Company one of the Sergeants is an old regular, and has been in all Scott's Mexican battles. 3 Corporals in my Company also are old regulars. Lieut. Murphy who was in the regular Army, says the Regiment is much more like a regular one than any about. We are getting an easy yet prompt way of doing everything and of drilling, which is very much better than the square and prim bearing of a military man. The men throughout have the most unbounded confidence in the Regiment and in our Officers, and in our ability to drill. The Colonel summoned us Commanders of Companies the other day, and told us an advance might at any time be ordered, and our Companies must be got into perfect trim. So I am very busy, seeing to everything, and if Company K is not perfectly supplied and ready for instant action when the time comes I intend that the fault shall be a good way from me. But the amount of labor necessary, together with the regular Company business for me, the Only Officer now, is great. I like Quarter Master Folsom very much and his brother too. They have (the younger I think) asked after you. I should like the Map of Virginia, but not that of Carolina. Please get the best copy, with a light cover (if any) and send it any time. Better wait till quite a number of things are ready. Send me a good supply of common red blotting paper. I have written for writing paper. I send by Lizzie another Balls /sic/ Bluff relic. I like the A.D. Officers, and hope Laurie will be frugal of the money. Who is Curator? My regards to Boyden, Jeffries and any fellows you may see. I have not received *any* of your Advertisers, but the one in the knapsack. Have you heard of the league against the M.P.C.? Jeffries will tell you. It is indeed diabolical. Today is rainy again and cold.

I am in *perfect* health. Do not feel the least anxious.

Your affectionate brother
Henry Ropes.

RIGHT UP INTO THE FIRE

Camp Benton
January 31st, 1862.

My dear Father.

I have just received your letter of January 20th with Mother's of same date enclosed, for both which please accept my thanks. The mail generally gets in by 8 o'clock P.M. and the Sergeant, who always gets the mail for the Company, usually gives me my letters before evening roll-call at 8 o'clk, at which I have to be present. Then I have the rest of the evening to answer them. We have now had a constant succession of snow and rain storms for 20 days. There was in that time only one fair day, last Sunday when I was on guard. The mud is terrible, and in spite of rubber boots, knee high, you get spattered terribly, and it is a regular journey to visit another tent. Generally however it has been cold enough to *freeze* at night but not much of late. I am much obliged for the tracts which I shall distribute. As to my money matters I felt that you had fitted me out most handsomely, and supplied me with a large sum at starting, and I also knew that my pay was more than enough for my support, so I felt anxious to put you to no expense for my own support. I feel very grateful at your and mother's kindness as expressed in your letters, and can only say that I shall accept most thankfully any gifts you may send, any articles of luxury for the table and the like, but I should still prefer to have John charge me with common things such as clothing, necessaries of food and the like. I think there is abundant room for presents outside of such ordinary matters. If I were at home, I should receive many presents, and at the same time pay for my coats and my shoes. I hope you will do as you see best taking this into consideration. In regards to my pay, I find my commission was purposely dated *November 25th* so that I should be on an equality in the Regiment with Lieuts. Patten & Mason, who both received their commissions before me. I am thus entitled to pay from November 25th and at the next payday, which comes as soon after the first of March as the Paymaster can come to the Regiment, I shall receive a little more than 3 months pay, in all about $330.00. Of this sum $100.00 will more than support me for the next 2 months, and $50.00 more will pay all bills I shall have out at that time, including any account I may have at Boston. I shall thus be able to send home about $180.00 to be credited to me by you, or placed in a Bank or otherwise invested. I shall in future be able to save ⅓ of my pay, and send that home every payday, and this without at all stinting myself in whatever is useful and needed here. This is of course in case all should go on well with me here.

The only time when I should want for money would probably be between now and next payday. Of the $100.00 you gave me when I started from home, I have already spent about $30.00 in travelling here, and in fitting up my tent, and other expenses necessary to set up housekeeping, as it were, besides paying Cash for daily food for myself and boy. I should however have been abundantly supplied had I been one day sooner, for then the Paymaster would have given me about $100.00 for December pay, but I was too late for the muster, and this amount will go to make up my $300.00 next time. I should therefore be very much obliged, if you would send to me about $25.00 any time before the middle of February, allowing me to repay the same when I send home my pay in March. It might be sent in U.S. bills, enclosed in letters, say $5.00 at a time, for safety, or sent by someone in gold, in which case I should prefer gold dollars entirely. Capt. Shepard would no doubt be happy to bring it.

I have written thus fully on this subject, that you may know exactly how I stand, and may feel that as soon as I begin to receive my regular pay I shall be well supported.

I am perfectly well, and have no news to tell. I am delighted to hear of Adjutant Pierson's /sic/ release and probable return to the Regiment.[9] I earnestly hope the Colonel will follow soon.

With love to all I remain

Your affectionate son
Henry Ropes.

Camp Benton January 31st 1862.

My dear Mother.

I have received your letter of January 29th with Father's, and am very much obliged for it, for the receipts, for the Almanac, and for your and Father's very kind desires to minister in so many ways to my comfort here.

Much obliged for Dr. Huntington's Tract, and for your kind advice in your letters. My boy is a Catholic, and will not read or hear the Bible or Prayer Book, but would be very thankful for a Catholic Bible, which I think it would be well to send him. Cannot you find some old child's story book? There is one of mine, I think in the Boys' Parlor, with pictures and some German stories, which I should be glad to give him. A boy needs something of that kind. Mary Ann can find

---

[9] Lieutenant Charles L. Peirson was taken prisoner in the battle of Ball's Bluff.

something, I know. I should find your receipts more useful, were I able to bake, and to get milk, and vegetables. The former is very scarce and for the latter we have "desiccated vegetables" so called, all kinds, cut fine, pressed and dried. I shall try the Rice and Bread puddings. I have as yet had no pudding but twice when one of my sergeants made me some. I often eat your nice strawberry preserve with bread.

I have written to Father fully about money matters. I am sure & do not want you to feel you cannot send me any presents you may wish and I assure you I shall be most thankful for anything, but I should like to be able to buy clothes etc. sometimes and have them sent on at my own expense. Do just as you think proper, but do not forget that the Government gives me $1000.00 a year, and I am a self supporting institution.

I shall try to go to church on Sunday, and think I can get off for I am Officer of the Guard tomorrow (Saturday) and am relieved at ½ past 9 on Sunday, and till afternoon the men who have just come off guard are always relieved from duty, being supposed to be tired. It is Communion Sunday, I know and I should esteem it a great privilege to go. Why do you persist in considering me unwell? I *never in my life* was in better health than I am in this moment.

Your affectionate son
Henry Ropes.

Camp Benton, 20th Regiment
February 1st 1862.

My dear John.

I have no letters to answer from you, but as I have a good deal of time, being on guard and as I want you to send me several things, I thought I would write you a short letter. It is rainy now and we had snow last night. Do not ever complain of Boston weather, but if ever it is cold and windy think of Maryland and mud. I should be perfectly delighted to get a week of cold weather when one could wear leather boots, and have one's tent dry and clean. I want you to send me a box of patent fire kindlings, I remember to have seen. It seems to be sawdust and pitch, dried in cakes and put up in paper boxes. It is very cheap, and I think it would be very convenient for me. Please find out the price of candles per pound. The Quartermaster charges me 25 Cents a pound for quite common tallow ones. If they are enough cheaper to make it an object, please send me a box, say 40 #. I have written to Father and shall have such necessaries charged to me. Please send me 4 of those bill files such as you use, with India Rubber straps.

I find my warm shoes a very great comfort. A tent is very airy, and in spite of an open fire the floor is a very cold place. Mother and Father have written about giving me things, and I have told them that I do not by any means mean to separate myself from them so far as to refuse to accept gifts, only I wish to pay for common things I send for. Of course I shall be most grateful in every way for every thing. I have received the Advertiser regularly for 3 days now, but I usually get the news earlier by a Washington paper. Would not the weekly do as well for me and be less trouble to you?

Your affectionate brother
Henry Ropes.

February 1st.

I have sent to you by discharged private Ballard of my Company, a small parcel for Mrs. Lee. It is a little photograph of our Camp. You will probably get it in about a week.

Affectionately
H. Ropes.

Camp Benton February 3rd 1862.

My dear John.

I am very glad to hear from Mary Ann that you are busy with your law case, and I hate to trouble you still further about my affairs, but I know you will appreciate my situation and find time to procure for me what I want. I find my boy Cornie will not do at all for me. As long as I /had/ nothing to do, and could look after him, he did pretty well and I rather liked at first to superintend his cooking etc., but now I have a very great deal to do. First, I have to do a Captain's duty and see to and sign all returns, requisitions etc., see to everything, hear complaints of all

RIGHT UP INTO THE FIRE

kinds, see to the rations, make and sign passes etc. etc. Then I do all the guard and police duty of a Lieutenant, no slight thing, and besides this, we all now recite daily in tactics etc. to the Colonel, and I as commander of a Company have to give daily instruction and recitations to the Sergeants and Corporals, and altogether I am perfectly full of work. I do not in the least complain, but only tell you of this to show the necessity of a really good servant, which I think can only be got in Boston. Cornie at first was quite attentive, but now he runs away and wastes his time in the men's tents and neglects his duty. Also he is very slovenly in managing his cooking matters. I do not want a man before the last of February or 1st of March, for I have advanced to Cornie some money for clothes. I want to explain fully what sort of servant I want. He must be honest, sober, healthy and smart. No lazy man will do. He must be clean in his management of all cooking matters, and he must have the rare quality of always getting along and putting up with everything. He must not expect very comfortable quarters. I want a man who can make the best of a little, who can get up something nice and comfortable out of an old tent and a few tin plates and cups and a rough board table, who can wash and cook, and chop wood, and run about and buy eggs and pick up things at farm houses and never be at fault or behind hand. I think a negro would be best. A man who had been cook and steward on board a vessel, who can make a little dirty galley look comfortable and clean. I think Kendall would find a man. I think a really smart, active nigger would be better than anyone else. Niggers, when not lazy, are apt to be bright and wide awake. After all there is almost no real hard work, but just such as a nigger likes. I have written a long explanation, but I feel almost unable to describe what I want, and yet I have seen such men. Mrs. Humphrey's Albert in Cambridge would be just right, I think, only he would not come of course. I think you know what kind of a man I want, if you only think of my position. I had thought of Mrs. Humphrey's present man, Edward, but I fear he could not cook and would not be neat. You know what a capability to get along in small and ill furnished quarters a sea faring life develops. You know a man who has been to sea has all kinds of little shifts and ways to make things convenient and comfortable. This is why I thought of a nigger ship's steward. A really good man, like Nash, would be entirely out of place. I do not have time to oversee my meals and to clean up my things, and I must have it done for me by a good servant, especially if on march, my time will be entirely occupied with my company, and at the end of a long march, I want a man who will fly round and get up something to eat, and extemporize a bed, or pitch a tent, and have a dry pair of socks ready, and do just what I want done without my having to oversee it all. You remember Albert at Cambridge, and how smart and ready he was. That is what I want, a cheerful make-the-best-of-it man.

 Now I have written this long letter merely for this purpose, because I feel its *immense importance* to me and my comfort and no doubt health. The man *must be* a good cook. Not one whom Mamma would care for in our kitchen, but one who can cook anything, in any kind of a pan or a pot.

I would be greatly obliged if (at your leisure) you would enquire for me of Nash, and of John McFeely and of Kendall, and in case you happen on one who you are sure would *exactly* suit, try to engage him. He gets his board and his lodging here, and needs only clothes, and blankets to sleep in. I would pay as high as $20.00 per month, if necessary, but this is *very* high.

Your affectionate brother
Henry Ropes.

Camp Benton, February 4th 1862.

My dear Mother.

I have no letter from you to answer, but thought I would write a few lines just to tell you what I have done. On Sunday I walked to Poolesville 2 ½ miles through awful mud, and got [*there*] in time for the last part of the Sermon and for the Communion at the little Episcopal Church there. I could not start earlier as we had dress parade at 9 o'clock and afterwards Company Inspection. Sunday and today were pleasant. Yesterday a snowstorm, and this evening cold. I was very glad to be able to attend even for a few minutes at a regular service, and particularly glad to be in time to commune. There was no afternoon service.

You were very kind to write so to me about presents. As to what I desire most, I assure you that one of your good pies or puddings would be far more acceptable than any expensive things you could buy at a store for me. I cannot get vegetables here, or puddings. I cannot bake, and can only rarely get anything done at the Regimental ovens. My standard food is bread, which is excellent, and meat, almost always fried. In no other way can I cook it so well or so soon. My attempts at Soup and at boiled Rice have been failures. My boy let them burn, and they have to be boiled a long time. I have written fully to John about getting me a proper servant, who can cook. I have plenty to do now during the day, but have the evenings to myself, and I really need a servant who will take all the care of my food off my hands. I can often get a bit of meat roasted but nothing in the way of pudding. I assure you, that *nothing* would be a more desirable gift than a good nice pudding, such a one as would keep, or a mince pie, which would also keep.

RIGHT UP INTO THE FIRE

But do not send anything by Express which you wish to come soon, for I have not yet received the box by Adam's /sic/ Express any may not for a long time. I am in need of nothing, and only mention these things that you might know what to send when you had an opportunity, and wanted to give me something. I have received the "Advertiser" quite regularly of late. I got yesterday a letter from Mary Ann which I shall soon answer.

Love to all from

Your affectionate son
Henry Ropes.

Camp Benton, 20th Regiment
February 6th 1862.

My dear John.

I have this morning received your letter of the 2nd, and I am delighted to know that your case has been so important a one, and I earnestly hope they may prove faithful to the charge you have committed to them and deliver me my box with speed and safety. I have just been out to my first battalion drill in command of my Company, and got along quite well on the whole. I feel greatly obliged to you for your kindness in getting me so many things and I beg you will thank Mr. Willard for his assistance in regard to the wrench.

I have not received any of the things yet. Tell me what you think of Capt. Shepard. He is a very kind man and all that, but not at all a soldier. I am very glad to be in command here, but by and by the Captain will return and a 1st Lieutenant will be appointed, and then my situation may not be so pleasant. The former Officers of Company K were Capt. Shepard, 1st Lieut. Beckwith, now a Captain, and 2nd Lieutenant Tilden, now 1st Lieutenant in another Company. I do not know who will be appointed to this Company. I think Lieut. Curtis is, on the whole, the most likely 2nd Lieutenant to be promoted, and I should be very sorry indeed to be obliged to room with him, and have him for my Senior in the Company. I cannot but think the Colonel should have put me at first into Company F, Capt. Cabot. I like Capt. Cabot very much. He is a real Gentleman and a soldier to the back bone. I like him as well as I like any one of the Officers, and I respect him as much as any. However, as I had got used to Company K and

Capt. Shephard [sic] liked me, I suppose the Colonel was unwilling to make a change, and when Hallowell came, put him at once into Company F. Capt. Shepard told me that he had asked the Colonel to put me permanently in his Company and I have found that the non-commissioned Officers have petitioned the Colonel to the same effect, and stated that it was the wish of the Company. I do not know what effect these things may have produced, and of course I am glad that I am thought well of, but I have still some misgivings as to my *future* life in Company K. Do not of course repeat all this I have written about myself. I only tell it you to explain exactly my position. On the whole then, taking into account the good will of the men, and other things, and that I have got used to the Company, and that we may soon advance, and that in all probability I shall have a good deal to do with the management of the Company, I am satisfied with my position and only anxious about my first Lieutenant.

As to Capt. Tremlett, he has the reputation here of a most excellent Captain. Whittier, his 1st Lieutenant, I like very much and he told me he should like to have me with him in Company A. I feel sure I could get along with Tremlett. I have got quite intimate with Harry Sturgis, whom I like very much. He is a very lively fellow, and frank and true hearted. I was very sorry to see the account of Adjutant Hodges' death.[10] I hardly knew him however, but remember his appearance well. Cabot has been quite ill of a fever attack like mine, only worse, for he had a relapse. I hope you will visit me in March. I hardly think we shall move before, unless a great victory farther South obliges the Rebels to retire and abandon Leesburg. Yesterday we shelled the Rebels from the ferry with a big Parrott gun. It kept booming away every little while all day. There is nothing to prevent them from shelling us here at Camp, except the fact that we should probably reply, and trot down Ricketts' Battery (Regular) which is camped near us to the river, and drive them off. As to the cold, yesterday morning was the coldest I have yet felt. I should think the thermometer must have been as low as 15° till say 10 o'cl. Often it is about 20° in the night, but warmer in the day and never any wind then. As to time, I should think the middle of March would be the best time for you to come here, and I cannot tell you how delighted I should be to see you. I have seen nothing of Professor Goodwin as yet. I wrote to Mr. Willard and said I hoped he would come on and see us and the other Regiments. I should be delighted to see him. If you come, merely bring to Camp a thick overcoat, a large Bay State Shawl, and a change of Underclothes. A valise would take everything.

As to the Germans. They are good soldiers, and *all* speak English, and the commands are invariably given in English. Of course they understand the

---

[10] Adjutant George Foster Hodges of the 18th Massachusetts Infantry (a fellow Harvard man) died of Typhoid Fever on January 31, 1862.

commands and such things much better than common English phrases, but the regulations prescribe that *all* soldiers shall speak English.

Tell me if the old Colonel is really coming back. His return would give a great start to the Regiment. Tell Mary Ann about the Company, for she enquired. I hope you got my letter about a servant. Do not engage any till you are *sure* he is *just* what I want. Try not to pay more than $10.00 a month. No one hardly gives so much. You might bring him on. He would be very convenient for you. You can probably send everything by Capt. Shepard.

Good bye.

Your affectionate brother
Henry Ropes.

Enclosed letters for Curtis and Mary Ann. Have received one from Sister Mary.

Camp Benton 20th Regiment
February 9th 1862 Sunday.

My dear John.

I received by last night's mail yours of the 6th for which much obliged. Lieut. Lowell arrived last night and looks well. He told me he had brought my nipple wrench. This morning the Sutler brought me from Poolesville the bundle containing the coat. In it I found an Almanac from you for which I am much obliged. Also a letter for Abbott which I have delivered. I have as yet seen or heard nothing of Wm. Perkins. I shall not give the coat to Cornie, as he does not deserve it. I am more and more dissatisfied with him every day. I cannot leave anything to him to do, as he will certainly neglect it if I am not by. He was a little sick for a day, and while he was so, I got a man of my Company, by name Morris, to do his work, and found a very great and immediate improvement. This Morris, when I first joined the Company, desired to be taken from the ranks, to be my servant. I did not want to take him from the ranks, and then thought Cornie would do. Morris has lost the use of one eye and as this unfits him for a soldier's duty, I got the Surgeon to certify to his physical disability (this is the term) and have applied for his discharge, which will no doubt soon be granted.[11] If Morris is

---

[11] Private Joseph Morris, age 25, was discharged for disability on April 15, 1862.

discharged I think I shall engage him until you can get me a first-rate man at home. The reason I did not want a man from the ranks is this. An Officer has the privilege of taking one man from his Company, as a servant, provided the man is willing and the Captain consents. This man still receives pay and rations from the Government, and is excused from all duty except occasional inspection. As the Officer generally gives him something additional, and as the work is not hard, the place is sought after generally by several soldiers. If the Officer thus takes a man, he is called in the books "Officer's servant" and the Officer in his account states on his honor that such a man is employed by him in such a capacity and places his personal description and name in the record. If however the Officer states that he keeps a servant, *not* an enlisted man, he is allowed $23.00 per month for wages for such servant and is required to write the name and description of the man, as in the former case. Now I will tell you how almost all the Officers manage it. They affirm they keep a servant, *not* an enlisted man, and thus draw $23.00 a month. Then they take a man from the ranks and keep him as a servant, and place a false name and a fabulous description on their account. Some even take two men from the ranks in this way, one for a cook. And this is defended on the ground of universal custom and the Paymaster knows and encourages it, and says it is only a legal form in the Government to require the certificates, and that this means is intended to increase the pay of Officers. For my part I cannot set my name to such a falsehood and then explain it away. I cannot but think it is cheating the Government. So I prefer to take a servant *not* enlisted and pay him regularly. They quite laughed at my squeamishness here, but I found that Cabot & Milton were with me. So I can take Morris as soon as he is discharged, and perhaps he will do for me. I hope you will not cease to look out for a really good man for me, and will engage such if you find him, but do not hurry so as to get at all a doubtful man, as I have happened on a fair servant here, and am not in positive need. I think by being not in a hurry you will at last fall in with exactly the article wanted. I have written a great deal about a servant, and I fear I shall put you to much trouble, but if you were here and could see how much I needed one, and how indispensable a good one was, I know you would not mind the trouble.

Thank you for getting my things. The kindlings are not *[at]* all bulky but come in a proper box about 10 inches square and 3 inches high. Do not send by Express. It takes a very long time. Capt. Shepard could bring a box as well as not. I have not yet received the box you sent by Express.

I am very sorry for Mother and hope she will soon be well.

Your affectionate brother
Henry Ropes.

Enclosed letter for Mary Ann.

RIGHT UP INTO THE FIRE

Camp Benton, 20th Regiment
February 11th, 1862.

My dear Father.

I have just received your kind letter of February 8th enclosing a bill for $5.00. You describe it as "No. 50005" whereas it is No. 1183, but I do not suppose this is of any consequence. I am much obliged to you for it and for your promise of sending a further supply. I have received sister Mary's letter, and shall soon answer it. We have now had 2 fair days, and a prospect of continued fair weather, but very cold nights. As it is dry, we do not mind how cold it is. I am rejoiced to hear of our success in the West[12], and hope soon to hear also a good account from Burnside.

This morning we heard of Genl. Stone's arrest. It may be a report, but I fear it is true. There has been a pretty general distrust in him for a long time.[13] As to sending me things, avoid the Express. Capt. Shepard will bring something. Capt. Cabot, just left on a leave of absence, kindly promised to see you and bring anything, and today a private of my Company, named John Smith, a very good man, has left on a furlough and will call at John's office on February 14th or 15th, and he will take anything. Better send any large box (if you have any) by him, even if you pay him something, (which I do not think he will take.) Please tell John when Smith will call.

I hope you will see Capt. Cabot. I have the *very highest* regard for him, both as a soldier and a Gentleman. He is one of the best Officers in the Regiment, and was with the British in the Sepoy Rebellion. I think with these 3 you can easily send everything. I have not yet received the box by Express. Col. Palfrey showed me today a letter from Col. Lee. It was written in a very cheerful tone, and spoke very kindly of Herbert Mason and myself. I have got a man out of my Company now as a servant, and am much more comfortable, as he cooks quite well. I had hominy yesterday for dinner and fried this morning for breakfast. I have also procured some parsnips and a goose, and anticipate a feast. I enclose a letter for mother.

Your affectionate son
Henry Ropes.

---

[12] Battle of Fort Henry on February 6th, 1862.

[13] General Stone was arrested for his supposed responsibility for the Union disaster at Ball's Bluff.

RIGHT UP INTO THE FIRE

Camp Benton February 11th 1862.
My dear Mother.

I have just now received your letter of Feby. 8th and thank you very much for it. I am very sorry to hear of your illness, and very glad to know that you are now getting better. If your weather has been like ours I do not wonder you caught cold.

Capt. Cabot, who has just got a leave of absence for a few days, has had just such an attack, only down here we do not have a comfortable bed and room to be sick in. I have received the coat, but have not given it to Cornie as he does not deserve or need it, and I intend to send him off as soon as possible. It is a very nice coat, and I shall send it back to you unless you wish me to make some other disposition of it. The Bible, when it comes I shall give him, and hope he will learn from it to be more useful to his next master. I have written to John about a new servant, and hope he will not send one unless he is sure he will do, for now I have got quite a good man from my Company who is very soon to be discharged because he has lost the sight of one eye. This new man can make very good coffee and dip toast (when I can get milk). Lt. Lowell has arrived, but looks thin. I have told Father that a private of my Company will call on John, and by him you can send me anything. If you do send a box and would put in one of your nice pies, nothing could be more acceptable. How do you boil a pudding? Is a bag needed? How long do you boil it? You see I am very ignorant. Today we have had snow, but on the whole it looks like better weather at last. Is there sleighing at Boston? I like to hear such little particulars very much. I am perfectly well, and so are all the Officers. Can you send me 3 or 4 prayer books? I think I could give this number away to the men, very well. Please also send 1 vol. Cameron's Infantry Tactics ($1.25) bought anywhere. This last for my Corporals.

Your affectionate son
Henry Ropes.

Camp Benton February 13th 1862.
My dear John.

I enclose a letter to sister Mary, which I shall be much obliged to you to forward. We were delighted to hear yesterday of the glorious victory of Burnside[14], but have as yet no particulars. I hope none of our 24th Regiment friends are hurt. It was

---

[14] Battles of Roanoke Island and Elizabeth City.

just tea time and the orders came to turn out the entire Regiment on the parade. This was most quickly done and there was Col. Palfrey and the Adjutant and another Officer. The Colonel read (from his horse) the splendid news "Wise's Army destroyed, 2000 prisoners taken, 1000 killed and wounded, 17 stands of colors taken, entire rebel fleet taken and destroyed, Elizabeth City burnt to the ground, our loss 300." He read this in a low, clear voice, and then called for three cheers for the Stars and Stripes, which, I tell you, were given with a will. The men broke up cheering and wild with excitement, and the camp was in a very excited state all the evening. The band came out and played "Hail Columbia" etc. etc. and all together it was quite an event. I was Officer of the guard for the day. What do you think of Stone?

Today 2 batteries are ordered to the ferry and we have been shelling the Rebels. They get off a tremendous gun every little while. I hear it is an immense Parrott gun.

What has become of my box sent by Express? You had better make enquiries, for I want the boots very much, and quantities of boxes have arrived since you sent that. Do not send again by Express. Yesterday Officers' baggage was weighed preparatory to a move.

Weather pleasant and warm, and mud drying up fast. I like my new man Morris quite well, but hope for even a better from you. Do not engage till you are quite sure he will do exactly. The whole Camp are now very anxious to move and are excited on hearing of our late victories. Our balloonist here, Capt. Steinburg (not Professor Lowe, as I at first wrongly called him) says there are a great many more Rebels opposite us than we have men here, and that we *could not* advance. He knows from his balloon. Have you received back my photographs, and are they being struck off?

Your affectionate brother
Henry Ropes.

Camp Benton
February 14th, 1862.

My dear Father.

I have just received yours of the 12th enclosing one from Mother of same date, one from Lizzy of the 10th, a small note about my box from Louisa, and a letter from Mary Ann of the 11th, for all of which I am very much obliged.

RIGHT UP INTO THE FIRE

I thank you and mother very much for sending me so many things in the box, but as I have written, the Express is a very doubtful means of transportation. If sent by a private hand I shall get them in 3 days after they leave you. I have as yet heard nothing from the Express Company concerning the box you sent weeks ago. I think enquiries ought to be made at the office at Boston. Please tell me how the box was directed.

Genl. Stone's arrest has been a good deal talked about. I very much doubt his guilt. Now we are under Genl. Gorman, a very old and I hear foolish man. He has begun to shell the Rebels near us here, and yesterday I went down with Lt. Abbott to see the firing. It was a Rhode Island battery of large Parrott guns, but the practice was very poor. None of the shell hit the place aimed at, some did not burst at all, one turned over in the air making a very peculiar sound, and none reached far enough. The guns are tremendous and the shell make a very loud whizzing sound, which gradually dies away, and then you watch for a cloud of dust where it hits a mile off. There is a rebel fort in sight at which they are throwing the shell.

We were all very much excited here at the good news both from the East and West.[15] I do not think we shall advance from this position. The Rebels are in great force opposite us, and have strong forts, and the advantage of position. Then the Rail Road to Leesburg can bring them up reinforcements with great speed. We are getting ready however, and perhaps we may be ordered to some other part of the line. I suppose the best sign of an advance would be the appointment of a good General to this Division.

I am very anxious to hear from the 24th Regiment where our friends were. I enclose a letter for mother and remain

Your affectionate son
Henry Ropes.

Camp Benton February 14th 1862.

My dear Mother.

I am very glad to get a letter from you and to find you so much better as to sit up. I went again to Church at Poolesville last Sunday, and hope to be able to do so in

---

[15] Battle of Fort Henry on February 6, 1862.

future. My present man, Morris, is a much better cook than I had thought and has made a most excellent bread pudding which I assure you I appreciated. Perhaps you think I pay too much attention to eating, but I think if you were here and were blessed with as good an appetite as I am and had so little else in the way of luxuries, you would pay quite as much attention to your dinners. I shall be very much obliged for the tongues and ham, but I am glad you did not send the chickens, for I can now get chickens here. If you should send me anything more, I would suggest pies, puddings or cranberry sauce, for these I cannot get here. Nothing would be so acceptable as a good mince pie, or one of those nice puddings which keep from Thanksgiving to Christmas. I am particularly fond of a good mince pie. I have now found out how to get Eggs, Poultry and sometimes Milk, and in fact am rarely unable to get any of the raw materials, the trouble is in converting such into a pie or a pudding. I have made arrangements with a man here to keep on the lookout for chickens, etc., and I find every day almost some new way of making myself more comfortable.

I do not think we shall move for some weeks at any rate, and if we do, there will be a way left to store or send home such baggage as we shall not take on a march.

Give all my love. I shall answer all soon. I hope soon to hear of your perfect recovery. If you have a chance, send me a few pounds of raisins or Zante currants to make puddings. Those of the Sutler are poor and very dear. I can get very good ham and Salt beef here. Please tell me how to make those nice Indian flapjacks. I think Morris can cook them. Sturgis Hooper arrived here yesterday.

Good bye.

Your affectionate son
Henry.

Camp Benton, February 18th 1862.

My dear John.

I enclose a letter for Mary Ann. I have not any letter from you to answer, but I must write to tell you of an event which will do me more good than you can well imagine in a military and regimental way. Billy Milton, whose place as Adjutant Peirson is soon to fill, is to be my first Lieutenant. I cannot tell you how relieved, gratified, and pleased I am. I must explain a little regimental politics first. You know what College politics are. We have something similar here. You see that somebody must be appointed 1st Lieutenant as there are not enough. Now there are two companies unsupplied, and Company K is one, and of course I began to think a great deal as to who was to be over me, and my room-mate etc. The Senior 2nd Lieutenant is Müller, but he has refused a promotion, not wishing to leave his German Company. Then comes Messer, a good fellow, kind and easy, and a man who went through Ball's Bluff under Caspar[16], but who is exceedingly lazy, and indolently neglects his duty. He has been skipped once, and is now the only 2nd Lieutenant who belonged originally to the Regiment who has not been offered a 1st Lieutenancy. Then we all come in a bunch: Murphy, Curtis, Herbert, Patten and myself, that is as to date of commission, but Curtis having been nominated by Col. Lee before the battle, would naturally come first of us. Now I find since I have come here, that there is an excellent class of men who think about alike on Regimental matters, comprising all the college men, Sturgis, Murphy perhaps, and in fact all but one or two. Captains Shepard, Beckwith, and Lieutenants Müller and Le Barnes are not exactly in the right set, but (except the last) are not disliked. Curtis is a great friend of Bartlett's, and a friend of no one else. He is young, about 19, and a surly, stuck up, cold, heartless kind of fellow. He makes a good enough Officer, but has been under Abbott all the time, and no one knows what he would do alone. He is a man whom I do not like at all, neither does Herbert nor in fact any one. Now this Curtis has yesterday been appointed 1st Lieutenant and will probably be with Herbert. Every one says it is Frank Bartlett who is shoving his friend quietly along. The old Officers are indignant that a mere boy, and a boy of no particular merit, should be put over Messer. The reply would be that Messer is unfit for the place, and Curtis, as he stands 1st to the 2nd should be promoted, unless there was a very strong reason to the contrary. Herbert is very indignant and hopes to be able to change his Company. Other things have occurred in regard to Sergeants etc. which show a very great partiality for Company I at Headquarters, and it is generally thought that Bartlett's long head has prepared his old Company for his return. This is of course between ourselves, or very intimate friends. Now I foresaw Curtis' promotion as probable, and felt very eager to have my company settled, for there is only one 1st in the field I dislike more and from Tilden I saw no danger. You may think then how delighted I was when the Adjutant opened the subject, and told me he could have any Company he wished, and should take Company K. There is not a 1st on the field I would rather have. He is a most excellent Officer, a splendid fellow, the most popular in the Regiment, I should think, and a man any Captain or 2nd Lieutenant would have been delighted to obtain. I feel now sure of Company K, and sure that my position in the Regiment will be as pleasant as it possibly can be.

---

[16] Captain Caspar Crowninshield.

RIGHT UP INTO THE FIRE

We shall chum and eat together, the Captain alone. Speaking of the men, I have alluded to Tilden. I formerly spoke well of him to Mary Ann so it would be better not to disabuse her of that good impression but I have seen ample reason to alter my opinion of him, and to consider him a vain, false, conceited and thoroughly cold-hearted man. He is moreover overbearing to his men and very neglectful of his duty, openly so. He is detested in the Regiment, but the Colonel seems to fancy him. I may have used strong language but I assure you I think it just. Herbert and another fellow both told me that after he had said a few words they felt always a very strong desire to take him by the collar and kick him out of sight.

His assumption of superiority in everything is perfectly ridiculous, and sometimes enough to make a man almost knock him down. He talks of the war as if he was McClellan, of the Regiment as if Colonel, and of women as if he was 50 years old, and had been the most perfect rake in the world and the most fashionable and was giving advice to a few boys.

I find the opinions you expressed to me about Captains Tremlett and Putnam confirmed by the men here. Both are good Captains, but neither fit for a higher post. Tremlett was remarkable for his obscenity and licentiousness. Neither have one half of Bartlett's ability.

I find Lowell is a shockingly poor Officer, and they say Holmes is as bad, yet, one will probably be soon a Captain. The more I study an Officer's life, the more I see the need of energy, and business ability, qualities which neither possess. Patten is doing much better, and he (as are Lowell and Holmes) is liked and in the best set of course. Little Pat as they called him made a name for himself by asking (when on picket) if he should fire into the houses which showed a light after 9 o'clock.

I am getting to like Capt. Macy more and more. He is a real true, sound man, very quiet and unassuming, very determined, and an excellent Officer.

Do tell me the prospects of a servant and the fate of my box. Perhaps you do not like so much of a letter about the men. I have made it long without thinking, and have given you quite an insight into the Regiment. I hope it will not bore you, but I know you like to talk of men, and so, as we cannot talk, I write. I have received the nipple wrench. Papers come regularly. Glorious news from Burnside. We are burning to do something here.

Whittier has been appointed on Genl. Gorman's staff for the present. Gorman is no Officer. O for Col. Lee. Then when he comes we may advance.

Love to all.

Your affectionate brother
Henry Ropes.

Enclosed one letter for M. A. R.

RIGHT UP INTO THE FIRE

Camp Benton, February 20th 1862.

My dear John.

Thank you for your letter of February 14th and 15th received on the 18th. I am very much obliged to you for all you have done, and have no doubt I shall like my servant very much. As you are all desirous at home, I will shave, so as to look just as I did before I left home, and then have a new card photograph taken here.

I have written to Mr. Case, Army Express Agent, Washington, enclosing full directions to Burckmeyer how to come to this Camp. I am perfectly satisfied with your agreement. Now, as to your coming. You know how delighted I shall be to see you, but for your own sake, after much thought on the subject, I do *not* advise you to come so early as February 28th, unless you have good reason to think this Regiment will move before or about that time. My only reason for this advice is a regard for your comfort. You can hardly imagine what it is to be surrounded with a sea of mud, and to have wet feet and a muddy flow all the time. They say that after March 1st we have here fresh, cool weather, and strong winds, and I cannot but think you would enjoy it more if you put off your visit till the middle of March. However we may move anytime, and I certainly should like very much to see you before we enter on active service. You must judge, only be assured I should be most delighted to see you, whenever you come, and will make you comfortable and give you enough to eat and a good fire and bed. I get to fare better all the time. Please bring me when you come a supply of *large size* writing paper, and one or two India Rubber bands for my pocket-book. When you come, better only bring a thick overcoat, a thick shawl, one change of Underclothes, and a change of boots. Wear the stoutest and highest top boots you have. Wear flannel travelling shirt, as we cannot get a white shirt washed and starched up here. Wear paper collars for the same reason.

I am very busy with the Court Martial now. Yesterday we sat from 10 A.M. till 4 P.M. Today we shall probably do the same. I cannot stop to write about this glorious news. Thank you very much for your description. May we not long be idle! Milton is going home on a leave, and will be in Boston about March 1st. If you have not sent my servant and would like to keep him to come on with you, do so.

Your ever affectionate brother
Henry.

RIGHT UP INTO THE FIRE

Camp Benton
February 22nd, 1862.

My dear Father.

I have received your letter of the 19th and my servant has arrived safely bringing the map and the kindlings for which I am much obliged. Adjutant Peirson stayed for a day or two in Washington, and sent Henry Burckmeyer on with Capt. Shepard via Poolesville. The box is with the Adjutant's baggage, and I expect it tonight. Henry enquired for the first box in Washington, but it was not at the office there. He brought me the receipt, and I have written to the Agents and expect to get it soon. I like Henry very much. I find him active and an excellent cook. I think I shall be perfectly satisfied with him. I am very much obliged for the good things in the box and have no doubt they will afford a great deal of pleasure to me and to my friends here. Adjutant Peirson is expected today.

Yesterday we sent down reinforcements to the river, and the Rebels brought down guns etc, and seemed to be about to cross, but as yet nothing has occurred. The pickets were firing at each other all along when I heard last. I think however it would be madness in them to attempt the passage of the river in the face of our guns, to say nothing of the troops they would need when they had got over.

Genl. Sedgwick was announced this morning at dress parade as Stone's successor. I hear none but good accounts of him. Genl. Dana has returned and was at this camp this morning. In him all our men have unbounded confidence. He was Colonel of the 2nd Minnesota Regiment now near us. The whole Regiment is now drilling in the bayonet exercise and practising long runs in double quick time and the movements in echelon. These latter movements are very beautiful movements. Capt. Shepard has got back. Capt. Cabot is to return tomorrow. Please thank Mother for her letters, and say I shall reply fully when I get the box.

I hear from the Captain that business is already looking up in Boston and the general opinion is that by next 4th July, there will be no vestige of Rebellion left.

I enclose a note for Lizzy.

Your affectionate son
Henry.

RIGHT UP INTO THE FIRE

Camp Benton Sunday, February 23rd 1862.

My dear John.

I have to acknowledge yours of February 17th received February 19th and yours of the 19th received 21st, the former I received from my servant Henry, and the latter by mail. This morning I have received the box from Adjutant Peirson, with everything perfectly safe. I will write to Mother of the box. I feel perfectly satisfied with Henry, and I am very much obliged indeed to you for getting so good a man. To be sure, I have had him but 3 days as yet, but I can see what sort of a man he is, already. We are delighted to see the Adjutant. As to your coming, I wrote you about the roads etc. They are now in an awful state, and only yesterday the Sutler's light wagon with *one* trunk in it, was stuck in the mud, and it took several extra horses to get it out. Still, as you know, the Army may move very soon. I therefore only tell you this and leave you to judge. Only remember, rubber shoes are of no use, and rubber boots are very uncomfortable to wear all the time, so the best things are stout, large leather boots, knee high and pants tucked in.

I will make you very comfortable for a Camp, and I cannot tell you how delighted I shall be to see you. It is no use for me to begin to write about political and military matters for I should never stop. Our reserve company (Capt. Macy) has just come up and reports that yesterday very heavy firing was heard in the direction of Drainsville, and volleys of Musketry distinctly heard. They think McCall was engaged, and if so it must have been a great fight.

Please say to Father that the Adjutant mentioned to me that he has some money for me, and that he would give me an account of it very soon. I have seen nothing of Professor Goodwin. 2nd Lieut. Perkins, lately appointed, arrived here yesterday. I have to tell you some bad news for me. Adjutant Milton (who I wrote you was to be my 1st Lieutenant) has received an appointment on Genl. Dana's staff, and will be detached from the Regiment and I shall have another 1st Lieutenant. O that it may not be Curtis! Murphy is the most likely 2nd to be promoted, and he is a fine soldier, and a good blunt, honest man, but he rose from the rank's [sic] and although well worthy of his post, is not a man I should pick out for a room-mate at all. He is an Irishman, was in the regular Army and was one of the 45 men who held Fort Pickens with Slemmer.[17] When you return I shall send home a lot of things I shall not want, including the Coat sent for Cornie.

I want you to bring on for me, or send if you have a chance, before you come yourself, a copy of Jane Eyre, same style as the Professor. I want to give it to

---

[17] 1st Lieutenant Adam J. Slemmer.

Herbert who has never read it. Herbert would be very much obliged if you would bring him a box of 6 bottles, 3 of Brandy and 3 of Whisky bought of Codman & Parker at $1.00 per bottle. They box it up at the store, and it is no trouble to have one more box. I hope you will bring it, as it would be a very kind thing to do for Herbert.

I shall send some books back by you, and my Buffalo, as it is warmer now, and they don't have a long cold spring here. If you could bring me some ale I should be very much obliged. You might have ½ dozen put up in Herbert's box. I should be delighted to get some ale.

Probably the clayey nature of the soil makes it more muddy here, and we might find a dry road after a few miles of mud. I know nothing of the kind of soil it is in Virginia. As I am Officer of Police today, I cannot go to church.

I remain your affectionate
Henry Ropes.

If you let me know exactly when you shall be at the Ferry or at Poolesville, I can probably have a wagon for your baggage.

H. R.

Camp Benton, February 23rd 1862.

My dear Mother.

I enclose a picture of myself, which my Sergeant took here at Camp yesterday. You see how fat I have got in the face. I have allowed the hair to grow on my face since I came, and this makes it look so indistinct about the chin and throat. I shall shave my chin tomorrow and then be taken on a card, just as I was before I left home. I think this is an excellent likeness, and our Sergeant is a very fine operator. He has a little log house, and has made a great deal of money already. You see it is my undress uniform with sword, just as I came off guard. So much open air, and enough to do, and no violent exercise has made me very fat and I weigh 163 lbs. I know you would see the picture first so I wrote about it before thanking you for the box which has just come. It contains a quantity of Gingerbread, 2 roast fowls, 1 plum-pudding in a tin, 1 pie in 2 tin plates, 1 pot marmalade, 1 pot Cranberry sauce, 1 tongue, 1 box candles, 4 bill files, large supply of blotting paper, 4 prayer books, 1 Cameron's tactics, 1 cod line, box writing paper, Kingsley's sermons, 1 towel, several pieces cloth, and several newspapers. For all these things I am very much obliged indeed to you and to Father and to everybody who thought of or made or sent them. I am sure you are very kind to send me so many luxuries. Everything is useful, for it is very queer to see what things we can, and what we cannot get here. For instance, the string (or rope rather) round the box was a most useful present to me. You cannot buy such here. The Cod-line will be invaluable.

If the war goes on at this rate, we may as well all come home in a week, for the Rebels seem to be evacuating every strong place they have made, and if they dare not wait behind their works, what will they do in the open field? We are now in Sedgwick's Division, and Dana's Brigade. The 19th Mass. are to be moved up to this Brigade very soon, and with us and the Minnesota 2nd and the miserable Tammany[18] and one or 2 other New York Regiments constitute one Brigade. We have 2 most excellent Generals and we consider our own Regiment and the Minnesota 2nd and perhaps the 19th Mass. excellent Regiments.

Love to all.

Your affectionate son
Henry Ropes.

Camp Benton, Monday
February 24th, 1862. 6.30 P.M.

My dear Father.

We have just been summoned by the Colonel and ordered to prepare ourselves for an immediate move, and told that no baggage nor tents will be carried, and that we must depend on our own backs for everything we wish to take. Although we may not start for several days, yet as I should have a great deal to do before setting off, I thought I would write that you might not feel anxious if you did not receive letters from me, after you heard that the Regiment had marched. The Colonel intimated that we might not see our baggage again for a very long time, and even advised us to send away home or to Washington everything we could;

---

[18] The nickname of the 42nd New York.

the reason for which I cannot make out. He said that Banks was to cross today and at the same time there was to be an advance at Aquia Creek, showing the plan of McClellan to be to advance at one time on both flanks of the Rebel Army of the Potomac.[19]

It is thought by some that we are going on some distant service, but I feel perfectly in the dark as to our destination. However, we may not go for some time, and I shall write before we leave if I possibly can. Today we have had a tremendously strong wind. A great many tents are blown down, and I think my tent was saved by stays which I put out, and which I should have been unable to make but for the strong cord sent out in my box.

Have just received Louisa's letter and three papers. Adjutant Peirson has given me $11.50 and the account of Henry's expenses amounting to $22.50.

Received from you $19.00
in gold 15.00
34.00
Paid for Henry 22.50
Leaving for me 11.50

Henry tells me he could have come much cheaper without the Adjutant.

I am very much obliged to you for this money, and it may be very useful to me, for the Paymaster does not visit a Regiment if there is any danger, and we may be in actual service very soon.

I have had my tent nicely fastened up with poles, and another bunk put up, all ready for John. If we march I shall send my baggage by him.

I remain

Your affectionate son
Henry Ropes.

Enclosed letter for Mary Ann and picture.

---

[19] The later Army of Northern Virginia.

RIGHT UP INTO THE FIRE

Camp Foster.
Poolesville, February 26th, 1862.
4 P.M.

My dear Father.

We left Camp Benton and marched to this Camp yesterday afternoon, and are in the tents left by the 15th Mass. who left yesterday to join Banks' Division above us. It is said Banks crossed yesterday. Heavy firing yesterday and last evening, at the river. We are as yet without any baggage but what we carried on our backs, but shall get everything in a day or two, and if we stay long here, we shall be very comfortable as we are right in the village. I hear that a large body of troops are coming up the Canal. No one knows how long we are to be here, and some say that we are to stay as a permanent guard, but the Colonel on leaving Camp Benton made us a speech and said we were now to take part in the grand advance etc. and that he hoped each would resolve to sustain the honor of the Regiment etc. and he also said to us Officers to reduce our baggage and that we would be obliged to be without transportation except for provisions, all which looks like an active Campaign but still there must be some troops here and perhaps we are to stay. I am delighted to hear that Col. Lee is released and could hardly believe the good news true. I suppose he will return to the Regiment. I will write to John of our movements. Please excuse this badly written letter, as I am sitting and writing on an old box, and have as yet no conveniences. I am perfectly well.

    Love to all from

Your affectionate son
Henry Ropes.

Guard House, Provost Guard.
Poolesville Md. February 28th, 1862.

My dear Father.

I wrote you that we marched to Poolesville on the 25th, and on the 26th just at evening. I was ordered to march to Camp Benton with Lts. Sander/s/ and Hallowell and 90 men to strike and pack our tents etc. It was raining and fearfully muddy and we carried our blankets on our backs and our provision in our haversacks and got back to the old camp by 8 o'clock. We all slept in one of the deserted tents, after being very well entertained by Dr. Hayward, who remained with the sick in hospital. It was a very rainy night but cleared off in the morning with a tremendous Northwester. We rose at daylight and had all the tents struck and everything ready by 10 o'clk and then marched back here. The Rebels have been throwing shell at night lately. One fell a little short of our old camp the other night and one went over. We have two guards here, the regular Camp Guard, and the Provost Guard in the town. I am Officer of the Provost today. We had hard work yesterday, for we struck all the 15th's tents and brought up and pitched our own in spite of the tremendous wind. Today is quite cold but very fine, with another strong N.W. wind. McClellan is above us, over 40,000 men have crossed, and vast quantities of troops are pouring up the canal. I hear we are to move in two days. I am making every preparation. It seems as if the grand advance is to be near us here. If we move of course my letters will be very irregular. I hope to see John first. I am rejoiced to hear of the Colonel's liberation and hope he will soon assume command.

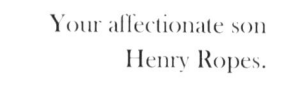

Your affectionate son
Henry Ropes.

March 2nd 1862 Camp Porter
Poolesville, Md.

My dear Mother.

We have now been 5 days quietly settling ourselves down in this camp. We have got our own tents and put them up in place of those left by the 15th Regiment.

I was delighted to see John on Friday. He came by stage and is now well settled in our tent. He has seen Col. Lee in Washington. We are delighted to hear of the Colonel's release, and expect him here soon. I do not think we shall be long here, for I think the whole army will be thrown across the Potomac. We can hear nothing definite about Genl. Banks, except that he has crossed and that McClellan is with him. We have had very cold nights and very strong winds here, and the troops who have marched and are without tents and baggage must have suffered. The roads are still horrible and it is impossible to transport the regular amount of baggage.

Today we have a snowstorm after a fine warm morning. John and I have attended the Episcopal Church and have communed. A very good sermon. James Codman came last night and is the Colonel's guest. He looks as stout and well as ever. I am much obliged for the prayer books which you sent, and have distributed them.

Thank you for the receipts. Henry I find, is an excellent cook, and I therefore live very well indeed now, and do not need them. I hear that all sorts of reports are in circulation about Banks' repulse etc. Do not worry yourself about any such rumors, and do not think, we are anything but comfortable till you hear so from me. I shall keep John here just as long as I possibly can. It feels very natural to see him again, and he is now quite at home, and enjoying himself. Had he come when we were at Camp Benton, I could have entertained him in a much more magnificent manner, but I shall soon be settled here and get up all my things from the old Camp.

I was greatly astonished to hear of President Felton's death.[20] He bade me good bye so very kindly and asked me to come and see him when I came back. He was a very good kind man, although often indiscreet. I wonder who will succeed him.

Your affectionate son
Henry.

Provost Guard House, March 4th, 1862.
6 A.M., Poolesville.

My dear Father.

You see by the dating of my letter that I am again on guard, much before my turn, but the Adjutant has not got his accounts in order, and in future I expect to be put on not more often than once in 6 days. John is still here and today we intend to go to the river and to visit the old Camp (Benton). The snow and rain we have had has prevented him from going far from the Camp as yet, but he has greatly enjoyed himself among us here, and I hope to keep him for several days. We have had no further signs of our moving. We have no news from Banks as yet.

---

[20] Cornelius Conway Felton, president of Harvard University, died on February 26, 1862.

RIGHT UP INTO THE FIRE

James Codman left for Washington and home yesterday. He must have had a very wet ride. Capt. Bartlett's father arrived last evening and brought the news of Genl. Lander's death. What a loss to the Army! In this division Lander was very highly respected and perfectly trusted in. We are hoping to see the Colonel soon, and then I think we shall move. I have not received letters from you all at home for several days now, and I suppose my letters have also been delayed. I have received papers as usual.

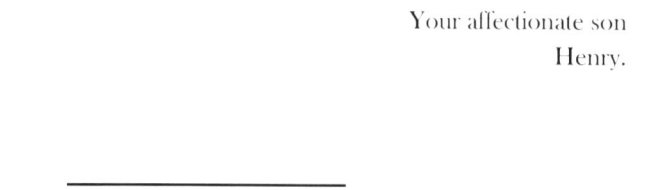

Your affectionate son
Henry.

City Hotel. Middletown, Va.
March 6th 1862.

My dear Mother.

I enclose a long letter to Mary Ann giving an account of my journey to this place, and this morning as I have a few moments to spare, I improve it by writing a continuation to you. First however, I must tell you of the long tramp John and I took to see Ball's Bluff. We started from Camp at 11 o'cl. I was off duty because I had just come off Guard, and we expected to be back by 2 o'cl., but the walking was so bad, and there was so much to see, that we did not get back till 6 o'cl., and then I found orders waiting for me to go to this place. I however passed a pleasant evening with John, saw him comfortably to bed, and then started on my expedition. We certainly had a very rough ride, for the roads, especially through the mountains, were horrible. At about 4 in the morning it was exceedingly dark and we came to the bank of a small river which we must cross. A waterfall, just above us, made such a noise we could not hear anything else, and the guide said he never knew the river so high before. We pushed in however and got through, although the stream was rapid and the horses up to their bodies. It was so dark, you could see hardly anything but the white foam of the water, and it was very cold.

Frederick, through which we passed, is quite a City looking place, and has several fine houses. There are large barracks here for troops now empty, for our troops from here crossed with Banks. The hardships of our ride were however amply made up for by the beauty of the scenery as we got upon the crest of the hills which encircle the valley in which is this town. At the farther end about 12 miles off, we could see the mountains of Harper's Ferry, which I have often heard you speak of.

Well, I had a most comfortable sleep here last night and am now (7 A.M.) waiting for the arrival of the cattle. I expect to ride slowly on with them, and reach Camp tomorrow evening.

Your affectionate son
Henry.

Camp Foster Poolesville March 7th 1862.

My dear Father.

On my return from my cattle driving expedition yesterday, I found your letter of March 4th enclosing one from Mother of the 3rd, the last page of which was written by Mary Ann. Please thank all. I have written an account of my journey to Middletown.

I left with the cattle on Thursday morning. I first saw to the weighing of the cattle at the public scales. We returned by a nearer road via Jefferson and Adamstown. At the depot at the latter place I was greatly surprised to see John, who I had supposed had left the day before. He had been detained on the road from Poolesville and had passed the night in the very house where I had just dined, but I did not know it, and had only time to say a word or two before he was off in the train.

I rode on with the cattle about 3 miles to the house of farmer Smith where we found corn etc. for fodder, and where I passed the night. On Friday I rode on to Camp, and the cattle followed all safely in about 3 hours.

We have no immediate expectation of leaving this camp, but all day yesterday and during the night before, the whole country around Leesburg was lighted up with great fires, and it is said they are burning all the Camps, barracks, corn stacks and everything which could be destroyed preparatory to evacuating. If they do leave I suppose we shall cross and hold possession. I hear they are collecting at Winchester and intend to make a stand there. We shall all know very soon. I am very glad to tell you that I have found my box at Adamstown at the Rail Road Office. Here it was forwarded by the Army Express, and had they notified me, I could have had it long ago. However I found it, and sent it along by a negro who drove a farm wagon, and expect to get it today. The negro took it as far as his master's farm about 2 miles from here and our wagons will bring it to me soon. I am busy for a day or 2 with the Court Martial again, but I shall answer Mother and the others very soon.

Your affectionate son
Henry Ropes.

Sunday evening March 9th 1862
Camp Lee, Poolesville.

My dear Father.

We are still at our old Camp Foster now called Camp Lee, but expect to leave by Wednesday. Leesburg and all the country round is evacuated by the Rebels and is occupied by our troops, and we shall probably cross very soon and join our Division under Banks. Beautiful weather now.
  In great haste

Your affectionate son
Henry.

Monday morning March 10th, 6.30 A.M.

My dear Father.

I open this to say that we are off at last. Orders came at midnight to cook 2 days rations and to prepare 2 uncooked, and we are to leave at 8 o'clk this morning. We go in light marching order and it is said to Harpers Ferry and thence to join Sedgwick and Banks. Perhaps however to Leesburg. I shall no doubt be able to write to you on the march. Love to all.
  In great haste

Your affectionate son
Henry.

RIGHT UP INTO THE FIRE

Camp Lee, Poolesville, Monday evening
March 10th 7 P.M. 1862.

My dear Father.

I wrote you yesterday, and this morning added a few lines to say that we were to start early this morning. As it has rained all day however, our departure has been postponed, and now it is about certain that we march tomorrow evening. Some of our tents and baggage go on tonight. I depend on my knapsack and have left my effects viz.: 1 trunk, 1 camp chest and one deal box in the care of Mr. Jesse J. Higgins, the principal Storekeeper of Poolesville. He does not insure them against war risk, or fire or theft, but agrees to take reasonable care of everything and to hold them subject to my orders. I have marked each as follows: 2nd Lt. Henry Ropes, Company K. 20th Regiment Mass. Volunteers, or William Ropes, 92 Beacon St., Boston, so that they may be sent home, or on to me, as I may afterwards see fit. I have nothing but these trunks and what I take on the march. We expect to be some little time at Harpers Ferry, as our Division (Sedgwick's formerly Stone's) is rather in the rear of the main Army. I sent home by John a box containing various articles of mine, no longer of use, which I hope will be made use of by any of the family, who may want them. Also a bundle for Herbert Mason, directed I think to Mrs. Sturgis Hooper.

I wrote you that I found the last box at Adamstown, and sent it on to a Farm near here by a negro slave. I have today got the box from the farmer's house, but all the Brandy etc. was gone, probably stolen by the negroes. This is a very great loss to me, as I shall have to depend on others if I need any stimulants. The box contained one pair Army shoes, one paper of Coffee, one box solidified Milk, one religious book, large quantity religious tracts and papers, several towels, copy of Putnam's Magazine and a letter from sister Anna. So you see the Gingerbread and Liquor was all that has been taken. I cannot of course recover anything, as we march tomorrow. When I handed the box to the negro at the station I heard the liquid inside and am thus sure that either he or my last messenger stole the things. Please thank sister Anna very much for her nice letter, and tell her how it was delayed, and how sorry I am I did not get it so as to answer it long ago. I shall answer it as soon as we get to a place where I can write with any comfort.

I wrote to you that I received $5.00 from you by letter, and $11.50 by Adjutant Peirson. The Paymaster has not yet been round, and now, as we are probably soon to be in an enemy's country, he may not come for a long time. The Government owe me $300.00 for pay up to March 1st none of which I have received, and I shall be much in want unless I get a supply soon. I dislike very much asking you to advance me any money, but as I have to buy food constantly for myself and servant, and pay all my own expenses, I have found that without any extravagance, the $100.00 you gave me together with the $15.50 advanced since, has been about exhausted. My pay of course is perfectly sure, and may come very soon, but I deem it prudent to be well supplied, and would therefore be very much obliged to you if you would send me as much as may be convenient, and allow the same to stand against me until I receive my pay and am relieved from all embarrassment on this score. If you would send a $5.00 bill in your next letter, and as much more as you see fit by Col. Lee, I think this would be the best way. The best form to have money in is gold dollars. I should be very unwilling to ask you for this did I not feel sure that after my first payday I shall be well supplied for the future. I have just received a letter from Mary Ann for which please thank her. I write the last pages to Mother.

Your affectionate son,
Henry Ropes.

My dear Mother.

I was very sorry to hear from someone that you thought of having copied that picture of me which I first sent you from Camp Benton, and which shows me as I appeared with half my beard of a 4 weeks growth. Now anybody will tell you how horribly a half grown beard makes any one look, and I am very much astonished to find you desire to keep a picture of me, not only in my roughest state, but in a state you never saw me in. I have the *very strongest* objection to having this copied and sent about as a portrait of me. Besides, I now wear *nothing* but the moustache, and I have sent you a small picture, which is said by all to be a most excellent likeness of me as I *now* appear. I have no objection to the one taken when I went off, nor to this which shows me as I am now, but I do not think it unreasonable to object to a picture which neither represents me as you ever saw me nor as I am now, but as I was when a long course of neglect of the toilet had brought me to a state resembling more nearly a barbarian than a civilized being. So much for this.

I have nothing to tell you beside what I have written to Father. We march tomorrow. I shall write as often as I can, but do not be anxious on account of lack of letters. I was much interested in the account of the Colonel's reception. Mrs. Lee sent me a very kind note by Lt. Milton. Please thank her, and say that I hope very soon to find time to answer it. Everybody is longing for the Colonel. Thank Louisa for her letter. I shall soon answer all, I hope.

Love to all.

Your affectionate son
Henry.

RIGHT UP INTO THE FIRE

> Harper's Ferry, Va. 20th Regiment
> March 15th 1862 10 o'cl P.M. Saturday.

My dear John.

I wrote to Mary Ann from Charlestown, Va. where we bivouacked on the 12th. On the 13th we marched in fine style through Charlestown. In the middle of the town we made a long halt. When we started again the band struck up Dixie, and it did my heart good to march to that tune with flying colors past the prison where John Brown was confined. We marched 12 miles to Berryville, and bivouacked again.

This is only 8 miles from Winchester, and in the evening a vast body of troops came marching back from Winchester, and we heard that we all were to return. The great fields and woods were perfectly filled with men for miles around and during the night in a blaze with the Camp fires. Yesterday morning (14th) we all started and marched back again to Charlestown, a vast Army, Mass. 19th, 15th and 20th, Minnesota, New York, Michigan and quantities of other Regiments, horse, foot and Artillery, the long line stretching farther than you could see in either direction from the highest hills. Last night we were told that our whole Division is to go to Fortress Munroe [sic] to be under Heintzelman; thence to Richmond. Today we marched from Charlestown here, and are now in deserted houses in the outskirts of the town. As it is raining hard, I write this in a little room of a small brick house deserted and containing no furniture. It has been used probably by troops, ours and the Rebels. We are said to be awaiting for the Cars. I depend entirely on my knapsack, and stand the hard marching as well as anyone. I have sent home my Buffalo, as I cannot carry it, and it is warm here and I do not need it.

I have written to Father about sending me some money. I now hear we shall not be paid till May. I have not been extravagant in any way, but one must have really money on a march, and as you know I have not as yet received any from the Government and have been obliged to borrow, and as the Paymaster has not come, and I know all the fellows need every cent of their money, I am therefore in *great need* of an abundant supply (of course as a loan till pay day). I hope you will see that I have some sent by the earliest opportunity so as to pay my debts as well as to live. I do not suppose this will be in the least inconvenient to Father. Please see to it for me, if you can.

Love to all.

> Your affectionate brother
> Henry.

RIGHT UP INTO THE FIRE

20th Regiment, Bolivar Heights
Harpers Ferry March 17th 1862.

My dear Father.

I wrote to John I think from this place on Saturday, and by mistake dated it Harpers Ferry. Bolivar Heights, where we now are, is about 1 mile from the Rail Road bridge at the Ferry. This town was inhabited principally by the workmen at the Arsenal, and most of the houses have been deserted for several months. We are in a little 2 story brick house of 5 rooms, and are very crowded, but expect to leave by tomorrow certainly. It was said at first that we were to go to Fort Monroe, and thence to Richmond. Now I hear we are to go to Ship Island. Another report is to reenforce Burnside. At all events it seems sure that we shall go first in the direction of Washington. This is a very beautiful place, but of course we are uncomfortably crowded. We bivouacked for 3 nights, and found it very comfortable except when it rained.

I have written to you and the others of the family from Charlestown and hope you received the letters. I have received nothing from you since we marched from Poolesville, but feel sure that letters are safe, as our sutler goes for them and expects to keep up to the Regiment. I have sent home my Buffalo, as it is so warm now I do not want it. It could be made an excellent sleigh robe, and I think it will be useful at home. I hope you have received my letter about a supply of money. As the Paymaster has not yet come, everyone is in great want. We have to pay Cash for everything here, even to the Commissary. If we go to Washington we can probably get something from the Government. I hope all the family will continue to write although their letters may be delayed.

I must ask you to excuse this letter and the want of ink, for I have no conveniences whatever here. Love to Mother and all. Continue to direct 20th Regiment Washington.

Enclosed letter for sister Anna.

Your affectionate son
Henry Ropes.

Bolivar Heights, 20th Regiment,
March 19th 1862.

My dear John.

I have received your letter announcing your return and giving me the intelligence of the Class elections. This is the only letter from home I have received since we marched from Camp Lee. Do tell me what has become of Hazeltine? Why was not he poet? I think on the whole McBurney was the best choice in the class, but I am very much astonished at Dennett's election. Do write me about it, and tell Jeffries and others to write. Do not let anybody cease writing for fear I shall not get letters, and still direct to "Washington, D.C." We get all letters, though late. I have written to you about having some money sent me. Please see to it that I have a supply in some way. You know the Government have never paid me anything yet, and this shameful delay of the Paymaster has troubled everybody, and I feel anxious to repay the about $30.00 I have been obliged to borrow of the fellows here. I do not think it would be at all inconvenient to Father to send me $100.00, but if you think it is, do not ask him for that amount, but borrow it for me, and use my name in any way you see fit.

It is very uncomfortable here, indeed, and I most earnestly hope we shall soon move on, but all is uncertain in war, and now the report is that the 20th are to remain and guard the Railroad between here and Winchester. I hope my Buffalo got along safely. I have not the least news to communicate, except regarding the Regiment. Lieut. Le Barnes and Capt. Beckwith have resigned. The former refused to obey an order to put out of the camp all but soldiers and servants very foolishly, for he could have accomplished his purpose perfectly without making a martyr of himself. He had brought a runaway slave into camp, and you know he is a great Abolitionist. Capt. Beckwith is you know a poor Officer, one of the old set, and lately got drunk, and had the horrors etc. and got into a row so the best way to settle both difficulties was to accept both resignations and pass over the matter quietly. Le Barnes might have put his slave just over the lines, and then had him registered as a servant and kept him as well as not; but you know how a certain class of men like to make sacrifices of themselves for conscience's sake, and Le Barnes flatly refused to obey and was immediately put in arrest by the Colonel.

Adjutant Peirson has received an appointment on some staff, and who do you think has been selected to act as Adjutant? Why, Curtis, Bartlett's friend, chosen over the heads of every 1st Lieutenant in the Regiment. Of course this has given the greatest dissatisfaction. There was however one pretty strong reason for this appointment, viz.: no Captain would take Curtis as his 1st Lieutenant. O for the return of Col. Lee, and for a strong head to the Regiment.

Your affectionate brother
Henry.

Capt. Shepard desires his regards.

RIGHT UP INTO THE FIRE

20th Regiment Bolivar Heights
March 21st 1862.

My dear Father.

I have received this afternoon your letter of March 15th enclosing Mother's of the same date, and a letter from Mary Ann also of the 15th. Please thank all. I am very much obliged for the $5.00 enclosed in your letter. I assure you I needed it very much. The Government now owe me pay since November 25th 1861 at the rate of $1266.00 per annum, so you see my pay is quite enough to support me, and my need of money is solely owing to the delay in paying me. I have borrowed about $30.00 in all from the other Officers here, who until lately were well supplied with money, but now everybody is short, and I want very much to repay my friends. Besides, on the march, it is impossible to get at the Brigade Commissary who alone supplies Officers, and who sells at a very moderate price, and Officers are obliged to buy anywhere, and anything, and at any price. Coffee, Sugar and Salt were almost unknown in Virginia when we came, and are only bought of the people at extravagant prices. I feel very much obliged to you for your kindness in offering me so bountifully.

Gold or U.S. Bills are the best money here. The only advantage of gold is that you can get dollars, while the bills are not smaller than Fives.

This afternoon we have received orders to prepare two day's rations and be ready by daylight tomorrow. I hear we are to go by the Canal boats to Washington, thence to our place under Genl. Sumner. I cannot see why we have delayed so long here. I am very much surprised at the astonishing attack on our fleet by the Merrimac /sic/. I had supposed that we had nothing to fear by water from the Rebels. I hope this will open our eyes to the necessity of always keeping ahead of our enemies in new inventions, even at a great expense. The English have done so for many years in regard to their steel clad Ships-of-war.

I think, and it is the opinion of many here, that if the Rebels fight at all, they will fight near Richmond, and if so, we shall be as likely to be in the engagement as any other Regiment. We shall be under McClellan, Sumner, Dana and Lee, Officers everyone of the first in their rank in the country, and I think the prospects of the Regiment for active duty and for success are especially good. Please tell John that the address of the box he took home for Private Murphy of my Company is "Wm. Manning, care Owen Mundy, 100 West Dedham Street, Boston". Please lay my bad writing to the lack of a seat and a table.

I enclose a letter for Mother, and remain

Your affectionate son
Henry Ropes.

RIGHT UP INTO THE FIRE

Bolivar Heights, Va.
20th Regiment, March 21st 1862.

My dear Mother.

You see we are still in this little town, awaiting every day orders to proceed to Washington. I have not received letters from you for a long time. Since we left Camp Lee, I have only got one letter from John, and one from Mr. Willard, the latter received last night. I wonder if you still continue to write and to direct as before. The mail comes regularly here.

I have been all about this most beautiful spot, and I often think of what you have often said about it, and about your visit to it when a child. Now however it presents a very martial appearance. The hills and fields are covered with troops, and you see them drilling, and hear the music all day long. Not a few Companies, or a half dozen small guns such as you have seen on the Common, but whole Brigades together, Regiment after Regiment of Infantry and Cavalry, and huge guns each drawn by 8 horses, and an endless line of them too. Day before yesterday there was a Cavalry review, and in the Afternoon a drill of Gorman's Brigade, 6 or 7 thousand men. Although there are so many men here, there is no disturbance at all, and very few drunken men, and no injury done to the few families who have remained. Everywhere Guards are posted, and strict discipline is enforced. I have been over the ruins of the Arsenal, and the vast destruction of property here is really frightful. The works were of enormous extent, and are now completely destroyed. It is like what you read about in a history of the French Revolution, to see fine houses completely ransacked and soldiers in what were once the best chambers, and actually horses stabled in the lower floors. Before one really splendid house, the fine fences and hedges are cut down, and the Artillery parked on what was once a beautiful terraced lawn overlooking the Shenandoah. We have had two days of rain, and the clouds hang very low over the tops of the mountains.

Another thing that strikes one is to hear the Massachusetts Bands playing the tune of "John Brown's soul is marching on" with the full force of trumpets and drums, on the very spot where he was taken. As far as I have been able to learn, the people are really sick of the Rebellion and heartily desirous of peace, and they of course see that peace can only be when the Rebellion is crushed.

There seems to be no doubt that we are going very soon to Washington, and to be then in Genl. Sumner's "Corps d'Armée". What a glorious victory by Burnside![21] I hear none of our friends are killed, but Sargent wounded. You must

---

[21] Battle of New Bern on March 14, 1862.

excuse this paper and writing. I am using a board for a desk and have no chair.

Your affectionate son
Henry.

Bolivar Heights, 20th Regiment
March 21st 1862. 3 P.M.

My dear Mother.

I have just received your letter inclosed in one from Father, and am glad you received my letters. I was very sorry to lose the brandy etc. but really have not needed it at all. I have not been in the least troubled with any sickness requiring either of the kinds of liquor. Still, if you send me a little of either, I shall be very glad of it; but do not send anything else, unless it is eatable, for we carry almost no baggage, and cannot. I find the Coffee *most excellent*, and the milk also. In marching, there is one thing to be observed above everything, viz.: not to be overloaded. Our men have thrown away coats, blankets, hats, and quantities of small trash to lighten their backs. I wrote you a long letter about my photographs. I represented the case, I thought, very clearly, and stated distinctly that I did not wish that one copied which was taken before I shaved my beard. I thought I gave good reasons for my choice, and was very much astonished to find in your letter merely a short postscript stating you preferred the one I had so positively condemned. If you have not received my letter on the subject, please let me know, but if you have, please examine the *reasons I there brought to your notice*. I am very glad we are to leave this crowded and dirty place, and hope we shall not again be quartered in houses.

I have no doubt you had a very pleasant evening at your party for Col. Lee. I am very sorry to notice the death of Mr. Homer, Instructor in Music at Harvard College. Mention it to Frank in your letters, for he knew him and studied with him. Please give my kindest regards to Mr. Willard, and say I hope to answer his letter very soon.

We are off at daybreak tomorrow, so I must bid you good bye for the present. Love to all.

Your affectionate son
Henry Ropes.

RIGHT UP INTO THE FIRE

Saturday evening March 22nd 1862.
20th Regiment Bolivar Heights

My dear Father.

I wrote you last evening that we were to go this morning, and so we all thought. The Drum beat at 4 o'cl. in the morning. The wagons were loaded, and everything made ready, but the final order did not come, and we are still here. It is said very definitely that we go tomorrow, but I believe nothing now.

I was delighted to receive today by mail a perfect pile of letters and papers, which I acknowledge as follows: 6 Advertisers, letter from you dated March 8th, with Post-script dated 10th, enclosing letter from John dated 9th written to tell me of his safe return. Letter from you dated March 14th enclosing letters (duplicate) on Messrs. Riggs & Co., Washington, and telling me of 2 packages of Fifty Dollars each, sent by Captains Dreher and Tremlett. Another from you dated 18th enclosing receipt for box, and a letter from Mother dated 12th March. This evening Capt. Dreher arrived and handed me the Fifty gold dollars, and also the other Fifty, which he said Capt. Tremlett gave him for me. These most liberal supplies together with the news of the box and the good things therein, all coming at once have quite overwhelmed me, and I feel at a loss how to sufficiently express my thanks. Let me assure you I feel deeply your kindness in thus ministering to my every want and supplying me with luxuries far more than the most dutiful son has a right to expect.

I felt some uneasiness about asking for money, at first not because I doubted your kindness and liberality, but from a desire to let you see that I now support myself, and earn my own money. I think most young men have this feeling when they begin to be their own masters, and to be independent. Your great kindness has now entirely relieved me from all anxiety as to my support.

I shall in future make it a point to leave no debts behind me, except the necessary one at the Sutler's, which is under the regulations of the Army and which is deducted from my pay at the pay table.

I hope it will not be much trouble to you to send the box brought by John for Murphy of my company. There is no hurry about it, but it will be a great benefit to him to have it sent, and he is a good man, and I should like to oblige him.

I have today visited a quite wonderful cave, near here. We entered through a small door, and proceeded by candlelight several hundred feet right into the mountain.

With love to all

Your affectionate son
Henry.

RIGHT UP INTO THE FIRE

Washington, D.C. March 27th 1862
Thursday.

My dear Father.

I wrote last from Bolivar. We left there at seven o'cl. on last Monday morning March 24th, and after marching a very short distance were halted, and waited for several hours. We heard that there had been a fight at Winchester, and we were ordered to be ready to move there instantly. At about 12 o'cl. we fell in again and marched through Harpers Ferry over the new Rail Road bridge, and down the river to Sandy Hook. Here we staid [sic] on the slope of a very steep hill overlooking the town till 12 o'clk. at night, when we marched down to the Rail Road at the foot of the hill and got into baggage cars, hastily fitted up with board seats, and of course very uncomfortable, and rode the rest of the night, and until 1 o'cl. on Tuesday when we arrived at Washington. We often stopped and waited, often for several hours and crowded as we were, it was very uncomfortable. The 19th Mass. and 7th Mich. preceded us in two trains. We were marched into a large wooden shed built for troops close to the depot, and slept there on the floor. On Wednesday we fell in at about 11 o'cl. A.M. and marched to an open field, about ½ a mile north of the Capitol, where we pitched tents and encamped, and here we are now. We are ordered to be ready at a moment's notice, and expect to go today. We hear we are to go by ship down the Potomac where a vast quantity of troops have lately gone from here. There is an immense body of troops all round us here, and the two other Brigades of our Division, Burns' and Gorman's, went off last night, so we shall undoubtedly follow very soon. I got an opportunity to visit the City for an hour or two on Tuesday evening, but shall not be able to see the sights at all. Yesterday afternoon Cousins Wm. Codman and Lizzie drove up in a carriage to see me. I was delighted of course to see them. They looked very well.

I have got my box and find it contains exactly what you said it did. I am indeed very much obliged for these many luxuries, and shall enjoy them very much. Do not however venture to send me anything more, for I shall not get it. We have reduced baggage to the last pound, by order, and therefore expect plenty of long marches. Henry Burckmeyer was very brutally attacked yesterday by some soldiers of a N.Y. Regiment, and quite cut and bruised, but not injured seriously. I have discovered who some of the men were and shall take the first opportunity to complain of them and have them arrested. Their Regiment left in the night and I could do nothing this morning. Do not be anxious if you do not get letters from me regularly in future, as we may be on shipboard.

Your affectionate son
Henry.

RIGHT UP INTO THE FIRE

Camp 20th Regiment Mass. Vols., near Washington,
March 27th 1862 3.30 P.M.

My dear John.

We have just received notice to start in one hour, and I hasten to acknowledge the following letters. One from March 21st by Lieut. Holmes, one from Mary Ann same date, and one from Mother, 24th, the 3 last pages written by you. This latter I got after writing to Father this morning. I have also received letters from Jeffries and McBurney. Some time ago I got a letter from Jack Reed. If you can please thank all these, and say I do not know when I can answer any. I think we are now going down toward Norfolk. One of the above letters was by Capt. Tremlett. I shall write whenever I can, but that may be very seldom.

Our Division consists of (at least) Burn's [sic], Gorman's, and Dana's (ours) Brigades. The 19th Mass., 7th Michigan, Rhode Island Artillery, Van Allen Cavalry, and several New York Regiments are in our Brigade.

Good bye. Love to all. In great haste

Your affectionate brother
Henry.

On board Steamer Catskill below
Washington. March 28th 1862 4 P.M.

My dear Father.

I wrote you from our Camp at Washington yesterday. I was Officer of the Guard then, and was ordered to say till all the wagons were loaded at the Camp, and then to bring on all the stragglers. The Regiment left the Camp at about 4 in the afternoon with the wagons which were to return to get another load. As this was our last day in a large city, an unusually large number of the men got away and were brought back drunk, so that I had a very hard duty. On account of the very great delay in getting the Regiment aboard the Steamer, the wagons did not return until midnight. Then everything was loaded up, and I marched down, not without a great deal of trouble from the drunken prisoners. However at about 5 o'clk. A.M. we got down to the river, and then had to wait till 7 o'cl. before all the baggage was put on board. At last we got all safely aboard, and I was relieved from my very arduous guard duty. There was still a great deal of delay in getting ready places for horses etc. and it was a quarter past 3 P.M. when we finally started from the wharf. We are now steaming down the river, and in about an hour I expect to get a view of Mount Vernon. The Captain tells me the house can be seen from the boat.

I do not know whether I distinctly acknowledged the receipt through Capt. Tremlett of your letter in regard to money, the first page a copy of the letter I before received at Bolivar. I am very sorry you were so troubled because of my want of money. I was at no time in absolute need, for I borrowed money from my friends, but now all are so short, that I was very glad to be able to pay my debts, and to relieve some of my suffering companions a little. If, when I get to Fort Monroe, where we are now going, I have reason to think that I shall be unable to get money for a long time, I shall draw the Fifty Dollars, to carry in case of need. I hope you were at no trouble to get gold for me. U.S. notes pass everywhere here, on both sides of the river, just as well, the only trouble is that there are none but $5.00 bills. I am indeed very much obliged for this timely supply, and hardly see what I should have done without it. I am perfectly well and comfortable.

Your affectionate son,
Henry Ropes.

On board Steamer Catskill, near Fort Munroe,
March 30th 1862.

My dear John.

I wrote to Father day before yesterday, soon after we left Washington. We proceeded well till night, but in the night we got aground and afire. We got off the one and put out the other, and laid at an anchor till daylight. Yesterday we ran till evening, and then anchored for the night, as the wind was East and some sea, and our crowded river Steamer very unfit for rough water. This morning at 9 o'clock it cleared a little and we proceeded on our voyage, and expect to be in tonight. I hear that there is a vast Army now at Fort Munroe.

As to my photographs I have expressed a very decided dislike to the picture which was taken when I had a half grown beard. I still, very naturally, feel unwilling that that picture should be multiplied and given to my friends. Of course, if any of you like it or any picture of me, why, keep a copy, but if you give away generally any of those pictures of me, you do so *entirely contrary* to my wish so often expressed. I very much prefer the excellent likeness taken of me just before I started, which you sent to me at Camp Benton, and which my friends here thought so good. I prefer that to any yet taken. If you still dislike all the pictures, wait till my whiskers grow, and if I can, I will then have another taken.

I fear I do not at all understand your theories in regard to the war. When we get to Fort Munroe I hope to get my trunk and my map.

Love to all.

our affectionate brother
Henry.

Holmes desires to be remembered to you and to John C. Gray.[22]

Camp 20th near Hampton, Va.
April 1st 1862.

My dear Father.

I wrote to you and to John from on board the Steamer "Catskill" on Sunday last. We arrived safely at Fort Monroe on Sunday evening, and found there an immense fleet of transports and war vessels, so that in every direction the lights were as thick as stars on a clear night. During the night our Captain left the Ship without a watch and she drew her anchor and drifted ashore, and into a schooner striking near the stern and breaking in part of the saloon. It was dark and there was a great commotion for a few moments, none knowing what had happened, but soon order was restored and we got off, and nobody was hurt. Our boat was an old North river Craft, utterly unfit for the voyage, and especially so when crowded with 800 men, beside horses etc. The Captain was a good for nothing fellow, and abused everybody and everything, and neglected his duties. I think we were very fortunate in meeting with no serious mishap.

On Monday morning we hauled into the wharf at the Fort, but the number of transports was so great and the quantity of troops so immense that we could not

---

[22] A fellow lawyer and friend of John C. Ropes.

land there, and therefore proceeded to Hampton, a very pretty sail through the harbor. I had a most excellent view of the Monitor lying with steam up, ready for anything. She is the most insignificant looking affair I ever saw, and I was very much astonished to see so small a Craft. You have no doubt seen pictures of her. To look at her, one would laugh at the idea of her fighting the Merrimac. The tower is very low, not up to the deck of a small ship.

We landed at Hampton, and soon marched 1 ½ miles on the Great Bethel road to this camp where we now are encamped, and where I suppose we shall wait till the rest of the Army comes, and the fleet is ready, and then we shall march on Yorktown and thence to Richmond. This is *probably* the destination of this Army. There is an immense Army here now, with the entire Regular reserve, which has been long collecting at Washington. It is a very flat country, and the troops are camped close together. It is warm and pleasant, and the trees are already budding. I have sent for my trunk from Poolesville by Adam's Express as I need a change of clothing.

As we may be now at any time called upon to march, I have determined to draw Fifty Dollars on Messrs. Riggs & Co. as soon as possible so as to be provided in case I should come short in an enemy's country. I think I can do this easily through the Quartermaster.

There seems to be no doubt that a vast army is to collect here for the great final attack on the Rebel power. There must be at least 100,000 men here now, and more are coming all the time. Almost all the Regular Artillery is now here. I suppose it will take a week or so to organize, and then we shall march on Yorktown 18 miles. After that city is reduced or evacuates, we shall proceed to Richmond, perhaps co-operating with an Army from Washington and with Burnside. I think letters had better be directed to Hampton, Va. near Fort Monroe via Washington, D.C. but probably the old direction will answer.

I have heard that Col. Lee arrived in Washington the afternoon we sailed, but have not heard whether his family were with him.

All well, love to Mother and all. Shall write more as soon as I get a tent and can get up something for a table.

Your affectionate son
Henry.

RIGHT UP INTO THE FIRE

Camp 20th Regiment 4 miles beyond
Big Bethel, Va. Sunday
April 6th 1862.

My dear John.

I write to Father by this mail. Have just received yours of the 1st April. We have got a tremendous Army here. Milton (who knows) tells me we have in all 135,000 men and 500 pieces of Artillery. The Rebels abandoned a very strong place at Big Bethel, the day before we came. When we had marched about 5 miles from Hampton, we halted, and soon about 5000 regular Infantry passed us, and the 6th Cavalry. I have met Lieut. Hartwell, Adjutant of the Regulars, here, a very fine fellow. Here McClellan past [sic] us, and we did not recognize him. I was very sorry. We bivouacked just beyond the Big Bethel earthworks on Friday, and yesterday we rose early and marched on passing the Regulars and vast quantities of the troops, and at about 9 o'clock made a very long halt. As I had been on guard and had had no sleep, and had marched since 5 o'clock, I was very tired. Where we halted several roads met and before us was a very large plain perfectly covered with troops, all halted. Soon we heard a distant cheering constantly coming nearer, it was said McClellan was coming. We drew up and presented Arms, and he rode through the whole Army to the front, with his whole Staff and Escort. We and all the rest cheered most tremendously and the amount of noise made by the shouts of the men was tremendous. I had a perfect view of him. He is a square stout man, with a light complexion, short sandy hair, small light yellow mustache and imperial, red cheeks, and a heavy, square wide head. He had his hat off, and was smiling and bowing all round, and seemed to notice everyone. He looks as if nothing could daunt him, and nothing discourage him. He looks frank and pleasant and hopeful. I was very much pleased with his appearance. He rode smiling by and evidently much pleased with his splendid reception. Soon after he passed we had a heavy thunder storm followed by a very hot sun indeed, and it was really oppressively hot. At about 9 o'clock came the heavy boom of a gun ahead, and another and then 2 or 3 together and so it continued, very heavy guns a long way off.

As I was very tired I fell asleep and woke at about 11 o'clock. The Cannonade was then one constant roar. The order came to fall in, and we went on, passing ahead of 2 or 3 Divisions and then turning off on a crossroad to the left. The Cannon now nearer and heavy. Soon we heard volleys of Musketry and a running fire. We marched through a very extensive Rebel camp, deserted very lately. Dr. Crehore came by and told me there were Rebel batteries 2 miles ahead which must be taken before night. The firing now became less, only distant guns heard. After a

RIGHT UP INTO THE FIRE

very tiresome and long tramp through deep mud, and over an awful road, we suddenly came out on to one of the great open places surrounded with woods which they have in this flat country, and I saw about 30,000 men (as I afterwards found) drawn up columns closed and the caissons in the rear and flanks. I really thought we were to find an enemy. Instantly the order came to close column by Division on 1st Division, which was done, and then we rested some time. The firing in front had about ceased and soon we stacked arms and quietly encamped, and here we are. Today we are resting and awaiting supplies. The regular Artillery cleared the way for us yesterday, and our gunboats are up the York river and shelling the Rebels, and thus are firing heavily. I am now speaking to a Rhode Island battery man just returned from a reconnaissance on the Rebels. He says they are entrenched in a semi-circle ¼ miles before us and that there has been fighting today. He saw our fleet shelling them. Several Artillery men have been killed and wounded. We are the central column, Keyes the left, Porter the right. We shall *undoubtedly* attack in one or 2 days, unless they surrender, and they cannot escape. Our men are perfectly confident of the result. They have only about 40,000 men under Magruder.

Today, an hour ago Capt. Bartlett came to me and ordered me to take 20 men of our Company, and go as a guard to Genl. Dana immediately, saying we might have skirmishing etc. I went with Generals Sedgwick and Dana into the woods. Before we had got a mile, the General told me to halt, and went a short distance forward, and then returned and dismissed the guard and me. I thought it quite an honor although it did not amount to much really.

Well, I expect that before this reaches you I shall have been in the greatest battle which ever took place on this continent. I do not like to write much, but of course I know what may happen, and I feel perfectly prepared for any result to myself, and feel only anxious to do my duty in battle. God grant I may! I do not feel much concerned for my own life, and am glad to rest the result in higher hands. Please do not read this letter to the family, for Mother, I know, will be *very* anxious when she knows how near we are. The letter I send to Father she will of course see. I am perfectly well, and the weather is delightful and very warm.

I think we shall take the entrenchments and Yorktown and 40,000 men! We have 135,000 men, 10,000 regulars, and 500 pieces of Artillery, a very great part regular. And we have McClellan and on the whole splendid troops, all perfectly confident and ready for anything.

Love to Mary Ann; shall try to write again and answer her letter.

Your affectionate brother
Henry.

RIGHT UP INTO THE FIRE

Camp 20th Regiment 4 miles beyond
Big Bethel, Va., April 3rd [6th] 1862. Sunday.

My dear Father.

I have just received Mother's and John's letters of April 1st. We marched from our Camp at Hampton on Thursday morning and passed through Little and Big Bethel and bivouacked just beyond Big Bethel. Here we found very extensive earthworks and barracks, just deserted by the Rebels. A vast quantity of troops were marching by our Camp all the night and after we had marched about 6 miles we made a long halt; while we were lying and resting by the roadside, a large number of Officers rode by, and just after they passed I found that it was McClellan and Staff. I was very sorry we did not recognize and cheer him. Yesterday we marched on to this place, and I have seen McClellan very plainly. He is a fine, open looking man, with a fresh complexion and sandy hair and only in the shape of his face resembling the pictures which make him look like a dark, severe man.

We have been here all day, and I do not know when we shall advance, but I hear the Rebels have fallen back somewhat. Our Army here is several times as large as their force, and we have an immense train of Artillery, so I suppose they will have no hope in resistance. Although our Army is so large that probably only a part will be engaged with the enemy, yet I feel of course that ours may be the attacking party. All is uncertain in war, but I hope you will not let your fears make you too anxious. Remember that I trust I am prepared for any event and that I feel happy in leaving all in God's hands.

Love to all.

Your affectionate son
Henry.

Camp 20th Regiment near Yorktown, Va.
April 9th 1862.

My dear John.

I wrote to you and to Father from this Camp on Sunday last. On Monday April 7th, the 19th and 20th Mass. Regiments with Capt. Saunders' Company of Sharpshooters all under Brigadier General Dana, made a reconnaissance, and as I was present, and as it came very near being a fight, I will give you a particular account of it all. But first let me say that on Monday a heavy North-East rain storm set in, and has continued ever since, and the roads are impassable, and the great advance must be retarded 4 or 5 days. We have been without tents, and have suffered very much sleeping wet and cold, everything soaked through and still no sign of clearing off. I write this in the Sutler's tent where I may be able to sleep tonight.

Well, on Monday the Regiment received orders to fall in without knapsacks at 7 A.M. and we marched off, the 19th just ahead of us. Capt. Shepard was Officer of the day, and he and Tilden, Officer of the Guard, were the only Officers left at Camp, except Captains Tremlett and Putnam who are sick. So I commanded Company K. We marched about 2 miles and halted on the edge of the woods and formed in line and then received orders to load, cap and halfcock, and to advance with perfect silence. The Surgeons accompanied us and got ready their stretchers etc. We advanced for several miles in the woods frequently halting. The roads very soft and bad. Often we went right through the thick woods. The object of the expedition was to reconnaître the enemy's position and advanced works and an Engineer was with us and rode with the General in every direction. We marched in a very round about way and at last came out on a road, and the 19th formed on the right, and we followed and formed on the right as we passed the 19th. Thus we were drawn up in line, the 19th on the right, and we on the left. There were thick woods on the right of the road, in front of our line. Soon I was ordered by Capt. Bartlett to select 4 good men, and post them, 2 in front of the line in the woods, just as far as we could see, and the other 2 as far beyond, and to tell them to keep a good lookout and report anything. The other Companies and the 19th did the same. I posted the men, and observed that just beyond the outer post there was an open place in the woods. I returned to the Company and we waited about one hour, when my picket sent in for me. I went out and they pointed to several men in the open place and on the edge of the woods beyond. I thought they were our men, and went out a short distance farther, and saw one man with a gun wearing a brown overcoat about ½ way across the open place. He soon retired to the woods and I saw several others on the edge of the woods. I returned and reported to the Colonel and he told me that the men must be Rebels, and that we were close to them, and should remain quiet and not let them know we were there. I returned to the outpost and told them not to fire if they could help it. I then returned to my post in the Company and before long the reports of rifles rang from the woods in front and on the left. It was kept up for several hours, sometimes only dropping, and often rattling in a very lively manner. The 19th men and some of our men, contrary to the orders of Genl. Dana, had gone over the open place I spoke of and found a rebel fort and entrenched camp, just beyond the woods at the other side. It was here that the firing took place. All this time of course the Engineer was examining the approaches etc. The Rebels only replied with musketry. It was now raining steadily.

RIGHT UP INTO THE FIRE

At about 3 o'clock, orders came to fall in, and we marched by the left flank along the road and soon came to an open field. Here we halted, and the 19th formed in line of battle here, and deployed the right flank Company as skirmishers. We then marched on and soon came to the burning ruins of a fine house. We here turned to the right and entered the woods, and came out on a large open place. We marched quietly along the edge of the woods and halted and formed. I will draw a little plan for you to see exactly how it was. Here the men were ordered to throw off anything that would hinder their process, and Rubber blankets and Overcoats were dropped. You see by the plan that we were now very near the Rebels, but I did not know exactly how near they were yet. I have marked the direction of our advance after we left the 19th by a dotted line.

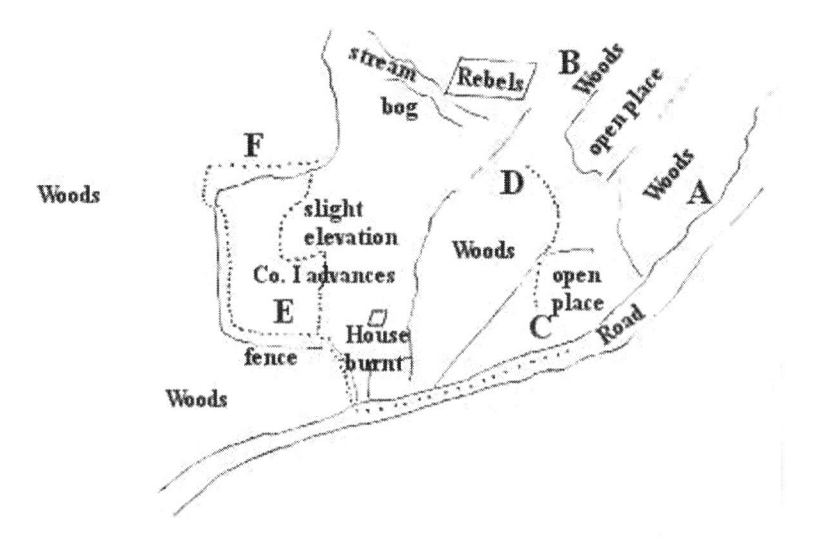

A. Where we halted and put out pickets.
B. Where our men first opened fire without orders.
C. Where the 19th drew up.
D. Where their skirmishers were sent out.
E. Where we formed and sent out skirmishers.
F. Final position.

Just as we got into the position (marked E) the 19th on our right opened fire suddenly from the woods, and kept up a very heavy and steady fire from this time.

Up to this time the Rebels had fired only musketry, but now they suddenly opened with a 32 lbs. shell gun and threw shells right into the 19th on our right. I have drawn it as if the 19th were nearer than we were. They were not, only a slight elevation in the field hid us from them. The shells exploded very rapidly, and Genl. Dana, who was with us all the time, ordered skirmishers forward, and

RIGHT UP INTO THE FIRE

Companies I, A & F were sent off. Co. I was first sent out alone, and Abbott marched them straight forward, and in another moment they would have gained the crest of the hill and been terribly exposed to the enemy. Dana instantly saw this and shouted out "March that Company more to the left, they will get a shell" and Dr. Crehore ran up and overtook them and gave the order, and the Company was thus saved from a close volley. The next Company in line is mine and after Abbott had gone up, I thought I should go next, but Capt. Shepard has never instructed the men in skirmishing, and of course they know nothing about it. So I explained to the men in a few words what I thought most important and awaited the order. But Capt. Bartlett, as soon as Abbott had entered the woods passed our Company K and ordered forward the next 2 Companies A and F as skirmishers, and ordered me to close my Company up on the remainder of the line. This I did. Our men received orders not to fire till they could see the enemy well. In the plan I have marked by a dotted line the advance of Company I. No sooner had I closed up my Company than we faced to the left, and marched round the edge of the field (where I place the dotted line) to our final position (marked F). Just before we advanced however, a detachment of sharpshooters went up, and soon the fire of the Rebel 32 lbs. slackened very much. We then halted and formed close to the enemy, but unseen by them and the firing continued. While we were waiting here, I asked Capt. Bartlett why he had passed over our Company when he sent out skirmishers. He said we could not skirmish very well, and told me that we were the main column still and would probably soon assault the enemy's works. However, I suppose Genl. Dana did not wish to bring on a battle, and as soon as the Engineer who was always in front, had finished his business, the Companies skirmishing were quietly drawn in, the firing dropped away by degrees, and we were marched back to the road as we came. It was 3 ½ o'clock when we sent out Company I as skirmishers, and 4 when we took our last position and we had marched 10 or 15 miles, and it was pouring with rain and the roads horribly muddy. The Tammany Regiment had been all day cutting a road for Artillery behind us and on this we marched back, after being led by mistake much out of the way. It was pitch dark when we got back tired and wet. The 19th lost one man killed[23] and several wounded, including a Captain.

The poor fellow killed was hit by a shell and when we passed was lying on a stretcher bloody and gasping. I saw 2 more wounded men. The Surgeons got everything ready just before we sent out Company I, but no one of our Regiment was hurt. For my part I did not hear a single bullet, and one only passed near me and broke a bough from a tree. But we were expecting every moment to be led on to the assault, and I doubt if even the General decided not to attack, till a few

---

[23] Private Andrew Fountain, Jr. of Company D.

moments before we fell back. There was a large force of Rebels behind the fort, and they had five Cannon mounted while we had none. I hear the reconnaissance was perfectly successful. Well, we got back to Camp soaked with mud and rain, and no tents or shelter. The Captain has got his rubber blanket stretched to form a shelter, and we tried to sleep, but laid awake cold and wet, the rain beating in and filling everything. It has rained ever since and I and every thing belonging to me is wet and cold, and altogether we have suffered more than I ever imagined we could stand. It is too bad to give us no tents, and it is awfully uncomfortable although I stand it perfectly well in health. The roads are now horrible beyond description, and the great advance must certainly be delayed for several days.

I have to acknowledge your letter of April 5th, and a letter from Father by Col. Lee, who sent it from Fort Munroe where he now is. I received at the same time a most kind letter from Mrs. Lee dated Washington. I have received several newspapers. I hope that before now Father has received my letters acknowledging the receipt of the $100.00, the drafts and the box, and knows that I have drawn for $50.00 from Messrs. Riggs & Co. I am delighted to hear of our class and the M.P.C. and ashamed of '63. I agree with you as to the cause of their weakness and want of energy. My love to all at home and to my college friends. Everybody must excuse my lack of writing for the present. We are on the eve of a tremendous attack, and God only knows what a day may bring forth. I thought you would be interested in all these particulars, even though we were not engaged after all. I hope to write fully about anything I hear. The 16th, 19th, 22nd and 7th Mass. Regiments are about here.

Your affectionate brother
Henry.

Camp 20th Regiment near
Yorktown, Va. April 11th 1862.

My dear Father.

I have to acknowledge several letters from you including one by Col. Lee, and one from Mother, of the date (I think) of April 7th. I have written fully to John of the skirmish of last Monday.

I have since learnt that the left flank Company of our Regiment (Capt. Putnam) which that day was under Herbert Mason was deployed on the road when the rest of the Regiment entered the woods, and Herbert was ordered by Genl. Dana to resist an expected attack of Cavalry. When it was decided not to assault the works and we returned to the road, Herbert formed the rearguard and before long came upon the poor fellow of the 19th who was mortally wounded, and had been left on a litter with 6 men to carry him back. These men were exhausted, it was pouring with rain, and very dark, and they were on the point of leaving him, but Herbert took him in charge, and his men carried the poor fellow the whole way back. Herbert was thus detained an hour, and his men had a very tiresome time indeed. They lost the Regiment and had to make their own way back in the darkness and mud. The poor fellow died just as they got him back. The 19th were very wrong in thus leaving a comrade. The Doctor should certainly have staid. A part of one of their Company left the field without order, and were sent back by the General, so the 19th have little to boast of for that day.

I hear we shall be unable to move for several days. I hear the Merrimack and Monitor are engaged today. Result unknown.

I have just heard of our glorious victory in the West.[24] It seems as if it only needed a great defeat here, to destroy the Rebel cause.

I enclose a letter for Mother. Shall hope to write again soon.

Your affectionate son
Henry Ropes.

Camp 20th Regiment near Yorktown, Va.
April 13th 1862.

My dear John.

We are still here, and the regular siege has not yet begun. Great re-enforcements, I hear, are constantly arriving for us, and heavy siege guns have begun to come up from Ship Point. I understand that regular parallels are to be opened, and the place will be a second Sebastopol. If McClellan knows any one branch of military knowledge better than any other, it certainly is the art of attacking earth-works, and no one has any doubt of our final success.

Henry desires me to say that he would be glad if Mr. Hichborn would please open the letter he speaks of, take the money enclosed, and make the purchases

---

[24] Battle of Shiloh on April 6-7, 1862.

requested, and send the same to Henry's family. Henry would thank you if you would afterwards send him the letter and if you have a chance, the Segars. Henry will write a letter to his family, and send it by me to you to be forwarded. Probably you could send any things Henry may wish to send to his family, by Messrs. B. C. Clark & Co.

We have beautiful weather again, though cold nights. I have drawn and received the $50.00 I wrote to Father about, by Adams' Express. I shall send to you very soon by Express a parcel containing some private letters to be given to Mary Ann and several little mementos of the Rebellion I have collected for you, of little value however.

I have just heard that our tents are to be brought up today, and this looks like a long stay here. I earnestly hope I shall get my trunk soon, and make a little better appearance in the way of clothes etc. We live here altogether on the Commissary stores, and hard bread, hominy, beef and pork are our regular food. I am perfectly well. As to when or how our operations will begin, I am sure you know as well as I do. I think not for several days at least.

The Paymasters are at the Fort, I hear, only waiting for the fall of Yorktown to come up and pay off all the Regiment.

Love to all. I hope to write often. You must excuse this writing done in open air on a hard bread case.

Your affectionate brother
Henry.

Camp near Yorktown Va. 20th Regt.
April 15th 1862.

My dear John.

I have just received your letter of April 11th; Mary Ann's of the 12th and 2 newspapers, and I hasten to reply. Here we are settled down and encamped in the same spot where we arrived a week ago last Saturday, expecting to take Yorktown the next day. We have our tents, the Captain and I have a nice wall tent together, and our men have built up 2 nice bunks and a table, on which I am now writing, and altogether I am perfectly comfortable. The great storm has passed entirely away and today is clear and really hot. We have dress parades and drills just as if

RIGHT UP INTO THE FIRE

we were in Camp Benton, and we now hardly ever hear guns. There is no skirmishing, because I suppose the Generals are perfectly acquainted with the situation and strength of the enemy. Our pickets are posted out every night a long distance in the woods, but I do not suppose the enemy have the least idea of coming out to attack us. I hear that large siege guns have been brought up from Ship Point, and that large bodies of troops have been landed there, but as the Ship Point road is above this camp I have seen nothing of these movements. We have no drumbeats or music now, by order of McClellan, probably for fear the enemy should know our position. Yesterday we had a grand Inspection. As our Company was inspected, and Genls. Dana and Sedgwick were looking at the men, guns etc., an old white haired Gentleman came quietly up, and seeing Capt. Bartlett and me standing a little apart, as he passed us said most pleasantly: "Good morning, Gentlemen," and we saluted, as he wore a General's straps. It was Genl. Sumner, Commander of our Corps d'Armée. He looked like a most excellent, retired, orthodox minister. Sedgwick is a man like Capt. Ths. Leach, only more refined and a very little pompous. He is exceedingly prompt and has things put through, and will not hear of delay about anything. Sumner has a long white beard and stoops a little.

I feel, as you say, that we are on the eve of a great contest, and yet it is perfectly impossible to keep up a state of suspense in one's mind. I did not know this before, but now I am satisfied that a man can get used to any state of things, and feel perfectly easy, no matter what is impending. This general feeling, however, is probably in a great measure the result of the perfect confidence in the result which all feel. We hear of Rebel re-enforcements, but we only think of how much greater will be the final success. I feel sure that we can bring an overpowering force against the Rebels and however many men they have, it is only for McClellan to telegraph and be furnished with any number he wishes. Then we have a splendid Army. I had no idea before how good other Regiments were compared with ours. I had thought the 20th was a long way ahead of all, but this is not so. Many other Regiments are our equals in every respect, and perhaps our superiors. Then there are about all the regulars, and regular Artillery and Cavalry that can be got together, and a large proportion of New England and Western Volunteers. Then we are most splendidly equipped, clothed and fed and altogether, I cannot well imagine a finer modern Army. As you say, there may be terrible fighting, but while each man's life is uncertain the feeling that the great cause is *certainly* to triumph makes every man only eager to be in the great final attack.

Last evening Jim Starr (57th) came over to the Camp. He is about 6 miles in the rear, brigaded with the 6th Regulars. I hear he has a splendid Regiment. He looks very well, and has shaved all but moustache and McClellan. As to my health, I never in the world was better. I am as perfectly well as I can imagine being, and I think I know how to keep well. We had several very cold nights, and before the tents came, I hardly slept for cold, but it produced no ill effect that I could see and last night I had a most comfortable rest in the tent.

I hear Col. Lee is still at the Fort. I *most earnestly* hope he will soon take command. I see *every day* and especially since we have been in active service that Col. Palfrey is not a real, active, wide awake man, nor a man of self reliance and force. Of course he is personally brave, but he does not keep up the Officers and the Regiment to the mark. The Officers do not respect him much. (This of course is private). Col. Lee has a will of his own and will put things through. Col. Palfrey, for instance, lies abed till ever so late, and many of the Company Officers do so too, and in many other small things the Colonel sets the example of sloth and delay in business. Col. Lee has a soldier's spirit, and plenty of energy, and a certain impatience of delaying and laziness. However, we are under Dana's eye, and he is every inch a soldier. He looks something like Mr. Joseph Willard (Senior) and is a perfectly cool man. I feel perfectly sure under him, and he likes our Regiment and always has his Headquarters close to us. I shall write often and let you know of any movements I see.

Did the box ever get to the family of Private Murphy of my Company? Please let me know. I sent the direction. Give my love to them all. Do not get uselessly anxious. At present we are as safe and comfortable here as you are at home. Friends and Capt. Shepard send regards.

Good bye, must go to Battalion Drill.

Your affectionate brother
Henry.

P.S. I have sent a letter from Henry Burckmeyer to his family, enclosed to you..

H. R.

Camp 20th Regiment, before Yorktown, Va.
April 19th 1862.

My dear Father.

I last wrote home from our Camp "near Yorktown, Va." It has been named "Camp Winfield Scott". On Wednesday last 300 of our Regiment were ordered out to work on the roads, and our Company among them. While we were just finishing a rough bridge over a stream, we saw the head of a column of soldiers come up the road, and soon we recognized our own Brigade. They kept passing on for about 4 hours, and among them the rest of our Regiment. Our whole Division passed on except Cavalry, and all the Generals, even Sumner. After they had passed we finished our work and marched back to our now deserted camp. After getting some supper we packed up, and followed our Regiment. It was very dark, but we marched only a short distance, and found the Army bivouacking in the woods. The next morning we marched out into an open place and encamped. During the night there was a very sharp firing of musketry in the advance. The Camp was roused and the whole Brigade formed under arms. Soon the firing slackened, and we were dismissed, but ordered to remain with arms ready and not undress. No further alarms roused us.

We heard in the morning that the Rebels made a sortie from their works and were repulsed by the 2nd Vermont. Every day one Brigade does picket duty in front of our Division, and yesterday was our turn. We were close to the enemy, and there was almost constant firing on both sides. One man of Comp. H was severely wounded in the side by a musket ball.[25] There was a great deal of firing in the night, but the woods are very thick and it is hard to see. I went down and could see the Rebel works and tents very plainly. Our pickets are as near them as from our house to Charles Street, and if anybody shows himself on either side, he is shot at. We hide behind trees. Things do not seem to move on very fast here, but I suppose it will all go well. Everyone is anxious for an immediate attack and all hate this constant picket fighting.

Your affectionate son
Henry.

April 22nd

All well.

Henry Ropes.

---

[25] Private Samuel Kershaw.

RIGHT UP INTO THE FIRE

Camp 20th Regiment before Yorktown, Va.
April 19th 1862.

My dear John.

You see by my date that we have moved our Camp nearer the Rebel works. We are now about ½ mile from them, and the guns are planted in front of us, and protected by a Division relieved daily. Yesterday we did this duty and were close to the enemy and firing most of the day and night. I wrote you a long account of our skirmish, and now find that what I called a Rebel fort, was really a part of their great works. It is flat marshy land here, and covered with dense fine woods, with occasional open spots so it is nearly impossible to form a clear idea of the enemy's position. You remember that I told you in the letter I referred to that the 19th Regiment formed in an open place and sent forward skirmishers.

April 22nd Tuesday.

My dear John.

I was obliged to leave off very suddenly, as you see, and have only now been able to continue. I will take it up where I left off.

In the open place where I said the 19th formed we went, and our Company was stationed on the edge of the woods as a reserve to Company F which was put out as pickets on the edge of the swamp. Company I was left with the Colonel at the road, and here also was a section of Artillery and some sharpshooters. I will give you another little map.

RIGHT UP INTO THE FIRE

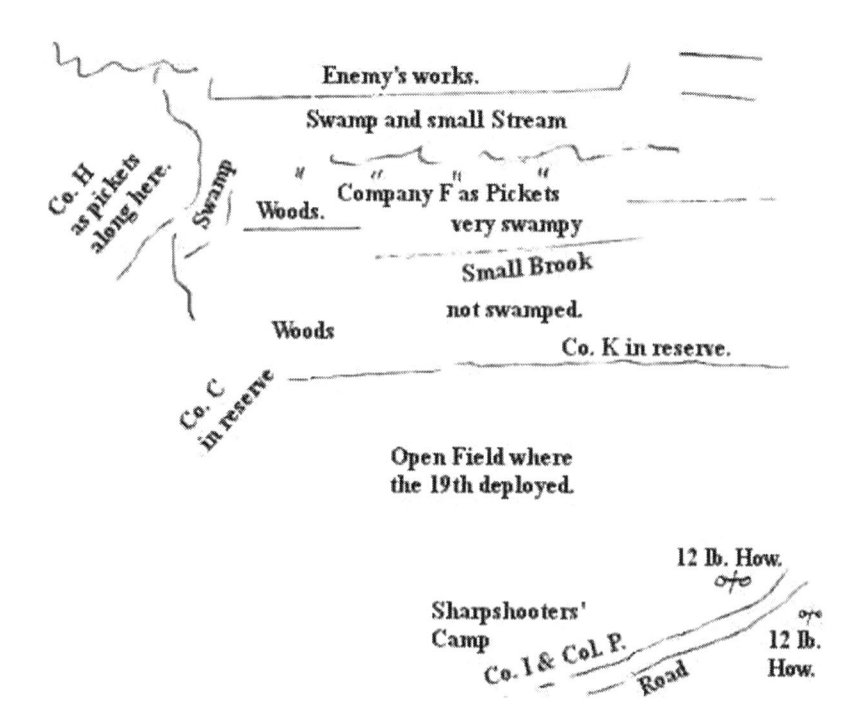

```
         Enemy's works.
         Swamp and small Stream
  Co. H              "    "     "
  as pickets   Woods.  Company F as Pickets
  along here.                very swampy
                         Small Brook
                         not swamped.
         Woods
                         Co. K in reserve.
  Co. C
  in reserve
              Open Field where
              the 19th deployed.

                                    12 lb. How.
              Sharpshooters'
              Camp      Co. I & Col. P.    12 lb.
                                    Road   How.
```

Of course this is very rough. The field is much wider from the road to the woods than I have drawn it, and it extends much farther to the left. When the 19th deployed the day of the skirmish, they went very much to the left and engaged a part of the fort which does not appear on my map.

During the night that we were on picket, we were not called upon, but Capt. Cabot's men kept up a very brisk firing with the Rebels. During the day one man of Herbert's Company was shot in the breast. His Company (H) was on a bluff, which rather overlooks the enemy, and they have some sharpshooters stationed on this part. The musicians and stretchers for the wounded were left with me and sent down to the points needed. Well, there was no real attack in spite of Cabot's firing and we were relieved and returned to Camp next day all safe. On Sunday at noon we were all suddenly turned out under arms. I had charge of the Company, as the Captain was Officer of the day, and while I was in the tent I heard someone say the Regiment was falling in. I ran out and saw the whole Brigade forming, and I then gave the order for Company K to fall in. Soon Generals Sumner and Dana rode off to the front. We fell in and the whole Brigade marched to the front and formed in line of battle on the road opposite the open field I have so often spoken of. Everybody expected we were to fight, for there were Regiments drawn up as far as one could see, but after waiting under arms till nearly sundown, we returned and found it was all a false alarm. Another alarm in the night called us all up. We were fast asleep in our tents, when I was awakened by the Captain.

RIGHT UP INTO THE FIRE

The Camp was perfectly still but there was a constant and heavy firing of musketry toward the front. Musketry at this distance (about ½ mile) sounds something like heavy wagons passing over a bridge. In a few moments orders came to fall in and put out lights, and in a very short time Company K was standing at ordered arms, ready for anything. However, after waiting till about One o'clock, we were dismissed and ordered to "hold ourselves in readiness" during the rest of the night. As usual the firing was only a false alarm of the pickets and reserves.

Yesterday it became our turn to go again on picket, and we went in spite of a heavy rain storm which turned our camp into a ditch and the roads into rivers. You can hardly imagine a worse country than this. It is all covered with dense woods, principally large pitch pine and is almost perfectly flat. Half of it is swamp, and you can get water anywhere by digging 2 feet down. Of course there are a few slight elevations. This time Company K was in the extreme advance, and occupied a sort of bluff where in my map I have said that Company H was stationed. However, we kept well behind trees, and nobody was hit, although the balls often whistled quite near us. In one place where 2 of our men were, we had a quite good view of the Fort. I saw a brass gun and several men. The Rebels have a rifle pit and some sharpshooters here, and both of my men at this point had the trees struck behind which they were. Toward evening we were obliged to extend the line of our Company much farther to the left to unite with Company C. Just as it got quite dark, we received the countersign, with orders to pass it along to the left. I told the Captain I would take it along to Company C, and started, following my own pickets. They were placed behind trees and stumps, about 150 feet apart but it was very cloudy and soon began to rain tremendously, and the darkness in those deep woods was extreme. At night the Rebels show lights to decoy our men to fire, thay *[sic]* they may know where and how many we are, and may fire volleys at random toward us. We were therefore ordered not to fire unless attacked.

I found the very greatest difficulty in getting from one post to another and frequently ran right against a tree or stump. At last, however, I got to Company C, gave the countersign and started to return. It was now darker than ever and raining very heavily. I got along to our last post but one, and then the picket told me it would be much easier for me to go back a few steps to a road which had been cut in the rear of the post and which ran right by the post where Capt. Shepard and I were to be. This I attempted to do, but did not succeed, for I could not tell at all when I got to the road. I attempted then to return to the post I had just left, but was unable to find it. I could not of course shout as this was close to the enemy, and I stood a good chance of a couple of shots from them had I thus shown where we were posted. I therefore pushed on in the direction I thought our men were posted, frequently stopping and listening, and giving low whistles etc. but could get no reply. At last I determined to stop and wait till I could see something by which to direct my way. I halted at the foot of a tall tree, and after feeling about discovered a stump on which I sat and waited for the rain to cease. After some time it stopped raining, and I saw a star or two. As I was quite tired and wet I fell into a daze. I was awakened by two shots, as it seemed to me, in front of me. I then thought that perhaps I had got between the enemy and my pickets. While sitting here leaning against the tree, I fell asleep, and when I awoke, the stars were shining and all was clear. I got up and before long saw in an opening of the branches the Dipper, and then the North Star. This gave me my direction, and I could then explain the shot I had heard as coming from our left. I found I had got quite turned round. Although it was still very dark near the ground in the shade of the trees, it was starlight, and much lighter than when it rained. I determined to proceed cautiously in an easterly direction, and thus hoped to strike our pickets or reserve. It was now still, and I could hear a long distance. Before I had got far I heard a man cough. I coughed in reply and advanced and heard distinctly the twigs breaking under somebody's feet. I then said in a moderate voice "Company K" feeling sure it was one of my men. He replied, I advanced, and in a few moments came upon Sergeant Faunce of my Company who conducted me to the Captain, only a few steps off in the very place from which I had started. The Captain and I were to have staid here with a reserve of 10 men, a little in rear of our line of pickets. The Captain was delighted to see me, for he had sent down to Company C soon after it cleared off, and learned that I had left them to return long before. I got back at about 2 o'clock. As pickets are allowed no fires, it was very uncomfortable for all till the sun rose and dried our clothes and warmed us. we were relieved very late, and did not get back to Camp till noon today. We had no alarms. The Rebels were at work at their forts all night, as usual, probably repairing the damage we do by shells etc. in the daytime. There is Artillery firing all day long but only at intervals. I really do not see what progress we are making here, nor why we do not do more. We have several batteries, to be sure, but there is no appearance of activity anywhere. Of course we know nothing of Genl. McClellan's plans, but the opinion is gaining ground that we are only to hold them in check here while Burnside and McDowell attack their rear. This picketing is bad work, and not very interesting or glorious, and I think bad for the men to lie out and wait for shots at each other, as if they were hunting deer. Besides, this swampy hole will be very uncomfortable and sickly soon, and already on a fine day the heat is oppressive, and one finds shirtsleeves the most comfortable rig.

We have now what are called "Shelter tents", which are little better than nothing. I am thankful to say however that the Officers are to have their wall tents today. We can be very comfortable then. I am perfectly well, and at present the Regiment is healthy, but the Doctor says we shall not be long.

I have received letter from you dated April 11th, Mary Ann's 12th and Father's 15th, for all which greatly obliged. Have received no letters since, but 3 papers. I shall write a soften as I can, and hope to have something more of interest another time. I hear it reported that we shall soon move to the rear, and be relieved in this picket duty by another Division. We are the first Brigade of our Division. I can hear nothing of the other parts of our line, and for what I know operations are being carried on vigorously at some other place, but we all trust to McClellan, and know that whenever he orders us to advance there will be some way of advancing. Mr. Henry Edwards is here now and looks perfectly well, and was very pleasant. He is on Government business. We Officers are much displeased that Governor Andrew should have filled the 2 vacancies in the Regiment by promoting 2 sergeants and this without any recommendation from Colonel Palfrey in the regular and usual manner. The Commissions, however are not yet given, I believe. I hear nothing about Col. Lee.

Love to all. Do not forget to write often.

Your affectionate brother
Henry.

Camp 20th Regiment before
Yorktown, Va. April 25th Friday 1862.

My dear Father.

I received yesterday your letter of the 19th enclosing a receipt of Adams' Express Co. for the box, *also* a letter from Mother, of the 18th, the last page written by Louisa, and a letter from Mary Ann of same date. This morning I received a letter from John of April 21st. I have also received 3 newspapers. Please thank all. I feel very much obliged to you for sending me the box. I am sure I never can repay the kindness you have shown me in so often supplying my wants, and furnishing me so often with so many comforts and luxuries. There is not an Officer in the Regiment who has received one half the presents from home I have, and I feel it quite impossible for me to express my gratitude.

In the midst of a wilderness like this, you can hardly imagine the value one places upon the things which one takes as a matter of course at home. I assure you I shall use the contents of the box with the greatest care, and I know it will contribute very much to my comfort.

We have this morning returned from another day of picket duty, and I grieve to say that yesterday our Regiment met with the greatest loss it could possible sustain. Capt. Bartlett was shot in the knee, and has lost his leg. He has been sent to Ship Point, thence to go to Washington. Our company was yesterday placed in reserve, close to the 2 Howitzers I have before mentioned in my letters, and we were not very near the enemy. Capt. Bartlett came up in command of the Regiment. Col. Palfrey remaining in camp, and after the different companies had taken their posts, he went to the advanced posts and was crouching down examining the enemy's works with a glass, when a ball, fired from a rifle pit by a Rebel sharpshooter struck his knee and shattered the bones down to the middle of the calf. He was brought up on a stretcher, and taken to a small house near our camp, where the surgeons, after a short consultation, decided on immediate amputation above the knee. He was placed under chloroform, and the operation was performed by Dr. Hayward. The last accounts were that he was quite comfortable. This of course ends the military career of one of the most promising young men in the Army. He occupied a very high place, and would no doubt have won a name in the coming campaign. He was the right hand man of the Regiment and I do not see who can fill his place. Capt. Dreher, the next in rank, is an older man and a most excellent Officer, and probably the best educated military man in the Regiment, but he is a German, and speaks English very imperfectly. In case of active service the Regiment will be in great need of Officers, and unless the Colonel returns very soon, we shall be very badly off indeed.

We go on picket every 3 days. The last time we were on, our Company had the exposed post, and I remember that Capt. Bartlett came up and told me he wished to visit the posts. I went with him, and when we were in the most exposed post, where a good view can be got of the enemy works, I told him of the rifle pit we had discovered, and cautioned him to pass without stopping - from tree to tree - that we might not give the enemy's sharpshooters a mark. We staid some time there, and saw the men in the rifle pit, and the stumps and logs piled round to deceive our men, and while there the Captain told me he hated this picket work, and felt sure he should sometime be shot while on picket. He said he would much rather meet the enemy in open fight. The very next time we came on picket, he was shot in this very place. I think it a very remarkable coincidence. The whole Regiment feels his loss deeply.

We seem to be settled down in this place. The Captain and I have now got a tent, and have had bunks put up of boughs, and are quite comfortable, and protected from the weather. Today is cold and rainy, but a few days ago the heat was oppressive. I shall never again complain of the great changes of weather at home. It is worse here. I cannot but think that McClellan is waiting for other movements before he attacks these works. We of course see only a small part of the line, and know almost nothing of what goes on elsewhere. There is no danger of our being surprised, as I see Genl. Grant was at Corinth. The picket duty is carried on with the very greatest regularity and care.

Henry desires me to give you his respects. He has received his letters.

Your affectionate son
Henry Ropes.

Enclosed letter for Mother.

RIGHT UP INTO THE FIRE

Camp 20th Regiment before Yorktown, Va.
April 25th 1862.

My dear Mother.

I thank you for your kind letter of the 18th received yesterday. I tell all the news I have to give in my letter to Father, but I must not forget to thank you also for the nice things you have sent in the box. You cannot tell how greatly such gifts contribute to my comfort and how very much obliged I am for them all.

I am very glad you have enjoyed Dr. Mercer's lectures. Do not think that I neglect my devotional duties. I always have time enough for that. On Sundays I read the service, and although I have no sermon, yet I find the regular observance of Sunday as far as possible, a great pleasure and benefit. Last Sunday was Easter, and while I was reading the morning service we were suddenly called out and marched to the front with every expectation of meeting the enemy, but it turned out a false alarm, and toward night we returned to Camp. Herbert's younger brother Philip, 2nd Lieutenant in the regular Artillery came over to see him the other day. He looks very well indeed. I believe he is very near us.

We have met with a sad loss in Capt. Bartlett. He was a man of fine military spirit and tastes and to be deprived of sharing in the coming struggle must be a great disappointment to him. He has lost a leg, but will no doubt do well, as he is young and strong.

Love to all.

Your affectionate son
Henry.

Camp before Yorktown, Va.
April 28th 1862.

My dear John.

Many happy returns of your birthday. I do not forget it here. Probably before your next birthday, this great question will be settled, and people will speak of the siege of Yorktown as they now do of Sebastopol. This morning I have come home from another day's picket. We were on the advanced post, where Capt. Bartlett was wounded, and as the Captain was ill I had charge of the Company. So my duty was arduous, and I feel a little spleepy [*sic*] this morning. Well, affairs remain about the same. The Rebels work all night on their fortifications, and from my stations last night I could hear distinctly the chopping of wood and the voices of the men. I could hear them even whistling when at work. We are ordered not to fire at night unless attacked and so they go on unmolested. But I understand that the main operations are on our right where a pontoon bridge has been thrown across the York River, and immense guns of 100 and 200 lbs. caliber have been mounted. From what I can learn I think that Gloucester Point will be occupied, and a position then taken which will enfilade their entire works. Then this immense battery I have spoken of will knock their earthworks opposite our right into a cocked hat, and the road for the Infantry will be open. This is my opinion of McClellan's plans, as far as I can learn. I have no news to tell you, and am perfectly well. Henry desires his thanks to you, and to Mr. Hichborn through you. He does not know what box you refer to. He wishes to know if any money was used by Mr. Hichborn for the benefit of Henry's family over and about the amount contained in the letter (if any was contained in the letter). He also wishes to know what could be the freight and duty on a small box sent to Hayti?

Love to all. No news. Just heard report of the Capture of New Orleans. Hope it is true.

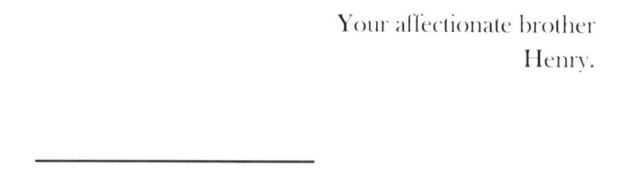

Your affectionate brother
Henry.

Camp Winfield Scott before Yorktown,
Va. May 1st 1862.

My dear Father.

I have no letters from you to acknowledge but this morning I received a letter from Mary Ann dated April 27th for which please thank her.

Yesterday the Regiment was paid off up to March 1st 1862. I received pay from the date of commission, November 25th 1861 to March 1st 1862, amounting to $333.05. I have still got about $40.00 of the $50.00 I drew from Messrs. Riggs & Co. and as we shall probably be paid up to May 1st 1862 in 3 or 4 weeks, I have sent home to you $280.00. I enclose a receipt for the amount signed by Mr. Folsom, which you will please present to the Mayor. I am very glad thus to be able to pay the sums you have been so kind as to advance.

RIGHT UP INTO THE FIRE

These are as follows:

> Feby. 11th in letter 5.00
> Feby. 24th by Adjutant Peirson 11.50
> Feby. 24th by Henry's Expenses 22.50
> Feby. 24th by do. wages, 1 month 15.00
> March 16th in letter 5.00
> March 22 by Capt. Dreher 100.00
> April 6th by draft Riggs & Co. <u>50.00</u>
> $209.00

These are all I have charged. Will you please therefore deduct this amount from the $280.00 and hand the balance $71.00 to John. I requested him to keep an account of the sums expended for me for clothes etc. etc. at various times, and I think the $71.00 more than enough to pay for these.

Should there be $25.00 left after deducting the amount John takes, I wish to have a silver hunter watch bought with it and sent to me. I find a watch with an exposed crystal a very great trouble. One is very apt to break a crystal by sleeping in one's clothes on the ground, and when the crystal is broken, it is perhaps a month before you can send it anywhere to be replaced. Then, besides, a watch which you can depend on is a necessity here, and mine is not at all trustworthy. I find most of the Officers have got plain silver hunter watches, and I wish you would get one for me not to cost more than $25.00. I do not care in the least how large or ugly a watch it is. The *only* things required are that it should be a *good time keeper*, and be a *hunter*. That is all. I would be very glad if you would buy such a watch and send it to me by Adams' Exp.

I have just got back from another day's picket. We were on reserve. We are used to this now and our men do not fire at all. Genl. Dana came up and I went with him along the line of outer posts and showed him what we could see of the enemy etc.

I was familiar with the ground as I was there the time before. I have not yet heard whether New Orleans is really taken. Have today received a letter from Martha.

Love to Mother and the rest of the family. I am perfectly well.

> Your affectionate son
> Henry Ropes.

RIGHT UP INTO THE FIRE

Camp Winfield Scott near Yorktown, Va.
May 1st 1862.

My dear John.

You see I now date my letters from Camp Winfield Scott. This is the regular authorized name now for the Camp of the entire Army before Yorktown.

I have been paid off up to March 1st 1862 $333.05, quite a pile of money for my first earnings. I am now due $210.00 more up to this date. We shall probably be paid this before long. I have sent home to Father through Capt. Macy, Agent for Mr. Folsom and the Mayor of Boston $280.00, and requested him to reimburse himself for the amounts advanced to me, in all $209.00 and to hand the remaining $71.00 to you. I know you have an account of my expenses for shoes, line etc. etc. written for by me while at Camp Benton. I never made a list of the things nor prices, but I beg you to sum up the whole and pay for it out of the $71.00. I suppose these expenses did not exceed $40.00 but I really have quite forgotten and I beg you to forward to me a list, if convenient. Then I wish you to take from the remainder $5.00 and expend the same in a birthday present for yourself, as you see fit, and let me know afterward what your choice may be. This leaves $26.00 in your hands, and with this I have requested Father to buy for me a silver hunter watch. I am in need of a watch to keep good time, and which has not a crystal to be broken. I do not care to spend a cent for beauty, and only desire a useful watch. I think $25.00 the maximum price such a watch will cost. No objection to a large one. Perhaps an American one will do very well. If I have passed over any money advanced by Father or have not allowed enough for your list of expenses, please let me know and I will send the money immediately. I would like to make all square behind me on this pay day, and I think the $280.00 will be sufficient, but it may not be.

It has occurred to me that perhaps the Harvard Boat Club will now need their house where our boat is stored. You had better write to McBurney, and ask him if he wishes you to remove the boat. She only needs painting to be fit for any use. Perhaps you will want her at Swampscott, but if you do not care much about it, I would advise selling her provided you can get $35.00 for her, complete with oars, awning etc. etc. Very likely Mr. Andrews would like her. If you want to sell her, *by all means* ask McBurney to tell Jim Holt in Cambridge. He is a boating man in Cambridge and would sell her if anybody would.

A long time ago Henry Jeffries asked me what he should do with my share of the Haidee Boat Money, about $6.00. Let him pay it to you, and you can credit it to Father, as it is his, not mine. Three Dollars are also due me from C. B. Porter for coal. This also is Father's. Jeffries asked me if I wanted to give the boat money to the A.D.? I should be happy to do so were it mine. By the way, Milton asked me about the A.D. and said he would give them $10.00 if they needed it. I should be happy to add $5.00 or $10.00 if it is needed. How is the glorious old fraternity? Do they need money? Better ask Jeffries or Grinnell.

In future all letters to me to be directed as of old merely "Washington D.C.".

We have warm weather now, but a good deal of rain.

Do not save the boat on my account, but act as you at home see best. No news. Constant firing night and day, but little damage. Frank Bartlett I hear, is doing finely. We are dreadfully in need of him or the Colonel.

Your affectionate brother
Henry.

Have received yours of 21st on the 25th.

Camp Winfield Scott, before Yorktown, Va.
May 2nd 1862.

My dear Mother.

I have received this morning your letter of April 28th for which I am much obliged. We are still here and likely to remain until the Rebel works are taken, as far as I can see.

I am afraid you make yourself needlessly anxious about me, for as yet we have not been in any danger, and very likely may not ever be in any, for it is thought the Rebels will evacuate when they see the preparations for attack completed. Since Capt. Bartlett was wounded we have had only Col. Palfrey for a field Officer, and he is confined to his tent by a lame foot, and we are in terrible need of Col. Lee and the Major. Lieut. Riddle has just returned from Fort Munroe, and he says that our Government released a Rebel Colonel, Major and Doctor from Fort Warren, and sent them on a parole of 15 days for Richmond as exchange for our Officers, and that the Rebel Colonel promised on his honor to return if not exchanged in 15 days, but the time is now out and he has not returned. He says perhaps the violation of parole by these Rebels will (according to the rules of war) release Col. Lee and his companions from their parole, but I suppose it will be a delicate question of honor. It is reported that unless in some way field Officers are supplied to us very soon, we shall be sent back to the Fort, and some full Regiment put in our place. The return of the Colonel would set all right. We have had a great deal of cold, wet weather, but now the sun shines again, and it is really hot. We have fully as great changes of weather here, as you have at home.

Our picket firing has now about ceased. The Rebels fire a little at night, but we do not return it, and keep concealed. If our men should return their fire, they could see by the flash of the guns where and how many we were. I have written to know if my box and trunk have arrived at the Fort. If I find they have, I shall send Henry down, and let him bring me many things from my trunk which I want.

If you could send me any good books by mail, I should be very much obliged. Nothing heavy or valuable of course, but some of the "Tauchnitz" editions might perhaps go thus. Perhaps you could cut one of these into 2 or 3 parts and send one at a time like a newspaper. At any rate an Atlantic Monthly or Living Age would go, but I should prefer a standard work. John would see to it.

Love to all. My eyes are perfectly well.

Your affectionate son
Henry.

Camp above West Point, York
River, Va. May 6th 1862 A.M.

My dear Father.

You have no doubt ere this rejoiced over our great success. We have been so hurried on in pursuit that I have not been able till now to write, and tell you what we have seen and done.

We were rejoiced on Friday to hear of the exchange of Col. Lee, the Major and his brother the Doctor, and on Friday evening they arrived in camp. The Colonel was very cordial to me and gave me your letter of the 30th enclosing one from Lizzy of the 9th, one from John of the 30th, and one from Mother same date. He looks very well indeed.

On Saturday the 3rd, we went on picket, our Company being under my command, as the Captain was Officer of the day. We were on the reserve with the Colonel. There was a good deal of firing during the day, and at 3 A.M. of Sunday the 4th we were all turned out under arms, as the Rebels fired smartly for half an hour or so. We waited till 7 o'cl. the usual time for us to be relieved, and then formed. As the 1st Company was on picket, our Company was first in line. Just at

7 o'cl. an Aide-de-Camp rode up at a gallop and ordered the Colonel instantly to advance on the enemy's works as they had evacuated. Col. Lee gave the order and we entered the woods in front, and came out on the open swamps right in front of the extensive works of the Rebels. We could see a few signal men on a part of the works, and no guns or flags left. The Colonel led the way, then the pioneers, then the Regiment. Our company of course first. We waded through the swamp and by bridges left by the Rebels we crossed 2 very deep and broad ditches, full of water, and mounted the principal redoubt. The Colonel instantly shouted for the flag, and in a few moments it waved, the 1st U.S. flag over the Rebel works at Yorktown. The Soldiers gave tremendous cheers, and it was altogether a glorious occasion. We have since marched to Yorktown, and were out all through a terribly rainy night and embarked in Steamers and this morning disembarked here, and are only waiting for the rest of the troops to begin our advance, perhaps on Richmond. I am perfectly well. Shall write more fully soon. I suppose we have headed them off now.

Your affectionate son
Henry.

Camp near West Point York River, Va.
May 8th 1862.

My dear John.

I wrote a letter to Father yesterday and despatched it this morning, and gave a short account of what we have seen and done.

Our Regiment entered the works before Yorktown at about ¼ before 3 on Sunday morning. Just as we mounted the works, after wading the swamp, I looked behind me, and it was a splendid sight to see the great glittering columns passing out of the woods in all directions moving on the forts. The horse Artillery galloped forward and took up position so as to command the woods in rear of the works in case the enemy should attempt to drive out our advanced Regiments. It was hot, clear, sunny morning. As Company I was away on the outer pickets, our Company was the first Company in, and as Capt. Shepard had remained in Camp as Officer of the day, I had the pleasure of commanding. When we advanced, we of course were not sure that we should not have to attack and drive off some small body of the enemy. The Colonel went first in. The forts are very extensive, and from where we were it was quite impossible to form an idea of their entire works. They were built of earth and in a regular manner, where we entered was a circular front. As near as I could see this would represent the front.

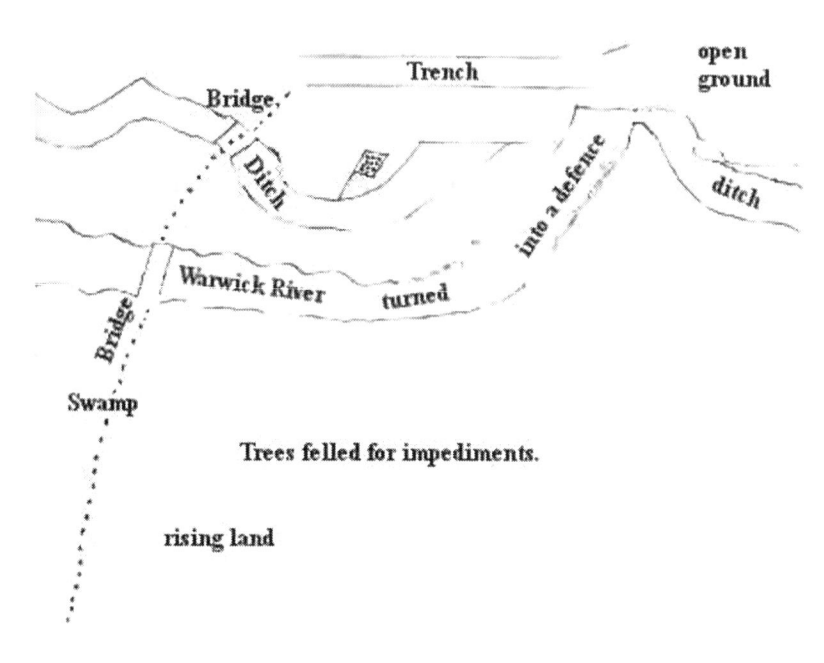

[Diagram: Map showing Bridge, Trench, open ground, Ditch, into a defence, ditch, Warwick River, turned, Bridge, Swamp, Trees felled for impediments, rising land]

The dotted line shows our course. In the interior ditch the men, who served the guns evidently lived, and had built shanties. The top of the works was piled up with sandbags, and pieces of our shells were scattered round quite thickly. As far as I could see, in this first line, the cannon used were only field pieces.

As to our having taken the place at first by an assault, I hardly think it could have been done. The ditches would have had to be bridged under a terrible fire, and the assaulting party would have been entirely broken up by the swamp and the fallen trees, arranged over a space of one or 200 feet wide, between the two ditches. From the Rebel forts our new works looked splendidly, and much more regular and workmanlike than theirs. I forgot to say that our flag was probably the first one raised over the Rebel forts, and in the position I have shown in my plan. Soon after we had occupied this part of the works, other Regiments came up, and we were moved in, and stacked arms and rested on a large parade ground inside. There were long rows of barracks all round, comfortably built of logs, and one or 2 old houses originally no doubt the farm houses, as the Rebel works were built on a place over cultivated land. These buildings were all in ruins and evidently not very lately occupied. Our shells had made this part very dangerous to live in. A great many old chairs, tin pots, papers and a few books were scattered about. I picked up a copy of Bunyan's Holy war, the blank leaves written over with blasphemous assertions of Northern cowardice and of the future success of the Confederate Arms. I have this, and a number of very interesting rebel letters and some Southern postage stamps etc. Some letters picked up refer to Magruder's drunkenness, and some abuse Davis. I have also a general order of Magruder's.

At about noon we marched back to our old Camp and were ordered to be ready for marching as soon as possible. Before we left, large bodies of horse Artillery, Cavalry and Infantry had passed us and gone on, no doubt in pursuit. We made all ready at Camp, but no marching orders came, and we spent Sunday night in the old place. It rained hard in the night, and all day Monday, but on Monday morning we fell in and marched to the right, and camped near the York River, about ½ mile from Yorktown. The land here is rather hilly and very pretty, grass green and trees in flower. We got very wet but pitched shelter tents here and built fires. I forgot to say that when we marched back from the Rebel works, we found the other Brigades packed up and all ready for a start, horses harnessed and Artillery men in their places. The Bands which have been silent for two weeks had begun again and were getting rid of their joyful feelings by sounding the well-known airs of Hail Columbia and Dixie in their loudest strains. Far down the Columns, you could hear the rolling of drums and the rumbling of Cannon and wagons. Altogether a very different scene from that we passed in our silent march to our picket-station only the day before. There was one thing the Rebels did before leaving, worthy of barbarians only. They left Percussion shells slightly buried in the earth inside their works, on the roads and in the fields. A person treading on one would cause it to explode. Several of our men were killed and wounded thus, and guards were stationed where ever these were found. I heard several explode, 2 of which wounded men. When it was found that this had been done, the Rebel prisoners taken were sent forward and obliged to point out and pick up these shells. As this burying shells could not in the least retard a large Army and could not benefit the Enemy in the least, I think, it was brutal and inhuman to do that which could only inflict injury on an enemy uselessly. Well, at 7 o'clock on Monday evening we were ordered to fall in and marched off to Yorktown. It had just settled down into a regular steady rain. We had only ½ mile to march, and it took us 11 hours! The time until 6 o'clock on Tuesday morning was spent on the road. It may seem incredible that 4000 men should thus needlessly be exposed for a whole night to a pouring cold rain and deep in mud, but such is the fact, and I really think I never felt so tired and exhausted and generally disgusted. The three roads from the Centre right and left of the Peninsula meet just before Yorktown, and along these roads the brooks were pouring in one steady stream the whole time. We first halted to let the right hand road empty itself, and we waded *[sic]* till it grew dark and until 1 o'clock, while the troops passed on. We then would march 5 minutes and halt 2 hours, and so on again. At last it ceased raining and at break of day we halted on a rather dry place, and men and Officers sank down, and in a few moments I fell asleep and awoke at broad daylight, wet and awfully cold. We were just on the edge of the ditch of a tremendous Rebel fortification, on which the great guns yet stood. This fort is altogether the largest and finest I have yet seen, and really is quite up to any description of the Redan or Malakoff I ever read. Inside this fort is Yorktown, i.e. about 6 respectable old houses. You would hardly know that the little group of houses was the town, and would suppose at first that they were the houses built for the Officers of the fort, not the town for the defence of which these great forts were built. We were allowed to go into the fort, and found the barracks inside quite comfortable and quantities of old chairs, tables, etc. etc. A large number of wagons, wheelbarrows, spades etc. were lying about, and there was an old Omnibus marked "Hampton".

Our men soon had immense fires lighted and cooked breakfast. The sun rose without a cloud, and in an hour's time everybody was luxuriating in warmth and comfort. I dried my socks etc. and had a good cup of coffee, and soon felt all right. At about 8 o'clock we marched down to the wharves, where the river was perfectly crowded with transports and men of war. Our Regiment was embarked in the splendid river Steamer C. Vanderbilt, and the 19th Mass. followed us on board. Our Company and Company I marched into the Ladies' cabin and stacked arms in two long rows. Here each Officer and most of the men had a berth to himself. Just before our Regiment went on board, I was detailed to attend to the getting the provisions on board and I was thus as busy as I could be till 3 o'clock, when the Steamer sailed. As I had been up all the last night, and on picket the night before, I was awfully sleepy, and immediately turned in and slept away, and was awakened for supper at 6 o'clock, when the boat was lying off the wharf of West Point, 30 or 40 miles up the York river. I of course did not see any fine scenery if there was any.

I left Henry Burckmeyer at our old Camp. He has been troubled with a lame back and colds for ever so long, and has not been able to do his full work, and when I found we were to march and he was quite unable to carry anything and keep up, I gave him leave of absence and let him go back and get well, and he is to let me know by letter how he is, and probably return when he is well. I do not think he is very ill, but he has not got any energy and spirit, and cannot put things through and stand all sorts of privations. When in good health he did very well, and I liked him very much, but since we have begun to march, I have seen his great lack of spirit, and that he is not a "man of many resources" by any means. He is a man who would make a most excellent servant for cousin Wm. Ropes, but a very poor one for a soldier in the middle of an active campaign. For the present I have got a private from my Company named "Walker", one of the best men in the

RIGHT UP INTO THE FIRE

world, and infinitely more active and enterprising than Henry, but of course not so quick and gentlemanly nor so good a cook. I should like to have Walker for a march and Henry for a camp always.

Well, I left off my narrative where we had just got to West Point. We soon steamed a little further up the river called "Pamunkey" on my map, and stopped for the night opposite to an immense open flat field on our left where a great many troops had already landed, and the river was crowded with steamers and barges and several black looking gunboats. The next morning (yesterday) we landed at about 6 o'clock A.M. in great barges, the Artillery being towed in on rafts. Altogether it was exactly like what you read about of the disembarkation of armies. We formed upon the shore and found ourselves about in the centre of the plain, close to the river, and several small houses near us. Troops were encamped in all directions, and our Division was just landing. We staid long enough to get some breakfast, and were then ordered into line without knapsacks, as some scattering firing had begun on the edges of the field where the woods began. This was about 8 o'clock Infantry and Artillery were rapidly thrown forward , and we were marched and drawn up in line of battle about in the centre of the field or rather nearer the river. Soon the plan of our attack was seen, for the troops were formed along the edges of the woods, and Artillery a little way behind. We were now marched to the left and drawn up in line of battle facing the woods, our left resting on the river. Our troops had now entered the woods all round, and the firing was getting to be very heavy. The Colonel walked along the line and told the men to keep cool, fire low etc. A battery was now drawn up behind us, we masking it. Soon the firing in front burst out volley after volley, and quite near. We then changed front to the rear on 8th Company, and of course unmasked the battery and formed, our rear on the river, and left toward the woods. We were marched a short distance to the rear and were then close to the river. Soon the musketry in front diminished, and for several hours a dropping fire was kept up. All this time firing was kept up on the farther part of the field, and our batteries on the edge of the woods kept up a steady fire for a long time, which was quite fierce some time after the firing in front of us had ceased. Col. Lee explained to me the military evolutions which were very interesting indeed, and of which we had a splendid view, for we could see the whole of our force, perhaps 40000 at first. Col. Lee told me that having engaged the enemy all round, it was determined to attack principally on our right, and we could see the Regiments and Batteries rapidly moving into the woods there. Altogether it was very much as I had supposed. Col. Lee told me we were merely getting and holding our position, and that this was not to be a general battle. By and by most of our troops had entered the woods, or were standing on the edge, and the firing had about ceased. The wounded had been brought in for some time, but I hear that our entire loss did not exceed 100 men. It seems very few for so much firing.

RIGHT UP INTO THE FIRE

Part of the battery we were supporting had been sent to the right, and we were resting on our arms when suddenly a Rebel battery from the woods on our extreme left opened and threw shell quite near to us and just short of the transports in the river. Every shot came nearer, and we heard them whistle by. One struck close to the Vanderbilt, and threw the water all over her. But their danger was short, for 2 gunboats immediately opened, and another coming up the river got into position and opened fire. The tremendous shot from these boats passed right by us and fell and burst right over the Rebels. Our guns only fired once for the General stopped them after the 1st fire, lest our position should be made known and fired on. The gunboats silenced the Rebels in about 10 minutes. It was a fine sight. The rest of the day there was no firing except a few shells thrown by us at a house where were some Rebels seen. Toward night we moved toward the centre of the field and bivouacked.

Today there has been no fighting. Have just heard of the evacuation of Norfolk. Part of the 6th Cavalry has just come through from McClellan. We beat the Rebels yesterday. They are to make their long promised "stand" at a little river back here about 20 miles.

Today I have had a fine swim in the river. It is like summer here, and very pleasant. Have received no letters, except from Col. Lee since I left our old camp. I am perfectly well. I have seen a great deal, which perhaps I can tell you about some day. The Rebellion seems about put down but there may be a fight here yet. Our dead brought in today are stabbed with many bayonet thrusts, and I hear some have had hair and clothes cut off for trophies by these savages. This and the Torpedoes left at Yorktown have terribly exasperated our men, and if we get at them I do not think they can hope for much mercy, and I think they deserve little.

Have been here all day. It is now 8 P.M. Hear we march tomorrow at 5 A.M. Love to all. Shall try to write again soon.

Your affectionate brother
Henry.

P.S. You all seem to think a great deal of my adventure in the woods. I suppose I unintentionally exaggerated it. It was not at all dangerous, and I wonder you thought it was. The 2nd line of rebel works were about ½ mile from Yorktown; The 3rd merely the fort enclosing the town.

H. R.

RIGHT UP INTO THE FIRE

On Picket about 8 miles above West Point, Va.
on the Pamunkey River
May 9th 1862.

My dear John.

I wrote you a tremendous letter day before yesterday, giving an account of my movements etc. up to date of letter. Nothing has since happened, except the advance of our Brigade about 3 miles along the bank of the river. We marched up yesterday, and today are put out on picket, although there are pickets beyond us, and the Cavalry today could not find an enemy anywhere within 5 miles. Our gunboats are pushing up the river and shelling the woods. McClellan arrived yesterday. He never moves without being received by tremendous cheers, and yesterday I traced his course a mile off in this way. Near our Camp on the open field I spoke of, the dead were buried yesterday. Many were bayonetted several times, and I hear one had his throat cut by these savages. 15 privates, 2 Captains and 2 Lieutenants of the 31st New York were put into one great grave, close to us. It was a solemn and sad sight. I am sorry to say some of the New York Regiments behaved badly on Wednesday. Col. Lee told me so. Col. Lee told me he expected we would be ordered forward every moment. I hear that it is very unusual to get such a good sight of real military movements.

I suppose we shall advance as fast as transportation and provision can be brought up. It is impossible to say whether or not we shall have a great battle here, but I think there is little chance of it. There is free communication between us and the Army which marched up the Peninsula from Yorktown.

Well, I write principally to you to ask you to get some *clothes* etc. for me, suitable for hot weather. It is very hot here now. I wish you would call on Martin Van Nason and order for me a pair of *light* blue Officer's pants and a regulation Officer's coat, both of the thinnest cloth. They must be strong, however and therefore let them be of the finest cloth. Of course I do not wish an unusually dear suit but they *must be* thin and *must be* strong, or I do not want them, and am willing to pay for a good quality of cloth. Let the holes for straps be made, but do not send straps. The measure for my last pants was very good. You know what trouble I had with my dress coat. As the new one is to be very thin, and worn without a vest, I think the old measure will do, only let it come up a little higher in the neck. Let there be no stuffing whatever, but let it be as cool a coat as possible. Of course so thin a coat must be smaller in the waist than the measure. Then I want also one flannel shirt, of the very thinnest material, and large enough. Any color will do. Also 2 pairs of my linen drawers, 2 cakes of good soap, one moderate sized sponge with water proof bag, and (if possible) a white havelock to go over my Cap. If however you can get a regulation Lieutenant's felt hat, of *very light* "matériel", I would like it with a nice bugle and "20" complete in every way. In case any regulation straw hat is adopted and you can get me one, send that. Remember my head is a little smaller than yours. I am in the very greatest need of these things and would be very much obliged if you would order the clothes immediately and send them on without any delay by Adams Express, directed as best you can to me whereever [*sic*] I may be. I want you to put them in a good waterproof valise or carpet bag, large enough to contain fully as much as your valise. I should rather prefer a bag, but let there be a wide bottom, and a good lock, and let it be made of rubber or glazed leather and strong, and distinctly marked: "H. Ropes, 20th Regt. Mass. Vol."

I should have written long ago for these things, but it has grown hot very rapidly of late, and besides I did not care to order new things till Yorktown had been taken. I need them very much now, and you are the only person who can get them, and I hope you are not so busy that you will be troubled by attending to it. Besides, I want a flask of glass or metal, to hold about a pint and strong and good. Should there be room, I would like you to buy and put in for me a bottle of good Portwine, and one of Sherry. I have not yet got the box or my trunk, but I expect to as soon as we get to some settled place, which must be, I think in about a fortnight, when I expect these new things will come. Probably we shall spend the summer in the South, if all goes well, and I shall need cool things. Do not send more clothing than I ask for. If anything more should be sent me, please do not let them put in Sugar, as I get excellent here. If possible, put a bottle of Lemon Syrup in my bag. Remember that I shall probably receive the box and bag about the same time.

It is delightful summer weather here, but insects are very troublesome in the woods. I have received no letters since those by the Colonel. The Colonel is a great man. He sees to everything himself. He is up at 3 in the morning, and everybody *now* has to toe the mark. He goes round and eats the rations, and examines the arms, and looks out himself for the smallest things. Then he has the profoundest respect of every Officer and man in the Regiment. I never thought he was so active a man as I know he is, now.

I think I have mentioned everything I want, and I assure you I do want the clothes very much. I have had a delightful swim in the York River, and this afternoon I bathed in the Pamunkey.

Love to all from

Your affectionate brother
Henry.

RIGHT UP INTO THE FIRE

Camp 20th Regiment above West Point, Va.
Sunday May 11th 1862.

My dear Mother.

I wrote a long letter to John yesterday asking him to send me some clothes etc., and today Lieut. Perry has arrived and brought me the watch and a letter from Father and one from Mary Ann enclosed. I am very much pleased with the watch, and very glad to get it so soon. Before I forget it, I will tell you that I should like you to put into the bag a good ball of stout twine, several fish hooks, of the "perch" and " tautog" size (John knows) and 3 or 4 little bags to hold say 2 or 3 pints each, for sugar, rice etc. to go in my haversack and knapsack.

I hear that Adams & Co. are to establish a great depot at West Point, and I expect that thus before long I shall get your box of good things, the new bag, and what things I need out of my trunk. It seems to me almost certain that in 2 weeks at farthest we must come to some settled camp, and then we can get up everything and prepare for passing a summer in the South. In case the resistance of the Rebels is prolonged several months, still this would be overcome by strong parties sent out from some great encampment. I think there must be either a great battle here in 10 days, or a general breaking up of the Rebel Army and perhaps a series of skirmishes for 2 or 3 months. In either case, we shall probably have at last some settled camp, and be able to get up our trunks etc., and make ourselves very comfortable. I am on guard today and yesterday was on picket, but no enemy anywhere near and nothing to do. McClellan has just ridden by, amid the usual cheers of the men. The battle at Williamsburg was severe, and but for McClellan's arrival might have been disastrous to us.

It is beautiful weather but very warm, and like Midsummer at home.

Your affectionate son
Henry.

Heard of evacuation of Norfolk today.

RIGHT UP INTO THE FIRE

Camp 20th Regiment near
Cumberland, Va. May 17th 1862.

My dear Father.

I have received no letters from home since those by Col. Lee and Lt. Perry which I have answered. We have had a very irregular mail of course, but I have received 2 newspapers, and I hope the next mail will bring me some letters.

We left our Camp above West Point on the morning of the 15th, and in a heavy rain and over an awful road we made a forced march to this place. There was no particular need of haste as far as I can learn but they marched us almost without a halt over a road at times ankle deep in slippery mud, during a heavy rain, and at a speed which forced ¾ of our Brigade to drop out of the ranks from fatigue. I did not expect a long march, and had loaded my knapsack quite heavily, and I found it the most trying march I ever endured. All our Sergeants but one fell out, and we came into camp with only about 12 men, and our Company stood it as well as the rest, and our Regiment much better than the other Regiments of the Brigade. We finally halted, and filed into the woods at the side of the road and our tired men put up what shelter they could against the rain and lay down for the night.

The next day we dried off and are now quite rested. I hear our pickets are beyond New Kent Court House. We get little news till we see the papers, and you probably know much more of our probable movements than we do.

Col. Lee thinks we shall enter Richmond without a battle and I hear that the Colonel has applied for the Provost Marshalship of Richmond, and that therefore we are likely to spend some time there. I hope this is so, for a rest, and an opportunity to get up our baggage etc. would be very pleasant.

It would be much better to spend some months in Richmond than in some out of the way place, or in some more Southern and sickly position.

I enclose a letter for Louisa. I am perfectly well as usual.

Your affectionate son
Henry.

RIGHT UP INTO THE FIRE

Camp 20th Regiment near New Kent, Va.
May 20th 1862.

My dear John.

I think you must have all forgotten me at home, for I have not received a letter for a long time, except the short note from you enclosing a letter to Henry. Henry is in Washington and getting better, and has written me so. I think he will soon return to me. I shall keep the letter for him.

We marched to this place on Sunday the 18th and expect to move on today or tomorrow. I hear that the Rebels have evacuated their position at Bottom's Bridge on the Chickahominy, and that a flag of truce has come in proposing the surrender of Richmond. Also that the Galena is sunk and the Naugatuck driven back on the James River. I do not know what to believe, and hope the latter is untrue. Yesterday there was distant but very heavy firing in the direction of the James river.

I hope you received my letter about clothes and will send the bag. You say that the $40.00 I sent will more than pay for the expenses on your list. Please give $3.00 of it to Mary Ann, and ask her to purchase with it a present for Lizzie from me. Her birthday occurred on the 14th and she must excuse my not thinking to send it in time. Government now owe me $220.00 on my last 2 months, and when we get this I shall send enough home to pay for the clothes, and considerable besides. I hope you have thought about our boat as I requested, for the "Harvard" may really need the room.

We are encamped now in a very beautiful spot, about ½ miles from New Kent, which village we passed through. There are no grand houses, but pretty little cottages shaded by trees, and a very pleasant looking place. We are about 4 miles from White House Landing. I hear that my box is there, and I hope to get it very soon now. I have had so much to write to you about that I forgot to mention something that I found out about a month ago, and which by the way you had better keep to yourself. I discovered that some time ago Col. Palfrey recommended to the Governor Herbert Mason and myself for promotion for 1st Lieutenants. This he did entirely without my knowledge, and indeed he never once alluded to the subject to me. However, Murphy heard of it and was very angry, as he and Messer and Müller are our Seniors in rank. Murphy indignantly complained to Col. Palfrey and even tried to resign etc. and spoke publicly of the matter, and really acted in a very foolish manner, but I never heard of it till afterward. However, you probably know that Col. Palfrey is not one of Governor Andrew's favorites, and his recommendation was disregarded and Messer and Müller were promoted. I never gave the matter a thought, and do not really care in the least for promotion, and certainly would not have taken a commission over my superiors but I certainly am glad that Colonel Palfrey has a good opinion of me. As to the promotions, and also Holmes', they are made in the regular way, but unquestionably all 3 men are miserable Officers and do not deserve a higher post. It has created a good deal of feeling in the Regiment that the Governor has promoted 2 sergeants, without consulting Col. Palfrey. The Officers have felt very indignant indeed. You have often asked about Lowell and Patten. Lowell is a much tougher man than I had supposed. I like him very much and we are excellent friends. He is really a much better Officer than I had supposed, and I find my opinion of him is constantly rising. Patten is good natured, but lacks judgment and tact. He is a very indifferent Officer. The more I see of Tremlett, the more I dislike him. He is only a Gentleman on particular occasions, and when he chooses, and has a good deal of the bully in him. He is a very gross, coarse man. However he is a good Officer and does his duty without any shirking or delay. There is no mistake about that. Abbott is the best Officer and the finest man in the Regiment, only the Colonel excepted, and he is not up to Abbott in military matters. Abbott is a great Company Officer. Colonel of course would make the best General, but he has forgotten a great deal of little things and drill that Abbott is always perfect in. I respect and admire Abbott more and more. There is not a pluckier man anywhere, and he makes none of that swagger, and puts on none of the prize fighter as Tremlett does.

I hope to get letters soon. Love to all. Tell me how business and the buildings are. Be careful how you repeat some parts of this letter. I am delighted that you have as much business.

Your affectionate brother,
Henry.

Postscript.

Dear John.

I open this envelope to acknowledge the receipt just now of yours of May 16th and of Luisa's, Lizzie's and Mother's of same date. Please thank them all and also Sister Anna for the latter part of Lizzie's letter. It was very kind of her when she is so ill. I shall try to answer all very soon. Henry has this morning returned well. He got your letter and the $2.00 in Washington but did not receive my letter to him. You had better see to it that Holt does not hurt the boat or let it. It will do it good to be used and especially to be painted. I am glad the H.P.C. goes on well. I do not care to make any present of money to the A Δ Φ unless they are really in need. I seem to be entirely forgotten by my old college friends. They never write now. As to publishing my letter I was indeed amazed. I really do not feel that what I wrote hurriedly and carelessly to you was fit for publication, but if you only wanted the facts, and could arrange the orthography yourself, and it was of any good to establish a fact, I do not object.

As to the Gunboats doing much, it is a mistake. They only fired about a dozen shots. The fear of them however might have kept the enemy back. As to Capt. Beckwith, all I can say is that I understood that Thorpe gave him the money to keep, without any particular condition and as a favor to him (Thorpe), and Beckwith went off on a spree and spent the money. Beckwith, however, is a man of some honor, and will no doubt pay. As to Thorpe's wife, I understand he shamefully abandoned her long ago and she has gone to live with her friends down East. I hope you will not get mixed up too much against Capt. Beckwith, for he was once a member, though an unworthy one, of the 20th Regiment, and besides I know him here.

I shall write soon again. I feel very sorry to hear of Dr. Brown's death. I always thought a great deal of him. He was such a kind, excellent man.

Affectionately
Henry R.

Camp 20th Regiment near Bottom's Bridge, Va.
May 24th 1862.

My dear John.

I enclose a letter for Mary Ann giving an account of our march to this camp, only a short distance from our previous camp. I acknowledged your last in the Postscript of my last.

Of course in case of a battle etc., or on many occasions I could imagine, where the safety of friends etc. was concerned, and even to establish a point which it might be important to maintain, I would not object to your allowing parts of my letters to be published in the papers, yet, as a rule, I should be *very sorry* to have you do so and I would rather not have seen the letter which I wrote about West Point in print. I hope in future that you will only publish in case of great necessity. I want to write freely to you all, and not to feel that I may be writing to a paper. Besides I hate any kind of notoriety, and even in such a little thing there are some questions asked and it is spoken of.

You say nothing about the clothes and bag I wrote about. I suppose you have not received the letter. Henry has returned well and in good spirits. There is no news. I long for home letters. Did you go to our benefit at the H.P.C.? Lowell has had a bill sent to him, so I see, it was a fine affair. We had a *tremendous* scouting march yesterday, through woods and swamps, and over farms. Some spots here are very fertile indeed, and I have seen some tremendous trees. The inhabitants at a few houses have remained and seem civil enough. It is evening now, and I have no news about starting. I am on guard, and a band nearby is playing the "Miserere" you like so well.

Phil Mason was at Williamsburg, and had a very narrow escape and was very much exposed. Sturgis was in a part of the fight. Today it has rained hard. Henry got into some difficulty with a Sergeant yesterday. The latter called him a damned nigger etc. without any cause and of course he got angry.

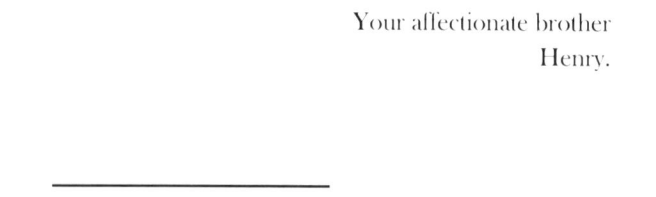

Your affectionate brother
Henry.

Camp 20th Regiment near Bottom's
Bridge, Va. May 25th Sunday 1862.

My dear Father.

I wrote yesterday to John and Mary Ann. There is no news today, only renewed reports of the evacuation of Richmond. We have moved about 4 miles from our last Camp to this one, but I date both "near Bottom's Bridge" because there is no name to either place that I have heard of. Our scouting march of 15 miles or so on Friday was not very tiresome as we had no knapsacks to carry. We marched through beautiful woods, and frequently stopped at fine springs of water. This is a fine farming country, and there is a great deal of wheat growing. We passed an old brick church surrounded by trees called Roper's Church, and near this we came upon quite a fine large country mansion, in the middle of a very extensive farm. Troops were camped all over the cleared land.

It is so hot here as we have it in June or July, and today is very pleasant. Some wild strawberries are found in the woods.

I am very glad you have settled to go to Swampscott and are to have such very pleasant society. The Rebellion seems now to be collapsing like a burst bladder, and it is possible that we may be discharged before autumn. It seems to me that there will be very little opposition made to the advance of the Army in any direction. Very likely the Army will be reduced one third or one half as soon as

Richmond is taken, and of course it is impossible to say what Regiments will be kept, and what sent back.

However, it may be that the Rebels will risk a great battle. In that case, McClellan will, I am sure, risk nothing but wait till he has collected an overpowering force. At any rate I think our campaigning is about over, and if successful (of which I have no doubt) we shall be settled down in some camp which we shall not leave till we retire to Massachusetts. We have just heard of the very valuable capture of Charleston, S.C.

My last letter was from Mary Ann, and as she said nothing about you all at home, I suppose all are well. I am perfectly well and we are now in a healthy place on a hill, near to a very pretty brook and not far from a fine lake.

We expect to move on tomorrow. Day before yesterday there was some Artillery firing in the advance.

Love to Mother and all.

Your affectionate son
Henry Ropes.

Camp near Bottom's Bridge,
Va. May 26th 1862.

My dear Father.

I enclose a letter for Frank. I am sorry I had no post paper, but I have written this all over and quite closely. Mother mentioned that a certain Wm. J. Temple, 26th Mass. Regiment, was reported wounded. I saw it in the paper and cannot think it was my friend and class mate, for he was in the 17th Regulars. Please ask John to enquire about it and let me know. I have no news to tell you. We are ordered to be ready to march, and expect to go into Richmond day after tomorrow, with or without a battle, as the Rebels may decide. Col. Lee says we have here 100,000 men and 120 pieces of Artillery effective for action now. I think this force will be irresistible.

I am well. Love to all.

Your affectionate son
Henry.

RIGHT UP INTO THE FIRE

Camp 20th Regiment
May 30th 1862.

My dear Mother.

Many thanks for yours of the 22nd. You all seem to think a great deal more of our hardships etc. than we do. It almost makes me smile to read your commiserations for the sufferings which I generally find difficulty in remembering when I get your replies several days after the events have happened. I am afraid I have given very exaggerated accounts, but I certainly do not recollect that I ever have. I assure you we think nothing here of what would be a great event at home. We have heavy firing in the advance, and are ordered under arms, and ordered to be ready at a moment's notice, and never think so much about it as we should at home if we saw in the paper that heavy firing was heard near Richmond. One gets very philosophical in the Army, and nobody ever gets excited on any occasion.

I am very glad there is some prospect for the stores, but would rather reserve the power to close the lease at the end of 5 years for instance by paying a certain sum. If trade revives after the war, there may be a much better use to put the stores to.

Do find out, if you can, who the W. J. Temple was, who was wounded and let me know. Please tell Mary Ann I shall write very soon to her, and thank her for her letters.

I have sent home by Mr. Wilkins to John a number of very interesting secesh relics. I am very well. We get some strawberries now, and there are a few peas about. It is quite warm now and very pleasant. This is a beautiful country covered with very large woods, and abounding in springs of water. The farms are tramped over and the people will certainly suffer for want of the usual crops.

Love to all.

Your affectionate son
Henry.

RIGHT UP INTO THE FIRE

Camp 20th Regiment
May 30th 1862.

My dear Father.

I have received your letter of May 22nd & 23rd enclosing Mother's, and the key of the valise and the receipt for the same. I am very much obliged to you for sending the valise and for getting the clothes etc. I hope to get it very soon. We are still at this camp, from which I last wrote, and I do not know when we shall leave it. Yesterday we returned from an advanced movement. We were marched 4 miles on Wednesday morning very early and halted in a field, with the rest of the Division. We left not knowing where we were going, and expecting an engagement, for the Colonel said it looked more like it that day than ever before. There was hardly a gun fired however, and we remained till night in the same place, expecting every moment the order to move. At 8 P.M. we began to march back, as we had left everything at the Camp, but before we had gone a mile the orders were countermanded and we marched back again and lay down without blankets or any covering or shelter. Some blankets were however brought for the men, and my man Henry finding I did not return marched up with blankets and overcoat and a pot of your nice chocolate, and I was perfectly comfortable for the night. We passed the next day in the same place, and just at the cool of the afternoon marched back to our old Camp where we now are.

The Captain's servant left to follow us long before Henry and lost his way, and got away up to Porter's Division, and only got back last night. He heard all about the brilliant action there[26] and conversed with the Rebel prisoners. He saw some North Carolinians and they told him freely that the whole Rebel Army was dreadfully disheartened and would not fight at Richmond. They say they are glad to be taken prisoners and fully believe the Rebellion is over. They want to go home, and they see no other way but by becoming loyal. The Officers and men were shockingly clothed and ragged.

We were all astonished at the news from Banks[27], but do not consider it very important, and were rather amused at the Home Guard demonstrations. There is a rumor today that we shall go to Harpers Ferry but I place no reliance on the report. I should indeed be sorry not to get to Richmond now. McClellan seems to be edging over to the North slowly. We are all disgusted with Governor Andrew's

---

[26] Battle of Hanover Court House on May 27th, 1862.

[27] Costly defeats in the Shenandoah Valley at the battles of Front Royal and Winchester on May 23rd and 25th, 1862.

letter, and foolish and bombastic manner.[28] There are men enough here to take Richmond and destroy Jackson too.

Your affectionate son
Henry.

Camp 20th Regiment May 30th 1862.

My dear John.

Thank you for yours of the 24th and for the trouble you must have been at to get the clothes etc. You have not yet told me whether the $280.00 has been received, and whether my old debts have been paid up, and whether there was enough money for all. For the clothes etc. I expect to send $100.00 from my next pay, now due since May 1st. I do not remember sending for my undershirts, or for but one pair of drawers, but you say there are 2 of each in the valise. Father speaks of my "trunk". I hope it is merely a good sized valise. Henry hopes you have sent his cigars. Please tell me if a box came for Henry, and, if so, what it contained. He says one of his letters mentions that his friends have sent to him a barrel of sweet potatoes, ½ of which were for Mr. Hichborn, and the other ½ for him. He desires to present his half of the barrel to Father if they should come. I have no doubt they would be excellent.

    I am very glad you have sent some Lemons and Syrup. One stands in great need of acid food and drink in this hot country. I have read Col. Lee's letter in the "Advertiser" with great pleasure. Very much obliged for the books you have sent. Can you send me the "Atlantic" for June by mail? I have sent to you by my friend Mr. Wilkins (who has long been connected with this Regiment and now returns home expecting a commission) a package containing a scarf I have no further use for, a package of letters etc. for Mary Ann to put in my box, and a packet of letters etc. I picked up in the deserted Rebel works before Yorktown. Also two $5.00 rebel bills bought for 5 Cents each by Henry Burckmeyer and sold at that price for relics. One he sends to you, and the other he gave to me. These things and

---

[28] On May 24th, the New York Tribune published a letter in which Governor Andrew mocked Secretary of War Stanton's urgent call for additional troops in view of the dire situation in the Shenandoah Valley.

others I may send home, I do not intend always to make over absolutely to you, for in case I should return I might want to keep them myself.

I am very glad to hear of Mr. Morse's engagement. Please to present my congratulations and kindest regards to him. I have sent a letter to Frank through Father.

Your affectionate brother
Henry.

12 o'clock M.

Heavy cannonade toward the city. No orders yet.

Camp near Fair Oaks Station Va.
at P.M. Tuesday June 3rd 1862.

My dear Father.

I take the first opportunity to inform you of my safety, that a kind Providence has mercifully preserved me in battle, and above all that I was enabled to do my duty there.

    On Saturday last, May 31st, we had not the slightest idea of danger being near till about noon when very heavy firing broke out from the woods West of us and at one time approached very near. We were ordered under arms, but I had no particular expectation of a battle, for we have been often called out in the same way before. The firing ceased, and we heard a report that Casey had been repulsed, but we did not know what to believe. At about 4 o'cl. orders came to fall in with one day's rations and we marched from Camp, and crossed the Chickahominy on the log bridge built by the Mich. Regimt. We came out on a low meadow where our Artillery was stuck in the mud. The 19th Mass. was on picket behind us, the Tammany we left here, and the 7th Mich. and we pushed on alone. After passing the meadow we ascended a small hill and found the country dry and hilly in front. Soon we halted, loaded and primed and then marched on again. In a few moments we heard guns ahead, and we pushed on rapidly, crossed a stream knee deep and took the double quick, for musketry and artillery were now heard in front, rapidly increasing. We drove forward out of breath and very hot, saw the smoke rising over the trees, and soon the road turned from along the edge of the woods, and we saw at the farther end of a large field our Artillery firing with the greatest rapidity, the Infantry forming, all hid in smoke. We again took the double quick step and ran through deep mud and pools of water toward the battle. The whole field in the rear of the line of firing was covered with dead; and wounded men were coming in in great numbers, some walking, some limping, some carried on stretchers and blankets, many with shattered limbs exposed and dripping with blood. In a moment we entered the fire. The noise was terrific, the balls whistled by us and the Shells exploded over us and by our side; the whole scene dark with smoke and lit up by the streams of fire from our battery and from our Infantry in line on each side. We were carried to the left and formed in line, and then marched by the left flank and advanced to the front and opened fire. Our men behaved with the greatest steadiness and stood up and fired and did exactly what they were told. The necessary confusion was very great, and it was as much as all the Officers could do to give the commands and see to the men. We changed position 2 or 3 times under a hot fire. Donnelly and Chase of my company fell not 2 feet from me. The shell and balls seemed all round us, and yet few seemed to fall. We kept up this heavy firing for some time, when the enemy came out of the woods in front and made a grand attack on the battery. They were met by grape and canister and a tremendous fire of the Infantry. They faltered and fell back. Some Regiment charged on them; the whole Rebel line was now in front of us, and Genl. Sumner ordered our whole line to advance. We rushed on with tremendous cheers, the whole together at a charge. The Rebels did not wait for the bayonets but broke and fled. Our Regiment came over a newly ploughed field and sank to the knee. We drove them to the edge of the woods and opened a tremendous fire for a few moments, and then

June 4th 12 M. 1862.

I was forced to stop suddenly yesterday for our Company went to occupy a house and yard in advance of our Regiment, and I expected to finish there, but the enemy appeared unexpectedly and opened fire on us and wounded 2 men of Company H, and I was fully occupied till this morning. I will continue my letter where I left it off.

We fired into the woods and then charged and drove them before us. We were then ordered back, and by the left flank and again charged the Rebels in a field on the left where they had rallied. We drove them and halted in the middle of the field and gave a few final volleys. It was then dark. We staid there that night. Ground covered with their killed and wounded. We took many prisoners. I will write more fully when I have more time.

On Sunday they attacked us tremendously. We were not in the heat of it and only lost one man. Fighting more or less all the time till now. No signs of the Rebels today. All Officers well and unhurt. Colonel well, but very busy. He desires me to ask you to send word to his family. I am on picket today. The Regiment will probably soon be relieved. Our total loss 30. My Company suffered most in the battle.

Love to Mother and all.

Your affectionate son
Henry.

Picket 20th Regiment near Fair Oaks Station, Va.
June 6th (Friday) 1862.

My dear John.

After the exciting events of the past week and the constant alarms and attacks of the enemy, I find a time of leisure and sit down to write to you as particular an account of this great battle or series of battles as I can and if possible to give you a truer idea of matters than I think you are likely to obtain from the newspapers. I have seen the New York Herald, and the account in the Baltimore Clipper taken from the New York Times, both of which are incorrect, and the latter shamefully untrue. The amount of the matter is that Casey's New York and Pennsylvania troops were *utterly defeated* and dispersed on Saturday in about one hour, that his position was taken and the centre of the Army well nigh pierced, and that Genl. Sumner, seeing the tremendous importance of the position on the South side of the Chickahominy, rushed his 10000 men across with only 5 or 6 guns, and engaged the overwhelming forces of the enemy, and by a desperate attack won back almost the entire ground by Saturday night. Sumner has done a great thing. He dared to t/*h*/rust his whole command, without reserve, in one magnificent bayonet charge on the best troops of the enemy and then he won back the position which if he had abandoned, would probably now be in the enemy's hands held by them between the right and the left of McClellan's army. He has dared to stake everything, where the tremendous importance of the point demanded it; this is in my opinion the greatest thing a General can do.

I have got a little excited on the matter because I see that the New York papers want to salve over Casey's disgraceful rout and Sumner's splendid victory;

and to make the battle of Sunday the important struggle. In one sense it was, but had not we cleared the way on Saturday night, the troops who fought Sunday's battle never could have come up.

Before I go further I will say that no Officer of the 20th is hurt, and that our entire loss to this date (2 P.M.) is 32 out of about 420 men who went into action. Well, I promised to give you a regular account. At about noon on Saturday 31st May we were in the camp where we had been a week or so, as quietly living as ever. I had had my hair cut and had shaved that morning, and was just putting up the razor when firing commenced in the direction of Richmond. It soon became very heavy, and approached rapidly nearer. There was very little Artillery. In about ½ an hour or ¾ of an hour it about stopped. After it began to decrease the order came to fall in. We have often fallen in on hearing firing by the pickets and often been marched toward the front on such occasions, and this seemed to be now about over and I thought nothing of it. I did not even put on my marching boots, but wore my Army shoes. I took my haversack with a little hard bread and a small amount of food, but only ordered Henry to get this ready, when I heard we were to march forward and I thought we might spend the night somewhere. Of our Brigade the 19th were on picket, and part of the Tammany, and so we were the right Regiment and the 7th Michigan the left of the Brigade. When we began to march, the firing had *entirely* ceased. I do not really think the whole firing lasted ¾ of an hour, and the only thing I thought strange was that it seemed to end at a point nearer to us than at which it began. We crossed the Chickahominy on the log bridge lately built by the Michigan 7th. Beyond the bridge is a large flat meadow. The river runs through a wide swamp. The logs are laid at the beginning of the marshy land, and reach to the firm ground on the other side. When one is about in the middle, there is a considerable stream of water, very muddy, and apparently not deep. As we emerged from the woods which are on each side of the bridge we saw the meadow I have spoken of before us and a brass gun stuck in the mud and a wagon beyond. Our Artillery, the Rhode Island battery, was behind us, and of course was stuck at the head of the bridge until the first gun could be got out of the way. We marched round the North edge of the meadow, and then ascended quite a hill, and entered a very pretty open country with fine trees and fields. After marching for one or two miles, we halted and loaded. This is not unusual, and I did not think then that the enemy was so near.

It was an open field where we halted, and here we left the Tammany as a picket guard perhaps to cover the retreat in case one was made. We pressed on, the 7th Michigan some distance ahead and very soon firing was heard in front, and then we were hurried on at a very rapid pace. We waded right through a stream and got over the rest of the way very quickly, part of the line at double quick, although it was very muddy. I was soaked with mud and water half way to the knee, and very hot, for the day was warm. All this time the firing was growing

RIGHT UP INTO THE FIRE

hotter and hotter, and I then began to think that we were going in in earnest. Soon after we started from camp, Sumner rode by and said to someone something about "a long step and a quick one" which remark was passed along down the line by the men, and we supposed we were to make a forced march. I enclose a rough map showing the various positions of the 20th in the battle.

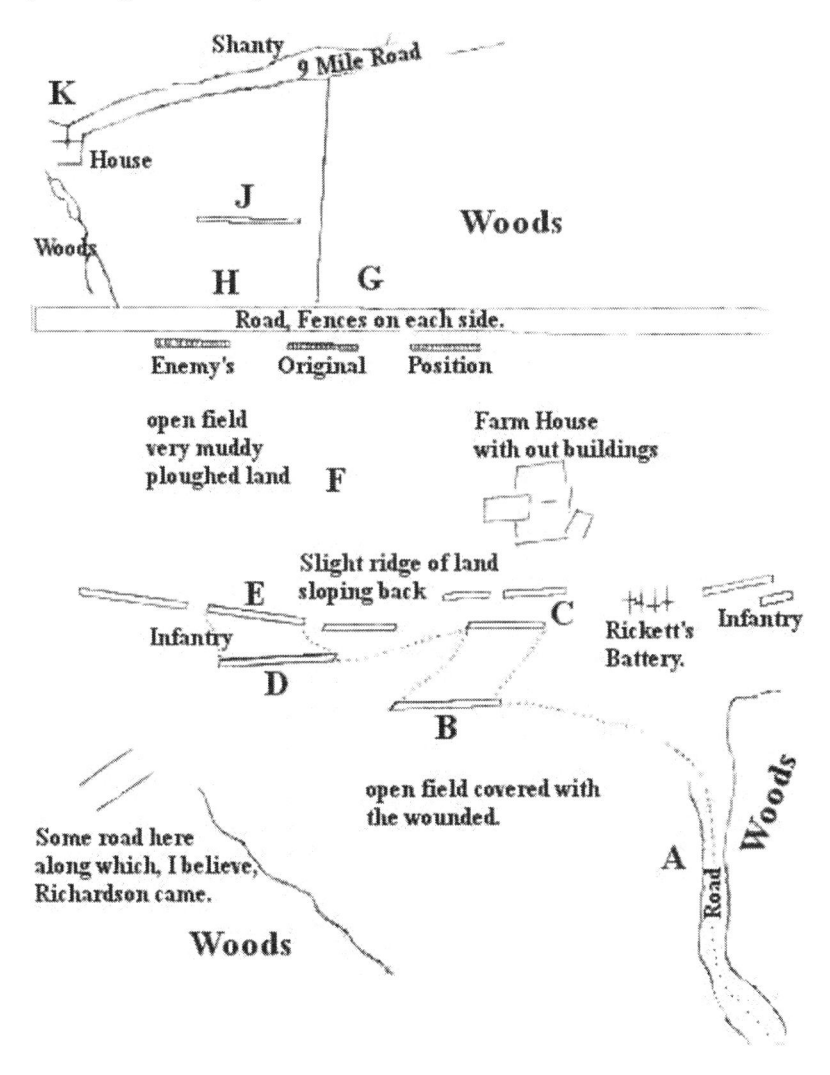

```
              Shanty
                   9 Mile Road
   K
      House                             Woods
                    J
   Woods          H   G
              Road, Fences on each side.
              Enemy's   Original   Position

   open field                  Farm House
   very muddy                  with out buildings
   ploughed land    F

                Slight ridge of land
              E    sloping back
                                    C
         Infantry                       Rickett's   Infantry
                    D                   Battery.
                          B
                    open field covered with
                       the wounded.
   Some road here
   along which, I believe,                A
   Richardson came.

              Woods
```

We came along the road marked A at about 5.30 P.M. and advanced double quick to the front. As we came out on the open field the sight was splendid indeed. Before us was the battery firing with the greatest rapidity, as also were the Infantry drawn up in line on each side. On the left fresh troops were just forming in line, and when we got about to the place marked A we heard the balls whistling over us and crashing through the woods on our right. We advanced by the right flank, and filed to the left, and rapidly formed on the right by files into line in the position B. As there was a slight ridge in front the balls principally went some distance over our heads, but I saw the shells bursting distinctly, especially near our battery. As soon as we formed we marched forward to C, then by the left flank to D, and here the men first began to fall. We finally advanced straight to the front to E, and opened fire in line on the enemy in front. The Michigan 7th was on our left where the land was a very little lower. I have stated we made these changes of position, but there was of course a terrific noise and smoke and confusion, and with the greatest difficulty we heard the various orders passed along, and before we got into our regular position E we moved right and left and forward and dressed up and back, all with regularity in the general movement, but with considerable confusion in particulars on account of the tremendous noise and probably the excitement of many of the men. Therefore I do not say that our Regiment made exactly these moves, in exactly this order and way, but only that this was the general series of movements which brought us from the road to the left and front. After we got well into action at the front, and the men were firing as fast as they could, I looked at my watch and found it ¼ of 6. This was the only time I had an opportunity to look and from this I guess at the time the action commenced. The men were now falling every few moments with a cry or groan and were carried a little back, and thence to the Surgeons in the rear. A man named Donnelly of my Company, just as a heavy fire was directed on us as we came to the front, threw himself flat down with a sort of cry, as I thought frightened. I ordered him up of course and even hit him with my sword for I thought he was frightened but instantly saw he was shot, and had him carried to the rear. He was hid *[sic]* in the breast. I did not hurt him in the least, but only took the only way to signify my command amid a noise that made it extremely difficult for the voice to be heard. The man who covered Donnelly in the rear rank fell almost at the same time. While we were still firing, the enemy advanced from the road where they were posted, and attempted to take the battery by assault. They got up about as far as the house, but were met by a concentrated fire of Infantry and by grape and canister and wavered, and were charged by the Infantry on the right of us. They fell back in confusion, and now old Sumner gave the order for the whole line to advance together. They did so at double quick charge bayonet and with tremendous cheers. It was a great sight, dark with smoke and lit up with the fire of the guns, and the line of bayonets reached as far as you could see. We came over an awfully muddy place (F) which completely winded us. We got to the road at the edge of the woods (G), but the enemy had fled, not waiting for the bayonet. We threw down the fence and were halted in the road and again opened fire into the woods of G. Then again came the order "charge" and over the fence and into the woods we went. It was very dark and smoky, and as the enemy fled, we were again halted and fired, and got into line. Then came the order to fall back which we did; halted, again fell back, formed in the road and marched by the left flank to the position H on the edge of the field. The enemy had made a last effort here and were drawn up in a dark line. It was now almost dark. We fired one volley and then over the fence and at them with the bayonet. They gave way, and after running some distance into the field we halted and formed, and kept firing into the darkness for 10 minutes or so, when the order "cease firing" came down the line, and we rested on the field, and the battle was over and won. It was now dark. The firing had about ceased, and only a few shots were heard at intervals. We waited in silence in line, and soon parties of men were sent out and a great many wounded Rebels were brought in, and many not wounded came and gave themselves up as prisoners. We lay down with arms in hands for a few hours, only during the night. Brigadier General Pettigrew of South Carolina and a Lieut. Col. Bull, S.C., both wounded, were brought in by our men. All the wounded lay in rear of our Regiment, all night on the wet ground, and in a rainstorm, and I could hear them groaning. Some of the prisoners lay down flat and pretended to be dead, and our men brought them in. When they found themselves discovered, they begged for their lives and were really convinced that we intended to murder them. The Colonel sent for me and ordered me to go with 2 men for a guard to Genl. Sumner, and deliver to him five prisoners (2 wounded) who had just come in and to ask for assistance for the wounded men. It was now very dark, and I started and went very slowly along the road and then over the meadow to the house which had been made into a Hospital. Right across the road lay a man. I thought he might be wounded, and lit a match, but he lay flat on his back with eyes glassy and fixed, and I saw he was dead. We moved him from the road, and passed on. The dead lay thick near the house but the wounded had been taken in. I must stop here, for I have no more paper. So far all well and unhurt. I hope to finish at length soon. Received Father's letter of 31st and yours and sister Mary's. Rebels seem to have fallen back.

Love to all.

Your affectionate Brother
Henry.

4 P.M. Friday.

Dear John.

I have been able to get some paper and therefore I open this envelope and continue my letter. I got to the house and delivered over my prisoners to Genl. Gorman, who was in charge, and then found Genl. Sumner. It was pitch dark. As I approached a group of horsemen I addressed one and asked for Genl. Sumner.

RIGHT UP INTO THE FIRE

He was close to me, only I could not see, and he spoke up in a loud voice "I am here, Sir." I gave him the Colonel's message, and he said we must send up the wounded and blankets as fast as we could without weakening our line. I then returned to the Regiment. The house was filled with wounded men shot in all manner of ways. The Surgeons were working as hard as they could, and the scene of suffering was indeed awful. When I returned, I looked again at the dead man by the road to see if he was one of our Regiment, but his brass plate was marked "6th Infantry, South Carolina". I talked with the prisoners as we went up, and found all had been impressed against their will, and wanted to go home. I talked principally with a Georgia man. He said he was poor, owned no slaves and only fought because he had to. He said when his Regiment advanced there was some confusion, and he lay down where we found him.

We were opposed to the famous Hampton Legion of S.C., and it was them we drove into the woods and over the field. Magruder's Aid [sic] was taken and he said Magruder told him that he was now convinced that his troops were no match for us, man for man. It was on the whole the most splendid victory of the war, I think, for it was straight out fighting, and in the final charge and in the Rebel attack on the battery resembled Waterloo very much.

Well, we were up before daylight on Sunday and at about 5 o'clock they began to feel along our front. They were in great force, as we learned since, and determined to make a desperate attempt to regain their lost ground and break our centre. At about 5 o'clock they attacked on our left, and the balls whistled by us, but no one was hurt, and they withdrew, and the firing ceased. Large re-enforcements had arrived during the night, including Artillery and Brigade after Brigade came up and entered the woods on our left and behind us. At about 9 o'cl. the enemy attacked, and in an hour all along our left the battles raged, and the musketry firing was perfectly tremendous. We were marched to our left and on the other side of the road, and drawn up for a support, but we were not needed, and although we could see the smoke through the trees and hear the cheers of our men as they charged, and sometimes hear the balls fly by, we were not actually engaged. By afternoon the enemy were driven back on all points with great slaughter and withdrew. In the afternoon they advanced several times a small squad, and twice threw volleys in on us, and killed one man of Company H, but this was the only loss during the day for us. We were under arms most of the night. On Monday there were constant alarms, and one of our men of Company B on picket was wounded by our own shell thrown at the Rebels. The Rebel Cavalry approached and we formed *square*, but they made no regular attack. During the night there was a picket alarm and we were marched back and resumed our place in the morning.

Tuesday we waited and there was only artillery firing and very little movement of troops. Abbott with his Company was on picket at a house I have marked K on the map. The enemy came to the shanty farther down the road and attacked him. The Regiment marched to his support and drew up on the edge of the woods. The enemy were driven away, but returned in the afternoon, fired a sudden volley just as our Company was entering to relieve Company I and wounded 2 men of Company H, who were in reserve there. We were on picket here during the night and all was quiet. We staid here Wednesday, and on Wednesday afternoon, as the enemy appeared to have left the shanty, the Colonel ordered me to examine the premises, with 10 men and a Sergeant. Abbott's men had been there when he was on picket at the house, but the enemy suddenly coming up drove the men back, they even being obliged to leave blankets and knapsacks. I approached my men as skirmishers and threw them round the shanty and posted them as lookouts, and then entered the house and found only a dog. I sent word to the Colonel and remained till Capt. Hallowell and his Company came up. Soon the enemy began to fire on us from pickets, and we kept it up till night, the men firing from behind shelters. No one hurt. At night our pickets were thrown out to this shanty and I and my 10 men fell back to the house K where we now are, behind barricades, as a support to the pickets. The Regiment is just in the edge of the woods, their left resting on this house.

Yesterday there was some picket firing and several shots thrown in here, but no one hurt. During the morning Porter advanced on our right and captured a battery, but today it has been quite quiet, and I hear the Rebels have fallen back. So here I am and you have a full account, although a tremendous letter. Large re-enforcements have come up on the Railroad from Newport News, and I hear we all advance tomorrow. We have had rain every day and have had little sleep, and been wet and muddy and no chance to dry off or change clothes for 2 days together. We have really endured a great deal, and have been and are in the advance and under fire almost all the time. I am perfectly well. I fear you have all been very anxious at home. You must try not to be. All will probably be settled soon now. The Regiment has gained great honor. Colonel well and full of spirit. He led the charges. Hope to write again soon. I have still quantities to tell you. Love to Father and Mother and all.

Ever affectionately
Henry.

RIGHT UP INTO THE FIRE

Picket Station Fair Oaks, Va.
20th Regiment, June 7th Saturday 1862. 7 A.M.

My dear Mother.

I know you must have been very anxious for my safety when you heard we had been engaged in so desperate a battle, but I assure you I wrote as soon as I could, and Henry tells me he sent a letter as soon as he heard of my safety.

We are still in the extreme advance and never take off equipments or clothes, and every day exchange a few shots with the enemy's pickets, but this morning and yesterday afternoon they have been unusually quiet, and have no doubt withdrawn. I am stationed in a barn, attached to a small house, very near the Fair Oaks Station, on the West Point and Richmond Rail Road. Our pickets extend ¼ of a mile in advance to a shanty on what is called the "9 Mile Road" to Richmond.

As the enemy brought forward their best troops and best Generals on Saturday and Sunday, and were utterly defeated, I hardly think they can make a long stand against our entire force now concentrated upon them. I hope they will stake all on a battle before Richmond, for it is worth a great deal to end this Rebellion by one great stroke. On Sunday (June 1st) they flooded the Chickahominy to prevent our troops crossing, and the bridge by which we came over was carried away, so had we been defeated then the result would have been most disastrous. Genl. Sumner managed the battle of Saturday in a splendid manner. He is a large, gray-haired, old man, with a flowing white beard, and was close behind our Regiment. When he ordered the final advance, he rode along, hat off, cheering on the men, and inspiring the greatest enthusiasm. The Michigan Regiment on our left once got into confusion under a very heavy fire and fell back, but our Regiment stood perfectly firm and the Michigan soon was brought up again and repulsed an attempt of the enemy to turn our left.

It has rained almost constantly for 3 days, and we have endured great exposure here in the advance, but today is fair and everything quiet.

Love to all. Shall answer Mary Ann soon.

I am perfectly well.

Your affectionate son
Henry.

RIGHT UP INTO THE FIRE

Camp 20th Regiment beyond Fair Oaks Station, Va.
June 9th (Monday) 1862.

My dear John.

I have written you a very long letter about the late battles, and yet I feel that I have not told you half. I am so disgusted with the falsehoods of the New York papers, and so angry to see these false accounts copied into Boston papers, that I feel disposed to write you everything, so that there may be at least one man at home who knows the truth.

There are two points that need to be well understood. The first is that there were two separate battles on the 31st. This the New York papers ignore entirely, and speak of Casey being driven in and fighting desperately *until* re-enforcements arrived, implying that *then* he in his turn advanced and shared in the victory. Casey was defeated in about an hour. I heard the firing when it began and when we fell in, it had entirely stopped. We marched up and engaged the enemy at about 5 o'clock P.M.. He had been re-enforced from Richmond in the mean time. We fought two hours or 2 ½ hours, and completely drove the enemy from his position, and only ceased driving him when it was so dark we could not see him. That very night our 20th pickets reached almost to the "9 Mile road" and the depot. During the night the enemy fell back. So you see Casey was routed, and Sumner came up 4 hours afterward and routed the enemy and occupied almost the whole of the ground Casey had lost. On Sunday the enemy made merely a tremendous attack to recover his lost ground and was repulsed and obliged to fall back still farther. Much larger numbers were engaged on Sunday, but with us it was a defensive battle, and as is usual in such cases, the enemy being defeated, fell back farther than the position from which he advanced. I think the honor and glory should be given to Sumner and his corps who advanced late in the afternoon and attacked a greatly superior enemy flushed with victory, and utterly routed him. The second point I wanted established was this, that Sunday's battle was on our part merely a defence of the position taken by Sumner on Saturday P.M. I want to correct some other errors. The papers speak of the "important aid" given by Sedgwick's division etc., as if we did not do as much as any other body of troops. Dana's Brigade is spoken of in the same way. Now of our Division the 34th New York was close to us and stood up splendidly and did their duty, and so did the 2nd New York *[82nd New York]*. But we did exactly the same thing, and the only difference was that we came up about 15 minutes later. As to Baxter's Fire Zouaves they did badly both they *[sic]* and again yesterday when their pickets came running in on us having left their posts.

The 20th especially occupied the advanced post during the night after the battle, and have since been constantly on picket and fought 2 or 3 skirmishes and been more or less under fire every day. As to our Brigade, the 19th and Tammany (or 42nd N.Y.) were not in the battle at all, and did not come up till everything was over, so of course they deserve no praise nor blame. There is one lie so very evident that I wonder that even the New York Herald published it. That paper said that a New York Lieut. Colonel took Genl. Pettigrew. He was taken by Corporal Summerhayes of Company I, 20th Mass. and brought to Lieut. Abbott commanding the Company, and Abbott now has his sword. Abbott took him to the Colonel who treated him in the kindest manner and had his wounds dressed and when the General expressed his surprise at his good treatment, Col. Lee told him he had fallen into the hands of a Mass. Regiment and would be treated as a Gentleman. He gave up his watch which was immediately returned to him. We also took Lieut. Col. Bull, wounded. He died during the night.

Our Regiment was opposed to the famous Hampton Legion of South Carolina and they fought well, and rallied in the open field just at the last, and we drove them there at the point of the bayonet which was no doubt the last charge of the day. Genl. Pettigru [sic] was found on this field.

So you see we have done our part. On Monday we collected Guns etc., and buried the dead. All over the field where we rested after the battle the Rebel dead lay thickly scattered, killed in every way. It was an awful sight. Men were mangled by shell in every way. The woods in all directions were full of dead. On Monday night I was up all night on guard. It was awfully dark and still while a terrible thunderstorm rolled up. At about 1 o'cl. the wind came out from the West and brought a sickening stench from the dead Rebels which filled the woods. Then we had a terrible thunder storm. On Monday we collected the muskets 112 in all which lay about us, and the Colonel sent me with the Company to carry them to Genl. Dana with a report. He told our Company that he gave them this honor, because they had behaved so well in the battle. We lost 6 men, out of 38 and 2 Officers, a heavier loss than that of any other Company.

Well, we have had some picket firing and some Artillery firing all along, and yesterday (Sunday) they attacked our pickets, and were after a while driven back. Then our forces advanced, and Sumner, Sedgwick, Dana and French were all at one time close to the house I have before mentioned and at which house we were stationed. We have moved a short distance, and now we are close to the Rail Road. Sumner's Corps has advanced about ½ a mile directly toward Richmond, and yesterday afternoon an immense number of men with axes were sent forward, and have cut down quite a forest before us and opened the path for our guns. Today however all is still, and there is a report that they are evacuating. I do not know what to believe.

I have received your letter and Mary Ann's. The 20th have gained great honor in this week's fighting, and the official reports will show it though the newspapers do not seem to know it.

RIGHT UP INTO THE FIRE

Well, I do not think of anything more to tell you, now. I shall try to write soon again and shall keep you fully informed, if I can.

Love to all. Write often.

Your affectionate brother
Henry.

Camp 20th Regiment 1 mile below
Fair Oaks, Va. Wednesday, June 11th 1862.

My dear Father.

We have just been withdrawn from the extreme advance and marched back one mile on the Rail Road and are camped here in comparative ease and comfort after 10 days of the hardest work soldiers can endure. I have just bathed and changed my underclothes and feel like another man. For 10 days we have not taken off equipments or boots or even cap, except for an hour or two, and have never been a moment sure of not having to spring to arms the next. We have been up night after night, and for 3 nights, only laid down in the mud and snatched a few hours rest. We have been soaked through and had to dry off when it cleared off and the sun came out, and have been every day within range of the enemy and had musket balls and round shot and shell thrown at us every day. But of course, men cannot long stand such exposure, and Genl. Sumner said that Dana's Brigade had done its full share, and therefore we are ordered to the rear, and our place is supplied by a fresh Brigade. Yesterday the enemy opened on us and threw shell very close to us and over us but hit no one. Our lines are now at least ¾ of a mile in advance of the position we took up on the night of the battle, and we have thrown up long lines of earthworks and cut down the forest in front for ½ a mile. The enemy seek to interrupt us by throwing shell, but do not often get the range. As yet we rarely reply. McClellan seems to be establishing a powerful base of operations and strong line of earthworks on which the Army could fall back if the necessity should come. I hear that McDowell is advancing, that Burnside has joined us on the left, that a mortar fleet to operate against Fort Darling, is at Norfolk, and that McClellan thus hopes to take them all round at once and capture or annihilate them. Of course it is hard to tell true reports from false, but I have no doubt McClellan will make sure work at the last.

I do not know whether we shall return to the advance in a week or so or not, but incline to think we shall be reserved for another desperate crisis. Sumner, Sedgwick, Dana, and especially the 20th Regiment have won a great name by the last 10 days work.

Please to thank Louisa for her and Lizzy's kind letters. So Lizzy is really gone to England. Please to give her my love when next you write. Also to sister Mary and thank her for her letter, and say I shall answer it soon I hope. I am perfectly well, and I think I stood the exposure of late remarkably well. All our friends here are well. The Colonel looks as well as ever, and I think better than he used to before he came to the war. He enjoys a military life and is very active and vigilant and up long before daybreak, and always on hand at the least alarm.

You must not believe the newspaper accounts of the battle etc. Wait for the Official reports of Sumner, Sedgwick and Dana. I have received Mother's and your letters, and am very sorry you were made so anxious, yet it could not be helped. A good many of our men are knocked up by our late exposures, but on the whole the health of the Regiment is good.

Please give my love to Mother and all. Have you ever received the $280.00 I sent? I think you have not yet acknowledged its receipt. I sent to John by Mr. Wilkins of this Regiment a small parcel which I hope he received safely. Please remind John to send me if possible some reading matter by mail. I want something to read very much. I hope to get my valise by the Rail Road very soon now.

Your affectionate son
Henry Ropes.

Camp 20th Regiment near Fair Oaks, Va.
Friday, June 13th 1862.

My dear John.

I received a letter from you several days ago telling me how anxious you were and am very glad to find from Louisa's letter (the latest I have received) that you heard of my safety before you felt sure I had been in much danger.

I have written very fully to you about the battle, and have nothing new to tell you. I wrote to Father that we had been moved ¾ of a mile back, and are now camped on the slope of a hill close to the Railroad. Our Brigade endured a great deal, with constant duty, fatigue and picket, and this during some of the heaviest rain I ever saw, and with a great lack of food and sleep. Water is the soldiers' great enemy. I am convinced of this. If a man can keep dry he can do almost anything but to get wet through and have no chance to change and to sleep on muddy ground after a week or so, breaks down most men. They do not "catch cold" as people at home suppose, but constant wet and the wearing of wet clothes gets up a sort of low feverish state. I really suffered a good deal. I did not remove my clothes from Saturday May 31st till Wednesday evening June 11th and was soaked with mud and water a great part of the time. Of course one gets actually dirty in such a length of time, and I found it brought about an irritable state of the skin. I had a boil under the arm, and was obliged to neglect it entirely, and did not even see it, but had to let it grow and burst of itself, irritated by my flannel shirt, and it had discharged 2 days before I could even wash the place. So you see there are some inconveniences of campaigning not down in the books. In fact one has to get completely over one's old ideas of necessaries and comforts, and finds out how little is really needed for a man to live with. With a field or staff Officer who has generally a tent, and horses, and who has no picket or night duty, the case is very different. He can always be comfortable.

Well, the enemy shell our lines every day, and generally are unable to get back any reply from our batteries whose positions they wish to find out. Very few, if any, are hurt by this process, for as soon as we see where they are trying to shell, we move a short distance off, and they have spent most of their powder in attacking an open field which *was* crowded with our men. All the time we are getting the most perfect knowledge of their batteries, and when our numerous batteries do open, I hardly think they will stand it long. Their firing range and shell are very inferior to ours. Only about ⅓ of their shell burst at all. We are vastly superior in Artillery, and the late battles have given our men perfect confidence in their bayonet charges, and must have produced an opposite effect on the Rebels.

We seem to be fortifying a position here to protect the Railroad, and to supply a firm base of operations for the great attack on Richmond. The pickets get firing a little every day at about 10 o'cl., and so do the batteries, but it is generally quiet afternoon. I am perfectly well and comfortable. The Quartermaster intends to send down for everything by Express for the Regiment, and I shall probably get my valise soon. You have not yet acknowledged the receipt of a parcel I sent you by Peter Wilkins. I hope you got it, for it was full of secesh relics. I send in this letter 2 very interesting relics taken from the bodies of two dead Rebels on the field of battle the next day or 2 after the fights. One is a small Rebel flag which was found as a mark in a pocket Bible which I saw taken out of the breast pocket of a Rebel killed in the woods, probably by the 7th Michigan Regiment on Saturday

RIGHT UP INTO THE FIRE

P.M. The hair in the paper was from the pocket-book of a Rebel who was killed by a shell very near where we stopped on the night of the battle. One of my men found a sort of diary, on a leaf of which was written: "I expect to go home one of these days". Another found a letter in which the writer said to his friend that they might meet in Heaven, but that he never expected to see him again on earth. Both these were found on the bodies of the dead. Many of the bodies were miserably dressed, and few wore uniforms. Several from a Tennessee Regiment wore a sort of red brown satined cloth, but most of those who had any uniform wore a very coarse grey pea jacket. The South Carolina men, I saw, were quite well clothed. The Rebels were generally good-sized men, but looked very dirty and sallow. The prisoners I talked to all said they were impressed against their will, and that they were very poorly fed, and that most of their comrades did not wish to fight anymore.

Some of those killed by shell were shockingly mangled, and in many places you could see pools of blood and perhaps a gun and haversack lying, showing where some dead or wounded man had fallen and been afterward carried off. The trees in the woods are terribly riddled with balls and shell and show the marks of very accurate aim, a very large proportion of shots being about breast high. I saw two dead men shot right through the heart and one shot in the centre of the forehead. Many wounded men lay for 2 and even 3 days in the woods before they were found and brought in. It was of course a very dreadful sight, but like everything else does not really affect one, because it is what you expect. So it is in battle. Such scenes anywhere else would move any one, there no one minds it at all.

Well, I have my little shelter tent pitched on short stakes here, and a pole bed, raised from the ground and am exceedingly comfortable. It is very hot today, and as the sun and moon set red, I think we are going to have dry weather for which I earnestly hope. You have no idea how much I want something to read. Can you send me the little German edition of Jane Eyre, by mail? I want to give it to Herbert. He liked the "Professor" very much. If you can send me such small books, please do, but if not, at any rate send some Magazines or papers, all by mail only.

We have to be ready all the time here, and yet are seldom called upon, and have quantities of time to read light books, but very little time for heavy reading. Indeed it is not worth while to send books one cannot throw away, for we move so often. Is the "Harvard" revived yet? I hardly think there will be much racing this summer. If all is successful and the Rebellion entirely put down, by next summer, there will be any amount of racing and excursion parties and travelling. If ever the Officers of this Army get safely home, they will take a month or two of recreation on their savings, and they richly deserve it.

Since McClellan has begun to entrench and collect, and since he now commands the Departments of McDowell and Burnside, I have thought that very likely Richmond will be a 2nd Corinth and the Rebellion will be quelled here without a great fight after all. But it seems to me sometimes that such an awfully wicked thing can only be finally done away by some fearful and bloody battle, in which all can see a pretty good share of retributive justice meted out.

Please tell me whether Temple of my class is wounded or not? I promised to write to him, but do not know where to direct to. Lowell, Capt. Shepard, and many others send regards. Love to all.

Affectionately
Henry.

Camp 20th Regiment near Fair Oaks, Va.
Sunday June 15th 1862.

My dear Mother.

I was delighted to receive your letter yesterday. We have been now several days at this Camp, about ¾ of a mile in rear of our advanced position on the Rail Road and "9 Mile road" as it is called. Picket firing has now about ceased, and yesterday and today we have been as quiet as if we were back in old Camp Benton again. Still we are under arms every morning at 3 o'clock, and at 3.30 the men are allowed to sit down in their places till 4.30 when they break ranks. At 3.30 the Whisky is given out, and indeed is very much needed. The Doctors recommend everyone in good health to take it as a protection against the early damp air of this country. I often take mine but generally give it to Henry as it is common Government stuff, and very unpalatable. We are now having hot dry weather which is no doubt more healthy than the constant rain and damp we have had.

The air is delightful, and there is generally a breeze. I have my little shelter tent pitched on legs, which keeps it 2 feet or so from the ground, and I have a bed made of poles raised from the grounds by forks driven down. Over this is a thick layer of leaves, and my blanket spread on top makes a most comfortable bed.

We suffer one great deprivation however: We get no fruit and vegetables. At the Camp we left before the battle we could get strawberries and peas quite often, but here there is such an immense body of troops that the few vegetables that are raised in the 2 or 3 little gardens near here are as nothing, and are probably all taken up by the Generals and guards. I have been able now to get fresh meat for 2 days, but before that I had nothing but ham for a long time. Indeed among the men there were one or 2 cases of scurvy, caused by eating too much salt food. You can hardly imagine how much one longs for acid food. The Doctor recommends vinegar, and I constantly drink it with water. Lemons and Oranges are brought up often on the Cars by the Engineers and others, and are eagerly sold at 10 Cents each, and then often very poor. Lowell managed to get hold of a pot of Pine Apple preserve, for which he paid $3.00 but which he was kind enough to share with Macy and myself. I hope to find that the Commissary has got some potatoes before long, and we daily expect the Sutler with a supply of pickles etc., but at present we are in great need of fresh and acid food. The Quarter Master has sent down for all Express things for the Regiment and I expect the valise daily.

You are very kind to speak of sending me more things. Should you send anything, I would suggest Lemons, Lemon or Lime Juice, pickles, etc. as being most suitable for this hot weather.

We are now on quite high ground, and therefore healthy, but the low swampy land which is the rule here, has a very depressing, enervating effect on the constitution in hot weather. Can you send me 2 or 3 toothpicks in a letter?

I hear rumors again this morning of the evacuation of Richmond. It would seem likely, had they not shown a desire to fight at last, and did not their leaders make such solemn promises to defend the place. I hear that 2 of our great siege guns are mounted now, and when we do open, if we ever have a chance, I think they will be sorry they staid so long.

Love to all at home.

Your affectionate son
Henry.

Camp near Fair Oaks, Va.
June 17th 1862.

My dear John.

I received yesterday your letter of the 10th enclosing a note for Henry, and 2 newspaper clippings, for all of which much obliged. Henry desired me to thank you, and I believe has expressed his thanks in a plainer manner in the letters he has sent to you and to Mother, which I mailed the other day.

RIGHT UP INTO THE FIRE

I am glad you understood my letter and there is nothing I recollect having written which I should wish now to contradict. You very likely saw in the "Transcript" a letter of Patten's, published without his knowledge, which says we were 20 minutes in the battle. He is mistaken, and now acknowledges his error, for 2 Officers besides myself looked at our watches and we all agree that the firing began at about 5.30 P.M. and that we arrived at about 5.45. Now we all know that when we ceased firing it was so dark that we could not see each other's faces, and this must have been about 8 P.M., giving us at least 2 hours in the fight. Of this there is no doubt whatever.

There is one thing I cannot explain fully. All the accounts speak of Casey being driven in, and giving way etc. at about 1 o'cl.. This was when we heard the firing. Then we got up at about 5.30 P.M. and at about this time the battle began again. Now, I am perfectly sure that I heard the first firing begin at about one, and cease by two, and begin again about ½ hour before we got up, and all this very near and distinct, and not at all dying away in the distance and gradually growing more and more plain; and yet the accounts speak plainly of a *continued* struggle of Kearney's [sic] Division checking the enemy, and of their final repulse by Sedgwick. How such a continued fight could have been kept up, and I hear nothing of it, I do not see. Of course I was most distant from the firing when it took place at Casey's advanced posts, and from that time till we were in the fight, I must have been getting constantly nearer to the firing, if there was any, and I am sure that it first broke out as clearly and suddenly as the firing of guns on the Common does to you at home, and ended as distinctly, and I cannot see why I (and everybody close who noticed it here) should have been struck with a sudden deafness from 2 to 5.30 P.M. of that day, and yet by this supposition only can I explain the accounts everywhere printed in the newspapers. The fact is I do not believe it was so, and I therefore suppose that Kearney checked the further advance of the enemy merely by a display of force, and by occupying good positions, and awaited our arrival before making an attack. The enemy probably having met with great success, were more anxious to secure the fruits than to pursue their advantage farther until re-enforced from Richmond and having received fresh troops they renewed the attack in the afternoon and were defeated. This I know, that we took prisoners who were not in the morning's fight, and who had marched that day from beyond Richmond.

I understand that Davis himself formed the 5 Regiments which constituted the column of attack against our batteries in the open field, where we passed the night, and himself directed the attack. Perhaps the attack was more extended than I at first thought and the fighting was continued far on our left after the guns I heard had ceased, and this firing was too distant for me to hear, but to me this seems perfectly impossible. I still think, in spite of the New York Herald and other false accounts, that there was very little fighting between 2 and 5.30 o'cl.

RIGHT UP INTO THE FIRE

As to the "Napoleon Gun" story you cut from the newspaper and sent me, I do not believe it. There was hardly any firing of Artillery at all, and nothing in the least like the regular and rapid firing of a battery. I rather think a battle is an exception to the usual laws of perspective, and those who have run farthest away give the most terrible accounts. As we marched up, quantities of New York men came running through the woods, with the bullets whistling after them, crying out that "no one could stand that" and something about "cut to pieces" etc. to which our men paid no attention, unless to damn them, and marched right up into the fire.

The 2nd night after the battle Company I was on picket, and there was an alarm, and volleys fired, and the entire pickets of the 19th *[Massachusetts]* and 7th Michigan came running in scared out of their wits, while our men everyone remained at their posts. So a few days later the Baxter Zouaves abandoned their posts and ran in saying they were "driven in", "cut to pieces" etc. all for nothing but a slight attack of Rebels, who were probably more frightened than they were. They do not seem to understand that if there is any danger of an attack, that is exactly the place they should be at to defend to the last, and give time for the rest to form. Never put any trust in any "Zouaves", "Tigers", "Chasseurs", or any such kind of soldiers. It is enough to spoil any man to dress him up in a striped monkey jacket and tell him he is a "Zouave". When Baxter's Zouaves ran in the other day, old Sedgwick was in a perfect rage. He ran out into the field, and saw a Corporal running in with the usual story "driven in". Sedgwick caught the fellow by the neck, violently kicked his rear before all the soldiers about, and ordered him back. I hear he says he means to have some of the Officers and men shot for cowardice. Well, I have run off into other things and have not answered your letter. As to the distances I should say that the house was about as far in front of our position, as Mr. Bates' house from our house at home, and about twice as far to our right, from the position we last took up. Then we charged down to the road, about as far as across the Public Garden, and a short distance say 300 feet into the woods beyond the road. If you imagine the houses opposite our house on Boylston St. to be woods and a ploughed field between, you have a fair idea of the distance. The enemy were drawn up this side of the woods, but how much I cannot say for I could not see them at all till we charged, and then I only could make out a dark line or wall, so dense was the smoke. If you imagine that we charged across the Public Garden, and into the houses, and then came back to Boylston Street and then marched by the left flank till opposite Park Square, and then that we charged at the Providence Depot, and that it fell back to Tremont St., and left us on its site, you have a good idea of the distances in the great battle of Fair Oaks. Going over the field in the charge, the mud was really knee deep at every step, and our line greatly broken up of course, and we all frequently had to walk and then run on being out of breath. I got along however as fast as the rest and was only hindered by the necessity of urging on the men, many of whom were much blown.

As to occupying the ground as far as I have been able to find out, the enemy fell back on Saturday night from almost the whole ground, from which they had not been driven, of the ground taken from Casey. Our pickets, Company A, were so close to them during the night as to hear their voices, but did not disturb them because they were searching about in the woods for the dead and wounded. By morning they fell back beyond the Richmond *[& York River Railroad]*.

As to the Commander in Chief, I say *without the least reservation*, that as far as I can see or hear, he has not lost in the *slightest degree* the confidence and respect of the Army. And I think justly. For, you must remember that our right wing has not yet crossed the Chickahominy, and that the reserve might have been called upon to resist an attack made on the East side. Besides, until the Railroad was made perfectly secure, and was well supplied with engines and cars, it would have been madness to risk a larger body of troops than that absolutely necessary, with such an uncertain means of supply as the bridges and wagon transportation.

Then remember that the enemy came on in overwhelming force and that Casey gave way instantly and that still Kearney came up in time to check the Rebel advance, and we in time to drive them back routed by the bayonet in spite of the greatest efforts of Davis himself and his best troops. When an attack is made unexpectedly and in overwhelming numbers, it cannot be stayed, and it is the duty of a General thus exposed in the advance, to see to it that he is *always* ready, so that he may hinder the assailants as long as possible. Casey, as far as I can learn was totally unprepared. His men should not have been allowed to undress, take off equipments or leave their stacks as long as he remained thus exposed, and, above all, his pickets should have given an early alarm, and made a desperate defence. If you blame McClellan at all, you can only say that he should have trusted such an important place only to Massachusetts troops; I can think of no other criticism.

In such a country transportation of provisions is the great thing to look out for. The muddy roads are something that must be seen and felt to be understood.

Well, our first parallel is nearly done, siege guns mounted and very soon I suppose we shall open, after that it cannot be longer. When these tremendous guns *do* begin let him who is in the field not go back for his coat, but skedaddle into the Virginia Mountains if there are any, while the way of escape is still open.

This morning I hear distant heavy guns on our left; Perhaps the Gunboats and Fort Darling. Cabot, Patten, and Tilden are sick, but the rest well. I was never better. I*[n]* consequence of the appearance of scurvy among the men, we are to have dried apples, onions and potatoes daily, at which I rejoice. Today it is delightfully cool and clear.

In speaking of McClellan, you seem to forget the terrible difficulties of the

RIGHT UP INTO THE FIRE

country. You must remember that he cannot be sure that a single battery can get 4 miles in a whole day. The roads are often actually impassable until trees are cut down and laid across the mud holes for Artillery to pass. Then this is a country of dense, swampy forest, and no one man could possibly see more than 2 Divisions at any one time, and the woods in front might conceal any number of the enemy, so that even the balloon can give no information. I think McClellan has adopted the only way of safety in slowly advancing, and not going again forward until he has got up enough provisions, and Artillery to make his place secure. Remember, a defeat now would be dreadful. He has now secured the Railroad, and a position 6 miles from the city, has got up his big guns, his Artillery, and his food, and his balloon, while it cannot give him much information of the enemy's movements toward him, is sure of giving early notice of an evacuation to the West, where the land is open.

I think he intends to *ensure the utter destruction* of the Rebel Army and of the Rebellion, and I think he will do it. I see what you mean, but I think you are mistaken. In this fight as yet there has been no opportunity for Napoleonic movements and victories. McClellan rode by us 3 days ago, and we received him in line. He has now a large red beard and does not look so well. He wore a straw hat. As to his ability to meet a great crisis I fully believe in him there. He seems to me to have a great deal of resolute confidence which he never has had a chance to display.

As to my feelings about which you enquire, I really hardly /k/now how to describe them, but I can only say that there was none of the indescribable excitement one sometimes hears of. I felt I was in danger of being hurt or killed, but I think one does not think so much of the pain of wounds etc. because death seems at times to be imminent. But I think no man of sense would act differently in a battle from the way he before determined and expects to act. I think that being killed does not seem so much to be dreaded and avoided when you are close to death, as when you think of it while in safety. My attention of course, was entirely taken up in directing the men, and seeing that they did not crowd together etc., and in passing along the orders. When we were merely standing up and firing, I had less to do and had an opportunity to look round and observe the battle, but as I have said, I could see very little on account of the smoke. I do not suppose it was at all a trying battle, but I certainly felt perfectly collected, and I do not think my conduct was at all influenced by the knowledge of the danger. I really do not remember that I had any particular feelings to describe, except perhaps a sort of eagerness and a strong desire to beat the enemy, the latter feeling I had not before expected to have particularly. Well, I have written a tremendous letter, but I want you to write long ones, and dare say you like to get long ones from me.

We are now quite comfortable at this Camp and may stay till the final attack.

I have today got the "Atlantic", for which greatly obliged. Can you send it to me regularly and make me a subscriber? I should like it very much. Try to send some Teubner boots [books], if you can. I expect the valise today. Lieut. Powsnell [Pousland] has gone down to White House to get such things. Herbert and I intend to petition immediately for our degrees. I hope you will do all you can to advance our claims.

Tell Mary Ann to write. I hope she and you will go out to class day and tell me everything about it and send me the papers. Perhaps Bartlett will be there with his one leg. What a lion he will be!

Your affectionate brother
Henry.

Camp Lincoln, 20th Regiment
June 19th 1862.

My dear John.

I have just received yours of the 14th and am delighted to attempt to answer your questions. You will see by my letter of the 17th that some things are as unexplainable to me as to you. You speak of Artillery. The Colonel told me yesterday that the Rebels used no artillery in the battle of Saturday P.M.. Yet I feel perfectly sure I saw shell bursting in the air, say 30 feet high, over the battery, and another Officer also has told me he saw shell burst over us. I suppose one of these days we shall know the exact truth. I think your plan of our position is no doubt correct, only probably our line is more in the shape of a semi-circle. As to the position of Couch and the behavior of his troops, I really know nothing. Your Division of McClellan's Army is no doubt correct, but I really have little means of knowing anything outside of our own Brigade.

You see we march into a field and camp, and never leave to ride about and see the positions of other Regiments and have very little notion of what we cannot see. You must remember

1st: that the general state of the country is forest, deep and high forest, and that spots of 200 to 500 acres are cleared for tillage, and perhaps to put up a little house, and the roads wind about from one clearing to the other, and that we march sometimes through the woods and often by the road.

2nd: there are no hills at all where one can see over the trees and have the least general view of the country. For these reasons I find it perfectly impossible to get any sort of correct idea of the land and the positions of the troops beyond the little field where we, or possibly our Division march etc. Every time we march I get completely turned around as to the points of the compass, and you know how confusing this is. If I could go a mile or two in different directions and visit other Corps, and get familiar with the general arrangement of the troops, I should get a good idea of every movement, but I never leave Camp, and cannot, and therefore can give you no information worth anything of the positions of Corps. I merely know that Porter is on the right and has not crossed, and that Hooker is our next neighbor on the left.

As I said in my previous letter (which you had not received when you wrote on the 14th) *I rather think* from what I can gather and *infer* that the troops whoever they were who checked the enemy first after Casey's rout did very little between 2 and 5 o'cl. but wait for re-enforcements from Richmond. There might have been some firing in the woods, which I did not hear, at this time, but nothing heavy at all. The reason we did not get up till 5.30 was this: We did not get orders to fall in till say 2 or 3 o'clock, and then had to wait till quantities of troops filed by, and we last of all. On the way we left the 42nd Tammany, and then pressed rapidly and gained up so as to get into action almost as soon as the 7th Michigan. You must remember that along these roads a Division cannot possibly make more than 2 ½ or 3 miles an hour, and often Artillery is much slower. In our case, for instance, the Artillery of our Brigade (Rhode Island) got completely stuck and got up a day or two after.

I have written to you about the impossibility of reconciling the continued fight spoken of by the papers and the evidence of my own ears. I have no further explanation to offer. As to my own evidence, I feel perfectly sure, and was under no excitement whatever at any time, which in the least interferred with my powers of observation or memory. I do not wonder you cannot reconcile the accounts, but I have heard that *no* newspaper correspondents were present and, if so, their accounts are no more to be relied on than mine, and not half so much.

As to the attack on our battery etc. I can only say that I did not see anything of it at all, and did not know they had attacked till afterwards, and only hear from others about it. Of this I am sure that they did not come up to *me* near enough for me to see them and in fact I only did see them very indistinctly when we charged on them, and when, as the line was somewhat broken on account of the muddy ground etc. I got ahead of the men and could see through. Some of our Officers, however, who commanded Companies did see the Rebels' attack, and I will enquire and answer your questions as well as I can. I have no doubt as you say (Mr. Shattuck says) that there was fighting (on our left) in the woods and fields, but our attack was made on the important point, where the Railroad and the turnpike road (as I believe it is called) and the "9 Mile Road" all meet, and where Davis and Pettigrew and the South Carolina Troops were. You see it was my first experience, and I have no doubt I paid too little attention to the enemy and never thought that we were engaged in a really great battle, or were doing our part in larger movements. Another time, if I have the opportunity, I shall try to look at the enemy and his actions more.

As to getting near them, when we charged into the woods, the backs of the rearmost were not more than 50 feet from our bayonets, but just where I was I could see none. Others tell me how near they got to them. I understand that there were no fences to impede the left of our line as we charged into the woods so they got there a little before us. I believe Richardson's Division *is* in our Corps d'Armée.

Our Regiment is, to be sure, very small, but I think you would be safe in averaging the actual strength of Regiments in a battle at 600 men. We now average about 20 sick per day, ¾ of whom are sent back to hospitals in the rear. There is some scurvy and a good deal of low fever and diarrhoea, the latter partly scorbutic. Now, we have dried apples and potatoes, and shall rapidly improve. The guard, sick, Quartermaster's Department etc. absorbs a great number of men. I know nothing of McClellan's strength, but I hear that McCall and 15,000 men have joined us.

I am very sorry for poor Jarvis *[sic]*. The 24th always does well.[29] As you say this picket danger is disgusting, but it is surprising how careless one gets. We have had our share. Officers are very much exposed on picket.

I am very glad the fellows are at last supplied with my photographs, and I hope the light of my countenance will induce them to remember the original. Which proof has the preference among them? I am delighted to hear of the success of the H.P.C. and my beloved A Δ. For that society I feel the greatest affection. I have past *[sic]* the pleasantest hours of my College life in that society, and my best friends are there. So also with the H.P., only that is less brotherly. I am glad you put my themes etc. away. Pay for my pictures out of my funds, if you have enough.

As to my bills I left no private ones at all. As to the expense of my fitting out it was distinctly understood, I thought, that Father was to pay that. I consider that as reasonable as his paying for Frank's medical books and instruments, for example. I thought he prepared me for a military life, after which I was to support myself. If I should return, I expect to enter the Counting room, and I suppose my business life would then be begun. I do not expect ever again to be a non-producer, or

---

[29] 2nd Lieutenant Horatio D. Jarves of the 24th Massachusetts Infantry was wounded on June 5, 1862, in the Battle of Tranter's Creek.

rather non-laborer, and I supposed my fit out was the usual expense to prepare for a self-supporting life. Still, please do not mention this to Father, and if as you imply, he expects me to save from my pay enough to pay for my outfit, I shall do it of course, though I really think it is a very different course from that he has pursued to you and to Frank in giving both a 3 years education beside College, and even now never hinting that either should do without his assistance. This, of course, between us. Tell me all about Class day. It is *perfectly impossible* that Tilden could have been in Boston since his leave of absence last winter from Camp Benton.

I believe now I have fully answered your letter. As to our news, all is quiet; Some Artillery this morning on our right.

Yesterday at 2.30 P.M. we were turned out under arms and heard that the enemy were advancing in force along the whole line and a general engagement was expected. At 4.30 musketry began, and dropped along for one or 2 hours, with occasionally a cannon shot. Then it slowly died away, and an Aide said it was thought the movement was made to cover an evacuation. We slept with equipments on, but hear nothing of importance today. Our picket lines, I hear, are advanced. Yesterday I heard from an aide of Genl. McClellan's that the General was yesterday in unusually fine spirits and remarked that he had found and secured the key to their position. The Army would be delighted to have the Rebels risk all on an attack on our lines.

Patten is now about well. All your friends here often send their regards etc. Capt. Shepard desires his. I have this moment sent Henry to White House to get my valise and expect it tonight. Please tell Mary Ann that I miss her letters dreadfully.

Very much obliged for the Atlantic. Do not forget to send everything of interest. I of course wish you to charge such expenses to me.

If there were no shoulder straps in the valise, please buy a pair of 2nd Lieutenant's straps done on Cloth and send by mail. You can get a kind that will go, I hear. Please do this soon, as mine are about spoiled.

Love to all. Write again soon, and tell all to write. I want to know all about Class day. Have you seen Frank Bartlett? If you do, give him my love and tell him how we miss him.

Your affectionate brother,
Henry.

P.S. We are still in the same camp now named "Camp Lincoln".

RIGHT UP INTO THE FIRE

Camp Lincoln, 20th Regiment
June 20th Friday 1862.

My dear John.

I got my valise last night and I need not tell you how delighted I was and how useful the contents will be. I wrote to you that I sent Henry down to White House and he there went on board a Steamer (where he was sent with a sword of the Colonel's and some other things) and saw Mr. Frothingham, Miss Lowell, and I believe other Bostonians, all well. I am delighted with the valise. It is acknowledged by all to be the very best in the Regiment. It is *just the thing*, and I am more than satisfied. The price ($13.00) is also reasonable. The pants I have not yet tried on, but I like the cloth very much, and I do not doubt they will fit. The coat is an excellent fit. I like it very much. So also the hat which however looks dreadfully swelly. I ought to have ordered new straps but thought I should get my trunk (where I have a nice pair) before my valise. As I have asked you, please send a nice plain pair by mail. I am greatly obliged to you for your kindness in getting so many things. All are what I want. I found the Sherry excellent. I have not opened the other bottles. Please thank Frank for his letter and tell him why my answer is so long delayed. I shall write to him very soon. In your letter (inside the valise) you speak of delay etc. in my letters. I suppose you have got all, however long before this.

I am very much obliged for your nice sponge bag. I fear you have deprived yourself to serve me. It was very kind of you. Very much obliged for your nice books. I shall read all with the greatest pleasure. Your supply of fish line is very abundant. I *may* never use it, but it takes up little room and it *may* give me a good dinner in place of a couple of hard crackers. I am very much pleased with your selection of books for yourself, and am astonished that you made the money go so far.

I like very much your idea of connecting family events by some little permanent thing, such as a military book to remember the (pro tempore I hope) military brother. I am very glad you enjoyed the A Δ and rejoice greatly at the prosperity of that glorious fraternity. Henry's Cigars are excellent, I hear. I shall try to read "Parson B.'s" speech.[30]

Love to all. Enclosed letter to Mother.

Ever your affectionate brother
Henry.

---

[30] Ropes is most likely referring to William Gannaway "Parson" Brownlow.

RIGHT UP INTO THE FIRE

P.S. Dear John. I am *very glad* you have published *nothing* of mine. Please publish nothing (except in case of battle) to relieve anxiety of friends. I mentioned to the Colonel that I had seen part of his letters in the "Advertiser", as you wrote to me. He seemed much surprised and said he knew nothing about it, entirely disapproved of it etc. and said it could not have been his letter. Perhaps you had better not publish any more of his till you get his leave. Pants fit perfectly. Cannonade on our left[31], perhaps 3 miles off (11.30 A.M.). Porter, I suppose.

Affectionately
Henry.

Camp Lincoln 20th June 1862.

My dear Mother.

I have now got my valise and I assure you I have appreciated its contents. Thank you very much for the Gingerbread, bags, havelock etc. and the book. Please thank Father and Louisa for their kind presents of books. I not only enjoy them myself but have given much pleasure to others by lending them. I think I did not describe clearly what kind of shirt I wanted. I do not want an Undershirt at all, as this would be superfluous when one wears a thick flannel shirt next the skin. Such as you sent are worn by those whose skins are so tender that they cannot wear flannel next the skin. I wrote to get some thin flannel shirts, but have since determined that my present ones are very good, and should I want more, I can get them of the Sutler who now has a good supply. I find the preserved Coffee you have sent is not very good or wholesome, and shall therefore exchange it for something else with the Sutler. I drink tea principally here. The Doctor says it is more healthy in the country. The chocolate is very nice, the Gingerbread beyond praise. The little bags are extremely useful and very nicely made.

I am now perfectly well, the weather is dry, though warm, and the health of the Regiment is improving. We had a sad death in the Company yesterday, a most excellent man named Thomas Whitman, Private from Stow, Mass. He leaves 2 small children. He has been ailing for some time, and was at times a little out of his mind, but lately has been getting better. Yesterday afternoon I was called by a

---

[31] Most likely Ropes meant to write "our right".

RIGHT UP INTO THE FIRE

Corporal suddenly to see him and found him in a fit, but perfectly quiet. I sent for the Doctor, but before the Doctor came he fell back, perfectly pale, and his pulse ceased. All said he was dead, but the Doctor coming up laid him back and the blood suddenly returned to his face, and he groaned aloud. He lay perfectly unconscious for a long time, and the most violent stimulants seemed to have no effect. Suddenly the fit became epileptic, and he struggled and cried out. Violent emetics were partially successful, and he finally quieted down, and was taken to the Hospital. Here he quietly died about ½ an hour after. He is to be buried this afternoon at 6. Col. Lee will read the service. He was a most excellent, faithful man, a widower, and seemed always to feel very much the loss of his wife, and to think a great deal about his 2 little children. I feel his death very much. I have no doubt the funeral will be a very solemn occasion.

All is quiet now, and nobody knows what is to happen the next hour. On the whole the belief is that McClellan intends to pursue his old plan, and conquer more by his fortifications and guns than by his troops. He always spares life as much as he can. The forts in our front are tremendous and it would be sheer madness for the enemy to attack us here. We have now good food, and everybody's health is improving. I keep perfectly well.

Today is Class Day, a day to which I had looked forward for years, but however much I miss the pleasure of the day, I am very glad I am here instead. I hope to get full accounts from you all. I am afraid Mary Ann quite forgets me when she goes away with her young lady friends. She has owed me a letter ever so long, and I hear she has been staying at Miss Blake's. You must make her write when she returns.

So you will soon be at the Seashore. It promises to be a very pleasant summer for you.

Best love to Father and all.

Your affectionate son
Henry.

RIGHT UP INTO THE FIRE

Camp Lincoln June 22nd
(Sunday) 1862.

My dear Mother.

I received yesterday your letter of the 17th. You have no doubt heard of the arrival of my valise by my letter to John. I think I may never have acknowledged the receipt by mail of the key, about 3 weeks ago. Beside this the key tied on came safely, and so I have two keys.

I think I have written to John about Herbert's and my Degrees. We sent in a formal petition and enclosed it in a letter to Professor Lovering, begging him to present it to the Faculty. Herbert has received a letter from his Father in which he says he desires that the Faculty give us our Degrees without our asking for them. Of course it is too late to carry out this now, as our petition has gone on. I always intended to petition, and President Felton advised me to do so. I rather think the Faculty will grant our request. I am very anxious to hear about Class Day.

Will you please send me 3 or 4 sheets of post paper by mail? I want to write to Frank and to sister Mary. I have really forgotten whether I ever answered sister Anna's last letter. I intended to do so, but I think the battle and the 10 days of hard work after it, put it out of my mind. However I shall certainly write and make sure. My books are going the rounds of the Regiment very rapidly.

Yesterday afternoon the Rebels attacked in front, but were quickly driven back as I hear with great loss. We were under arms of course but did not leave our Camp. It is expected that our Guns will open tomorrow. Please tell John that I made a mistake in writing to him that Lieut. Abbott had Genl. Pettigrew's sword. Pettigrew gave his sword to his fleeing friends. It was Lt. Colonel Bull's sword that Abbott got. Both men were taken and brought in about the same time, and I got them a little confused. Col. Bull died that night. After the attack yesterday McClellan rode up and was received as usual with tremendous cheers.

I hear that we had notice of the approach of the enemy yesterday, and being all prepared let them get well into the open land and then suddenly opened from our lines and with a terrific cross-fire of Canister. They fled leaving their colors, and the slaughter was awful. We had one slightly wounded. This is the report I have heard. I am well as usual.

Love to Father and all.

Your affectionate son
Henry.

RIGHT UP INTO THE FIRE

Camp Lincoln June 24th 1862.

My dear Father.

I believe I have no letter from you to acknowledge, but as I have got no letters for 2 days I expect some by the mail today, and very likely I shall receive one from you.

Yesterday we were paid off up to May 1st 1862, two months. My pay was $212.50 and I send home of this $110.00. I enclose the receipt by which you can draw the money as you did before, at the Mayor's Office.

I have not yet received from John an account of my expenses, and therefore do not know whether the whole or more or less is required to meet my expenses, but should any balance remain in my favor I beg you will credit it to me. I know that my valise and its contents must have been quite expensive.

Yesterday I was on a fatigue party at the fortifications in front. Our forts are very extensive and the batteries that are being moved up very formidable. A battery of Siege Howitzers, tremendous affair, throwing a 64 lb. shell has just arrived.

Yesterday afternoon there came a report that Richmond was being evacuated, and so our pickets were thrown forward and the woods shelled in front of them as they advanced, and a small body of men was sent forward from Hooker's Division. But they soon returned and reported the enemy still in force in his old position. However, these constant reports of evacuation mean something, and as at Yorktown very likely precede the event. The Rebels have been very quiet lately, and have no doubt now quite settled the fact in their own minds that they cannot drive McClellan off.

The key tied on the valise was so nicely tucked away that Henry at first did not observe it. Please tell Mother that I have begun to wear the undershirts she sent out, although I did not expect to, and find them very comfortable.

We had another terrible thunderstorm last night. They are very frequent here, but are rarely accompanied with wind. Today is cooler and cloudy.

Love to all.

Your affectionate son
Henry.

RIGHT UP INTO THE FIRE

Camp Lincoln June 26th 1862.

My dear Father.

I have been at the works in front with a working party two days, and have been unable to write in answer to your kind letters before.

I now acknowledge two from you dated 19th and 20th, and one received yesterday of the 19th enclosing receipt for a box. I have also received one from Mother of the 17th and one from Mary Ann 21st giving a very interesting account of Class Day.

In regard to my degree at College, I believe I have written that Herbert Mason and I have sent in a joint petition to the Faculty and written a joint letter to Prof. Lovering, requesting him to present it. This we did before we knew that you and Mr. Mason had done anything for us.

I cannot think they will refuse us, as they have often given degrees to Students, who have been absent longer than we, for sickness.

It is very kind indeed of you and Mother to send me another box so soon after my valise. I feel that I cannot thank you enough. If we stay here, I shall undoubtedly get it without any delay.

I must close, for I have little time. It is now 5 o'cl. A.M. and we go on a working party at ½ past 6. Yesterday our entire left advanced, driving the enemy. Quite a severe battle. Our Regiment not engaged of course. I was in a redoubt in the front and we opened for about 2 hours with 6 guns. Genls. McClellan, Sumner, Sedgwick, Dana, Meagher, Smith, French, and others were at our redoubt, a very central place.

I suppose we have occupied the enemy's advanced works. Firing in the night quite heavy, also this morning. Our central works are very strong.

All well. Love to mother and all.

Your ever affectionate son
Henry Ropes.

RIGHT UP INTO THE FIRE

Camp Lincoln June 27th 1862.

My dear Father.

I enclose a letter for Mary Ann.

We had the Regiment out yesterday evening to cheer at the good news of Porter's victorious advance on the right. I hope it is as good as our report of it was.

We may move at any time. Considerable firing today. I saw by the receipt of the valise you sent that $1.00 was paid for freight. Yet the Agent at White House charged Henry $2.25 in addition for freight. Can this be right? I have written to the Agent for an explanation, but he has not answered my letter yet. I think $3.25 a very extravagant freight. My box you sent was charged no additional freight.

The last box which you have so kindly sent has not yet come. I expect it daily now. Its contents will be very useful and contribute much to my health and enjoyment.

Thank John for the books by mail (Halifax etc.). I am perfectly well. Weather warm and fine. Love to Mother and all from

Your affectionate son
Henry Ropes.

Camp Lincoln 20th Regiment
Saturday June 28th 1862. 5 A.M.

My dear John.

I received yesterday your letter about Class day. I need not tell you how interesting it was. I enjoyed it very much and have read most of it to Herbert.

We have been so constantly disturbed by firing going on in front for 2 days that I have really been unable to write much, and I have great doubts if this letter is finished without interruption. We had quite an alarm at 2 this morning.

I hear Porter advances this morning. There have been great movements of troops during the night, and I really expect a very important day. We were marched down to the works last night, but immediately returned.

I am very glad that all my relics have gone safely. As to the "Atlantic" I should be very glad to get it regularly, and I beg you will read it first, and then send it to me by mail. Please also send the May number.

RIGHT UP INTO THE FIRE

I am very glad that your business increases. Thank you for your kind present of books. They are all very interesting, but I am afraid I do not appreciate "Phenix".[32] One has to be in a particularly jovial state to enjoy such a book. In regard to the box they have sent me. In case anything else should at any time be sent I hope you will see that no Coffee in cans, or Chocolate is put in. Of course, I am exceedingly obliged for these boxes Father and Mother send so often, and I do not feel like hinting to them, that this or that is not desired, but I wish privately to tell you what really I want, and what I do not care for, so that you can direct without my seeming to presume to dictate in the least.

You see that we are in a hot, damp country, and the tendency is to getting run down and lazy and languid. One does not in the least need such a rich hearty drink as Chocolate. I drink what they send, but do not care for it, and of course the room could be much better filled. As to this preserved Coffee, it is a miserable substitute for real Coffee. You must remember that one cannot get milk at all here. I gave away one can, have two now on hand, and Father writes that he has sent out *four* more in the box. These cost at least ½ a dollar each and the 7 cans with the Chocolate must have thus cost at least $4.00, enough to buy 4 bottles of brandy, or whisky, or cheese, or quantities of useful things. I have got to enjoy tea here in this debilitating country. In case any other box should ever be sent, please see that some of the following articles are sent, in preference to anything else. For liquors: 1st Brandy, then Cherry Cordial, or wines. For useful food, salt mackerel, salt fish, perhaps 1 dutch cheese, a very small amount of best tea, and ground coffee, 2 small cans solidified milk, bottle or pot preserved ginger, perhaps dried ginger, paper Cayenne pepper, paper black pepper, box yeast powder, tongues or ham that will keep in hot weather, white sugar is very well, but I can get good sugar (brown) here. Pickles, Limes, figs, lemons, oranges, lemon or raspberry syrup, wine or other crackers and gingerbread, preserved fruits are always excellent. Curry powder (for rice) would be very nice. I merely give you this list in case anything else should in future be sent, not of course expecting anything, and I beg you will keep it to yourself and merely give your advice when necessary. Should you ever have an opportunity of sending anything to me by any other way, I would be glad to get anything of the above list on my own account. Sardines are not desirable, because one does not fancy such cold weather food here. Remember this is a damp, weakening country. One wants stimulating food like Curry etc., and astringent drink like tea or wine (such as Port, Sherry or Claret) more than rich food like sardines and chocolate.

Now do not on any account show this to Father or Mother, or let them think that anything they send is not desired, or that I want anything I do not get.

---

[32] Ropes is possibly referring to "The Phoenix", a comedic play by Thomas Middleton.

Herbert is quite sick. Not much the matter except a little fever, but very weak, the usual illness here. Recovery is very slow here always. Tilden is better. Curtis very sick. Cabot quite unwell. The Colonel stands it remarkably, but he is feeble. Constant loss of sleep runs down almost everyone. As for me, I am perfectly well, and I really think I feel "smarter" than any of them. I do not mind the great heat so much as the rest, I think.

Thank you for your information about my friend Temple. I am delighted to hear that Dick is a "brother". I shall try to write to him about it. Is Sturgis or Mifflin (65) in? I am very much interested in Hazeltine's plan. When he writes, I shall hope to reply fully. I was rather astonished that Tom should go however. Hazy will get on well but will be laughed at for some of his crotchets. I long for Hazy's letter. You know he has so long neglected me. I am very much interested in everything about class day, the H.P. and the A Δ, and am delighted the last is getting on so well.

I have no news. We have conflicting rumours as to Porter's Corps. Quantities of troops were moving yesterday and in the night. The Rebels shelled heavily yesterday. Some passed over us here, and very close. I shall try to send home the books I have read and other things by Express.

Love to all.

Most affectionately
Your brother
Henry.

Camp near landing on James River
Va. July 5th 1862.

My dear Father.

Again I have been preserved from all harm amid the greatest dangers; dangers to which those I have so lately passed through seem nothing.

I feel that I can never be thankful enough for my preservation, for I am perfectly untouched although about one half of my company are gone. We have fought 4 regular battles and covered the retreat the whole way. We have really marched 3 successive nights and fought 3 successive days.

Now, however, we are encamped some distance to the rear, and fresh troops which are pouring up from the river are in the advance. I was fortunate enough to save my valise and a small box of food etc. but my knapsack was left behind, the wagons being overloaded. In this however I only lost a shirt, pair drawers, blanket and a few books. What most I regret was the loss of the little Prayer book given me by Mother just before I left, and which I have always had by me. Had I had the least reason to suppose we were going to leave I could have so packed my valise as to leave nothing useful behind; but I left the Camp fully expecting to be back by night, and I never returned to it.

I will not attempt to describe all I have seen now, for I have not time. All I can say is that of the 4 battles the 3rd at "Nelson's Farm" was the one in which we met with so heavy a loss.

We marched over an open field exposed to a heavy fire of Artillery and musketry halting 3 times to dress, and drove the enemy before us, and passed beyond a battery of ours which had been taken and retaken once already. On the open field my Company lost nearly a third of their number. A shell burst right among us. One shell dashed Sergeant Holmes' head in pieces and spattered the brains and bits of flesh all about, pieces remaining stuck to the faces of the men. Another (or a ball) took off Corporal Sampson's leg above the knee knocking it far away. Another tore away the whole breast and bowels of Sergeant Compass. Many were wounded beside these. All this was while we steadily advanced over a wide field and before a gun was fired by us.

Still the Regiment never faltered an inch. It was nothing but "close up" "guide left" as the line pressed steadily forward. Our Company lost most by the shell etc. When we got to the abandoned battery the sight was indeed awful. Horses and men were spread over the ground torn to pieces in every way; some alive, and gasping and crying out. We passed right on beyond the battery to support our own troops who were rapidly being driven out of the woods in front. They all fell behind us, but did not reform well.

We were ordered to fall back to the woods. The enemy came out on us. Our Brigade withstood them. Then the Michigan 7th gave way before the close fire, and we were soon the only Regiment left, the enemy pressing on in large numbers. The order was given "about face" "forward march". So we fell back through the woods, twice halting, facing to the front and delivering fire. The enemy pressed yelling on, firing and soon opened with shell. It was quite dark in the underbrush and dense smoke, so many of the men got separated, and although Colonel Palfrey (Col. Lee was in command of the Brigade) led the way to the right to a road there, many of the men lost their way and did not find us in the darkness and confusion. We formed on the road, sadly diminished in numbers, and very soon Meagher's and other troops passed up farther to our right, and I understand drove back the enemy, captured again our abandoned battery, and also 2 guns from the Rebels.

We fell back to the road near the position from which we started, and here I learned our loss. Poor Lowell is gone, shot like Putnam in the bowels. Patten, Abbott and Miller are wounded. Col. Palfrey slightly, a mere scratch. Col. Lee was run over by a runaway horse and bruised, but has gone back to be well taken care of. Capt. Hallowell also scratched. Our Company lost in killed and wounded 12 men (not counting one or two contusions) out of 30. Capt. Shepard and I were entirely unhurt.

Abbott was shot through the arm just before we fell back, yet he stuck to us, although suffering great pain, and would not go to the surgeons till all was over.

I cannot describe the other battles here. We lost no one there, but a few were slightly scratched. This battle was altogether the greatest. Our marches have been terribly tiresome, and we have been without clothing to change for several days, though wet through. Herbert is quite used up and has gone back. So have Tilden and Curtis. Hallowell (Lt. Edward N.) went back long ago, and Sturgis has been for some time on Berry's staff, so we are very short of Officers. Our Regiment now numbers a little over 200 men.

But the 20th has done splendidly, everyone says so. In fact I hardly know how men could have done better than obey orders and keep formation under the heaviest fire and in a trying repulse. Our colors are of course safe, though torn with balls. The State Flag is torn to shreds by a shell.

I have only hurried off this account. I shall try to write long letters and full accounts soon. As to the strategy etc. I will not now speak. Opinions are divided here. Form myself I have still the fullest confidence in the cause and the Generals. It cannot be denied however that quantities of our Regiments do not and will not stand. If all were 20th, there would be no need of re-enforcements or anything else. As far as I have seen the Rebels *always* give way before a steady advance. Re-enforcements have landed in very large numbers and I think have gone to the front. We are now perfectly quiet and safe and expect to remain here and recruit our energies a little.

Please ask Mother to send me another little prayer book by mail. Please ask John to send by mail one or two of the spring clasps, or hooks used to connect the Sword with the belt strap. They are of brass and are of this shape *[drawing missing]*. The scabbard is attached in the way I have rudely represented. Please show this to John, and he will know what I mean.

Best love to Mother and all. I stood the hardships perfectly. I feel I never shall cease to remember these events in the most vivid manner. I fear you have been very anxious. I really could not write before. Received today letter from Mother, 30th, I think.

Your ever affectionate son
Henry.

RIGHT UP INTO THE FIRE

Camp 20th Regiment near Landing
on James River July 6th 1862.

My dear John,

Although it is about a week since I wrote to you and 3 days since we settled down into a quiet life in Camp, I have only been able as yet to write a hasty letter to Father yesterday, and today to try to give you some connected account of the important events and terrible scenes of the past 10 days.

On the morning of Saturday June 28th our Regiment was ordered out on a working party. There had been a great deal of heavy cannonading, especially on the right, for several days, but, so far as we knew, nothing particular had happened, and I went out on the working party that morning just as I had gone out so often before, expecting of course to return at night and leaving Henry at the tent to see to my things and to get me some dinner when I returned. We went to work on a Magazine being built some distance in the rear of one of the principal redoubts. I was overseeing the digging of a trench when an Officer rode up and hastily enquired for the Commander of the party and at the same time told me to collect the men and stop work. Capt. Macy was in charge of the party, for the Field Officers did not think it worth while to come out on a working party. Capt. Shephard /sic/ had staid in camp to do some writing. The men were collected and we marched farther to the left, and took up position on the edge of a piece of woods behind part of the earth works occupied by the 19th Mass. Col. Lee, Col. Palfrey, the Major, and most of the other Officers soon joined us. Herbert was quite sick and was in the Camp. So was Curtis. Tilden had been ill for some time, but was with us quite weak and lying down under the trees. Suddenly he became worse; Dr. Crehore was sent for and he was taken back to Camp. I hear that he and Curtis were sent on in an ambulance from Camp, probably to the James river. Neither of them have been with us since.

Soon after we got to the woods, say at about 10 o'cl. A.M. an order came to dig traverses. We attempted to do so, but the ground was so very swampy we were obliged to give it up. In the earthworks, however, they dug them. Then we heard that our right had been turned and that we must expect a flanking fire. Capt. Shepard came down, and in the most excited and secret manner told me that it was all up: Our right turned, we were going to retreat, and were in a most precarious position, etc. However, we did nothing all day, and were not fired on. Henry came down and told me that the whole camp was packed up. I sent him back with orders to see to my baggage and precede us on the march. He left me a good supply of food and my Rubber blanket. At night a guard was posted and we slept just where we were. At 3 A.M. on Sunday morning (29th) we fell in and quietly marched off down the Railroad and past our old camp.

RIGHT UP INTO THE FIRE

All the troops were gone and the Camps were entirely deserted. Many tents were left behind and quantities of blankets, pots, boxes, knapsacks, etc. At the Railroad was an immense amount of Stores which were being rapidly destroyed. Barrels of flour, Sugar, Coffee, Whisky, etc. were knocked in and poured into the mud. Clothing was cut to pieces, Ammunition thrown into a bog near, and they were knocking a new rocket battery to pieces. It was terrible to see this great destruction of property. A few Cavalry were out to give the alarm of the enemy's approach, and a couple of guns on a slight rising ground were unlimbered and ready to check the advance of the Rebels. We marched down the Railroad for about ½ a mile, and then came out on an open field on the left of the Railroad, where we found our troops drawn up in battle array, the guns on a rising ground. We were formed along the edge of the woods nearest our old camp, and of course closest to the enemy. We sent out pickets. The 1st California[33] and the 5th New Hampshire were on our right and left and also had pickets out. Here, after all those still behind us had passed down, we awaited the advance of the enemy. The troops drawn up on the open field were Sumner's Corps, charged with covering the retreat. They were passing down the Railroad for perhaps an hour before the enemy came on. We heard the Rebels cheering as they came out and took possession of our deserted works and camps. Soon they came farther on, and before long engaged our pickets. The picket firing was at times quite heavy and then would about cease. But all this time the enemy were pressing on in increasing numbers, and our forces filing off along the Railroad and a road made by it. It was very trying to stand up and know this, and yet do nothing. At last the enemy brought up Artillery and shelled us and advanced and opened heavily with musketry. Our guns opened and the shell blew over our heads, and the enemy's shell burst over us and near us. The battle lasted for some time, but at last ceased, the Rebels probably waiting till more of their troops should come up. All this time, our Regiment, except Companies I & B which were advanced as pickets, remained expecting the enemy every moment. It was to me much more trying than any battle, knowing as I did that our own troops were falling back, and the Rebels advancing every moment. All our troops had now left the open field and were marching along the Railroad, and the order came for us quietly to draw in our pickets and march after them. We did so, and silently and rapidly crossed the open field and marched down the Railroad; on the farther edge of the open field we found another line of troops, a mere picket line, left to give us notice in case of the enemy following very closely. But no alarm was given, and we marched down to Despatch Station about 5 miles and here was a very large open field and our Corps being again drawn up.

---

[33] Known as the 71st Pennsylvania since October, 1861.

So this was the first battle, near Fair Oaks. We lost no men, but one or 2 were just touched by bits of shell. I hear the enemy lost a large number. It was awfully hot. Some of our men were sunstruck, and almost all threw away their blankets, and knapsacks. The way was strewed with these, in great numbers. I have not an opportunity of writing more now, but will take up the story here in my next and try to give you a connected account of the whole.

The shoulder straps have arrived safely. Can you send me two more keys for my valise? I have lost one, and like to have extra ones. Please also send some toothpicks and stamps by mail.

I hope someone keeps the newspaper accounts of any things of interest for me. I especially want to keep college things. It is Joe May's old sofa in the A Δ, I gave it. I will try to get you a "Fair Oaks" stick.

Love to all.

Most affectionately
Henry Ropes.

P.S. Just received yours 2nd July and Father's 28th June.

Camp 20th Regiment near Landing
on James river Monday July 7th 1862.

My dear John.

I wrote to you yesterday and gave an account of our retreat after the 1st battle which I see is called in the papers "Peach Orchard". I made a mistake in saying than [sic] then we marched to "Despatch" Station. I should have said "Savage's" Station. Well, we marched to this immense open field, and it was terribly hot. The Railroad ran through the field and our forces were soon drawn up on the South side of the Railroad, where the ground was quite elevated. I here will give you a rude outline of the place.

RIGHT UP INTO THE FIRE

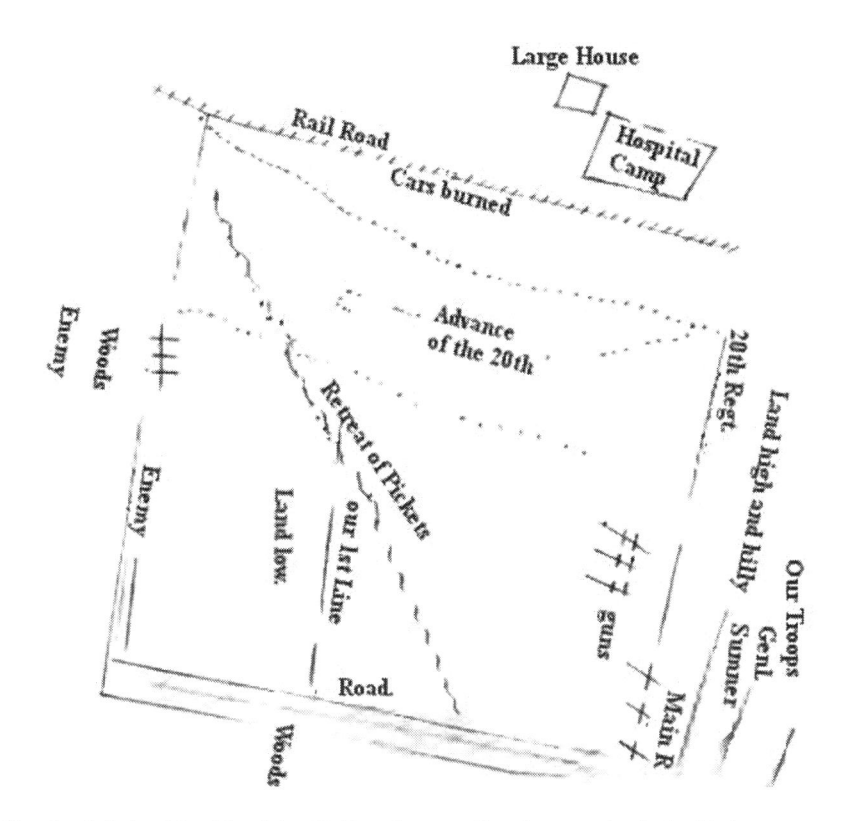

On the left (or North) of the Railroad was a fine house, shaded with large trees, and a little in the rear about 50 wall tents placed in regular order, in which a large number of the sick and wounded, who could not be carried off, had been left with suitable attendants. This camp of tents was formerly Heintzelman's Headquarters. Soon after we got on the field a large number of Cars filled with ammunition were burnt, and an immense quantity of powder blown up. It was a fine sight. A tremendous column of smoke was forced high into the air and looked like an immense white balloon. When we first came on the field we were drawn up in a position at right angles to the one I have drawn, our front toward the house, and our left on quite a rising ground. We waited quietly till near 5 o'clock and ate our dinners, and then Genl. Sumner advanced a long line of troops toward the woods. The distance from Genl. Sumner's position (as I have drawn it) to the woods where the enemy were, was I should think as far as from the State House to the Providence Depot. The enemy opened the battle by firing from a battery, just at the edge of the woods upon us. Our left being, as I said, on high ground was much exposed, and several were wounded. Soon we were marched by the right flank to the position I have shown. The shell flew and burst close to our right Companies and several came exceedingly near, yet it was about ½ an hour before we received orders to change our position. Then Companies I and K were drawn back from the high ground and placed behind the 2nd Division. The Rebels threw many shot and shell right among the Hospital tents far on our right, and at last a man came out with a white flag, and I think they stopped then. After the Artillery had thundered away for about an hour, our Infantry advanced and engaged the Rebels who had now come out of the woods in front, and there was the usual roar and smoke. Just now also a heavy thunderstorm rolled up, and altogether it was a very splendid sight. Our Infantry had driven the Rebels back into the woods, when we received orders to go back into line, and then to advance. We went forward with the 2nd line, we the extreme right, and partly at double quick and with cheers ran forward. Old General Sumner was there on horseback, cool as ever. A shell burst right among his staff but he seemed to take no notice of it. We crossed the field and got to the edge of the woods. Here we halted and after a short time of heavy firing from our troops in front of us, the Rebels left, and we were in position /possession/ of the field. Our Regiment did not fire a shot, but were considerable /sic/ exposed both to Artillery at first and to musketry near the woods. It was now getting dark, the other Regiments were drawn back, and we left on the edge of the woods. We threw out pickets in front, the 7th Michigan had a few pickets on our right on the other side of the Railroad and the 15th Mass. on our left. Our Company and Company A all under Capt. Tremlett went on picket. It was awfully dark. We posted the men and communicated with our neighbors on either side. Soon a heavy squall came up and the rain was tremendous. Part of the plain was still lit up by the remains of the still burning cars. The woods were filled with dead and wounded Rebels, many groaning and crying out and begging for assistance. We could see nothing, but I spoke to several and told them I would do what I could as soon as our pickets were established. There was a Colonel, a Captain and a Lieutenant close to us. They were all from South Carolina, and the Lieutenant told me we had been engaged with a Brigade of South Carolina troops, 4 Regiments. We gave them water, and I expected every moment that men would be sent to take them in, but none came. We could hear them groaning some distance out beyond us in the woods, and some of our pickets said they heard the Rebels coming to them and taking them off, showing how near the enemy was.

At about 11 o'clock, I should think, Capt. Tremlett, who had been round in the dark to see exactly where we were, came and told us that the Regiment and all the troops were gone and the plain empty, yet no orders had come for us to withdraw. He could not find the Michigan pickets on our right and therefore sent a Sergeant to explore. You must remember that it was pitch dark, and we in a wood. While we were waiting thus, an order to draw in the men was quietly past /sic/ down and Capt. Shepard drew in our Company, and sent word to Company A. Just now a volley of musketry came from the other side of the Railroad.

RIGHT UP INTO THE FIRE

The Sergeant sent had found no Michigan pickets and had been fired at by the advancing pickets of the enemy. Silently we fell in and marched across the open field, obliquely, to the right. It was deep mud and we constantly ran against stumps and trees, so deep was the darkness. The fire lit up the deserted plain. We at last struck the road on the right and followed it along, and took the main road to the right, and before we had gone over two miles, came upon the rear of our retreating army, and marched with them, without adventure till we gained up with the Regiment at about 3 A.M. It was a very muddy, tiresome march, especially to us who were tired before. This picket adventure was, you see, very close, for the enemy must have learned of our departure from the wounded men, and could easily have headed us off with a few Cavalry. It was a very tight place, and certainly we were all quite anxious until we had got a good start. The whole Division halted at about day break, and I lay down and got about an hour's sleep. When I awoke I saw Sergeant Compass with a cup of Coffee, which he kindly had made for me. I drank it and ate something and felt much revived. Poor Sergeant Compass was killed that day, and it is pleasant to remember this act of kindness.

At about 6 o'clock we marched on some distance farther and then again halted and soon the Artillery opened on our right. Before long we got orders to fall in, and marched in the direction of the fire and halted and formed some distance in rear of the actual conflict. The enemy's shell all fell to our left in a wood which was soon on fire. It was very hot, and we all had suffered much from thirst. This was really terrible, and the only water the muddy pools on the road side which were eagerly drunk up. At about noon the firing ceased and we lay still till about 3.30 P.M. when firing suddenly broke out on the left and was soon very severe. We were marched very rapidly, although it was awfully hot and dusty, toward the left. Soon we came out on an open place, where the shot and bullets and shells were plying very thick, and the Artillery playing, and our troops evidently engaged in the woods in front, where all was hid in dense smoke and the roar of musketry was incessant. Sumner was here and ordered us instantly to the front. As we had marched by the left flank, our Regiment was first on the field, and immediately formed in line and advanced in face of a tremendous fire of Artillery and musketry toward the woods. Our advance was perfectly steady although men fell at every step. We halted and dressed 3 times. Our Company lost dreadfully here from shell and cannon shot. As this was our great fight I will give you a little map.

RIGHT UP INTO THE FIRE

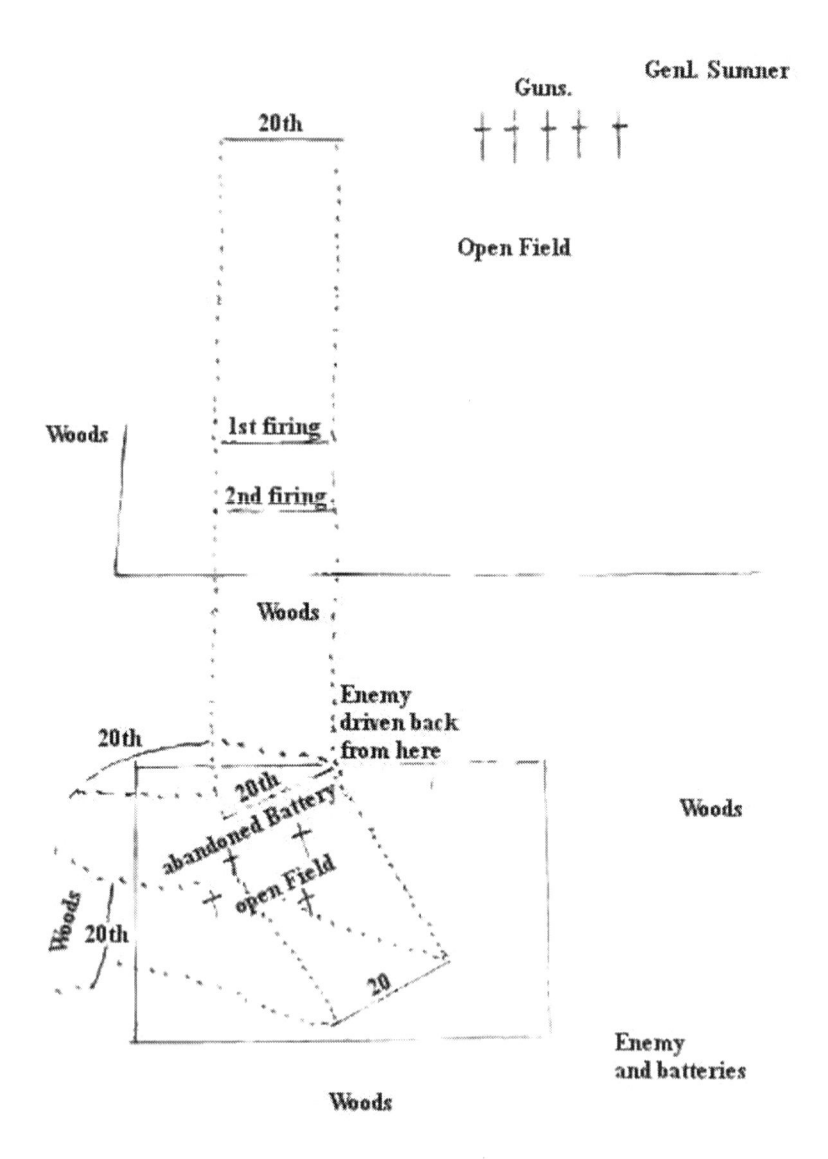

[Diagram with labels: "20th", "Guns.", "GenL Sumner", "Open Field", "Woods", "1st firing", "2nd firing", "Woods", "Enemy driven back from here", "20th", "20th", "abandoned Battery", "open Field", "20", "Woods", "Woods", "20th", "Enemy and batteries", "Woods"]

Sergeants Holmes and Compass were instantly killed here. We got pretty near the woods, halted, fired and after a few moments again advanced, halted and fired again, and continued firing for some time. Then we had orders to file to the left oblique and then to cease firing. Some of the Regiments on our right and left however got excited and did not cease and soon an Officer came running out of the woods throwing up his hands and begging us not to fire on our own men who had advanced from the right and driven back the enemy. Soon we were advanced through the woods in front and came out on an open field, where was the most

RIGHT UP INTO THE FIRE

terrible sight I have ever yet seen in war. There was one of our batteries abandoned, the horses lying dead and wounded and some dreadfully torn by shell, and some kicking and bellowing, and the ground covered with dead and wounded men, Rebels, and our troops in front engaged with the Rebels at the edge of the woods beyond, and the smoke darkening all and the shouts of the combatants often rising above all. Our men were just being driven out of the woods. We halted and the broken Regiments tried to rally behind us, the re-enforcements. I should have said that before we crossed the open field where the battery was, we filed to the right in the edge of the woods, and then advanced. The enemy were evidently in great force, and after covering our men who were falling back, we about faced, wheeled to the left and entered the woods as I have shown in the plan. Here we halted and opened fire on the enemy who had come out and filled the field. We stood here a long time, the fire very severe. It was here Abbott was shot, he fell to the rear and said "Ropes, I have got it at last; take my Company." It was awfully hot, we all were covered with sweat and black with smoke and powder. Poor Abbott was in great pain. I went to the right of his company. His men were firing away perfectly cool, and taking steady aim. All these woods as well as the field were full of the dead and wounded. On our right were the remains of the broken Regiments in no kind of order, but firing away, some far in advance of others. I tried to get them to form a line, but I could see no Officer, and they paid no heed to my orders. They seemed brave men enough, but too much excited, and did not seem to know the necessity of keeping regular formation. Suddenly I looked to the left, and to my great astonishment saw the Regiment on our left running back in disorder. This was the 7th Michigan. I have since heard that the Colonel gave the order to fall back and is now under arrest for it. At any rate I saw our entire left running back in disorder and the 20th alone, about 250 men facing the enemy.

I knew of course that we must fall back, for it would have been foolish to have staid and been surrounded, as the enemy had nothing to oppose them on our right as well as our left. Abbott now rushed up. He had refused to go back, wishing as he said to see it out. In a few moments the order came, "About face", "forward march". So we fell back, but twice we halted, faced about at the order and fired. We were descending quite a hill. The enemy pressed on with yells, firing constantly, and in a few moments opened our abandoned battery on us. As we got to the foot of the hill the underbrush was very thick and although Col. Palfrey filed the Regiment to the right, a large number kept straight on and got separated from us. I hear that the enemy did come in on our right and took many prisoners. Here (i.e. on the right) there was a road and we halted and formed and marched a little farther back. The shells were still bursting over us, and it was getting dark and the enemy were near and firing still continued. The 19th formed also and parts of other Regiments were there, some of the Officers greatly excited, waving their swords, begging their men to come on etc. Our Regiment halted quietly and formed calmly. Soon Aides rode up and said that 2 Brigades had advanced to our right and now the heavy fire broke out and we heard the cheers of our men. Before long it died away somewhat, and another battery came up, and we heard that our fresh troops had driven the enemy back. Afterwards I learned that we not only recovered the guns but took two from the enemy besides. We remained here at the road till it was long after dark and then marched along a byroad toward our old position, and halted by the road side, and Col. Palfrey went to report. Then we heard of Lowell's death and of our other losses. Col. Lee was in command of the Brigade and was knocked down by a battery horse running off, and badly bruised. He is now, I hear, gone back and is well taken care of, no doubt. Col. Palfrey was slightly wounded, Hallowell just scratched. Abbott shot through the arm, yet he managed to march with us to the river, and has now gone back to be attended to. He is about the bravest man I ever saw. He is always cheerful and hopeful and never gives up. Patten was hit in the leg, but came along on horseback. Miller was wounded and I believe left behind. Herbert was so ill he had just been able to get along the last 2 days on a horse, and had not been with his company and was not of course able to be with us in the battles at all. I feel very sorry for him.

Well, we were dreadfully exhausted and lay down and got a little sleep. At midnight we were roused, fell in and again marched and about 4 A.M. we got to a perfectly immense extent of open land, very hilly and pretty and where we had a fine view, and the river was in the distance. Here we got some breakfast, food was given out and we dried ourselves and got rather more comfortable. This place was called "Malvernton", I hear. The battle which I have just described is called the battle of "Nelson's farm." Some of the papers speak of the battle of "Oak Swamp" which may be the same.

Well, I have written a tremendous letter, and I dare say you are tired at reading it. I will finish the account of this great retreat in my next letter. We have been now nearly a week in this camp, and are beginning to get comfortable but it is awfully hot. I long for the box of Lemons, etc. We may be here some time. Henry would like you to find out from Mr. Redpath how his family are. I enclose a Rebel stamp which Henry found in a deserted house and sends a present to you.

I have sent by Capt. Macy, in a trunk he has just sent home, by Express, a package directed to you containing "John Brent" which I enjoyed very much, and would like to have kept. Also a lot of private letters to be put in my box, a little prayerbook which I picked up at "Fair Oaks", and an old letter I found at the shanty which I took possession of with 10 men, soon after the battle of "Fair Oaks". Also my gold watch, of which the crystal is broken. Please let these things be kept against my return. Henry also sends a Secesh letter which he thinks will be interesting to you.

I am very well, and we are perfectly quiet now. Genl. Dana has gone to the rear sick. We have a new Regiment, the 59th New York, added to our Brigade. We all feel Lowell's loss very deeply, but since we all were with him in the danger, and have been so busy and excited since, it does not seem like a death at home. Yet, you will feel it very much. I liked him very much indeed.

I want exceedingly to get your letters after you had heard all the news. Thank Grinnell for his letter. I shall try to answer soon, but we write under great difficulties here. Love to them all at home. I owe letters to sister Mary, and Frank, but do not know when I can write. Do write and tell me everything, and what they think at home, and what the war is coming to. I do not like the aspect of affairs abroad.

I remain

Your affectionate brother
Henry.

Camp 20th Regiment July 9th 1862.

My dear Mother.

This is I find my last ½ sheet, or I would write you a longer letter. It is often very hard to get paper, and this is you see very bad. I must hunt about now for a Sutler's wagon and get some more.

We are in the middle of a Southern July now, and it is hot enough, but we get up shades and drink lemonade when we can get it, and manage to get along quite well.

Of course we have none of the usual summer luxuries, ice, milk, and fruit, but there is no knowing what enterprise will accomplish if we stay here long enough for any Yankee to open a store, and I dare say we shall have an ice cream Saloon by and by.

We are perfectly quiet and there is no appearance of a move. I do not see what is going to be done. I have really no news to tell you. I am well and quite comfortable. Henry is quite well too. I hope you will soon be at Swampscott and enjoy the sea air. I should delight to be with you.

Best love to Father.

Your ever affectionate son
Henry.

Enclosed letter for Mary Ann.

RIGHT UP INTO THE FIRE

Camp 20th Regiment Mass. Volunteers
near Harrison's Landing, Va.
July 11th 1862.

My dear John.

I have just received yours of the 7th, and I hasten to reply, but first I will continue the narrative of the retreat which I believe I left off in my last letter at "Malvern Hills" [sic] or Malvernton, as, I think, it is called.

We are now quite comfortably settled in this camp, and I am perfectly well. It was early on Tuesday morning (July 1st) that we arrived at this beautiful place (Malvernton), after another fatiguing night march, following the terrible excitement of the battle of "Nelson's Farm". We found ourselves on a hill overlooking an immense open tract of country, broken by hills and with several fine pieces of woodland, and several large good houses on it. As it grew light we saw the ground was occupied by our Army as far as the eye could reach, except in a northerly direction where a ravine separated our position from another open place beyond which were dense forests. Our forces were gradually taking up positions, and it was a magnificent sight. We were not marched to the extreme front but lay in the 3rd general line in a beautiful clover field near a house. We were in line of battle, and lay down and rested. It was perhaps 9 o'clock before the battle opened. Then we could distinctly see the black masses of the enemy emerging from the woods and taking up position on the open land beyond the ravine in support of batteries which advanced and opened fire. Few of their shots at first came near us, and before long the Artillery had got pretty generally into play, and there was the usual amount of smoke etc. After an hour or two the enemy got up nearer and then commenced throwing shell right in among our Division. At about this time our batteries unaccountably ceased, and we were, seemingly for no reason, exposed to a very close fire of shot and shell. We several times had changed our position. At last the fire was very accurate, shell bursting right in the middle of Regiments on all sides of us, and many being killed and wounded, but none of our Regiment hit, although quantities of shell came not more than 8 or 10 feet from where I was. At last came the order to move, and we marched off by the flank, still exposed, and were placed for shelter behind a hill and in some woods. Just about this time the fire ceased suddenly, and we afterwards learned that we had taken the whole rebel battery by throwing troops in their rear, and that they were allowed to play upon us so long, that they might be kept in position while our men surrounded them. The next day I saw some of the captured guns. During the remainder of the day we were very comfortable in the woods. On the afternoon there was firing again, and our Division ordered out of the woods, but were immediately ordered back, our aid not being needed.

RIGHT UP INTO THE FIRE

We slept till about 1 o'clock A.M. of the 2nd and then again marched, and got to Harrison's Landing at about 2 o'clock P.M., or a little earlier. It rained heavily. That night and the whole of the next day and night, we were close to the river, and it was rainy and very muddy and we suffered greatly. Then we marched here about 1 ½ miles from the river and are in quite a comfortable place. It has been very hot indeed, of late.

Well, as to our state, I suppose we can now muster in the Regiment 300 men for a fight, and perhaps 10 Company Officers. Companies F and G are consolidated and so is Company I and part of Company D under Capt. Hallowell. The rest of Company D, about 20 men, have been for months detailed under Lieut. Messer, as a special guard for the Balloon, and have seen no fighting.

I have read your letter with a great deal of interest. I tell you truly that when we got to the river, i.e. on July 2nd, and for 2 or 3 days after everything looked pretty gloomy, and I heard from various sources great distrust etc. in McClellan. But now everyone has gained heart, heavy re-enforcements have arrived, the men are rested and refreshed, and I think the old Army would today fight better for its number than ever before. The new troops would probably do well, too. But a great deal of faith in McClellan is gone, and I fear will not return. For my own part, although sorely tempted to fall in with the general spirit, especially after reading your letter, I cannot after carefully considering the whole history of the campaign blame McClellan, and all I can say is that I suppose Napoleon would have invented some way of overcoming difficulties, through which I cannot see the least light. For instance, I have heard that orders had been sent for a general advance of the entire army on the day after the battle of "Fair Oaks", and that Porter was obliged to say that the state of the Chickahominy would not permit him to bring over a *single piece* of Artillery. The difficulties are not such as a little skill and energy can overcome, but so tremendous that the most energetic soul would wilt at the thought. To my mind it is the greatest wonder that we got off the great guns. The roads baffle description. There seems to be no bottom to the mud. Fortunately, the last half of our retreat was over a better and harder road. Now, as to the general charge against McClellan, viz.: "that he did not attack Richmond before", I answer that never, at any one time has he had a force that justified him in the attempt. True he was as strong then as now, and the enemy much stronger now, but my first remark is still true. He needed enormous re-enforcements, and above all a system of enlistments which would keep the Regiments pretty nearly full.

Then there is one other thing which I am almost ashamed to own, but which must be said and which I know is true in spite of all the flaunting newspaper accounts. It is this. With the exception of some Mass. Regiments, and a very few others, the troops *do not fight*. They will go in and fire and run up and run back and make a splendid charge as long as the Rebels run the other way, but they will not stand up and fight steadily in regular formation, and keep at it and stick to it. If the Rebels do not run back in about 15 minutes they certainly will. To be sure the Rebels generally do run first, but still the great majority of our troops are not persistent soldiers, have nothing of the steadiness of veterans. This is too true and the reason is in my opinion, because the line Officers are not Gentlemen. I say this after deliberate reflection. In a battle the tendency to give way to fear is of such a nature that a merely good, honest, plucky man is very little good as an Officer. An Officer, if he feels afraid, must hide it and be above his men. With good Officers the men will do anything. I have taken some pains to notice what kind of men do best, and I find that a merely naturally brave man (I mean a common man) is of no particular good as an Officer. His men are his equals, they see just how he feels, and they feel just the same, and if anything goes, all goes together; but Officers, as a class, must be men to whom the slightest taint of cowardice or the exhibition of fear before an enemy would be perfect destruction and everlasting indignity. They must have a Gentleman's sense of honor and regard for character. A substitute for this would be the contempt for death shown by martyrs and religious Enthusiasts, but the bully style of man, the sham Gentleman style of man is good for nothing. As for our Regiment, I see that as usual the papers praise everyone close while no one did what we did. When we advanced over that open field, so important was it at that critical moment, that Sumner himself followed us half way, and an Officer of the Regular Battery on our left, by which we passed to the front, told Lieut. Murphy that there was almost a shout of admiration from them, and every one cried out "What splendid Regiment is that?" They said they could see the shells and canister tearing through us, and our line never waver a hair. As you know, we drove the enemy back, and had we not been so very much advanced would probably have not been ever forced to retire. I have wandered from my subject, however.

 I think with you that Sumner is indeed a splendid General and fully capable of anything. He is not afraid to give the word to advance, when the time has come. He is *always* on the spot and exposes himself very much. We admire him and the men have perfect confidence in him. On that Sunday morning when we all felt that great things were impending and knew that we were the very last of the Army, it was great to see old Sumner ride quietly along with his full white beard, and his calm, benignant yet perfectly confident and resolute face. He does not get the credit he deserves. He covered the main part of the retreat. In the falling back from the earthworks the 20th Regiment was actually the *very last* Regiment that marched out, and we with the 5th New Hampshire and the 1st California extended in line were the first to repel the enemy from the Peach Orchard, and the *very* last to retire. After the battle of Savage's Station also Company A and my Company were the *very last picket which left* some hours after the Army. We have not got credit for what we did. We never do. No matter, History will show, and the Official Accounts will prove all. The 19th is by no means so cut up as you suppose. They were not in the heaviest fire by any means, and only lost about 60 men in killed and wounded. Our loss was perhaps about 70 or 80 and our number engaged very much smaller. Yet you see the 19th praised to the skies.

At present I think the morale of the Army is good, but certainly we must have more men. As to the enemy I know they lost terribly. They had no Artillery to speak of, and Artillery does the work when you can get it to play. They fire very well and aim low.

For myself, in spite of all different opinions and gloomy forebodings, I think we shall all come out well, and I mean to stick it out if nothing happens, and see the end. Sturgis has resigned and gone home. I think he has made a mistake. Macy sends regards and says you are dreadfully fallen away to condemn McClellan, whom he still earnestly supports. Macy and Sanders lost their servant, and now we 3 mess together, and Henry cooks, and it is very pleasant.

The Express runs freely now and I expect my box very soon. Will you please send for our mess by Express a box containing a salt Salmon, some salt Mackerel, a few Herrings, a Ham, several Tongues, a bottle /of/ Pickles (in mustard), can preserved Milk, 2 lbs. good Coffee, and some biscuits. These I think will fill a good box. Please let me know the total expense, as it is divided among us. Send if there is room anything else you may find, but no Chocolate or Cocoa, or preserved Coffee, or Sugar. Any small thing for me could be put in the same box. I expect to get hold of my trunk in a day or two, and shall find there everything I need in the way of clothing, etc. I have sent in a trunk of Macy's a parcel for you containing a book, some relics and some private letters. I believe I wrote to you about them. Be very careful of the letters and have them put (by Mary Ann) in my box. Do send me some toothpicks by mail.

Henry Burckmeyer is well and desires regard, and would like you to find out about his family from Mr. Redpath. Please send a box "Yeast Powder" for making cakes. Preserves of all kinds always acceptable, especially (to me) Ginger. Please take from my money in Father's hands a proper amount and get some present for Mother's birthday. I wish I had thought of it before. In case you all join in a present make me one. We are to be paid again very soon, and I can send home a good supply of money. Mary Ann's birthday comes on the 14th. I fear I am very late for her present, too. Please get her a nice present. Let it be a good one. I leave it all to you. As to the price, let that be not less than $8.00 and as high as $10.00 if you see anything you want to get. Do not be jealous because I am a little liberal towards her, just now. I have got more than I want with me, and $200.00 just coming. She is the only girl, you know. I would rather you spend $10.00 than $8.00, but there is no need of her knowing what anything costs. Give Mother and Mary Ann my best love and my wishes for many happy returns of their birthdays. With God's blessing I may be home by their next.

RIGHT UP INTO THE FIRE

I have written a long letter, and really have nothing more to say till you ask some questions. Write soon and tell me all home news, and what people think and what they feel and what they say? I hope you enjoy Swampscott. Where is the boat? Tell me how the Colonel is, if you hear. I fear he is pretty much used up.

Ever your affectionate brother
Henry.

Camp 20th Regiment Mass. Vols.
near Harrison's Landing, Va. July 13th
Sunday 1862.

My dear Mother.

I am somewhat astonished that I did not get any letters at all either yesterday or today, but I have this morning received an Advertiser so I suppose you are all well or John would have written.

I felt very sorry to leave you uncertain about me for so long a time, but I really could not write before. Major Revere wrote from Malvernton and Col. Lee went back soon after, and I knew you would hear of my safety from one of these sources. Capt. Cabot wrote very soon, and promised to have word sent to you of my safety. I lost my knapsack containing writing materials, the prayer book you gave me, my tactics, and 3 or 4 of the books John sent out. Besides this my woolen blanket and my overcoat cape. Henry lost his knapsack and all his things, but it was his own fault partly, for he might have carried it, or at any rate thrown only part away. I have drawn for a new knapsack, blankets etc. from Government. Besides I lost a woolen Shirt, pair drawers and a pair socks, but I have plenty more of all these things in my trunk which I had sent to Fort Munroe long ago, and which I expect daily by Express.

The Express boat has come, and there is something for me, but the goods cannot be landed till tomorrow. I have no doubt that the article for me is the box you sent containing Lemons, Limes etc. It will be most acceptable. We have to look out and keep the scurvy away. A great deal of sickness in Camp is laid to the scurvy by the Doctor. Now we get fresh meat, onions and potatoes. We eat quantities of onions. They are a delicious vegetable, and I shall never despise them when I get home. For soup they are invaluable, and they are most excellent boiled or fried, and make a delicious salad cut up raw with pepper and vinegar. The Doctor especially recommends this last way of eating them. We have got very comfortable now. The Officers have wall tents, and as there are so few of us we have quite room enough. I have had a table put up and a bed and a bench, and am most comfortable. This is a very healthy Camp and I was never better in my life. There is a brook close to us and a large pond a short distance off, and so we have abundant chances for bathing, and this is a great luxury and adds very much to the health of the Regiment.

We have had some terribly hot weather, but today it is pleasant, and a fine breeze. I do not suffer from heat, but can stand it perfectly well.

To all appearance, we are to make a long stay here. Our earthworks in front are very strong and are being rapidly pushed forward. The enemy do not trouble us in the least, and it is a rare thing to hear a gun fired.

I am getting to think that (as at Corinth) the fighting is over, and that McClellan is making this point so very strong that he may use it as a permanent base, leaving a part of his Army here, while with the rest, and with Burnside's aid perhaps, he cuts off the Rebels' supplies from the South, leaving Pope to do the same on the West. Then they must evacuate or break up their Army. However, no one can do anything but surmise.

I have heard nothing from the Colonel. He needs rest and good nursing more than anything else I think. Tell John to send me another copy of Alton Locke. You spoke of sending me some religious books. I should be delighted to get some. You could easily send sermons, as they could go by mail and are so often published in a pamphlet form. Always send everything by mail in preference to Express when you can, for the Express is very often delayed.

I had almost finished & forgotten my principal reason for writing. Many happy returns of your birthday, my dear Mother. May you have many more, and many happier ones than this. With God's blessing both your absent sons may be with you on your next birthday. I hope it may be so and that you may be kept well and able to enjoy so happy a day as that would be. Always keep cheerful and hope for the best.

Your ever affectionate son
Henry.

RIGHT UP INTO THE FIRE

Camp 20th Regiment near
Harrison's Landing, Va. July 14th 1862.

My dear Father.

I have just received your letter of the 7th enclosing one from Louisa, together with Mother's of the 9th (mailed at Swampscott). John's enclosing 2 sword clasps, and an Advertiser. For all these I am very much obliged. Please thank John for getting and sending the clasps. They are excellent, though much larger than my old ones.

I assure you, my dear Father, I feel deeply grateful to God preserving me amid so great dangers and hardships, and I never forget that you all pray constantly for me, that I may be preserved from harm and this is a most comforting thought. I feel that I have been supported in the greatest danger by putting my whole trust in God, and in feeling perfectly resigned to whatever may happen, and I know I have thus been enabled to preserve calmness in battle, and the better to discharge my duty. I never can be grateful enough to God for giving me such parents and such friends.

You speak of my losses. I really feel that I have lost nothing so little has been my loss in comparison with that of others. Dr. Hayward lost *everything* except the clothes on his back and the horse he escaped on, and this he sacrificed that the wagons might be used for the wounded and sick. He got every one of his patients safely off. Almost every one lost more than I. I lost nothing I cannot easily replace. I have quite enough clothes with me, and an abundant supply in my trunk, which I now daily expect by Express. My overcoat cape I cannot easily replace, but in this weather the coat is quite heavy enough without it. I only use it occasionally to sleep in. The books lost (perhaps $3.00 worth) can be easily replaced. My valise is perfectly safe. I have written on for two more keys. I find it very easy to lose keys here.

I am now more comfortable than I have been since we began the campaign. I have a wall Tent. I have had a bed made of poles, very comfortable, and I am writing on the top of a bread-box put up for a table. I have the sides of the tent looped up, and although the sun is hot, a fine breeze circulates. We are in a very healthy part of the country. None of the languid feeling we had on the Chickahominy. The soil is sandy, and the land high. Very soon the Express will run regularly, and then we shall have everything. Soft bread is now a great luxury. It is brought up from the Fort and eagerly bought at 25¢ a loaf. Lemons are 12 ½ cents each. No milk, eggs, butter or poultry are to be got, but we get beef, potatoes, onions and flour and do very well. The box will no doubt come up today. I shall greatly enjoy the limes etc. The Doctor says scurvy is often caused by sameness of food, and advises as much acid food as possible. You see we have no fresh fruit or vegetables at all, and some acid is always eaten in these.

RIGHT UP INTO THE FIRE

I wrote yesterday to Mother. Love to all. I hope you will enjoy Swampscott.

Your affectionate son
Henry.

Camp 20th Regiment near Harrison's Landing, Va.
July 15th 1862.

My dear John.

I received yesterday your letter of July 10th enclosing the 2 clasps for my sword. These are larger than I have had before, but very nice and strong and I am much obliged to you for getting them. I have just now received yours of the 11th enclosing 33 stamps, some toothpicks and 2 keys both of which fit. I will answer that of the 10th first.

I know nothing of the position of "Nelson's Farm", but suppose it was the Northern part of the battle of White Oak swamp. This was the action of Monday afternoon, and in it we lost most of the men. Eight I think were wounded (of our Regiment) at Savages. Holmes was 1st Sergeant, and Compass 3rd. Campion was 2nd Sergeant and is now acting as first. His wound was slight. Corporal Sampson, reported wounded badly, could not have lived but a few hours. I have been unable to find out what troops have re-enforced us, but the new Regiment of our Brigade is the 59th New York. I have heard nothing of the arrival of Western troops. I dare say Hayden is right about McClellan.

I have received today the 2 Atlantics, and last night the box of good things. Also letter from Frank and one for Henry. Henry thanks you and says the remainder of the money in Mr. Hichborn's hands may be spent for paper and envelopes and these be sent to Hayti. Henry stood the march well, but is now quite ill. The usual bowel complaint. My valise and a small box of food came safely in the wagon. Only a few wagons were burnt, and these might have been saved. No wagons or guns fell into the enemy's hands during the retreat.

I have told Col. Palfrey of the pickles, onions, etc. He is glad they are coming and will make a proper distribution of them. I feel very sorry for Herbert and shall write to him very soon. My love to Abbott, if you see him. I shall write immediately to him and tell him the Regimental news and how we miss him. My love to Bartlett, also. My kindest regards to Joe May. I hope he is improved in health.

RIGHT UP INTO THE FIRE

I am glad you are getting to know more about McClellan. I have not changed my opinion about him. A man cannot do the deeds of a Napoleon without an old guard and a few Murats and Soults, nor fight a Waterloo with New York troops. Better wait a good while before you judge McClellan. I think he is a man who will land on his feet. Did I tell you he spoke to me the other day? He rode in unexpectedly among the troops, and seeing me asked if the Whiskey had been served. This was the day after we got to the river, a cold, wet day.

Well, I have answered your letters and can only add that I am perfectly well and the weather is clear and hot. I have distributed most of the little books Mother sent in the box.

Inches and Wadsworth visited us yesterday. The Sanitary Commission presented us the other day with some dried fruit and some ice, both most acceptable.

Please send some books. Good standards if possible. Also some good steel pens by mail. When next you send any box, please put in a few Seidlitz Powders. I used one a few weeks ago and found it a most excellent thing. I enclose letters to Tom Curtis, to Mother and to Mary Ann. Your list said "2 doz. Lemons" in the box. There were none. I suppose there was not room.

My trunk is coming up and I expect it in 2 days.

Your affectionate brother
Henry.

Camp Harrison's Landing, Va.
July 15th 1862.

My dear Mother.

I received yesterday your letter of the 9th and today I have received your beautiful gift the prayer book I so much wanted to replace the one the Rebels got. I am indeed very much obliged for it. I hope I shall always read it and benefit by it, and that I may yet be permitted to open it in the old pew at Trinity.

Last night I got the box, and I assure you the contents were most acceptable. The limes and lime juice are particularly desirable, and will no doubt prove a great advantage to my health. The figs are *very* fine. I am particularly fond of figs. The Whisky will be invaluable if we have any bad weather or exposure. I am delighted to find 2 cans of Milk instead of condensed Coffee which I do not care for. The milk will be very useful.

I am sorry to say that Henry is quite unwell. He has quite a severe turn of diarrhoea, but sees Dr. Crehore, and will no doubt soon improve. I am very glad you are at the Seaside. I think Father is always better for his regular afternoon ride and for the sea air. I hope you will enjoy the season. Do you have Dr. Huntington this year? I shall value a church in future. They do not have any to speak of in this country. We have seen one since leaving Fort Munroe. I have a great many letters to answer today, so I must close.

Best love to Father.

Your affectionate son
Henry.

Camp 20th Regiment, Harrison's Landing, Va.
July 17th 1862 (Thursday)

My dear John.

I received no letter from home since I wrote last, and have no Camp or Army news whatever to give you. The weather is hot but very pleasant, and not particularly debilitating, at any rate not to me.

I have several things of importance to tell you. First, I have discharged Henry, and I shall probably get him a pass very soon to Washington, as he wishes to go there. Henry has always served me well and faithfully, and until lately I have always supposed that his behavior to others was always proper. But I find he has considered that he is not bound to pay any regard to anyone but me, and he has several times acted and spoken in a surly and almost impudent manner to some of the men, cooks and others about camp, and even to Officers. Now, this cannot be allowed in a camp where he, like every other camp follower, is under military discipline to a great extent, and must obey orders given by other Officers than me. He had some words with Capt. Cabot, Officer of the day, a few days ago, and yesterday he behaved in a very improper manner to the Captain in my tent and before me. I had a long talk with him and I apologized to Cabot for his conduct, but Henry, although he said he was very sorry indeed he had offended me, and would do nothing to offend and vex me, etc. yet appeared to defend his conduct to the Captain. Now, this is really unsafe for him. If he should give any impudence to an Officer before the men he would get knocked down and perhaps tied up or if he resisted like enough, get his head broken, and I told him so and told him I could not have him unless he entirely alters his manners to others, especially to Officers. He however seemed to feel that he was constantly insulted, and could not endure it longer, and I finally settled it that he should go, although his feelings to me are the very kindest possible. I am very sorry to part with Henry, yet it is his own fault, or rather the fault of his excessively resentful and sensitive nature and bearing. If he comes to Boston, you and the others had better not talk to him about the cause of his leaving and consider only that he was tired of our hard life. Well, now that he is to go, I must have another man, and the only way is to have another man sent out. I feel very sorry to trouble you again to get me a man, but I know how kind you are, and I do not like to trust anyone else about such a matter. You, at home, can hardly estimate the necessity and the value of a servant to an Officer. I have written you before a long letter about the qualifications for a servant, and will not repeat, but would only add what my experience with Henry has taught me. And first, I should *much prefer* a white man. He *must be* strong, healthy, tough, very willing to work and to work hard on a pinch, perfectly honest, *not above his place*, not liable to get angry because he gets a very prompt order from me or from any other Officer. He must have a proper respect for military rank and must not be pugnacious and liable to get into quarrels with the non-commissioned Officers. Then he must be a fair cook, and a generally handy man. I want a brisker man /than/ Henry was, and a prompter and a man who is always civil to *everybody* and not all the time on his dignity. He must be able and willing to carry a load on a march and to put up with hardship. One of the best servants here is a man from Cape Cod, who has been fishing, and farmed a little at home, and who has been for several years cook and steward on board a ship. He has the ready and always civil manners that a man gets on board a ship under a ship's discipline, and he has got used to being a "man under authority" and respects Officers and Sergeants as he used to respect the Captain and the 2nd Mate. Then he can get up a dinner out of hard bread and salt beef and make fish-balls and hash. This is the kind of man I want. Do you remember Albert or Tim at Mrs. Humphrey's in Cambridge? I want a man as brisk, lively and as civil and ready as he was. I think you understand. Try for an old Cook and Steward of a ship. Above all, send no one till you are *quite sure* of his qualities, especially of his readiness to work. Let him "look alive", much more alive than Henry. Good health is indispensable.

As to wages, I *would* pay $18.00 per month, and although I will not agree to keep him in clothes and pay him this, I will agree to do so and $15.00 a month in case you are *obliged* to make this agreement. Fifteen Dollars per month is good wages for the kind of man wanted, for he can save the whole of this. I of course feed him. If he would like to come for say 2 months on trial, you may send him with the agreement that he must pay his own way home. I should like to get a good man at $15.00 and no agreement about clothes. If he has a family he could have part or the whole of his money paid by you to his wife at Boston, monthly, and I would send it on. Now, John, do not hurry in the least, and do not send till you are sure. I can get along very well with a man from the Company for some time. If you do get a colored man, get one of the good natured kind who will be: "Yes, Massa" to everybody, not such a dignified individual as Henry. Of course, in regard to cooking, if the man is clean and smart, he can probably soon pick up enough. If he can make good tea and boiled rice, and broil a steak, and perhaps make hash and fish balls this will be enough. As to his passage on, I do not wish to pay $22.00 as I did for Henry. By applying properly you can no doubt get a free ticket for him here. Perhaps you can send him on with some returning Officer, free of charge, and this would be the best way. I do not wish to pay a large sum for having him sent on, for I *know* he can come on free or almost free, by waiting and looking round. If you get one and send him on, and can send anything with him, please send as much as convenient of Salt Mackerel, Lemons, Crackers, etc. etc., for these articles are much in request here, and what we cannot use for our own Mess we could easily let others have. If however there is reason to suppose the Army is about to move, do not encumber him with much baggage. Let him provide himself with a rubber, and a light wool blanket, and if he has a light overcoat let him bring that, but do not let him load himself with many clothes etc. So much for my servant.

My trunk arrived safely yesterday. I have taken out of it as many underclothes etc. as I want, and expect to send it right back by Express to Father at Boston to be kept subject to my orders. In it is a parcel of private letters, among them my Commission and some military letters etc. all of which I should like to have safely kept in my box under Mary Ann's care. As to the rest of the contents of the trunk, better leave them in Mother's care, and tell her that should we be camped permanently during the autumn and winter, I should send on for these things by Express. Some of the woolen things (coat etc.) as also the woolen pants left at home in the other trunk, had better be wrapped in Camphor. I shall also send home "John Halifax" which please have neatly bound and kept. No hurry, of course. I shall probably send also several packages for Officers here, which you can have sent round to their directions. The key I shall send by mail when I send the trunk.

The mail today and yesterday brings me no letters. I do not remember that I mentioned to you that I had to pay the Express Agent at White House $2.25 for my valise, in addition to the $1.25 you prepaid. Was not this an imposition? If you send anything more by Express, please enquire about this. I wrote to the Agent asking an explanation but received no answer.

As I have nothing more to say, and no letters to answer, I will close.

Your affectionate brother
Henry.

P.S. I have plenty of paper etc. in my trunk, do not send more. Cannot you give Hazeltine and Tom Curtis letters to Sister Mary, Bros. William and Frank? Hazy, you know, is my intimate friend. Frank would like Tom and be of great use to him in directing him how best to study. They would like Hazy in England.

Affectionately

H. R.

Letter for Sister Mary enclosed.

July 18th 1862.
Camp 20th Regiment.

Dear John.

I send my trunk to father today by Express. I probably cannot prepay it, so you can pay the Express there and charge it to my account. Please have my knife in the trunk taken to Bradford's and put in perfect order. It needs 2 new blades, and the saw sharpened and made to open more in the teeth so as not to bind.

Will you please buy for me a haversack like the one I started with. It should be made very strong and of good leather. Get the kind of this shape when shut up.

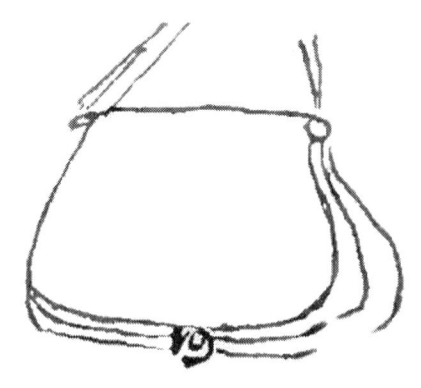

It opens at the bottom and fastens with a strap. When open this is the shape.

RIGHT UP INTO THE FIRE

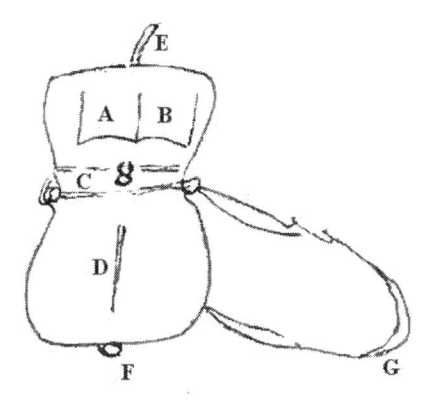

A and B small pockets; C opening to large lined pocket for food; D a split opening to a pocket not lined; E strap; F buckle; G strap to go over the neck.

They are made of enamelled letter [*leather*] generally. They should be water proof. The reason the [*r/*] open at the bottom is to avoid the water leaking in.

No matter if the arrangements are not exactly as I have drawn it. It costs about $3.00 and may be bought best at Holmes', Tremont Row, or Baker's Court Street. Get a good one and a strong one. Also please send me a small metal soap box to put in a cake of soap. I have sent back your English "J. R." bag for sponge. This hot weather here has caused the rubber to melt and become sticky. I am very sorry but fear it is ruined. Please send me a *small* rubber bag for soap. If you would attend to these things and send them on to me I should be greatly obliged. Send them by Adams' Express.

I have no news to tell you. We are perfectly quiet. What do you think of that Senator's abuse of McClellan?[34] Love to all. I shall write to Mary Ann and answer her letter very soon.

Your affectionate brother
Henry.

---

[34] Several times in July 1862, after the failure of the Peninsula Campaign, Senator Zachariah Chandler (MI) attacked McClellan sharply on the Senate floor, calling (among other things) his generalship a disgrace and demanding that the general "should suffer the extreme penalty of the law".

RIGHT UP INTO THE FIRE

Camp 20th Regiment, Harrison's Landing
July 18th 1862.

My dear John.

I have just received yours of the 14th with the map, and Mary Ann's of the 14th.

I am very much obliged indeed for the map. It is of a very convenient size, and I should think very accurate. I am glad the watch etc. has come safely. You might have a crystal put on and use the watch.

I am glad you have sold the boat. A boat is a great trouble to anyone but a boating man who can take care of her himself. The price is not bad, considering the times and the age of the boat. The money is Father's, not mine.

I feel not sure that it would be well to draft. I rather think not. Better enlist men for one or two years. We have called for 300,000 men. We do not really need more than 150,000 at any rate now. I go in for a heavy bounty rather than a draft. Let States, Cities and Towns pay extra bounties and feel an interest to give at least their quota without a draft. I hope Massachusetts will be up to the mark. Are any new Regiments to be officered by Gentlemen? I hope so but have not the least confidence in Governor Andrew. He has done as much harm to Mass. Regiments as any living man. A Regiment officered by young Gentlemen can be made efficient in half the time a Country Regiment can be. I hope the Regiments now in service will be at least partially filled as well as new Regiments raised.

Henry has gone. He was very sorry to leave me, but it is best he should go. He got to think everyone intended to insult and abuse him, and resented every word almost and would have got into endless trouble. But he was an excellent servant to me. Henry was partly of Indian blood, and I think his Indian traits are too prominent. I have a man from the Company at present but may get a contraband if I can see a good one. Henry will eventually go to Boston. I paid him up in full of everything before he left.

Enclosed letter for the Doctor.

Your affectionate brother
Henry.

RIGHT UP INTO THE FIRE

Camp 20th Regiment
Harrison's Landing July 19th 1862.

My dear Father.

I have today sent home by Adams' Express my trunk, which I left at Poolesville in March, and which I wrote for and which came on to me here by Express. I have taken out of it some underclothes, books, papers, etc. etc. and now send it back only half full. There is a dress coat, pair thick trousers and waistcoat and some stockings and drawers which Mother had better have put away for fear of moths. There is a bundle of private papers (letters, my commission etc.) which I have directed to John, and which he understands what to do with. There is a small tin box containing fixed ammunition for my pistol and another box containing a little powder, caps and ball. I send back a fatigue cap which I would like to have carefully kept against my return. As I have worn it ever since we marched from Camp Benton, and it has been on my head in all our battles and skirmishes. I send my knife, the one Mary Ann gave, which has a great variety of blades. I have found this exceedingly useful and would be very glad if John would take it to Bradford's and have it fixed up. I enclose a short note to John asking him to get several things for me, and telling him about the knife.

The trunk and the rest of its contents can either be laid aside or used by the family. Should I pass another long season in any fixed Camp or Garrison, I should probably send on for it and my things. I enclose the key.

Beside this trunk I have now a box and a Camp chest, both full, at the Store of Mr. Jesse J. Higgins at Poolesville, and my valise with me here. I have told you I think that I have parted with Henry. I shall perhaps pick up a contraband here, but would prefer a good white servant from home. However there is no haste whatever. Yesterday and today have been cool and comfortable.

Best love to Mother and all.

Your affectionate son
Henry.

RIGHT UP INTO THE FIRE

Camp 20th Regiment, Harrison's Landing.
Sunday, 20th July 1862.

My dear John.

I have not received any letters from home by today's mail, but I see by the papers that Bartlett, Herbert and I have our degrees. I am very glad indeed for this. I have no doubt you have seen to it all. Commencement seems to have gone off well. I hope you were there. I have sent the key to my trunk to Father in a letter, and was much surprised yesterday P.M. when my trunk was brought back, the Express Agent refusing to take any goods from this place. They say they are too overwhelmed with business coming to us, that they can make no arrangements to take anything from us. I shall probably soon have a chance to send it by a private way.

I wrote yesterday asking you to get me a haversack etc. Please also send on an India Rubber water pail. They are made to roll up, and are very light. They are of this shape very flat like a basin and easy to wash in.

They hold about 3 quarts and are very light. Can probably be bought at Hall's, Milk St., or South Side of Bromfield St.
No news. All quiet. Weather hot.

Your affectionate brother
Henry.

RIGHT UP INTO THE FIRE

Camp 20th Regiment near
Harrison's Landing Va. July 23rd 1862.

My dear Father.

I received yesterday your letter of the 18th and Mother's enclosed, for which I am very much obliged. I was very glad to see your name among those who are helping forward the good cause by personal exactions in such a time as this.[35] I hope you will urge the filling up of the old Regiments to at least 600 men each, before new Regiments are formed. A recruit learns his duty much more rapidly when placed beside old soldiers, and besides, the new Officers cannot be so fitted to instruct recruits as those, who have had recent experience of actual service.

Beside this, a Regiment partly composed of men who have been previously under fire, is much more to be depended upon in battle. A new Regiment is almost useless for picket and outpost duty. Nothing but experience fits either Officers or men for this.

I received yesterday two rolls of writing paper by mail. They will come into use very soon, and I am much obliged for them. I have sent you by mail the key of my trunk. As I still have the trunk here and may not be able to send it for some time, will you please send me the key back? I shall perhaps want to open the trunk again.

All is quiet here. We had a grand review yesterday. The river is full of Gunboats and Steamers and provision vessels.

I enclose a letter for Mother.

Your affectionate son
Henry Ropes.

---

[35] William Ropes was part of a committee that on July 14th laid a communication before the city government in which it was recommended to pay to each new volunteer a bounty of 100 dollars.

RIGHT UP INTO THE FIRE

Camp 20th Regiment near Harrison's
Landing, Va. July 23rd 1862.

My dear Mother.

I have received your letter of the 17th and am very glad you date it from Swampscott. I often envy you the sea-breezes and fresh invigorating air of Swampscott. As for me, I am passing a summer in the country, and I must say I prefer the sea shore.

I am glad to hear such good accounts of Col. Lee's health. I think he needs rest and the comforts of home more than any regular Doctor's treatment. You must not allow yourself to look forward to any possible dangers I may be exposed to. We are now heavily entrenched here, and it would be madness for the enemy to attempt to attack us, and I incline to think the next great battle will be on the other side, and that Genl. Pope will manage to make Richmond an untenable place. The Rebels have so concentrated their Army at Richmond that they can offer no resistance to columns sent out by Pope to cut off supplies etc., and you know such a vast army cannot stay where there is the least danger of a lack of food. It is very likely that Richmond will be taken, and the Rebel Army dispersed without much more fighting. So you must be thankful all has so far gone well and not look out for future danger.

It is very kind of you to be thinking about another box before I have disposed of this one I now have. Do not send expensive luxuries. I assure you a loaf of real home made cake or bread, or a pot of home made Cranberry sauce, Rhubarb, Apple Sauce or Jelly is to me far nicer than the best of Sardines or other things you may buy. Will you please send a small piece of netting? We are greatly troubled with flies, and it is very convenient to put a piece of netting over one's face while reading or sleeping.

I am delighted to find my name among the list of Graduates. I have no doubt I owe it in great measure to Father's exertions. My kindest regards to Joe May, and my congratulations upon his engagement, if this is not so great a secret as yet, as not to admit of congratulations. I shall of course say nothing to anyone about it. I have written to Frank and sent on the letter. Tell me if any of my young friends have entered College? Let John send me on a catalogue when they come out.

We are getting more comfortable every day now. Soon we are to have Ovens built and to really eat fresh soft bread. After such a long time on Government hard bread you can imagine how good this will be.

We have had cooler weather lately, and it is very dry and I think healthy. We do not have much to do. Please give my kindest regards to all my relatives and friends who may enquire for me.

Ever your affectionate son

Henry.

RIGHT UP INTO THE FIRE

Camp 20th Regiment near Harrison's Landing, Va.
July 23rd 1862.

My dear John.

I have not had a letter from you for several days, but the Advertisers come regularly, and yesterday I received a barrel by Express, containing the articles I wrote for, for the use of our mess, to viz.: 1 ham, 6 tongues, tub fish (mackerell [sic], I suppose), 1 salmon, box herrings, paper, Coffee, 1 can preserved milk, 2 parcels biscuits, 1 box yeast powder, 1 bottle lemon Syrup. I think this was all. They are very nice and I thank you very much for getting them for me. I do not remember that I wrote for herrings and Lemon Syrup, but at any rate they are very nice and very much wanted. The milk, I am sorry to say, was not good. I do not know whether the hot weather had spoiled it, or whether *all* "preserved" or "condensed" milk is bad. The old fashioned "solidified" milk is, I think the only kind worth having. I am getting to distrust all of the sealed up preparations for drinking. Is there not some way of putting up common fresh milk, so that it will keep in bottles? I think I have heard of it somewhere. If you happen to come across any, please send some, if you have a chance. I hear, however, that the Government intend to stop Adams & Co. from bringing on more boxes. I do not know what can be the reason of this. Is it possible we are to leave this position? I have found it impossible to send on my trunk. Still I may meet with somebody any day who would take it. Please let me know the price of each article of the barrel's contents that I may charge it to the mess.

Hallowell (Ned, Company F) has lately returned, and brought some very fine Brandy, very old and Choice, and he most kindly gave me a bottle, saying that the Cherry Cordial I once gave him just before the battle of Fair Oaks saved his life. I know it did him a great deal of good, as it always does, and it enabled him to go through with that trying day. I shall keep this brandy carefully in case of sickness or exposure. Macy received 2 dozens of Claret from some unknown friend in New York, a few days ago. It was merely directed to him and sent by Express. Very nice, was it not? He is very liberal with it. Macy also received a tremendous box, perfectly filled with good things, from some of his Gentlemen friends. Of course there was an abundance of brandy etc., and all of the best. It is very convenient to mess with such a man. In fact the Camp is full of liquor of all kinds now.

We had a grand Review of Sumner's Corps yesterday, perhaps 40,000 men. It must have been very fine to the Generals, but it was very tiresome to us. I would very much have liked to have had you see it. The finest review of troops I ever yet saw, however, was the battle of Malvern Hill. I suppose 100,000 men were then in view, counting the Rebels. It was a magnificent spectacle.

RIGHT UP INTO THE FIRE

In learning more about the recent battles, I find that our fight at "Nelson's Farm" was the left, or perhaps centre of the "Oak Swamp" battle, not the right, as I had thought. We were marched to the right in the morning and only held in reserve. Then in the afternoon they attacked farther along, attempting to cut us off from the river.

Our Regiment has got a splendid reputation in the Army. We do not care at all what the newspapers say about others. Some of the Officers have seen the official accounts from Dana, and they say we are spoken of most particularly and honorably. When our Regiment advanced alone at "Nelson's Farm" Sumner followed us half way, and it must have been a critical moment, indeed, when the Commander of a Corps takes the personal direction of a single Regiment in a battle. Our reputation among other Regiments is really most flattering.

Your onions, pickles etc. have arrived and been distributed by Col. Palfrey. I hear some rumors about changes in the Regiment. I hear that Col. Lee may resign, and that Major Revere will be appointed Colonel. Of course Colonel Palfrey could not stand this, and if he leaves, a great many good Officers will leave with him. I also hear that Captains Tremlett and Shepard may receive Majorities in the New Regiments, and so leave us. Both are pleasant in their way, but neither good Officers. Tremlett has for a long time been half sick and lost all the bone out of his back (if he ever had any). He thinks we are going to the devil, Rebels will beat us, etc. etc. Tremlett is utterly wanting in that hopeful reliance and calm and persistent determination which distinguishes Abbott, for instance. He is of course brave in battle but has got no moral courage at all. I would not give much for such a soldier in times of disappointment like that we have just been through with. If Tremlett and Shepard go, we shall have Abbott and Whittier as Captains, which will be a great improvement. I hope the Governor will not again appoint Sergeants without consulting Col. Palfrey. You know he did appoint Pouswall *[Pousland]* and Hirschauer thus. Pouswall is very good on drill etc., Hirschauer is a miserable Officer, good for nothing, especially in battle.

We tried the Salmon and Ham and find them most excellent. Biscuits very nice, too. Macy sends kindest regards. So does Murphy. He took a great fancy to you in Camp Foster, and desires particularly to be remembered. So do many others. Did you ever receive anything on my account from C. B. Porter? I left him some coal and several things and asked him to dispose of them for me.

Your affectionate brother
Henry.

RIGHT UP INTO THE FIRE

Camp 20th Regiment near Harrison's Landing, Va.
July 28th 1862.

Dear John.

I have just received yours and Mother's of the 25th yesterday. I received "Barchester Towers". Much obliged for getting this book and the other things you have sent on by Express. I do not need religious Books now, as I had 2 volumes "Sermons" in my trunk. I write for various things as I need them, and leave to your discretion how and when to send them on. I have now a great abundance of writing paper etc. You can perhaps send on the Rubber coat by Herbert. Can you send a bottle of Cherry Cordial? It is invaluable here, for it is next to impossible to keep clear of a slight diarrhoea in this climate. Nothing painful or serious, but troublesome. I shall *always* value a bottle of Cordial above anything else of the kind.

Lieut. Col. Ritchie was here today on Government business. Do not tell this which I now write:

We are secretly preparing for some movement. Probably we shall go to Fort Munroe. What next, I do not know. I have this secretly from very good authority. You must not whisper it. The Artillery Officers and Hospitals are silently preparing for a move. Probably when the news comes out you will hear we are to advance, but I think this is to cover a retreat. Can we be all going to Genl. Pope? Now this is *strictly secret.* Keep your eyes open and do not send things to me after you hear we have moved. I think there is little danger from the Rebels here. Please ask Mother to send me 3 or 4 darning needles and a few large pins by mail.

If you see Stone, thank him most kindly for the flowers etc., and give him my love. I shall enjoy reading the Oration etc. very much. Macy and others desire kindest regards. Everything continues quiet here.

It is very foolish to think that digging trenches tired our men and wore them out. The work was very light and only about 2 days a week ever and did the men good. They also worked slowly, and rested between reliefs.

There is a good deal of low sickness still in camp, but very little dangerous. Mess barrel arrived safe. Send list of prices.

Your affectionate brother
Henry.

RIGHT UP INTO THE FIRE

31st July 1862
20th Regiment Harrison's Landing.

Dear John.

I have no letters to answer from anybody. All is quiet here. Yesterday we were ordered to prepare 3 days' rations and be ready to march. Today this order is countermanded. I heard that were [sic] was some fear that Rebel gunboats might come down, and this order was in case anything should happen unfavorably. I do not know anything more, but on the whole feel my suppositions of an early move confirmed. 18 very heavy guns were at the landing yesterday in position, pointing up the river.

I am going to trouble you again. I wish you would send me 1 doz. Quarts of American bitter Ale. I wish to have it for our Mess. Macy and Sanders have provided Claret, and I wish to do my share. This will be very little trouble to you. Only leave my address at a respectable Grocer's, and he will box it up and forward it immediately. Please send a good quality. It is not expensive. I suppose you have still a considerable balance in my favor in your hands, I cannot quite tell till you send me my accounts. We ought to be paid every day now, and then I shall send about $100.00 more. Let me have also a bottle of Cherry Cordial or dark Brandy, next time you send on a box. If convenient please send a bottle of Raspberry Preserve. Ned Hallowell brought out some, and it is very nice and very wholesome for this climate. I think the bitter ale will be particularly wholesome. One needs tonic and astringent drink about every day. Is there not some kind of bitters you can recommend as a *pleasant* as well as wholesome drink? I do not at all like common bitters such as they make Cocktails of. If convenient send a bottle of such bitters. I always think of ½ a dozen things when I begin to write for one but I dare say you can get everything at one place and merely stop in and leave the order. I hope you will get a servant soon. As I now mess with Macy cooking well is not so important a requirement for my servant. I hope you liked Maine. Tell me exactly where you went.

Love to all.

Affectionately,
Henry.

RIGHT UP INTO THE FIRE

Camp 20th Regiment near
Harrison's Landing, Va. August 3rd 1862.

My dear Father.

I received last night your letter dated Swampscott July 30th and was very sorry to find your cold was so serious as to confine you to your bed. I had no idea it had been so severe, but I am very glad to hear you have got over the worst and are now getting better. Hot damp weather such as I hear you have had is very unhealthy, and very apt to tempt one to expose oneself to colds.

I received the key of the trunk some days ago, but have not yet been able to send the trunk home. I am waiting for somebody to go back at least to Fort Munroe whence it can be sent home by Express. It is your black English trunk with which I left home in December which I intend to send home now. It is too large to be carried in a campaign, and the smaller new trunk (or valise) is quite big enough. This has been so much admired here that 2 of our Officers have written for valises just like it, and one has come out to Capt. Macy, which is the exact counterpart of mine.

Mr. Alford *did* send a supply of Jam, Jellies etc. to the Hospital of the Regiment. I have not distributed all the tracts yet, and cannot, for there are more than are wanted. I fear very few are read, and great quantities wasted. We are most bountifully supplied now with everything needed in Hospital, and the Tract Society can give us nothing we need. Mr. Alford has a nice carriage and drives about, visiting Camps and distributing tracts, and I have no doubt enjoys himself very much. If all this is paid for by the Society, however, I really think he might be better employed as a Preacher or Missionary.

It is very well of course to have good books supplied, but they are so plentifully given away here that by far the greater part is wasted. I have not heard from Mr. Alford since he left me the tracts, and have not received the $10.00 worth of comforts you say you sent to me. I am indeed greatly obliged, and will acknowledge them as soon as I receive them. I think there is no better way to send things than by Adams' Express. As to what we most need, I would suggest a few loaves of real brown bread, lemons or Oranges, Syrups, such as Raspberry, Lemon and Ginger or Sarsaparilla, which are excellent to drink with the very soft water we get here. Then such luxuries as Jellies, Jams, Sauces and Preserves, or Honey, would be of course most acceptable. Of any preserve I would suggest Ginger, as this has an excellent effect on the bowels. We need tonics, astringents and some stimulants here always. It is almost impossible to keep clear of a light kind of diarrhea, accompanied with languor and weakness. Above everything else I should put Cherry Cordial. It is perfectly invaluable for the bowels. I should think some kind of tonic bitters would be most excellent.

RIGHT UP INTO THE FIRE

Do not think that I am sick and in need of anything, for no one keeps up better than I, although of course I am not so strong and tough as I should be if I was in Swampscott. I am somewhat troubled with this unavoidable diarrhoea but nothing of any consequence.

Today a very heavy force has gone out to have a look at the Rebels on the Charles City road. We do not anticipate any serious action. Probably they will meet no resistance.

Best love to Mother and all.

Your affectionate son
Henry.

Enclosed letter for J.C.R.

Camp 20th Regiment near Harrison's Landing, Va.
August 3rd 1862 (Sunday)

My dear John.

I received your most interesting letter of the 30th yesterday, and am greatly obliged to you for it. I am delighted to hear that you have so much to do and hope your clients do not leave you empty handed. The green netting I shall not need as I have already plenty here. I forgot I asked for any. Much obliged for the Sermons received yesterday. Please thank Mother and Cousin Ritty for them. I shall read them with great interest. The yeast powder was for the mess, like the rest. As to my servant, I need him very much and shall not know what to do if we march soon. Better advertise in the "Journal" (not "Herald", I think) without stating terms.

I am very much astonished at Henry's writing to you for money. I paid him up in full for everything, and always was very liberal with him, giving him clothes, etc. I always had perfect faith in his honesty, but am surprised he should try to get any money from you. He had $55.00 from me when he started. If he comes on, be careful of him for I might possibly de deceived. He is fond of money. In my trunk is the prayer book Mother gave him. He asked me to send it home for him in the trunk, and said he would call for it.

I hardly think Col. Lee will resign, but I fear he will not be fit ever to take command of a Regiment in active service. I have written 3 times to Herbert, care of Sturgis Hooper, Esq., Cotuit Port, and care Reed and H., Boston. I hope he has got them all.

I am much pleased with your selection of Mary Ann's present, and she seems delighted. Very much obliged to you for your trouble in getting the books.

Brother Morton and the A Δ call up memories of pleasant times. I see the 'shadowy forms' and can hardly believe that those happy days and scenes have gone for ever, and that my class has passed away from "Harvard", and their places are filled by other men. If you see Brother Morton, please give him my kindest regards and my best wishes for his health, prosperity and happiness.

I am delighted you intend going to Lennox *[Lenox]*. I hear it is a beautiful place. You may meet the Gardners there, and that will be very pleasant for you. Go by all means. Of course Swampscott is dull. Go anywhere for a trip. It does one so much good to make a short pleasure trip. As to books, I have only read of Dickens' "Pickwick", "David Copperfield" and part of some others. Send any of Dickens'. I can generally borrow the latest novels here. Have not read "Mill on the Floss", or any of Thackeray's, but "Pendennis" and "Vanity Fair". Can you send the whole or part of Scott's Poetical Works? Have not read also "Bride of Lammermoor", "Castle Dangerous", "Peveril of the Peak" and many others, and should like very much to re-read "Kenilworth", "Ivanhoe", "Heart of Midlothian" and others.

Please send me Cameron's Tactics (1 vol. $1.25). I lost mine in the retreat. Tell some of them at Swampscott to send me a few papers of Radish seed & string beans. Thompson sells them. We may stay 4 or 5 weeks here, and it is worth while to make a trial of a small vegetable garden.

As to the battle. There were 6 guns of ours abandoned and two rebel guns (perhaps more) beyond. The other Regiments followed us up and formed on our right and left. We marched first. The Michigan 7th came up behind us and formed on our right before we got beyond the first open field. You see we were 3 or 4 hours in the fight.

I begin to think now that it would be well nigh impossible to draw off this Army safely. But as you say, we might cross, attack Petersburgh and then depart for Fort Munroe under the cloud of a sudden dash and make a brilliant thing of it, too. I hardly think the Rebels will make a real attempt to destroy us here. They are very glad to have 90,000 men shut up here.

I see exactly how you feel about McClellan, but for myself, I desire to postpone my judgment. I do not feel I have seen enough yet. I earnestly hope something brilliant will soon be done to enliven the country. Genl. Dana has I believe not returned. Mr. Peirson returns to the Regiment today as Adjutant. 40 recruits have joined us. Our Company has one.

Your affectionate brother
Henry.

RIGHT UP INTO THE FIRE

Camp near Harrison's Landing,
Va. Thursday, 7th August 1862.

My dear Father.

I have this morning returned from a three days' expedition to Malvern Hill, and am glad to say that not only I feel no worse for the tiresome trip but a good deal better and stronger than I did before I went. I think we have let the Rebels see that we are alive still and that we need a pretty careful watching. Our Regiment was not in the battle, and we have no loss of any kind to record.

We were ordered to get ready on last Monday afternoon, and at 6 o'cl. our Division began the march. Our Regiment is the rearmost one and we started at 7 P.M. We marched with hardly a halt till about 2.30 or 3 o'cl. A.M. of Tuesday, and during that time had gone first about North on the Charles City road, a wide good road, and then Westerly through all sorts of back roads where it was very dark. At about 3 A.M. we drew up in an open field and lay down and slept about 2 hours. Then, when it became light we marched on, and could hear Gunboats firing on our left. We finally came out on the main road to Richmond close to our old battle field of Nelson's Farm, and turning again to the left, approached Malvern Hill from the North. We had been entirely round Malvern Hill. We now heard some Artillery and soon after we got to Malvern Hill, and found that the enemy had been scattered by the force which preceded us after a very slight resistance, and that the enemy had escaped over another road between us and the river. Our horse Artillery and Cavalry were in pursuit however and about 200 prisoners were taken, and I believe two Caissons. They managed to get off their 2 guns. We had marched about 18 miles now, and were glad to rest and eat something. We had all brought 2 days' rations. The remainder of the day we staid on Malvern Hill, and slept there, and the next day (Wednesday) 2 days were [sic] rations were sent for, and it was reported that we were to occupy the hill permanently. It was dreadfully hot, and we did as well as we could by fastening up our rubber blankets for a shade. McClellan was here, and fresh troops arrived. In the afternoon we were marched to the front and added to Gorman's Brigade in the extreme advance. At night we heard that the enemy were advancing in great force. I forgot to say that as there were very few Officers, I was put in command of Company I, the right flank Company. At night the whole Regiment went on picket. I was on the extreme right of course, and I met the left of Genl. Hooker's pickets at a little shanty, on an open field, which I picketed to the left of the shanty, and he to the right. It was bright moonlight, and very open country. A squad of Cavalry were at a barn, on a hill in front of us. I placed the men, and went to the right hand part myself, where was the shanty. At about 10 o'clock P.M. my vidette gave the alarm, and I was astonished to see the pickets on my right

RIGHT UP INTO THE FIRE

(115th Pennsylvania) running in. One cried out "Retreat". I had received no orders, and after looking about and finding nothing to cause an alarm, I went back to the Officer in charge and he told me he had been ordered to withdraw silently. I put out an extra sentinel in my right flank and waited about 3 hours when Hooker's pickets were put back. I had heard Artillery moving in my rear for a long time, and felt surer we were falling back. At about 1 o'cl. Hooker's pickets were again withdrawn, and about 2, just as the moon set, I received orders to draw in and fall back to a certain house; which I did with my company, and very soon Capt. Hallowell, in command of the right pickets arrived with his men, and we all marched back, joined the Regiment and marched to the Malvern Hill road, where we found the last of the troops filing off, and joined in behind Gorman's Brigade. The retreat was of course covered by Cavalry. We marched back by the road along which we retreated a month ago, and when we had gone about 3 miles we met cavalry outposts, and sometime after passed through Casey's troops drawn up to cover our retreat. Horse Artillery passed to the rear, and we felt sure that all was right. It was now broad daylight. We marched on, and about 6 A.M. this (Thursday) morning we passed through our lines of earthworks and arrived safely in camp. Of course we were glad enough to get back and enjoy rest and get a good bath.

I thought I was somewhat weakened by the late hot weather etc. but I found I stood the long marches and tiresome picket duty remarkably well, and now feel better than ever. I find one only wants something to do to be able to do it. We have been very successful and made a decided diversion in favor of Pope, and scattered a Brigade of Rebels and taken about 200 prisoners. It was of course rather an anxious 3 days.

I have received the Ind. Rubb. pail, haversack etc. all right. No letters from you all for 3 days now.

Best love to Mother and all.

Your affectionate son
Henry.

RIGHT UP INTO THE FIRE

Camp 20th Regiment near Harrison's Landing, Va.
Friday, August 8th 1862.

My dear John.

I received last evening your letter of the 4th. I had then already written to Father giving an account of our late expedition to Malvern Hill. All has been quiet since.

I see, as you say, that it was openly discussed whether or not our Army was to stay here, but the private information I got was through Capt. Macy who had got a letter from Le Barnes. Now, Le Barnes knows Wilson, Sumner, and other great men of that set in Washington, and he said that the Army was to be ordered back to Fort Munroe. However, Halleck has taken command since, and plans may be altered. Do not of course mention names.

I am rejoiced beyond measure that you have got me a servant. I shall need one very much if we march, and I have no doubt your choice has been a good one. I expect him every day. No doubt Abbott or Herbert would be glad to have him come on with them.

I shall be delighted to get the Cordial and indeed everything you may send. As to sending boxes etc. now, I really think you would be quite safe in doing so. I have now about made up my mind that we are to stay here. If, however, we move to the Fort, anything you may send would reach me safely there. I wrote to you about some ale, etc. I am perfectly willing to risk this, so send it if convenient, without delay. If English Ale should be in better bottles etc. and so safer, perhaps you had better get that.

I am astonished at your fears. We feel perfectly secure here, and it is the general belief, as far as I can discover, that our position is impregnable. It could only be taken by a siege which would employ 150,000 men for a long time, and which the Rebels could not possibly support so far from Richmond. The only cause for anxiety is the possible obstruction of the river, and I have no doubt our Naval Officers are alive to their duty there. Our Army was never more effective than it is now, and would fight magnificently. The lack of confidence in McClellan seems to exist in direct ratio to the distance. We have no fears here, and this last movement has given additional confidence.

I am very glad Tom Curtis and Hazy have letters.

I am not astonished at Mr. Willard's going, but wish he could be Major as soon as his 170 men have enlisted.[36] He would make a great Major, and any Colonel would be delighted to get him. He would do plenty of work and his great personal energy would keep others well up to the mark. He is indeed an Officer

---

[36] On August 16, 1862, Sidney Willard was mustered into the 35th Massachusetts Infantry as Captain of Company I.

of the old New England stamp. I am very much obliged to him for inducing men to enter my Company. Mr. Willard of course could not possibly come into this Regiment as a Captain. Such appointments are never made. I have heard nothing more about Capt. Shepard's promotion to another Regiment.

Capt. Tremlett and Capt. Cabot, and Lieut. Messer all leave us today to recruit their health, so we are dreadfully short of Officers. Major Revere and Lieut. Perkins are ill. As for me, I was never better, and the late marches have done me good.

You have probably seen in the paper that Herbert and Sander/s/ are promoted. I am very glad for both. Both are well worthy and excellent Officers. Sander was educated in a military school in Germany and was an Officer in the regular Army there, and has been with us through all the late battles etc. and well deserves promotion. You know how much of a friend I am to Herbert, and I tell you truly that I have not a particle of envy at his promotion, and shall not have, but I cannot but think that in strict justice, the promotions should be given to those who have borne the burden and heat of the day. Now it is very unfortunate for a young Officer to be sick and be obliged to be absent from 4 battles and all the tremendous labors and sufferings of the retreat, and the heat and sickness of this last month here, but it is his misfortune, and certainly it seems to me that those whose health did hold out, and who really did stand the duty and brave the dangers of battle, are richly entitled to the rewards. Now the only ground of seniority Herbert had over me, was that he got his commission and went to Camp Benton 20 days before I did. Both of our Commissions are of the same date. Now I did duty from about June 15th till July 4th, all through the retreat, while Herbert was barely able to be carried to the rear on horseback, and since then I have done duty here and been on the late expedition, while he has been at home. If my *real claims* are not superior to his I am no judge of what a soldier's duty is. Of course, it can be said that he would have done everything had he been there, and that an unavoidable illness only prevented, but the fact remains that he was not there and I was.

Now perhaps you will not believe me when I say these two things: 1st I honestly think that I deserved the promotion before Herbert. 2nd that I do *not* feel the least envy toward him. Yet, this is true. I really care nothing for the name and for advancement etc., only for the slight additional comforts I should get, but you know one cannot help looking at such things. Do not of course mention this, it is of no importance, but I write very fully to you. With the single exception of Lieut. Murphy against whom Col. Palfrey has a spite, I have done duty as a Lieutenant in this Regiment longer than any Lieutenant whose commission dated the same as mine. This includes Sander, Curtis, Herbert and Patten. Well, let the matter drop.

I was speaking to Mr. Folsom the other day about the possibility of getting some Champagne. He and Sander would like to join with me and get a basket. Now could you speak to Mr. Andrews? He used to have some most excellent at $10.00 to $12.00 a basket. It could be boxed right over and I think would come very safely, and only cost us perhaps $1.50 per bottle when here. If it is not too much trouble please send me a basket by Adams' Express. If, however, you feel quite sure that movements are taking place and that it would be a long time before we should get it, do not send. I leave it to you. If it should be troublesome to you, do not mind about it. I suggested Mr. Andrews' Champagne because it is good and cheap. Use your own judgment.

We are to be paid off today, and I shall probably enclose a draft for $100.00. This makes in all $490.00 I shall have sent home, more than enough, I should think, to cover all expenses, is it not so? Do not let me ever overrun. The India Rubber pail etc. came all right. The bags are much too small for a sponge. Can you not send an Oil Silk bag large enough for my sponge?

I forbear to write more about the Malvern Hill affair till I see the newspaper accounts.

I shall try again to send the trunk today. Write soon.

Ever your affectionate brother,
Henry.

Camp 20th Regiment near Harrison's Landing, Va.
August 10th 1862.

My dear John.

I received yesterday by mail your letter giving me a list of articles sent in the two boxes to me. Lieutenants Abbott, Curtis, and Wilkins arrived yesterday and with them my new servant James, whom I like so far very much. I am indeed delighted to read over the long list of good things that you have sent. Abbott found that it would be impossible for him to carry them with him all the way, and so left them to come on by Express, and I expect to get them tomorrow. Please let me know what things are presents and what are charged to me, and the prices of the latter. When the boxes arrive I shall answer fully and shall take the first opportunity to thank Mrs. Jeffries for her kind and most acceptable present.

When I look over the list I cannot but think that my order for Champagne was almost superfluous, but as I shall probably get only 2 or 3 bottles of it, I will not countermand it. I often fear that I trouble you greatly about sending things, but no one here has any mercy on friends at home, and others are now receiving quantities of good things.

Father wrote some time ago that he had sent to me $10.00 worth of good things by the "American Tract Society". Did he sent [*sic*] this to me or for me to distribute to the Regiment? And were the Tracts etc., or Jellies etc. such as the Tract Society sent to the Regiment? Father did not specify and I did not quite understand what he sent and for whom? I have not received it yet.

We now get plenty of vegetables here, onions and potatoes, and of late even turnips. I eat hardly any meat, the vegetables being still such a luxury to me, that I cannot but make my dinner of them. On the whole we have plenty of good food. Still the delicious contents of the boxes will be as welcome as ever, and I shall enjoy every article. Raspberry vinegar is *especially* nice, and very good for one here. The liberal supply of Cordial will be indeed appreciated. Not a drop shall be wasted. Be assured that everything sent is keenly enjoyed and does a great deal to help us keep up our spirits in this rather trying climate.

I am delighted to see Abbott back and looking so well, but I am very sorry to hear from him of the gloomy and desponding feeling at home. He said he was glad to get away, and into a place where people were cheerful and hopeful. I am astonished at the fears of people at home. We have none here. Our Army is in splendid fighting trim and ready for anything. As to an evacuation, the more I look about, the more evidence I see that we are not to move. We are safe and comfortable here, and if well handled can oblige the Rebels to keep large forces at Petersburgh, Richmond and Malvern Hill, and be always ready for a move and a blow. We have no idea of giving up and if the people at home could only come out and see the Army, they would hurry to enlist so as to be in time to see the last struggles of the Rebellion.

Some of our men have just got back from Richmond where they were prisoners. I gather from what they say that the Rebellion is as good as gone now. They met with Union people in plenty. Women would snatch a little United States flag from their bosoms and wave it at them. The people in the streets showed every mark of sympathy. The Soldiers were downhearted and openly said that everything was going to ruin, that they were sick of the war, that they were forced into it and would desert at their first opportunity. They have no tea, Coffee, sugar and salt in the rations. They cursed Jefferson Davis and said he was watched lest he should escape and leave Richmond to its fate. In short their immense Army is miserably fed, miserably equipped, and full of dissatisfaction and distrust. And, besides, it is impossible that it can be supported much longer. Our United States Notes were eagerly taken at $9.00 for a $5.00 greenback, and gold for double its worth. Yet these secesh Notes passed normally at par in the streets. One of my men paid a quarter of a dollar for one onion. Pies miserably poor for 50 Cents each, coffee $1.00 a pound, etc. etc.

Our Army is healthy, well fed and confident. I fully believe that we shall *utterly crush* the Rebellion before cold weather. We only want the hearty, hopeful support of our friends at home. Our Army is veteran in every sense. It cannot (humanly speaking) be badly beaten. The Rebel Army is just such an [*sic*] one as can receive an overwhelming defeat, be utterly disorganized and cut to pieces. Its very size is against it. In manoeuvring [*sic*] it certainly will get confused, and I repeat, I fully believe that with the blessing of God we shall destroy them yet. Do not be dispirited. We are ready here. Only our old grumblers, Tremlett and Cabot, are glum here. They are both trying all they can to get home on a sick leave, but cannot make it quite go. If they do get home they may give a doleful account drawn from their own scared imaginations, but do not believe them. The Army is all right. Send out a few more men, and have a big reserve, and then we will take Richmond and close up the account.

Captains Hallowell, Shepard, Macy and many others constantly desire kindest regards to you. The first said he intended to write very soon to you. Good bye! I hope you enjoyed the fishing excursion.

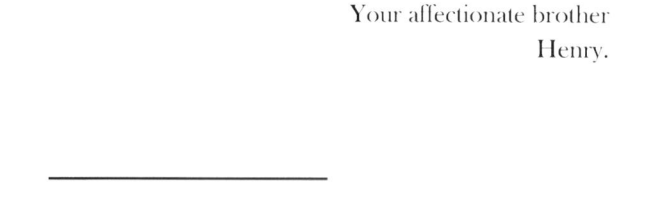

Your affectionate brother
Henry.

Harrison's Landing Sunday P.M.
August 10th 1862.

My dear Father.

I wrote to John this morning that I did not expect to move for a long time, but this afternoon I hear from a Staff Officer that this Division will move tomorrow at 2 P.M. down the river. This may not be true but it probably is, and if it is you may not hear from me for several days. No attack is expected. It may be we are going to Washington and thence to Pope. Perhaps to hold the position lately occupied by Burnside, perhaps we are the first instalment, and the whole Army is to follow. I think it most likely we are going near to Fort Munroe first, and I cannot guess further. At all events it is decidedly most probable that we shall be for some days away from active operations.

If I learn more and can write you I will. I only write now lest you should be anxious at not getting letters. My boxes are still with the Express, and will remain safe with them.

Your affectionate son
Henry.

P.S. Just received Mother's and Mary Ann's of the 6th. Enclosed is key of trunk. We leave tomorrow.

Henry Ropes. 10 P.M.

Wednesday 13th August 1862
Camp near Harrison's Landing, Va.

My dear Father.

We are still here, all quiet, and no signs of the enemy. All our baggage except a very small amount we take with us has gone on transports. As far as I can learn the whole Army is still here, but in light marching order, and ready for an instant move in any direction. There are transports here somewhere, yet it is said we are to march. All the sick have been sent off. Just heard of a great battle with Pope.[37] Do not know the final result. One account says Capt. Abbott of the 2nd *[Massachusetts Infantry]* is killed, but the Herald does not give his name, and we hope it is not true.

I suppose we are awaiting news of the result. Our pickets are out nearly to Malvern Hill, and at last accounts all was quiet. Have not received boxes etc. Just received letter from John. Will try to answer soon.

In haste

Your affectionate son
Henry.

---

[37] Battle of Cedar Mountain on August 9, 1862.

RIGHT UP INTO THE FIRE

Camp 20th Regiment near Harrison's Landing, Va.
Thursday morning
(6 A.M.) August 14th 1862.

My dear John.

I did not think I should be able to answer your letter from this camp, for we have been under marching orders since Monday, and everything packed up, but still there is no sign of a move, and I hear that only the reserve Artillery has embarked.

We have just heard of the battle with Pope, but cannot see much of a victory in it. Milton has seen a Richmond paper which acknowledges a decided reverse to the Rebels. We have heard of the death of Captains Abbott, Russell and Goodwin of the 2nd, but the Richmond paper has Russell's name among the prisoners, and Abbott's name is not in the corrected list so we hope for "Lit's"[38] sake he is not hurt. Poor Abbott does not know what to believe, and of course we all are anxious to get true accounts and know the worst.

Major Revere is, as you know, very ill, and has gone home. He has received an appointment on Sumner's staff, and will leave the Regiment. Adjutant Peirson is quite ill with inflammation of the bowels. Capt. Cabot and Lieutenants Whittier and Messer, and Perkins are all ill with the jaundice, which is very common now. Dr. Hayward says Cider is the best thing for prevention and cure, and should be drunk freely in this climate. So if you can give any advice to the Sanitary Commission or Tract Society, tell them to send Cider for the jaundice patients. James did not tell me he had received $2.00 from you. Did he understand it was a present or an advance on his wages?

I am glad you have seen Henry, and that he is well. He is very apt to get into trouble, but I am very sorry for him, and especially for his loss of his money. Perhaps you can help him to get a place. I fear I shall not be able to raise my radishes now, but if I had had them at first I might have had quite a crop.

I am very glad you are going to Lenox, and that you will meet the Gardners there. Please give my very kindest regards and respects to Mr. and Mrs. Gardner and their family.

Balch ('59) is now here as a private, and goes about, and /be/comes the heavy respectful, and salutes and tries to make himself a most exemplary private, but it is impossible for any of us to treat him personally as a private. He is a splendid fellow, and really tries to do everything a private should do, and rather avoids the Officers and will not go with them and be treated as one of them. I think however,

---

[38] Lieutenant Henry L. Abbott's nickname was "Little".

he is right. He has come as a private and he means to be a real private, and do a real soldier's duty. He is in Company I. Then we have 2 other recruits, both in some sense Gentlemen. One was a Clerk, and robbed his employer and ran away with some girl, but was taken and imprisoned. Now he is released to enlist. Your account of the fishing excursion and the party at the Mudge's quite brings me back to Swampscott. Tell me what other men are coming out here? I am very glad to hear of Chs. Codman's splendid position. I think he will make a most excellent Colonel. Sourdon is hardly strong enough, but very likely the 9 months men will not get farther than Washington, and will see no service. Hartwell, I remember well. I was introduced to his brother by Patten and found him a most agreable [sic], Gentlemanly man. I fear there is not the least chance for him in this Regiment.

There was no regular column of Regiments at the battle, but each Regiment as it came up was pushed forward, and we came first. We stopped and opened fire twice and each time fired 15 or 20 minutes, so there was plenty of time for other Regiments to come up.

My Company is now quite full again. Many have returned from Hospital and 3 from Richmond. Some have returned who left us for the General Hospital at Yorktown. We can turn out 38 rifles now for action.

As to our moving, everybody is entirely ignorant of what McClellan's plans are. No one can even conjecture. Perhaps we shall move right on Richmond, perhaps to the Rappahannock and perhaps on Petersburgh. At any rate all is quiet now and no one excited or anxious. If we go down the Peninsula part of the Army will march with the trains. We are ready for anything.

Good bye! Love to all. Shall try to write again soon, but do not be anxious if you do not get letters, for sometimes one cannot get a chance to write for several days.

Your affectionate brother
Henry.

RIGHT UP INTO THE FIRE

Camp 20th Regiment, Newport News, Va.
Saturday August 23rd 1862.

My dear Father.

We arrived here safely after a week's march from Harrison's Landing, and are now camped on a high bluff overlooking the river. It is cool and pleasant.
We fell in at our old Camp at 5 P.M. on Friday the 15th inst., and our baggage was sent on before us. We did not get orders to march till 6 A.M. on Saturday the 16th, and then we slowly left the entrenchments and marched to Charles City Court house where we camped for the (Saturday) night. On Sunday (17th) we marched to the mouth of the Chickahominy, a very dusty and tiresome march. Very early on Monday (18th) morning we crossed the Chickahominy in a pontoon bridge, and stopped on the opposite Bank long enough to get a most refreshing bath in the James (River). Then we marched on 5 miles and camped for the night. Tuesday (19th) we marched to Williamsburgh, passed through the town and camped 4 miles beyond near Fort Magruder. Williamsburgh is quite a fine old place. A great many very old looking fine houses. The College is quite a large fine Building. Wednesday (20th) we marched to Yorktown, camped on the North side of the town and had a good bath in the York river.

Here I met with an unfortunate accident. James had just made me a pot of coffee and placed it close to my foot. I did not see it and moved my foot, and spilt the hot coffee on my ankle and instep. I received quite a severe scald, and suffered a good deal, as there was no remedy at hand. One of my Corporals however brought me a bottle of Haynes' Arabian Balsam which he recommended most highly, and which I applied liberally, and bound it on with a handkerchief. It caused a very intense pain for about ½ an hour after which the pain entirely passed off, and I have not been troubled since. The Doctor however told me I must keep my foot bound up and not wear a shoe, as if I wore off the blisters I should have a very serious wound. So for Thursday and Friday I was obliged to ride on horseback, without a shoe and with only a handkerchief bound lightly round the place. I now have it properly dressed, and the Doctor says it will soon be well, but tells me not to walk. It is very fortunate that our marching is now over for the present.

On Thursday (21st) we made a very tremendous march from beyond Yorktown to Big Bethel, during the heat of the day, and yesterday (22nd) we marched here. Here we got our baggage and are most comfortably off in every way. We expect our Express boxes today from the fort. On the march we got corn and apples from the farms, and often chickens, ducks and Turkeys. Now we expect abundant supplies of food from the fort.

I understand we are to stay several days here. Beyond this, I know nothing, but it is rumored that a considerable force is to be kept here to threaten Petersburg, and we may be a part of such force.

I received yesterday the mail for the last week, and acknowledge the receipt of the following letters etc. From you of August 14th enclosing one from Mother of the 12th. Also one from you of the 12th, one from Louisa of the 8th dated Robbinston, Maine; one from Mary Ann of the 12th, 8 newspapers, Tactics, 4 volumes Dickens' "Bleak House", and the Atlantic for September. Before leaving Harrison's Landing I received letters from Mother and Mary Ann of August 6th which I do not think I ever acknowledged.

I am deeply grieved to hear certainly of the death of Capt. Abbott and Lt. Perkins of the 2nd. Lt. Abbott is very much affected, but bears up nobly. They were most affectionate brothers.

John will feel Stephen Perkins' death very much. We are all well here. I am in most excellent health, and hope soon to be quite able to march.

My best love to Mother and all. I hope soon to acknowledge the receipt of the boxes.

Your affectionate son
Henry Ropes.

Camp 20th Regiment Newport News, Va.
August 23rd 1862.

My dear John.

I have just written to Father an account of our march to this place and will not trouble you with a repetition of what you have no doubt heard.

Thanks for the books. I shall greatly enjoy to read "Bleak House". Tactics all right. James I find is strong and willing, but stupid and careless. However, I think he will do, for he works well. He lost my new India Rubber pail on the march. Will you please buy me another just like that one, and send it on as soon as convenient, either by Express, or better still by some Officer or man coming out to the Regiment. Please send at the same time 4 cakes nice soap of a size small enough for my soap case.

I shall send home by Express, as soon as possible, a parcel containing my old blouse, which I have worn steadily since a few days before the battle of Fair Oaks.

RIGHT UP INTO THE FIRE

The shoulder straps and buttons I have worn throughout the entire campaign, and I would like to keep them. Please lay the old blouse aside just as it is. I also send a dressing case I do not need, 2 volumes "Barchester Towers" and some private papers for Mary Ann to put away. You will find an old legal paper tucked under the string, which I picked up near Charles City Court House. I may send something else which I will write you about. I have sent home my trunk and the key by mail to Father. Please open the trunk and send me by mail the shoulder straps from my thick Dress coat. I have got a thin sack coat here and need these straps. I have no news to tell you. I have just heard a report that we go to New Orleans! I do not believe it of course. It is delightful here. I expect my boxes very soon from the Express. Weather cool and good salt water bathing.

How dreadfully the 2nd has suffered! I can hardly believe that Abbott is gone, and Stephen Perkins, too. You will feel the latter loss particularly.

Please send me a shaving brush. I left one behind. In the dressing case I send home is a nail brush belonging to my English dressing case, which please keep.

Good bye!

Your affectionate brother
Henry.

Macy, Shepard, Hallowell and others send kind regards. Please send me a few stamps.

H. R.

Camp 20th Regiment, Newport News, Va.
Sunday, August 24th 1862.

My dear John.

I wrote to you and to Father yesterday, and have nothing more to tell you of particular interest. Sumner's whole Corps are ordered to be ready for embarkation, and we expect to be off tomorrow or the next day. Our destination is still a secret., but the rumor of our going to some Southern port gains ground. Officers are ordered to provide 10 days' rations, rather a large quantity to last us merely for a trip to Acquia Creek. I have heard we are going to South Carolina.

I shall send home a box containing the things I spoke of in my last letter, and, besides, my revolver etc. I find this one rather too large and heavy to march with and should prefer a smaller one. I send with it some ammunition and caps. Please take the revolver John Bradlee gave me from the case, and buy a small holster to fit it and send it to me together with 5 cases of fixed ammunition to fit, and a small box of caps. Perhaps the caps and ammunition I send home will fit the smaller pistol. Better send these on by some Officer or man returning to the Regiment. I have just received notice that we shall probably move today, but I do not think we shall. There is always great delay. My foot is much better and I hope will soon be quite well.

I was very sorry and very much astonished to see an extract from one of my letters in the Advertiser. I did not see the slightest reason for putting it in. I have not heard from you why you did put it in yet. I thought I had distinctly expressed my wish that extracts from my letters should only be put in to relieve anxiety of friends as for instance after a battle.

We have today received an abundant supply of peaches and melons from Fort Munroe and are feasting on them. All well here. Love to all. I may not be able to write for some days.

Your affectionate brother
Henry.

Alexandria, near Washington,
on board Steamship "Atlantic" Thursday
August 28th 1862 10 A.M.

My dear Father.

We have just arrived here after a most comfortable voyage from Newport News. We know nothing of our future movements, but expect to land soon. The 42nd and 50th New York and the 10th Mass. are on board beside us. We saw part of the 1st Mass. Cavalry at Aquia Creek where we stopped last night for orders.

This is the old Collins steamer, Captain Eldridge. Officers had staterooms and the regular table was set for them. All perfectly well. My foot very much better and rapidly healing. Shall write again very soon if I have a chance when I get ashore.

Your affectionate son
Henry.

RIGHT UP INTO THE FIRE

Camp 20th Regiment, 3 miles South of
Alexandria. Friday August 29th 1862
3 P.M.

My dear John.

I wrote to Father when we arrived at Alexandria in the Steamer "Atlantic", Capt. Eldridge. We marched through the town and camped for the night on a beautiful slope, with many Regiments of our Division near us. Alexandria is quite a city and has many quite fine houses, and altogether looks busy and rather prosperous. The country here is hilly and looks quite fertile.

This morning we had orders to march at 9, but they were countermanded, and we are here still. The 59th and 42nd New York of our Brigade have gone to garrison the forts commanding the Long Bridge, and I hear that the 19th and 20th [Massachusetts] are to do like duty for the Chain Bridge forts. This report is from good authority and seems very likely, as part of the Brigade are already gone. Of course we may go on to the front but on the whole I think it more probable we are to be stationed in the Forts. Of course we are all glad to get a little rest, and enjoy the comforts one can get near a great city, but I think we should all be sorry to be permanently detached from the Army of the Potomac an from McClellan's command, just now when such great events seem to be at hand. However, we are such old soldiers now that we take anything that comes, and are glad for its advantages whatever they are. Any hour we may get orders which settle the question.

We had a delightful voyage up, and pretty good fare. The State Rooms seemed horribly close to us who have so [sic] slept so long in the open air. The miserable Tammany Regiment got into a fight on deck and the Lieut. Colonel of the 59th was considerably bruised in attempting to quell it. No other event of interest occured.

I am perfectly well, and my foot a great deal better. I now wear my shoe and walk a little. If we march I shall ride. I have no news to tell you at all. I cannot send home the blouse, pistol etc., as it is not allowed by a recent regulation. I shall try to send it by a private hand.

James does as well as he can I suppose, but is dreadfully stupid. I cannot trust the least thing to him. If ever you fall in with a really good man such a man for instance as Albert or Tim, whom you knew in Cambridge at Mrs. Humphrey's, keep your eye on him, and I will get rid of James. James means well, but I would give anything for a really good servant.

About 75 recruits just came.

Your affectionate brother
Henry.

RIGHT UP INTO THE FIRE

>August 31st Sunday near
>Fairfax Court House, Va. 2 P.M. 1862.

My dear Father.

We marched here this morning from near Washington. Herbert and Patten have just come. All well. A great battle yesterday[39], but all quiet today.

In great haste

>Your affectionate son
>Henry.

>Camp 20th Regiment Mass.
>near Alexandria, Va. September 3rd 1862.

My dear Father.

After 4 days of tiresome marching and picket duty, we are brought to the same place which we left on Saturday last. I wrote you from Chain Bridge that we were to occupy some forts permanently. Then orders were changed and we crossed the Chain Bridge, and went to some hills N.W. of Washington. Here we heard all day Saturday the heavy Canonading [sic], and we knew a great battle was going on. We marched again at 3 A.M. on Sunday, passed through Georgetown, crossed the river and marched through a heavy rain to Fairfax Court House, Va. where we arrived at 12 M. after a march of 22 hours. We had several long halts however, and the march was well conducted and not very trying.

As we expected fully to go to the front and be engaged with the enemy very soon, I kept with the Regiment although my foot was very lame. We lay down for a few hours at Fairfax my Company and Co. I being advanced and pickets thrown out for a body of Rebel Cavalry etc. had appeared in rear of our main Army. Monday morning we advanced about 5 miles and occupied a road and rested all day. Our pickets were thrown out, and met a few of the enemy and we had one

---

[39] Second Battle of Bull Run.

man of Company C wounded.[40] We found a large body of Cavalry had got in between us and the main body of the Army at Centreville. In the afternoon Hooker advanced, and attacked them, and we formed part of the 2nd line, behind a hastily built breastwork. I hear he drove them off. A rain storm made the night very uncomfortable, but Tuesday was a very fine day, and very cool. Our Army now fell back, leaving us as the extreme Infantry advance. Casey & Slocum formed line of battle behind us[41] and the Cavalry were a little in front of us. At about 5 P.M. we fell back, and afterward halted and let all the other troops go by, and our Brigade covered the retreat. We were still detached from our Division and were now under Hooker. The enemy pressed us, but a section of horse Artillery was ordered to the rear and kept them back. I at first rode with the Regiment on the Adjutant's horse, but before long got a chance to ride on a Caisson of a Regiment of Artillery in Banks' Corps, and thus reached Alexandria soon after midnight. The Artillery went much farther than the Regiment without my knowledge, and I could not find the Regiment in the darkness and therefore got in at a house and slept till this morning when I found the Regiment. I am now with it here. I rode because my foot was very lame after my long march. This morning I have seen Col. Lee and Major Revere, and they both look very well, and we are delighted to see them again here. We shall no doubt have a season of rest here. The Army needs a month to recruit and refit, and then I hope we shall make our last advance. I am in perfect health and have no doubt a few days rest will restore my foot. I have received from Col. Lee's servant the shoulder straps, pail etc. and thus I see you must have got my trunk and key. I hope to write again very soon. Excuse this letter written under great difficulties.

All well in the Regiment.

Your affectionate son,
Henry.

---

[40] Private Andrew Beska.

[41] Brigadier General Silas Casey's Division was detached from the Army of the Potomac in June, 1862, after the Battle of Seven Pines. Ropes is possibly referring to Major General Darius Couch's Division.

RIGHT UP INTO THE FIRE

Camp, 20th Regiment near Alexandria, Va.
September 3rd 1862.

My dear John.

I have just received from the Colonel your letter, the pail, soap, stamps, straps, and shaving brush for all of which I am very much obliged. Col. Lee looks very well and so does the Major. The Colonel asked me to mention in my letter that he arrived here last night safely and well, and requests you to send word to Mrs. Lee and the family.

I think we shall move toward Chain Bridge and stay there for some time. All quiet now. I believe I never acknowledged the receipt of the following letters. From Father August 23rd and 27th, Mary Ann 19th and 26th, and you of the 19th and the one by Col. Lee. Please thank all. In answer to your questions, Sedgwick sent word to Col. Palfrey that he might want an Officer for 2 or 3 days, and asked if he could send one in case he should need him. Col. Palfrey said he could spare one and asked me if I would go. I said I would but was never called for. Sedgwick had before asked for Peirson or Whittier, but both were sick. Whittier is now on his staff. I was detailed to command Company F, but now Patten has returned and assumed command, and I am still in K. James does pretty well, but *do* keep a look-out for a really good man. Strength to carry a heavy load and willingness to endure discomfort are absolutely necessary. About 75 recruits joined us but were unarmed, and had to be sent to the rear when we advanced.

I feel very sorry to trouble you so much in getting so many things for me, but you see my equipment has to do for a house, pantry, kitchen, bath room, and everything else, including butcher, baker and tailor, and all this has to be carried on my back to be of use to me at the right time, and so I have to be very particular to have good articles and of the lightest materials. You no doubt will think it silly of me to give such particular directions about small things, but remember that to have a couple of eyelet holes in the wrong place in a tent may make me wet to the skin for 24 hours, instead of keeping me dry, and a slight alteration of the straps of a knapsack may cut my shoulder and disable me, instead of leaving me perfectly sound and well. Now I wish to be perfectly prepared for active operations immediately, and therefore, after much thought, I have determined on what I want and ask you to see to the procuring of the same, in accordance with the enclosed directions. I want the following articles:

Pair of Boots. Rice made me a perfect pair of Army shoes last December, and probably has my measure yet. Those shoes were very loose and comfortable, and very long, exactly as I want the boots. They must go on easily, even when wet. Please order a pair at Rice's, not of excessive thickness, but of the leather best calculated to keep out water. Perhaps it would be well to have Cork soles put on (not inside Cork soles covered with Lamb's wool). Let them be loose about the ankle bones, high, nearly to the knee, and very large in the calf. My calf is very large. Let no expense be incurred for ornament and none be spared for strength and durability. As they are to be worn in rain and mud, let the "counters" be very stiff. Should Rice not have the measure, perhaps Rogers has (who made the Army shoes you sent out.) But let Rogers make them a little wider than the shoes. Clauser [*Clausen*] has my measure in Cambridge, but if he makes them, tell him to make them large. I prefer Rice.

    2nd. A knapsack. Please call at Roulston's [*Roulstone's*], Tremont Street, and order a knapsack, made exactly like the ones he made lately for Lieut. Wilkins and Herbert Mason, with this alteration: Instead of side straps for shoes on the outside let there be on each side a small pocket, large enough for a sponge, for instance, fastened by a lappet and button, or buckle. Let the knapsack be made as light as possible, and of the very best material. Its cost is, I believe, $4.00. I will give you a little representation of the pockets I wish. He will understand what I want, for Wilkins is my model.

I wish to have "Lieut. Ropes, 20th Mass." distinctly marked in small letters in white paint just above (or under) the left hand pocket, as I have represented. This is very necessary. Wilkins' had a little inside pouch or pocket for comb tooth brush etc., and I wish one like this, with a lappet and fastening.

    3rd. Wool Blanket. I wish one of some color not very light, blue preferred. Size, regulation about 6 feet by 4. I want a *very* light thin blanket, not more than ½ as heavy as the common kind sold. Let it be as warm as possible for its weight, and therefore I suppose it must be made either of fine wool, or of silk and wool. Do not spare expense, but get the *greatest amount of warmth* and the *least weight possible*.

4th. India Rubber Blanket. I wish the lightest Rubber that is strong enough to bear careful usage. Patten has an excellent one. Let mine be very large, say (if possible) 7 feet by 5, with strong edges, and an eyelet hole in each corner, and besides 3 others along each long side and 2 along each short side. Let this and the wool blanket be marked with my name "H. Ropes". Do not get a lined blanket, only the light "linen rubber" (as I believe it is called).

5th. Rubber Pillow. I have lost my old one. Please get a very small light one. Let it be marked with my name "H. Ropes".

6th. A crockery Plate, Cup and saucer. Perhaps this seems to you to be very luxurious, but I assure you to eat so long from tin is very tiresome, and a crockery cup is a great luxury. These must be very small and light. I should prefer some of that old set which you remember I had in Cambridge. The Cups were small and the material was light. If you buy anything, get it white.

7th. A Shelter tent. As this is an article of the very *greatest* importance, I enclose a description.

8th. A Lantern (Ropes' Patent) Description enclosed. *[Description missing.]*

9th. A very small light and sharp Hatchet with a little leather case and strap to go over the shoulder. This for James to carry.

This is all, I believe. I really feel ashamed to trouble you to such a fearful extent, but if you were here and could go to the front a week or so with me, I am sure you would appreciate my wants, and see the absolute necessity of everything I have sent for, and the need of having the best of everything and thus the lightest.

Everything I have written for can be packed in the knapsack, and if possible let it be sent on by some faithful man. If you can find no man, let Adams & Co. take it. One thing Mother can send me, if she pleases, 4 little linen bags like the former ones she sent. If three of these are filled with white sugar, tea and coffee, I shall be much obliged.

Another thing: 2 small boxes, tin or pewter, very light, to hold each about 1 gill, for salt and pepper. *Not* with holes in the top for scattering the contents over the food.

I think everything can be made and sent off in 10 days after you get this and so in 3 weeks I can get all.

I expect a campaign in Autumn, and I want to be as well protected from wet and cold and as generally comfortable, as possible. I have no news. Very sorry for your eyes. You had better go to Lenox and try to enjoy that female society you say you consider so dull for a "steady drink".

No news. All steady here; no desponding. We have arrived at our "Torres Vedras", and I look forward to our last advance before long.

RIGHT UP INTO THE FIRE

Herbert, Macy, Hallowell, Abbott, Murphy, Shepard, Patten and others desire kindest regards.

Your affectionate brother
Henry.

P.S. Black India Rubber for the blanket, unless white is stronger or lighter.

[Enclosed description of the tent.]

Dear John.

I wish to explain to you the triangular end of the tent. It is a triangle divided in the centre into 2 right-angled triangles, each of a base of 3 ½ feet (because the tent is to stretch 7 feet wide) of a hypothenuse of 6 feet (because the 2 sides together are 12 feet long) and 4 feet 10 in perpendicular, because of the other dimensions. But to keep out rain I want a flap 6 inches wide, and to fasten this securely there must be 2 sets of tapes or strings, one outside, one inside. Then the ridge pole must have room to come out at the end, and be supported by a fork stuck in the ground, so the tops of these triangles must be cut off a little. The piece of strong canvas will sufficiently cover this opening.

I hope this description is plain, and that it will not trouble you very much.

Herbert has seen this and wishes one just like it. Can you order 2? Please do so for him. Better make one first and show it to you. Hall's, Milk Street, is the best Rubber store, I think.

Yours
H. R.

Camp 20th Regiment
Tenallytown near Washington, D.C.
September 5th 1862.

My dear Father.

I wrote to you last from Alexandria day before yesterday, telling you of our heavy marches to and from Fairfax Court House. Yesterday the Brigade (under Col. Lee) marched to this place, crossing at Chain Bridge. Our Corps, and Banks' is here, and I understand Banks is today to move up the river to Poolesville. I was unable to march yesterday and came in an ambulance with Col. Hinks of the 19th Regiment, a very pleasant man. He told me that we marched 30 miles on Sunday, from 2 A.M. till 12 P.M., and that taking the 3 days together we marched 65 miles in 64 consecutive hours. This march quite used up my foot, and I found yesterday that I was quite unable to march, but today it is much better and I have no doubt a few days' rest will quite restore it.

We are now on very high land and shall probably be very comfortable. I have written to Poolesville and ordered my two boxes there to be sent home to you by Adams' Express. I enclose the keys. They are filled with Camp equipage which I could not carry with me from Poolesville. Please open the boxes and make any use of the contents. Some of the things I may need and if so will send for them.

From all I hear McDowell made a bad job of his retreat and our loss was heavy, and a great deal of valuable stores and many wagons fell into the enemy's hands. I can see no excuse for this. A good firm rear guard can stop almost any pursuit. We have now twice covered a retreat, and both times with success.

Jackson seems to strike terror everywhere. I hope Sumner will meet him some day and turn the tables. We expect to be here several weeks. I am perfectly well as usual. Herbert is quite strong and well and stood the hard marching perfectly. I have written to John to get me a number of things, and I have no doubt it will take up much of his time to see to them, but he is very kind in attending to everything, and I think I have now found out exactly what I need.

Best love to Mother and all. I shall write soon and answer all letters when I can get a tent up.

Ever your affectionate son
Henry.

Camp Defiance near Rockville
Md. Monday September 8th 1862.

My dear Father.

We marched from Tenallytown on Saturday last and drew up here in line of battle in support of batteries and sent out pickets. We had heard of the invasion of the Rebels, and we quite expected a battle, as their pickets occupied Jamestown a few miles before us. However, they have not molested us, and now we have an immense force here. Banks is on our left, and the 2nd Mass. is close to us in the 2nd line. I was really very much astonished to hear that the Rebels had crossed, but I think it will be their ruin, that is if they are here in force. I do not think they will attack us here, for we are in a very strong position, and they seem to me making to the North. Perhaps after all they will retire after supplying themselves with what food and clothing they can get.

Mr. John Gray has just been here and is getting a good idea of military matters. We are in a most beautiful and healthy Camp, and as Genl. Sumner has today given it a name "Defiance" and as our baggage has just come up, I think we may be some time here.

My foot is much better. I enclose 2 bills of $2.00 each of N.E. Banks. I understand both are good but they will not often take N.E. bills here. If they are good will you please send me back the $4.00 in U.S. $1.00 or better still postage stamps and small change?

I received yesterday yours of the 4th and Mother's of August 28th enclosing a letter from Frank at Berlin and Lizzy at Lewisham. Please thank all and say I hope to answer soon. I am delighted you gave such a handsome present to Mr. Willard. I know he will value it accordingly. All friends here well. The Colonel as brisk and active as ever. He already looks much better than when he came, for he is sunburnt and ruddy. Very much obliged to you for attending to my little matters, and for sending to their owners the contents of the trunk.

Letter for Mary Ann enclosed.

Your affectionate son
Henry.

Camp 20th Regiment near
Middletown, Md. Monday September 15th 1862.
6 A.M.

My dear Father.

We came here late last night having marched very far to the North during the day. We marched from Rockville to Frederick City via Clarksburg and Middlebrook, and camped day before yesterday close to Frederick. The people show every sign of joy at our arrival. There was a severe battle here yesterday before we came up, about which I have not yet heard much, but we drove the Rebels at last.[42] All quiet as yet this morning, so I suppose they have retreated in the night. I hear the 35th Mass. was engaged. Genl. Reno is killed, his body was carried by us. The houses were filled with wounded where we passed up. We are about 2 miles from the position the Rebels occupied last night. My foot is well. All the Regiment safe and well, except Lieutenants Abbott, Murphy and Beckwith who are ill and left at Frederick. I do not think Abbott is much ill, but it would have hurt him to march and we persuaded him to stay behind for a day or two.

Received letter from mother of the 8th. No other letters. Please do not send on the pistol if there is no fixed ammunition to fit it.

Love to Mother and all. Shall try to write soon. Our force here is very large and we are in reserve and in all probability should not be engaged in case another battle takes place in a few days.

In great haste

Your affectionate son
Henry.

Field near Sharpsburg, Va. [sic]
Friday, September 19th 1862.

My dear Father.

We have had a tremendous battle and again I have been mercifully preserved from all harm. It began at 6 A.M. on Wednesday, day before yesterday, and we have been on picket ever since the fight. Last night the enemy left and have probably crossed the river. We are drawn back, our forces in pursuit. Col. Palfrey is wounded in shoulder, and I believe missing; Capt. Holmes in neck; Capt. Hallowell in arm; Lt. Milton slightly in three places; Lt. Col. Revere in arm; Col. Lee safe and well; Genl. Richardson mortally; Genl. Sedgwick badly; Genl. Dana in leg; Col. Hinks killed. Our Division suffered awfully. I was bruised slightly twice, once by a spent ball in the shoulder, and once by a cannon shot, which passed between my legs, just grazing my knee. Herbert and all the rest safe. Abbott and Macy not there.

Most affectionate son
Henry

P.S. Have just heard that Dr. Revere is killed, may not be true.

---

[42] Battle of South Mountain.

RIGHT UP INTO THE FIRE

Camp on Battlefield near Sharpsburg, Md.
Saturday, 20th September 1862.

My dear Father.

I wrote to you a pencil note yesterday just to tell you of my safety etc. We have had a really terrific battle. Our Division was formed in three lines, the first line Gorman's Brigade, the second ours, the third Burns'[43]. The principal musketry firing was done of course by the first line. We were under a heavy fire, however, and suffered from artillery while advancing. We drove the enemy before us with tremendous loss on both sides. The slaughter was horrible especially close to the Hagerstown turnpike where the enemy made a stand by the fences. We finally advanced down a slope, beyond which the enemy held a cornfield and farmhouse with barn and outbuildings, all on an opposite slope. The enemy had cannon planted on the top and constantly swept us down with grape and shrapnell [sic] shell. Our line was advanced close to the first, exposing us to an equal fire, while we could not fire at all because of our first line. The third line was finally advanced close to the second; all this time we stood up and were shot down without being able to reply. Sedgwick and Dana were shot, and we had no one to command the Division. The enemy in the meantime came round on our left and rear, and poured in a terrible crossfire. Sumner came up in time to save the Division and ordered us to march off by the right flank. We did so, but the left Regiments gave way in confusion, the enemy poured in upon our rear, and now the slaughter was worse than anything I have ever seen before. Sumner walked his horse quietly along waving his hand and keeping all steady near him. Although the Regiments in rear of us were rushing by us and through our ranks in the greatest confusion, we kept our Company perfectly steady, did not take a single step faster than the regular marching order, and brought off every man except those killed and wounded, who of course were left. Ricketts' regular Battery and some Regiments drawn up at right angles to us stayed the enemy, and the broken Regiments reformed in the rear. Our Brigade suffered awfully, the 7th Michigan has only four Officers left. The 42nd and 59th New York Regiments broke and gave way most disgracefully, our Regiment fell into perfect order as soon as we halted, and was immediately advanced to the front, and our Company and Company I sent out on picket. We staid on picket till yesterday morning, when we were advanced as skirmishers and found the enemy had evacuated. We had heard them moving all night, and had given constant information of it, and were sure they were retreating. Now we are camped on a part of the battlefield. I hear

---

[43] At the time commanded by General Howard.

that McClellan is pursuing the enemy and that Sumner's Corps is left behind here. We are all quiet and are burying the dead etc.

A Pioneer of our Regiment, by name Bean, wishes me to send word of his safety and good health to a Miss Hill who is at the same water cure that Louisa is at. Will you please ask Louisa to do so?

Of our Regiment Dr. Revere was shot dead on the field while dressing a wounded man's leg. His body was immediately rifled of everything of the least value. Col. Palfrey badly wounded in the shoulder, taken prisoner and released, or rather left behind. Capt. Holmes shot through the neck, and Capt. Hallowell in the arm; Milton slightly in three places. Lt. Col. Revere in the arm. The losses of the Regiments of the Division are enormous.

Shall try to write again soon.

Love to Mother.
Your affectionate son
Henry.

Camp on Battlefield near Sharpsburg, Md.
September 20th 1862.

My dear John.

I have written to Father giving an account of the late battle. I have received 2 letters from you of the 12th, one from Mother of the 8th and one from Mary Ann, and one from Father of the 9th inst, which I have not yet acknowledged.

Yesterday I went over the field, and it was really a most awful sight, the dead were really piled up and lay in rows. The slaughter was more awful than anything I ever read of, for it is not a small field on which the dead lay thickly scattered as if there was a desperate fight at that one place, but a vast extent of country several times as large as the Commons where there is no place which you can stand and not see the field black with dead bodies as far as the eye can reach. Then the wounded gathered into barns etc. are an awful sight. The Rebels let them lay for 2 days without care, and would not allow our men to either take them off, or dress their wounds, as they lay, although their own men robbed them of everything and often stripped their clothes from their bodies. No description I ever read begins to give one an idea of the slaughter and the horrible sights of this battle-field.

We drove them for about 1 ½ miles, and they then repulsed us from the ravine into which we were too hastily advanced. The Artillery was by far the heaviest we have ever yet heard.

The 20th has lost about 150 out of about 400, and it never acted better or better supported its reputation for perfect steadiness. The advance of our Division was a splendid sight. I had 2 very narrow escapes. The spent ball made a hole in my coat and only scraped up the skin a little and made me lame for a day. The cannon ball I saw distinctly. It first hit the branch of a tree, glanced, passed between my legs slightly bruising my knee and leaving a black mark on my pants. It struck the ground behind me and again glanced up and smashed the shoulder of Corporal Campion of my Company. A great many of our men were killed by the grape shot they piled into us from the top of the hill about as far off as from our home to Charles St.

Well, it is over, and we may not see another such battle for many months.

Much obliged to you for your attention to my things. Your recruit has not yet come. James is doing better of late and seems capable of improvement. I should not take an enlisted man for a servant. Col. Lee is well and in command of the Brigade; Genl. Howard of the Division; Capt. Dreher of the Regiment. Herbert is all right and unhurt. So are all other friends except those I mentioned as wounded. We have beaten the enemy badly and they acknowledge it. I should not wonder if the war was now brought to a speedy end.

I have heard that our left was unprotected in consequence of Genl. French taking a wrong road. He should have been there. I have received the pistol etc. and have determined to keep John Bradlee*[s]* and send home the heavy one. Have not seen Lieut. Morse of the 2nd *[Massachusetts]*. They were only near us for 2 days. Saw Caspar and Forbes of the Cavalry the other day. Murphy and Abbott were left sick at Frederick and were not in the battle.

Your affectionate brother
Henry.

RIGHT UP INTO THE FIRE

Camp 20th Regiment on field near
Sharpsburg, Md. Sunday September 21st 1862.

My dear Mother.

I have not written to you for a long time, but I know it was the same thing to write to Father, and I have kept him as well informed of my movements as possible. Even since we left Harrison's Landing, August 16th, I have not had a day or even an hour when I could be sure we were not to get immediate orders to start.

I have written fully to the others about the late battle, and have no more to say. You have no doubt seen full lists of the killed and wounded. I am entirely ignorant of the movements of the Rebels and even of our own troops. I hear however two reports, one that Genl. Sumner's Corps is not to cross into Virginia, but be left to protect Maryland, probably to stay near the Potomac, the other that Dana's Brigade is reported unfit for service. As you know Genl. Dana is wounded; and of our Regiments the 7th Michigan is almost destroyed, the 42nd New York (Tammany) dispersed and almost broken up, and the 19th and 20th *[Massachusetts]* suffered heavily. Col. Hinks mortally wounded, Lt. Colonel Devereux and the 1st Captain wounded, the Lieut. Colonel of the 59th *[New York]* killed, and we have lost Col. Palfrey. Col. Lee is quite broken down and ill. Do not of course needlessly alarm his family, but it is the opinion of all here, that he is quite incapable of enduring the hardships of a camp life longer. He ought to go home and be attended to and nursed. He does not take care of himself at all, and gets wet through, and sleeps without a tent on the wet ground etc., when he could just as well be comfortable and leave such rough duty to younger men. Then you know he is by no means a young man, and, as far as I have observed, an old man cannot endure hardship like a young one. Cold and wet and exposure use up an old man, when a young one gets over anything after a few hours of sleep and a good breakfast. The reason why some old men do flourish so out here is that they take things easily and take great care of themselves, like old Sumner for instance. So as we are very short of Officers, and the Regiments greatly reduced in the number of men, we shall probably be left to lie still and recruit for a time.

I am delighted to find Mr. Willard is Major. I have tried to see him but have been as yet unable. Capt. Macy saw him, and he enquired particularly for me.

If you have an opportunity please send me 2 pairs of my blue woolen socks. I like them rather better than the Government socks, and they wear better.

We are now camped on a part of the battlefield, and the trees are marked with shot and often split by balls and shells. Most of the dead are now buried, but large numbers of horses still remain and pollute the air. The farmers about here have shown the greatest patriotism and kindness.

They came on the field the day after the battle and took great quantities of the wounded to their own houses to nurse and attend to them. I hear that in the midst of the battle a farmer brought 5 horses to one of our batteries from his own barn, and generously gave them to supply the place of those killed. Herbert Mason was particularly exposed, as he was on the left. He lost all his non-commissioned Officers, and half of his men. Our Division lost about one half. A very good man of my Company, named Riley, was killed instantly. He was poor, and worked in a foundry in Chelsea, where he has a wife and 7 children. They may possibly be in want. Perhaps you could visit them when you make your charitable rounds.

James does very well now, and I shall no doubt keep him.

Love to Mary Ann and all. I shall try to write to her next.

Your affectionate son
Henry.

Camp 20th Regiment, Bolivar Heights, Va.
September 23rd 1862.

My dear John.

I answered your two last letters and have only to tell you that we marched here yesterday and forded the river. Sumner's Corps is here and he in command.

I enclose a letter for Mary Ann. I have sent home by Mr. Folsom, who was kind enough to take charge of it, a bundle containing my heavy revolver, cartridge boxes, ammunition etc., some books I have done with, some private papers, a knife, etc. Please have "Barchester Towers" bound, if you think it is worth it, and "Bleak House" too, when I send home the other volumes which Herbert is now reading.

Please have new plates put in the knife and send it to me when you have a chance. Let the pistol be cleaned, oiled and put away, and the fixed ammunition kept for it. Give the private letters to Mary Ann to put in my box. As I know you like to keep some relics of a battle field, I send a piece of shell and a grape shot I picked up. It will give you some idea of what sort of a buzzing we had about our ears. Please tell me if you ever got my Buffalo skins sent home last spring? I have forgotten whether or not it went safely. Please send me by mail $6.00 in U.S. ones, and $4.00 in postage stamp change. I have nothing smaller than $5.00 and find great trouble in making change. Charge the $10.00 to my account. By the way, can you not tell me roughly about how much you have charged to me? I feel sure I must have a considerable balance on hand, but would very much like to know how much.

We ought to be paid every day now, and when we are, I shall send home another $100.00. Herbert is very much obliged to you for attending to a tent for him. I advised him to wait till mine came, and see how he liked it, but he read my description and felt sure it would answer. I hope it is of white Rubber, that is if both are equally strong. Very likely you will find some light lantern all made which will be quite as light and compact as the one I described. If so, buy it instead. If the tent is what I expect it will be, it will be invaluable. Especially at this season, it is important to keep dry at night. The rubber coat will be very useful, I know. I hope the boots will not give you trouble. If Rice has saved my measure it is all right. Do not let the soles be of extravagant thickness, as was formerly the fashion for "Army Shoes".

I have not seen the 2nd Mass. since we were at Rockland, but hope, if we are near them again, to get acquainted with Capt. Morse. The 2nd is now at Sandy Hook about 6 miles from here, across the river.

I am at present quite lame from a boil which has selected a very unfortunate position. It is exactly on the cord or tendon which connects the extremity of the heel with the calf of the leg. It is very small, however, and will no doubt be well in a couple of days.

You never tell me how business matters and the estates are getting on, and whether the general affairs of the family are in a flourishing state. Please do tell me.

I suppose you now have quite an income from law. Write soon.

Your affectionate brother
Henry.

P.S. The Colonel's man, George, desires respects.

RIGHT UP INTO THE FIRE

Camp 20th Regiment Mass. Volunteers
Bolivar Heights, Va. September 26th 1862.
Friday.

My dear Father.

I have received no letters from home since I wrote last to you from this camp. We are still quietly recruiting ourselves, drilling our new men and getting things generally to rights.

Col. Lee is, as you know, in command of the Brigade, and today he detailed me to act as Aide-de-Camp. Lieuts. Hallowell and Milton the two regular Aides of Genl. Dana being away ill. I am to remain "during the absence of Lt. Milton". The Colonel asked me to share his tent, and I am now with him. He has quite a cold yet and is not well, but I hope he will soon improve. I of course get a horse by this arrangement, and many other comforts. It is of course only temporary.

We are camped on the brow of the hill, the air is very pure and healthy, and I think I never saw a better place for one's health. If you can find a recruit or Officer coming on, I should be very glad if you would send me my buffalo skin. By the time it gets here the nights will be cold enough for it.

I am perfectly well. Best love to Mother. Please thank sister Mary for her letter and say I intend to write very soon. By the way, I believe I have not acknowledged yours of the 20th enclosing sister Mary's letter.

You seem to overestimate the battle of Sunday[44] compared with that of Wednesday the 17th. Sunday's fight was a decided victory, but the battle of the 17th was the greatest battle ever fought on this continent and the loss fearful. Our Corps of about 15,000 men lost between 5000 and 6000, our Division more in proportion and our Brigade the most of any in the Division although it is the smallest. Col. Lee says except at Ball's Bluff he never was under such a fire. It seems to me an awful responsibility rests somewhere. The 2nd and 3rd lines were advanced under the heaviest fire for no purpose, and the left flank left entirely exposed. Had the 3rd line covered the left, the 2nd been placed on the open field and ordered to lie down and the first kept the enemy at bay by skirmishers till a battery could have been brought to bear on the enemy's position, I think things might have resulted differently, and lives saved. However it is easy to criticise after all is over.

Col. Lee sends his respects.

Your affectionate son
Henry.

---

[44] Battle of South Mountain.

RIGHT UP INTO THE FIRE

Head Quarters, 3rd Brigade
Bolivar Heights, Va. September 27th 1862.

My dear John.

I received your letter (written by Mary Ann) last evening. I am *very sorry* your eyes are so weak. I know what a hopeless feeling one has, when one begins to find out that there is a settled weakness of the eyes. It seems as if everything was doubtful, and you are not sure what you are able to do. I hope you are able to read this letter. If anybody reads it to you, let it be only Mary Ann, for I shall write to you on the next page what I do not wish every one to know. I am now with the Colonel, and while he is here, I shall stay and do everything for him I can. But he ought to resign *immediately*. The fact is he is completely broken down and is not fit for duty. He has now got the chills and fever (not badly), the diarrhoea, and a cough. It is beautiful weather but cold at night, and I know he suffers from it, yet he still keeps about and generally is in good spirits. Should we have one week of active service, I know he would completely break down. You know he is pretty old and not of a very strong constitution. He will not hear of getting a leave of absence, and says if he cannot do full duty, he had better do none and leave the service.

Now we are quiet and no immediate prospect of an advance. We have just been through a short but active campaign, and have done well, and this is exactly the time for Col. Lee to resign. There would be time to fill his place and arrange things before we are again called into the field. He has done his duty well by the Regiment. He has been in every battle and escaped unhurt. He would retire now most honorably. If he stays and breaks down when we are in active service, it may not be so well for him or for us. I write this of course for your private eye or ear.

Capt. Leach of Dana's staff, a very able, clear headed man, is here, and Col. Lee places great trust in him, and he manages Brigade matters almost entirely. He has told me privately that he probably will soon get an order to report to Genl. Dana in Washington, and wishes some one to get into the harness here before he leaves. He first asked Herbert but he could not leave his Company, and then (at the Colonel's request) he asked me to come to Head Quarters. Under any other circumstances I should have refused, but while I feel I can be of any use to the Colonel, I shall remain. I shall not leave the old Regiment for any bed of feathers in a Staff. I intend to stand by the 20th as long as we both last, but for the present, while Col. Lee is here, I shall be here.

Do not let all this go far. I write in confidence to you. I think Col. Lee will resign before a month has passed. This is only my opinion.

Well, to answer your letter. Lieut. Beckwith was formerly a Sergeant, and was promoted 2nd Lieutenant a few months ago. He is of the kind Capt. Shepard describes as a "wet rag". No relation to Capt. Beckwith as far as I know.

As to the Strategy: Everyone thinks and I think that old Sumner made a great mistake in dashing Sedgwick's Division so recklessly against the very key of the enemy's position. We never should have gone down into that ravine, where the dead were piled closer than in the orchard at Waterloo. We lost between 2 and 3000 men there out of about 6000, all in 2 hours or so. It was a slaughter pen. I think that our 3rd line should have been held far back, our first advanced to the edge of the valley and skirmishers sent down, and our 2nd line taken to the left to hold that part of the field until a connection could be made with French on the left. Then batteries should have been advanced and used against the enemy in the Cornfield, house, barn, etc. Had this been done and we gained the elevated land beyond the house, then Sumner's whole Corps could have advanced and driven everything before them as they did on the open land this side of the ravine. Then the whole of the enemy's left would have been turned and our guns could have been placed on a hill sweeping the whole right of the enemy, and Burnside would have had an easy victory, and I do not see how the Rebel Army could have been saved. Sumner was too impetuous and too sure of victory. However, you underestimate our success. With the exception of this ravine or valley we gained possession of the whole field and it was a most decided advantage to us. It forced the enemy to retreat. Then none of you seem to appreciate what a tremendous battle it was. Fair Oaks, White Oak swamp, Malvern Hill and the others do not compare with it. It was from daylight till dark, and most obstinately fought, and at very close quarters. As you see the comparative loss in our Corps, Division, Brigade, and Regiment greatly exceeds that of the British at Waterloo, or the Alma, or of the French at Magenta and Solferino.

It was the first time I ever appreciated what I have often read of "men mowed down in rows like corn", but it was so. When they came in on our left and rear the fire was awful. I was once covered with stones and dirt cast up by a shell striking close to me, and the trees of the wood were crackling as if on fire. Then, when the New York and Pennsylvania troops were rushing by us and through us like sheep, our Regiment showed its discipline, and my Company did not take one step at double quick, but marched out at shouldered arms without the loss of one man, except those left dead and wounded on the field.

If you want to know more of the battle, you must ask questions, and I will try to answer them. I think McClellan was right in keeping troops near Washington. How did he know the whole rebel force was here? The day after the battle he got a despatch from Halleck, telling him this fact. It would have been wrong to leave Washington in the *slightest danger*. That should be protected at *any* cost.

I am sorry you found so much trouble with the tents. Please also send me from my trunk the pair of dark blue pants I sent back, also 1 pair woolen ribbed drawers. Let straps (for riding) be put on the pants, to unbutton, of course.

RIGHT UP INTO THE FIRE

Probably the Express will soon run to Harper's Ferry. Grafton's Regiment (the 2nd Mass.) is not with us, but at Sandy Hook, 6 miles off. I can send there easily, however. Please send me $1.00 worth letter stamps. I have none at all now. I hear poor *Abbott is very ill indeed.* I am exceedingly sorry for him. Glad you are well. Mary Ann must not be sickly. Make her ride on horseback, and walk etc. Love to all.

Your affectionate brother
Henry.

P.S. Direct in future "Lieut. Ropes, Head Quarters, Dana's Brigade.

H. R.

Head Quarters, Bolivar Heights,
September 30th 1862.

My dear John.

I have not got letters from home for several days, and have nothing to write to you about. I am still quietly living along here at Head Quarters. I have almost nothing to do. Col. Lee is better, but still rather feeble and quite unable to endure exposure, should he be called upon to do so. I have just heard of the death of Robert Ives, aide to Genl. Rodman in the late action. It will of course be a dreadful blow to his parents, especially his Mother.

I have thought for a day or two what a good thing it would be for you to come out here and spend a few days. You could be perfectly comfortable at some house in the town here, close to us, and you could ride over from here to the battle-field and get a most excellent idea of the battle.

Then of course it would be delightful to me to see you again and talk out everything and tell you anything about the battles etc. You could probably get a pass at Washington which would take you round everywhere. If you came now you would be a good deal here at Head Quarters, and would see Col. Hall of the 7th *[Michigan]*, Col. Sully and others. Col. Sully is a great man, and is very often here, and I know you would enjoy hearing him tell of what he saw and did. You get more military knowledge in ten minutes out of him, than in reading a book. He is about as truly jolly a man as you ever saw. Then you would see and perhaps get acquainted with Sumner, Howard and others. I know you would greatly enjoy the trip, and I need not say how delighted beyond measure I should be to see you. I have plenty of time now and the use of a horse, and you would be very comfortable.

Do think seriously of this.

Your affectionate brother
Henry.

Headquarters Bolivar Heights, Va.
October 1st 1862.

My dear Father.

I received yesterday your two letters of September 26th and one from Mother of the 25th. Thank you very much for again sending me so many comforts and luxuries.

I have not yet received the two boxes sent on with Lt. Abbott, the parcel of fly netting you sent nor the box by Lt. Grafton. The two first were sent last July or August and probably went to Harrison's Landg. In a very few days the Express Company expect to open a depot here, and then I shall probably receive all. When we were at Harrison's Landing you wrote to me that you had sent through Mr. Alford, Agent of the American Tract Society $10.00 worth of "Goodies". Perhaps they were for the sick, I am not sure, but at any rate I never got them. Mr. Alford brought some tracts to the Regiment, and gave some Jams, Crackers etc. to the Hospital of the Regiment, but if I remember correctly your donation was after this.

You say you fear letters miscarry. Please tell me if you received lately a letter from me containing $4.00 in Mass. Banks to be changed for U.S. notes. I sent such a letter. I believe I am right about the boxes etc. I give the list as I expect to get them. Please tell me if it is right.

Boxes to be sent to me.

1 box Ale etc. by Adams Express
1 box Ginger Mrs. Dr. Jeffries, etc. by Adams Express
1 parcel Netting by Adams Express

RIGHT UP INTO THE FIRE

1 supply Goodies American Tract Society
1 box Brandy etc. Lt. Grafton.

These I have received notice of and expect.

Please tell Mother that I long ago sent my thanks to Cousin Kitty for the sermons. I have written for some letter stamps. They are very scarce here now.

I think you underestimate our loss. Our Brigade lost most heavily of all. The day after the battle Col. Lee took command, and it then numbered 960 men for 5 Regiments. He reported officially a loss in all of almost 900 men. Our Corps of about 13,000 or 14,000 men lost between 5000 and 6000. I think our entire loss must be 12,000 to 14,000.

We are all quiet here and no news.

Your affectionate son
Henry.

Head Quarters, Bolivar Heights,
October 5th 1862.

My dear John.

I have before me your two letters received October 3rd through Lieut. Wilkins, with $10.00 enclosed. Much obliged to you for sending them. I am very sorry your eyes are still troublesome, and very much obliged to you for sending on my things by Express. I shall probably get everything together now.

As to the battle, I cannot begin to give you a good idea of things by a letter, you must come on and have a talk and see the ground yourself. The enemy had an immense advantage of position. As to an attack on the next day, I can only refer you to the list of losses, especially to the loss of General Officers, which was tremendous and which would have greatly crippled us in an offensive movement. A shattered Army can often hold an old position when to attack would have been impossible. It took the whole of Thursday to re-arrange the Army, to place the newly-arrived troops and to assign the different Generals etc. As to the enemy's crossing, why the water is so low, even here, that we could march across in line of battle and not wet our knees. They could cross anywhere, and in any number of columns. As to your ideas of the rapidity with which troops can be moved and formed, I can only say that you have as yet no conception of the vastness of great movements, and the time it takes.

RIGHT UP INTO THE FIRE

Why, suppose Sumner's Corps to be drawn up in line of battle on the Mill Dam, opposite our house, fronting Cambridge bridge, and the right resting at the corner of Charles and Beacon Streets, and you find it necessary to change front so as to make a line of battle on Charles Street, the right resting on the New Jail, and fronting toward Brookline and Longwood. It would take from day-break till 11 o'clock for the men to march steadily by together with the batteries and the necessary Ammunition, wagons and Ambulances, without any halt or delay of any kind beyond the absolutely necessary halts for rests. I feel perfectly unable to describe to you what is so perfectly plain to me, for we seem to have no starting point.

You write of this and that delay and length of time employed etc. etc., and it seems to me perfectly natural that such should have been the case. I can only describe it by an example, as if one should expatiate on the immense time, viz.: one year employed by the earth in going only once round the sun. Yet we know how tremendous is the earth's speed although the daily change of climate etc. is imperceptible to us. Or as if I should wonder at the long time, say several months, taken up in deciding a most important and difficult case of law and wonder why enough lawyers were not employed to do it up in a morning.

However, besides all this I acknowledge that the action of some Officers high in command so generally acknowledged to have been reckless, to say the least; and if I could have a talk with you I think I could explain to your satisfaction why McClellan's *most admirable* plans were not successfully carried out. I do not care to write everything. Of course, do not on *any consideration* repeat this or give my authority for the statement. I write in perfect confidence.

I have never seen Walcott. Macy was sent to Washington to arm and equip the recruits arrived there, a few days before the battle. He was unable to get up till the next day. He, however, heard the tremendous fire, 30 miles off, at Rockland, and hurried on as fast as his poor broken down horse could go. He said it was awful to him, the suspense and his entire ignorance of how the day was going and where we were, and all day long from dawn till night the tremendous roaring of Artillery. He met a man riding back from the field and hailed him: "Is Sumner's Corps in?" Answer: "In! Yes, in all over." He said he probably suffered more by suspense and anxiety, than if he had been wounded. As to whether the battle was fought well, I should say most undoubtedly yes. Both parties closed up and took and gave the most destructive fire at very short range, and both parties remained under fire from batteries at short range, till almost destroyed. I doubt if soldierly qualities were ever better displayed. I believe I have now answered everything in reference to the battle that I feel at liberty to commit to writing. I do not know whether anything I have written commends itself to your judgment or not, but I wish here to repeat in the most positive and emphatic manner that the English language can express, that it is my earnest wish that no part whatever of this letter, or of any subsequent or former letters be in any way ever printed, published or proclaimed. I am and always shall be delighted to write to you and to my relatives and friends generally, about everything of interest that I see here, and to answer any questions whatever respecting battles, etc., but I cannot bear the idea that my letters should be printed or used in any way but the way in which I write them to be used, to viz.: for you to read, and if they wish it, for any others of the family, or of our familiar friends to whom you may choose to show them. Excepting always the one case where my letters state facts in reference to the safety etc. of Officers and others whose friends may be anxious about them.

I hope you will not think I have written too much on this point, for I wish to make it perfectly clear. All well here. Mrs. Lee came yesterday P.M. quite unexpectedly, and has lodgings in the town. She looks perfectly well. Colonel better. Love to all.

Your affectionate brother
Henry.

Head Quarters, 3rd Brigade
Bolivar Heights, Va.
October 6th 1862.

My dear Father.

I received last night by Express the two boxes you sent on by Lt. Abbott to Harrison's Landing, and the bundle of fly netting. The damage to the contents of the boxes was less than I had expected., considering they had been so long on the way and had been carried once to Harrison's Landing and then back, and been exposed to so great heat. The box of Ale was broken, and two bottles taken out, and one broken, but I thought it very fortunate that I got 9 bottles safe out of 12. In the other box the Lemons of course were rotten. One bottle of Cherry Cordial was broken, and the top of the Ginger preserve was loose so the liquid part of the contents of the jar had soaked into about everything that would absorb it. The shirts can easily be washed, and nothing was spoiled but the Sedlitz Powders, which I do not now need. The ginger bread was quite dry, but of course rather stale. The rest of the Cordial, the Brandy, Bitters, Syrup, Sugar, Tea, Figs etc. etc. were all safe and in good condition and are most acceptable. I assure you I shall use them all most carefully and shall greatly enjoy them. I expect the other things by Express in a day or two.

Mrs. Lee is here now at Head Quarters with the Colonel, and today is to dine here at the Mess. It is cool today, and windy, and seems quite like Autumn. There is nothing stirring, and no prospect of a move, and everybody is getting settled down into as comfortable quarters as they can get.

I enclose a note for Mrs. Dr. Jeffries, thanking her for her kind present of Ginger preserve. It is in perfect condition, very nice indeed.

Your affectionate son
Henry.

Head Quarters Bolivar Heights
October 9th 1862.

My dear Mother.

I was delighted to meet John at the Cars yesterday afternoon, and to find him well. He is enjoying himself very much, and today has gone over to the 2nd Mass. with Lieutenants Mason and Whittier. Robby Lee was with him, and is now with his mother at her lodgings in the town. His parents were delighted to see him as you may suppose. Mrs. Lee and Robby have been to ride with Capt. Le Duc this morning and seen everything to be seen here. The Colonel is on a Court Martial today. John expects to visit the battle field with me tomorrow. I am very much obliged for the books, and shall write and thank all soon. John has other things for me which have not arrived yet, but will be here this P.M. I received from him 3 letters, one from you, one from Louisa and one from Mary Ann. Shall answer all soon.

Mrs. Lee is very well and the Colonel about the same. Mrs. Lee talks of returning with John and Robert.

Love to all.

Your affectionate son
Henry.

RIGHT UP INTO THE FIRE

Camp 20th, October 15th 1862
Wednesday

My dear Father.

I am trying to induce John to remain a day or two longer, and have no doubt I shall succeed. He unfortunately left his valise in Washington, and ought to wait here till it is sent to him. I have now returned to the Regiment as Lt. Milton of the Staff (whose place I took) has got home from Boston, and I can make John perfectly comfortable here. I think he really owes me a visit of 2 weeks at least, and hope he will stay. His eyes will be much benefitted by the rest and change of occupation etc. We went day before yesterday to Antietam, and saw the whole field. We passed the night at Keedysville very comfortably. Robby Lee went with us, and he and John have secured quantities of bullets, shells etc. for relics.

You asked once about letters miscarrying. A thief has been discovered here, at Genl. Howard's Head Quarters, who has for some time robbed the mails. I hope all letters will in future go safely. Best love to all. Have received no letters for 3 days. John will probably visit John Gray and the 2nd Regiment today.

Your affectionate son
Henry.

Camp 20th Regiment, Bolivar Heights
October 18th Saturday (11 A.M.) 1862.

Dear John.

I returned about an hour ago from the expedition on which I started just after I bade you good bye. We drove in a small force of Rebels and occupied Charlestown, and left it at noon yesterday, because a large force of Rebels were approaching. Porter, I hear, crossed above, and we heard his guns. Our Regiment, of course, was in the advance as much as possible and picketing the whole time. No Infantry fighting. The usual amount of hard marching and exposure. The affair very well managed, and on the whole as little disagreeable as is possible for these most unpleasant of all military movements. No news.

I shall send your pipe by Col. Revere's servant who leaves in a few days for Boston. I enclose the Power of Attorney. Nothing yet of the boxes or valise.

No letters from home. Write soon and tell me about the boxes, tent, etc., and if the box is lost please order a duplicate copy immediately. I hope you had a pleasant journey. John Gray came to see you the day you left, thereby proving that you ought to have staid a week longer, at least.

Please ask Nason if he can make me a cape for my overcoat, and if he wants the measure. There must be 5 button holes, one in the middle, behind. Let the cape be only long enough to reach the waist, that is about ½ way between wrist and elbow. Cape must nearly match in color, of course. Please send on some time when you have a chance 1 lb. best *green* tea. I am told it is very good for a night of picket or guard, and very nice. I hope you will get your valise all right. Give them all my love at home, and tell them to write. I shall acknowledge the receipt of the boxes etc., when I get them.

Please let me know (if convenient) whether Mrs. Dr. Jeffries ever got my note of thanks for the Ginger. I fear very many letters have miscarried of late, for a letter thief has been found at Division Head Quarters. Genl. Hancock is a good Officer, careful and wide awake. McClellan came up to Charlestown day before yesterday. We took 1 gun, some prisoners and 3000 bushels wheat, which last were carried back by a special train sent up from the ferry.

All friends here desire regards. I hear another expedition goes out somewhere today.

Your affectionate brother
Henry.

20th Regiment, Sunday,
19th October 1862.

Dear John.

I have just got your letter dated Baltimore 16th and am delighted to know that you found your valise. I have not yet got the bundle. I wrote you of our safe return etc. Had you staid one day more you might have seen John Gray and a battle, and then driven over to Charlestown with Genl. McClellan, and finally got to Washington and home as soon as you now will. But you would none of our counsel and advice, and hape reapened the bitter fruits. I want my Buffalo and the blanket *awfully*. It is horribly cold at night, although so warm in the daytime that we enjoy a bath in the river.

A number of us want to get quite a supply of preserved meats, fruits, pickles, etc. etc. from Boston, better than those we get here. Can you call at W. K. Lewis & Co., or Davis Underwood & Co.[45] (whichever is the better and cheaper) and get one of their printed catalogues and make some enquiries as to price etc. in case we should order a quantity to be sent on by Express.

I am *perfectly disgusted* with my position here. That little cocky fool, Curtis, is my First Lieutenant. I think this is shameful considering I have been more with the Regiment and seen more service and been in more battles than *any* Lieutenant in the Regiment, 1st or 2nd. I think now Capt. Shepard is acting Major I *deserve* to have command of my Company. I have spoken to the Colonel about it, and I think he will make some change in the assignment of Officers, but he of course does not see it in the same light I do. My friends here, Herbert, Macy, and Milton *all* say it is abominable to treat me so, etc. However, I shall hope for the best and at present of course I must only endure. Time generally brings all right.

Your affectionate brother
Henry.

Camp 20th Regiment
Bolivar, October 20th 1862.

My dear Father.

I received yesterday your letter of September 30th enclosing one from Mary Ann of September 20th, which were delayed by being sent to the 20th Maine Regiment. The Captain of Company K, 20th Maine sent them to me. Perhaps the direction in Mary Ann's handwriting was not quite clear enough. The best and surest direction to me is "Lt. Ropes, 20th Regiment Mass. Volunteers, Washington, D.C." This is enough and is always right. You speak in your letter of Lt. Robert Ives' death which was indeed very sad. I wrote about it at the time. I observed in the paper the death of Stephen Codman. So he is gone. I shall no doubt hear from you about his death. I do not know what to make of the Mail now for I get almost no letters. I have as yet been unable to get anything from the

---

[45] Ropes is possibly referring to William Underwood & Co.

Express Office, although they acknowledge they have one box for me.

I see by your letter (of September 30th) that you have received my letter asking for the buffalo skin and I dare say it is already sent on. We have had warm weather the last few days, but a week or so ago we really suffered.

Col. Lee has been quite ill owing I think to his great exposure during the reconnaissance, but he is much better now. Yesterday a rumor was current of his death. I do not know whether any newspaper correspondent, anxious for an item of news has taken it up or not, but for fear Mrs. Lee should hear of it, I wrote to her (care of Mr. Hare, Chestnut Hill, Philadelphia) and explained how the Colonel was. I did not telegraph for fear the mere reception of a dispatch would alarm her, and induce her to come on. Colonel was much better yesterday and nicely today. He is in a comfortable house in the town.

I received the pistol etc. with a letter from Capt. Cabot. Grafton was obliged to send the box back, but I expect it by Express. I believe I received a letter or two from him. Best love to mother. Enclosed letter for Mary Ann.

Your affectionate son
Henry.

Camp 20th Regiment, Bolivar
October 21st 1862.

My dear Mother.

Thank you for yours of the 4th received before John arrived. He is now with you, I hope, and will do instead of any letters from me.

I have just received Father's of the 16th October. Please tell him I never received the $2.00 in change he sent, but have no doubt that that letter, with many others, were taken from the mail bag at Head Quarters, where a mail thief has been discovered.

I hear there is a box for me at the Express Office. I suppose this is the one John left containing the much needed blanket. Please let there be no delay about sending on the Buffalo skin I wrote for.

There are rumors of an advance today, but I hear we are to garrison this place. Best love to Father and all. Enclosed letter to Mary Ann.

Your affectionate son
Henry.

RIGHT UP INTO THE FIRE

Thank you very much for the books John brought, the small ones of which (Prayers, Sermons, etc.) I have just got. They will be very useful. Also the other things, peas etc.

Your affectionate
Henry.

20th Regiment Bolivar
21st October 1862.

Dear John.

We very likely shall advance soon. Everything looks like it. We of course may not go, but Milton (who generally knows) says we shall. It is awfully cold and I have suffered very much for want of warm clothing for the night. I *most earnestly* await the arrival of the box containing knapsack etc. Please send on as soon as you can by Express 2 very large and warm blankets, or 3 if you cannot find any very large and warm. Also another pair of my thick ribbed drawers, another woolen shirt, 2 moderately thick undershirts, and 3 pairs blue woolen socks. All these in addition to the Buffalo skin and the other things I have written for. Also send the extra pair dark blue pants left in the large trunk. As to the blankets, any white ones would do as well. Better get coarse ones, only warmth wanted.

If we march I shall need money, for we shall not get paid. Please, therefore, send me by mail $25.00 say $10.00 first, then $5.00 at a time. Send, if possible, U.S. ones and small change.

Herbert is much obliged for the contents of the bundle, and desires you to tell his father he has received them.

On the whole, better send also the thick dress coat sent home in my trunk from Harrison's Landing. These things cannot reach me before we are in winter quarters, and then I shall need everything.

No news. I hope we shall be settled soon.

Your affectionate brother
Henry.

Enclosed letter for Louisa.

RIGHT UP INTO THE FIRE

Camp 20th Regiment Bolivar
October 28th 1862.

My dear John.

I have received yours of the 24th and am delighted you had such a pleasant trip home, and that you have received the Power of Attorney, etc. The man by whom I intend to send your pipe has sprained his ankle and will not go for several days. I shall send probably a small parcel by then. I shall enquire today for the trunk. All the Expresses converge into Adams & Co. here.

We have had a very heavy rain and I find that my rubber tent lets in water in the seams which fasten the canvas to the top of the tent. I never saw Rubber goods before in which the seams were left in this way. Any man could see at a glance that water would leak in. Always the seams should be covered with the India Rubber in the gum state and allowed to harden. I shall cover the seams with wax or tallow.

Do not let the new tent be made in this way. Let every part be waterproof. If it is not too late let the back be made whole in one piece with a hole for the ridge pole. If necessary to bring it within weight, reduce the size to 5 ft. 2 inches each way, instead of 5 ft. 6 inches. If still Rubber cloth will be too heavy, let the tent be made of common cotton or linen cloth, whichever is lighter, and more waterproof. Let the back be whole not divided. In every respect like the rubber tent would be.

I cannot but think $20.00 an enormous price for the tent I have, but I suppose one must pay for experiments. As it has turned out I have already had $20.00 worth out of it. Whenever you send on a box put in a bottle of dark Brandy (Hennessey's) such as you sent lately. Boxes are often delayed and the Brandy rarely comes amiss.

Curtis is changed to Company I and I now command K, and we are now full of business. Regular drills and Company duties well occupy the time.

Last night we had ½ inch of Ice. Rather tough for shelter tents and an insufficient supply of blankets. Everything is comfortable now with this exception. Send me some more stamps. I never got those you sent nor the legal letter nor the $2.00 (or $4.00) Father sent. Send the $25.00 I wrote for as soon as possible.

Captains Macy and Shepard, Herbert, Murphy, Milton, and others send kind regards, etc.

Your affectionate brother
Henry.

RIGHT UP INTO THE FIRE

Camp 20th Regiment, Bolivar, Va.
October 30th 1862.

My dear Father.

I got the trunk by Express day before yesterday, all right containing buffalo, 2 blue blankets, knapsack, India Rubber Blanket, 2 bottles wine, gingerbread, Coffee, Tea, Sugar, Lantern, Cup, Saucer, plate, hatchet, ditto and some Cherry Cordial for Herbert, and I believe everything I sent for.

You can hardly imagine how much more comfortable these things have made me. Everything is of the best, and exactly what I wanted. The buffalo and the Blankets are very great comforts especially. There is still a box at the Office for me which they cannot find yet but which I suppose is the one sent by Grafton, containing Brandy, Tea, Sugar etc. It will no doubt turn up soon, just when most needed. There is a general movement going on. Hancock moves today. Gorman's Brigade was under marching orders at 5 A.M. and we are ordered to prepare 3 days rations. We may follow, where, I cannot tell. Col. Lee left yesterday for Washington on a leave of absence. He certainly needs it. Capt. Le Duc accompanied him. In consequence of the burning of some freight cars, the trains have been delayed on the other side of the river, and he was obliged to pass the night in Knoxville. Mrs. Lee came on from Washington yesterday afternoon, hearing that the Colonel was ill. She must have passed him on the way, as she came in the same train he went back in. She passed the night at the Colonel's old quarters, and returned to Washington this morning, by the early train. I saw her off at 5 A.M. in Capt. Le Duc's ambulance under charge of Mr. Bronson, Capt. Le Duc's brother-in-law, who was to see her safely into the cars. I could not go because we might be ordered to move at any moment. Mrs. Lee looks very well. Colonel went off without trouble, a little weak, but decidedly improving. The Regiment is gone out on picket, but I was obliged to remain as I am Judge Advocate of a General Court Martial here. I expect to get through today. I enclose a short note for Mother. Please excuse this scrap of paper, for we are all out of paper now.

As to our move, no one knows anything, but it is thought we are only to be held in readiness, or moved a little forward to be near at hand. At any rate 135,000 men have preceded us, so it is about impossible we shall see any service. I shall write when I can, but may of course be unable to do so for some days.

Your affectionate son
Henry.

RIGHT UP INTO THE FIRE

20th Regiment, October 30th 1862.

Dear Mother.

Everything came safely in the trunk but the saucer which was broken. Thank you very much for the Gingerbread (which is delicious) and all the other nice things. I am now perfectly comfortable, and ready to stay or go as it may happen. My new knapsack is perfect. I dare say you never use the old set of which you sent me the cup etc. If so, will you please send when next a box comes another small cup and plate, and 2 saucers? Also (if not in use) the little covered dish, I remember, of that sauce set. It would be very useful for me. By the time these get on I shall be in some permanent place of abode I suppose.

Mrs. Lee was here last night as I wrote to Father. She will probably join the Colonel today at Washington. My new blankets are splendid ones, and I am now perfectly protected.

Your affectionate son
Henry.

20th Regiment on the march near
Bloomfield, Va. November 3rd 1862 Monday.

My dear Father.

We left Bolivar on Thursday last (30th Oct.), halted Friday and marched Saturday and yesterday to this place, some Artillery in the front. All quiet today. I received the knapsack etc. in time for this march and I am in consequence more comfortable than I ever have been on a march. I have received a great many letters, viz.: yours of September 30th giving an account of Lt. Ives' death and alluding to the death of Mr. Lodge and Dr. Adams' daughter; and of the 24th October about John's visit and loss of valise etc.; Mother's of October 20th and 27th , Mary Ann's of October 13th, 28th and 29th and John's 2 of the 27th enclosing $13.00 in U.S. two's and 50 Cent Stamps. Please thank all. You speak of a large letter from abroad. I have received none but perhaps you mistook one from Henry Jeffries for a foreign letter.

The blankets etc. were all of most excellent quality and exactly what I wanted.

I am very comfortable indeed and have quite enjoyed the march thus far. Please say to John I have no doubt Linen or Cotton will do for the Tent, and that he had better not hesitate to reduce the *size* to save weight. Very light material is quite strong enough.

John's new blankets will be very useful in the winter and will arrive quite as soon as I want them. Enclosed a note for Mary Ann.

My love to all. I cannot write often now, and cannot write to Frank for some time probably.

Your affectionate son
Henry.

20th Regiment, near Paris, Va.
November 5th 1862.

My dear John.

We have now been nearly a week on the march, beautiful weather, though cool at night, and a very beautiful country to travel through. We have as usual been worked to the advance and been often on picket, and day before yesterday we drew up to support a battery, loaded and primed, and there was considerable Artillery on our right, but we were not engaged. The enemy seems to be retreating and we advancing on every road. I have appreciated fully the value of the Buffalo, in which I have slept comfortably every night, although my rubber blanket has often been covered with ice, from the dew frozen. I hope you will succeed in getting a light and dry tent. I wonder if it would be possible to get oiled silk, a coarse kind, but strong and light. I should think this would be excellent, if not too expensive. However, I have no doubt you will get the best thing.

I have written to you of the disposition of the things that came in Mr. Folsom's box. I shall try to send home very soon several books etc. by Express. Do not let them send out any more solid books till we come to some stopping place. I always like some small books to carry, but as I have on the whole little time to read, I prefer to read only the most important books. I have not yet read ½ the best novels, histories and books of poetry and therefore do not care to have any but such standard books sent out. I should very much like a "Tauchnitz" Edition of Scott's Poems (or a part of them), or (if possible) a volume of Napier's Peninsular

War, or some good history of Cromwell. I am rather poorly posted on both these important epochs. I have heard of a "Camp Kettle" sold at home, consisting of an iron pot of moderate size, inside of which plates, cups, a frying pan etc. fit. If you happen to see such a thing, please let me know and tell me the *size* and contents.

As to the delay in my letters, it may have been partly owing to the direction. No need of putting on "Dana's Brigade", as the letters are taken by a Division mail carrier, who knows every Regiment in this Division, and does not leave letters at the different Brigade Head Quarters. Better always direct "Lieut. Ropes, 20th Mass. Regt. 2nd Corps, 2nd Division, Washington, D.C." I have no doubt "Washington D.C." is generally enough, but I often get letters thus directed endorsed in pencil "Sedgwick". Perhaps "Sumner's Corps, Sedgwick's Division" is better than the number.

But /Best/ love to all. Thanks for the $13.00 received all right. The people about here are real Rebels and often refuse to sell anything for our money. Gold and Silver however are most eagerly sought after. Can you send me a few gold dollars in a letter? I dare say they would go a great way here although they may cost at home $1.20. Some 5 and 10 ¢ pieces of silver would be very convenient. You must tell all to excuse my not writing while on the march, it is very difficult. The people here are mad for tea and coffee, and will give you a sheep for a pound or two of either.

Your affectionate brother
Henry.

Camp 20th Regiment near Rectortown, Va.
November 7th 1862.

My dear Mother.

You see by the date of this letter that we are mowing still down the valley towards Manassas. We marched to this place from Paris yesterday. It is very cold and today a driving N.E. Snowstorm, very like home. We have only shelter tents, a miserable protection and I have no doubt the men will suffer a good deal. I get along very well for I have India Rubber clothes and my invaluable Buffalo, and I dare say a few tents for the Officers will soon be sent up. This is a beautiful and fertile country, but most of the inhabitants Rebels. I have heard that Col. Lee arrived safely at Washington, and met Mrs. Lee at Knoxville. I have since heard it reported that he had gone home. I hope he has for he can of course be more comfortable there.

The Rebels appear to give way as we advance, and I have no doubt they will avoid a battle with a force so superior to their own. We are in the rear again now, and likely to remain there. Capt. Le Duc has accepted the Quarter Master Ship of Sigel's corps and ranks as Lieut. Colonel. Capt. Macy of our Regiment is detailed as acting Brigade Quarter Master in Capt. Le Duc's place.

All friends must excuse me for not writing often now, it is so very difficult without chair or desk and often without any shelter.

Love to all.

Your affectionate son
Henry.

Camp, 20th Regiment
Warrenton, Va.
Sunday November 9th 1862.

My dear Father.

You see by my date that we have now marched to a point nearly opposite Washington, and not so very far from Fairfax Court house where we were 2 months ago, having since travelled round a complete circle through Maryland, to arrive at last at the old battleground of the war.

Weather is cold but not unpleasant for marching. Roads excellent. We had a snowstorm for one day. We are now well in the rear of the Grand Army. Yesterday we saw McClellan, Sumner and Burnside together, at the little town of Salem, through which we passed. We shall probably spend 3 or 4 days here, and if we get tents I shall be able to write quite often.

Please ask mother to send in a letter a few pieces of tape marked "Lt. Ropes, 20th Mass." I wish to sew one on each blanket etc. I have. Herbert and all friends well.

Your affectionate son
Henry.

Letter for J.C. enclosed.

RIGHT UP INTO THE FIRE

Camp 20th Regiment, Warrenton, Va.
November 9th 1862.

Dear John.

Thank you for your very interesting letter of the 31st October and 1st November. I am delighted to hear of the prosperity of A Δ Φ. Please inquire if any of the $10.75 received from C. B. Porter belonged to Herbert, and, if it did, let me know how much, and I will pay him here, and you can credit the whole to me. Perhaps part (for coal) is to be credited to Father. Please see to this. As to my tent, I see every day the necessity of its being as waterproof as possible. It occurred to me that to save weight, the back might be of cotton or linen, and the sides only of Rubber. If you find a material light enough, you can have not only a whole back, fastened to the sides, but a *front* also, to open just like the *back* of my present heavy tent. I dare say you can get a kind of coarse oiled or prepared silk, like a balloon. I give these directions all in case you have not yet decided upon a material and given orders, not by any means to interfere in case you have already decided on style and material. I feel sure Adams' Express will soon run to the Army. I shall be delighted to see Abbott again. I hardly know what to think of the Regiment now. Dreher was drunk the other day, when we were before the enemy, and in line of battle, and Shepard had to take command. Macy is detailed as Brig. Quarter Master and no doubt is glad to get into a decent place. (Do not mention that about Dreher, of course). I believe I did not tell you that Col. Hall, commanding Brigade, asked me to be on his staff, but I declined on the ground of duty to be with my Regiment and Company, especially as we expected active service. Do not mention this either. Herbert, Abbott and Patten are my only friends now in the Regiment. I am exceedingly sorry to lose Macy, but he came and had a long talk with me, and I know his reasons are good and he does right. I do not dare to consider the future of the poor old 20th. Col. Lee, I suppose, will never return to us. Col. Palfrey laid up for months. No Major. Bartlett gone to another Regiment, and the probability of Dreher, a crazy drunken Dutchman, for Major, and Commanding Officer! If we have another fight, and the Lord deliver us, we have one good thing however, as good a Brigade Commander as there is anywhere, a young man with a clear head.

 I am much interested in what you and Mary Ann say about Mr. Boulnois. Perhaps he would like to visit the Army when we come to a stop. I should be delighted to show him round, and do all I could for him.

 There is a terrible feeling against England in the Army, especially among the Western troops. I believe that if we put down the Rebellion this Autumn, that an English war would be hailed with joy by the great body of the Army. With the Irish there is a settled determination to have a Rebellion against England as soon as this war is over, and they really seem to consider this war as a sort of preparation. I feel very sorry for this, but it is true.

Give my love to Holmes, if you see him. I am glad he is recovering so well. He had a bad looking wound. Send me some stamps and the rest of the $25.00 I wrote for. I have now received $13.00. If possible, send a little gold and silver.

Your affectionate brother
Henry.

Camp 20th Regiment, Warrenton, Va.
Wednesday, November 12th 1862.

My dear John.

I have been so busy with my Muster Rolls etc. for the last few days that I have been unable to write home. I received today the "Atlantic" for November, and 3 papers, no letters for some days. I have received a most interesting and able letter from Hazeltine dated Nimes, France.

The whole Army is depressed and broken spirited, and full of depondency [sic] and indignation at McClellan's removal. He bade us farewell, and I thought he never looked better, though very sad. Burnside is no doubt an able man, but I have never yet heard of his doing anything on a very large scale. He seems to assume the Command unwillingly, and I hear he only is to hold it until Hooker gets well. Everyone feels gloomy and reckless of what may come. When I consider this in connection with the recent elections, I almost despair for the Country.[46]

The Regiment is in a disgusting state. Dreher and Shepard make fools of themselves every day, and the poor old 20th is the laughing stock of the Brigade, whenever either attempt the simplest movements. A letter has been written to our old Major Revere stating our lack of Officers and begging him to assume his old command. I have signed it most willingly. He is our only hope. Dreher and Shepard are furious at the letter and would not sign. Murphy goes with them.

---

[46] In the 1862 elections to the U.S. House of Representatives, the Republicans lost 22 seats in Congress and were only able to retain control of the House with the support of the representatives of the Unionist Party.

Beside this letter which is a perfectly respectful, proper and public one, another letter has been written privately, which only Cabot, Mason, Wilkins, Curtis, Patten and I have signed, stating the true case, and plainly setting forth Dreher's ignorance, violence and conceipt, and Shepard's foolishness and (of late) insufferable self-confidence. I hope these will succeed. If they do not, we feel that any relief would be eagerly snatched at. I mean to stick by the 20th to the last, but the present horrible state of the Regiment is unendurable. Shepard and Dreher know how much they are despised by the old Officers and are both uncivil and overbearing to the last degree. I suppose this is a gloomy letter, for so I feel. However, I keep heart, and hope for better things both for the Regiment and the Country. I do not anticipate an advance or a great battle. A Winter Campaign is as impossible as an Army without food, and amounts to much the same thing.

Love to all.

Your affectionate brother
Henry.

Camp 20th Regiment (Mass. Volunteers)
Warrenton, Va. November 14th 1862.

My dear John.

I have been so busy as not to have had time to write anything but a hurried note to you for some days. I received last evening yours of November 3rd enclosing $5.00 and 12 stamps, but no agreement about the mortgage you spoke of. This I suppose you omitted to put in. I shall expect it in your next. I/n/ consequence of our march, the pay-rolls are again delayed, and although 4 months were due on November 1st, I suppose we shall have to wait a long time yet for our pay. So please continue to send small sums say $5.00 or $6.00 in your letters. U.S. money, gold or silver, is the only kind which passes here. Send ones or twos, or postage currency, if possible. Food is very scarce here, and very dear, but if we stay, the Commissary will soon supply us quite well. I have now received $18.00 in all. Please send up the $50.00. In a campaign one must guard against every risk, and it is of course possible to be taken prisoner, when to be without money would be very awkward.

James is now quite ill, and like all simple fellows as he, thinks he is about used up and probably will never recover. He has a slight fever turn and is getting along nicely. I have had some trouble with him of late. He is, as you know, a very foolish, simple, "green" fellow, and of late he got into a way of neglecting his duties and loafing about with the men, and occasionally grumbling. Then he became surly, and finally I told him that he might either leave or change his conduct, to which he promptly replied he would go, only wishing to remain till pay-day to collect some debts due him from men in the Regiment. I then found he expected me to pay his passage to Boston, perhaps $20.00 and said you made a distinct agreement with him to the effect that whenever I should discharge him, I was to send him back. Now, I never understood this to be the agreement, especially when a man is discharged for bad conduct. I have sent back, among my private papers, the written agreement with James signed in your Office, and I think it is there distinctly stated that I would *not* agree to pay his passage home, that is of course unless he returned with me. Of course, I shall abide by any agreement you made, but I wish you would write to me what the stipulation was, and if you like, open my box, and take out the original agreement from among my papers. It seems to me absurd that a man can at any time behave badly and be discharged and then get his passage paid back to Boston. The only hold I have on him is the fear of discharge and this takes that away. Since James behaved so badly, however, he seemed to repent, came to me and said he was very sorry indeed to have to leave, and then set about his duties in the most active manner and showed by his energy and faithfulness that he wished to atone for past defects. I saw this and had determined to keep him after all, but since then he has fallen sick and I may be obliged to part with him. If I do now, I shall pay his way to Boston after all, because he fell sick in my employ, and was at the time doing well, but I wish to know what the agreement was with him.

  Please send by mail to me when you can, some writing paper and envelopes. Cannot you fold them square instead of rolling them up?

  I understand "Casey's tactics" are now adopted. Please send me a copy. I also want (when you send a box) 4 pieces soap, ball Twine, my "Army Regulations" (in trunk), a box shaving soap and a pocket penholder. These things, I suppose, will reach me in some winter quarters, if at all. I have written you what I think of McClellan's removal. Still we must support the Government. At present my confidence in Lincoln and Halleck is about gone. Tell me what you think of the "Peoples" party and of the recent democratic victories. I hope the country will sustain the war at least one year more. For my part I can see no way but war. Peace means truce, nothing more. The South must be crushed, or the North, i.e. the country, the Republic will perish. If the South conquer, I see nothing but war forever, unless indeed we become so far demoralized as to consent to be the South's servants. They will rule or perish, and as they have placed this as the issue, I see our duty clearly to utterly destroy them as a united people. The governing class destroyed and their places filled with Northern emigrants, the two would unite and become with the old North a great nation once more. We must look solely at the end to be accomplished, the total subjection of the Rebellion, and overlook everything between, no matter what expense or what sacrifice of life is to come. The more I see and the more I think, the more I am convinced this is so, and the more willing I am to help to gain the great end.

My situation here is very uncomfortable, but we hope for better things. How are the Colonel and Mrs. Lee?

Your affectionate brother
Henry.

Camp 20th Regiment near Falmouth
opposite Fredericksburg, Va.
Tuesday, November 18th 1862.

My dear Father.

I last wrote home from Warrenton on Friday last, November 14th. On *Saturday morning* soon after daylight we packed up and marched 3 miles beyond Warrenton Junction. *Sunday* we marched all day (reveille at 4.30 A.M.) and camped in a field at night, and yesterday we had an easy march to this place which is I understand about 1 mile from the river. There was a good deal of Artillery firing yesterday, which I hear was our forces shelling at the Rebels across the river. Weather has been cloudy and rainy for 2 days, but not cold. There is a large force here, and Sumner is with us. We are now merely camped for a night or so, and shall probably move this morning a short distance. We can learn nothing of Army movements, and do not in the least know our destination, but I suppose we shall not cross the river until the whole Army is ready to cross, that is if we cross at all. I still think that the Army of the Potomac will not move on Richmond and risk a great battle this autumn. I think we shall lie about here, near this City and Culpepper [sic], with the Gaps well guarded, and plenty of troops behind at Warrenton, Centreville etc. The roads are now good, and we are near Railroads and can get supplies, but when we begin an advance we must, to a very great extent, depend on our trains, and these cannot be moved when the heavy rains of winter set in. Then besides the men must have tents soon. If we attempt what they call in the papers the "Winter campaign" we shall labor under every disadvantage as an attacking force, in comparison with the Rebels, a defensive force. The men would sicken and die by hundreds, and before Spring this vast Army would be about used up. Especially the new troops would suffer. The enemy are now probably in their well fortified position near Gordonsville comfortable in log houses. Behind this they can have another position prepared, and after our Army, after enduring every hardship, has perhaps driven them from Gordonsville, they can fall back to a 2nd comfortable position, and so on, avoiding a battle, using our Army up, and keeping up the spirits of their people by the excitement of continual skirmishes and attacks on a small scale. Then when Spring opens they have a fresh Army and we have a broken down one.

It seems to me perfectly clear that unless Burnside is almost certain of meeting with no opposition he cannot at once overcome (a very unlikely supposition) he will not dare to expose the Army to such perils and will content himself with drawing a complete chain round the Rebels, shutting them out completely from North West Virginia, and then attending to the wants of his army and making them comfortable, while attacks from the South weaken the enemy and compel him to undertake frequent and harrassing marches.

For my part, I do not expect to get farther South this winter, and I earnestly hope the popular will will not overcome our new General, and oblige him to take risks his military judgment would not permit. I see clearly now that we must expect to be defeated until the people at home learn to mind their own business and let the Generals mind theirs.

I am as usual, well, so are all our friends here. I must beg you to excuse this bad writing, for I have no desk or table but my knee as I sit on the ground. However I know you would rather have this than no letter at all. Best love to mother and all. Please thank Dr. F. *[illegible]* for his last and say I will answer as soon as I can.

Your affectionate son
Henry.

RIGHT UP INTO THE FIRE

On Picket, near Falmouth, Va.
Wednesday, 19th November 1862.

My dear John.

I wrote to Father yesterday, giving an account of our march to this place. Capt. Holmes and Lieut. Abbott have just arrived, safe and well, and I have received from the latter your letter of the 11th and Father's of the 12th, enclosing $25.00 in Government money. Please thank Father for sending this. I am *very glad* you have at last got the tent. Tell me if there is a "whole back", as I wrote about in one of my last letters. I have received no letter about the Estates. As to McClellan, I have begun to feel a little as you did. As *far as we can now judge*, I think McClellan should either have advanced as ordered, or refused and resigned. I can hardly account for his delaying and not refusing, especially as you seem to think he *intentionally* delayed. Since we came here *vast columns* of troops, I hear 5 Corps in all, have moved up. Burnside passed this morning, and the troops are still passing, 3 columns abreast. It is a heavy rainstorm, but warm. It rained all night and much of yesterday. No signs of clearing off. It looks like an advance beyond the river, but I still hold to my former opinion that nothing will be accomplished from this side till spring. I hear old Sumner says a "winter campaign" is possible. No one else I think would say so. Sumner has his old Corps again and leads the way. I think the Army has got over the depression caused by McClellan's removal, and it is in good heart for anything, but in case of serious reverse, there would be a great want of confidence. Of course, in one sense, I know no more of McClellan than you at home, but I still retain and shall retain this feeling, that I am perfectly satisfied with him as Commander, and only wish to see him left to himself untrammelled. I do not care much for McClellan's complaints about the Quarter Master Department. Delays may easily have occurred which would make both his and Halleck's statements true. I think McClellan is a far-seeing man. He knows another year is necessary, and prefers a good Army next spring to a smaller and poorer one for a few weeks this Autumn. The people say the war *must* be finished in *9* months. McClellan lays his plans merely to finish the war, whether 9 months or 9 years are required.

I am very glad to hear Mr. Boulnois' health is improved. I hope he will succeed in getting on some good staff. He had better try for some Major General's Staff where the staff is large, but I dare say he will meet with difficulty, on account of the feeling against England, and the claims of Line Officers to Staff appointments.

Please send me some gold dollars and silver change, if possible. The $25.00 are full enough for present need, but in this country gold will buy what no paper will. People *will not sell at all* for paper often. I should be glad to pay 25 per cent premium for $10.00 in gold. If you can some time send me a small true pocket-compass, please do. I wonder I never thought to ask for one before.

I have many letters to answer which I must postpone till we get to some sort of settled camp. I will write you as often as I can and tell you everything I can about matters. My own opinion is that if a winter campaign is attempted, it will signally fail. This I say not without fairly thinking of the matter, and I think not influenced by a desire for comfort and a dislike to face hardship and danger again. We shall soon see. Did you ever place $30.00 to James' credit at the Savings Bank? Let me know. I am much interested in a book I have borrowed here "Tom Burke" by Chs. Lever. Is it a fair picture of the era of Napoleon? It seems quite so to me. I hear Col. Lee is to return to us, and I am amazed beyond measure. Can it be his intention? I thought he had gone home.

Your affectionate brother,
Henry.

Camp 20th Regiment near Falmouth, Va.
November 22nd 1862, Saturday.

My dear John.

I have received yours of the 14th enclosing 20 stamps. The lantern, hatchet, etc. were all right, and so were Herbert's bottles and hatchet. I hope you will be able to send on the shelter tent very soon. I received the $25.00 all right. I have asked for a small amount of gold and silver. I find it often is of great value, and passes when no paper money will. Abbott's baggage has not yet come, but he tells me he has Schalk's work, and a shirt for me. I have received no letter or agreement whatever about the Estates. I see you allude to the sale of the Hanover street Estate. When I get your letter I will fully consider the matter.

As to the kettle-stove, I think I shall not want it this autumn. I do not believe the stove part is of much use. I am astonished to hear that Col. Lee expects to return. I am sure he cannot stand it. He was really very ill at Bolivar. I am very glad for Stone, though I look upon joining that Regiment very much like joining the Boston Cadets, for there is small chance of their ever seeing service, and Cavalry service at best in this war is a mere sham. Herbert is much obliged to you for promising to get him the blanket etc. Capt. Le Duc has been made Corps Quarter Master to Sigel, with the rank of Lieutenant-Colonel. You do not appear to know that we left Capt. Schmidt sick at Bolivar. He never did 2 days duty but fell ill immediately.

We have moved our camp ½ or ¾ mile to an excellent place on a hill and have begun to make ourselves a little comfortable. I see no signs of a move. We have had tremendous rains for 3 days, and the mud is very deep. I have no doubt the river here is very high. I am glad you did not order a cape for me. My old Coat is pretty well worn out now, and I think I must have a new one. I enclose a description for Nason's use. It ought not to cost more than $22.00 but I dare say you will have to pay as high as $28.00 or $30.00. My old one, made very large and thick and with a tremendous Cape was $26.00 only. I have found by experience that a great coat should be very light in the skirts for marching, and close at the waist to allow the belt to meet.

Herbert has just reminded me of the Class photographs. Please get for me a complete set, including every one, Tutors, Professors, and all the extras such as buildings, trees etc. Let me have *everything*. Better ask Jeffries about it. Herbert has a splendid likeness of himself, class-book size in uniform, bust only. He promised me one of these which he says you can ask his father for, and then have framed and kept for me. Many of the fellows here ask me for my pictures. I hardly know what cards you had taken of me. Please send me on a few, including at least one of each kind. Abbott wants one *without* whiskers, if you have any. Please send me about 12 sheets post paper, and ½ doz. post paper envelopes. I think you had better send (when you send a box) ½ doz. pocket handkerchiefs and ½ doz. small towels. Also a nice leather stock.

I am very sorry to hear from Abbott and Holmes that the general state of feeling at home is so unfavorable to a continued support of the war. They both say that the eventual separation of the country is considered certain by almost all, and that they hardly think the Country will support the war a year longer. If so, I am disappointed in the American people. I had thought the country was in earnest, but I fear the effect of party division. The Army absolutely needs a rest of 3 months, needs it just as /a/ tired horse needs rest, needs to get into comfortable quarters, drill, get well of sickness and wounds and become ready for another campaign. Without such a rest the troops will be fit for very little when spring comes. If the country will not endure this, it is a very hard master. No General in his senses would undertake a winter campaign in this country against an equal enemy. We ought to be allowed a rest after what we have done and suffered. It must be, and the country may as well make up their minds to it first as last. The Army is all right for another year, if the people at home back down, they are a pretty poor set.

I believe I have no letters to acknowledge. Please do not send any more books but what I ask for; I can hardly find room for them and do not like to throw them away.

RIGHT UP INTO THE FIRE

It is more pleasant here now Abbott and Holmes have returned. Both and several others send regards etc. to you.

Best love to all.

Your affectionate brother
Henry.

Falmouth, Va. November 27th 1862
Thanksgiving Day.

My dear John.

I dare say you are getting up an appetite for a most excellent dinner while I write this, in a room of an old house in this town, where the Court Martial sits, during a recess of the Court. It has been found impossible to get a turkey, the nearest approach is a chicken, obtained by Capt. Cabot and Lieutenants Curtis and Wilkins. For my part, after the Court adjourns at 3 o'clock, I intend to go to Camp and dine on a can of sealed Oysters and a can of sealed tomatoes, the most extravagant bill of fare I can get up. However, perhaps I may enjoy a better Christmas dinner, that is if we go into our long wished for winter quarters. I shall try to be with you in spirit and have no doubt you will think of me.

I hear that the Colonel has got home, and am very glad of it, and hope he may now have a season of rest and be comfortable, which I know he cannot be while he is constantly expecting to return. I see no signs of a move here, but we have twice had preparatory orders issued. We had a heavy rain day before yesterday, and I hear the roads to Acquia Creek are in an awful state. I do not see how we can make any move till the Railroad is completed, nor of what use a move will be when the Railroad is made, except to hold the city which might be used to quarter part of the Army. The Rebels are easily seen on the other side and have erected batteries.

I have received, as you know, the $25.00 but still wish you to send on some more, for you know we may possibly move, and I like to be well supplied. If convenient, send a small supply of gold or silver. Have you continued to take for me Copies of the "Pictorial History of the War?" and the "Rebellion Record"? I hope you have. As to my new Coat, if the light blue is hard to get for any reason, let it be of the dark blue. I have little preference but prefer light, if the color and quality are good. The Coat ought not to be a heavy or bulky one.

I have really no news to tell you. I am very busy on the Court Martial, and shall be for several days to come. I get letters very irregularly now, and I fear that letter of yours about the Hanover Street property is lost. I have perfect confidence in your judgment in the matter.

Best love to all.

Your affectionate brother
Henry.

Camp 20th Regiment, near
Falmouth, Va., November 28th 1862.

My dear Father.

I received yesterday yours of November 22nd, enclosing a letter from Frank, and also a letter from you dated September 12th enclosing $2.00 in postage currency. I can hardly imagine what has caused this delay, but am very glad indeed to get the letter. I have also received a very kind letter from Mrs. Lee, dated Washington, November 17th. I am glad to hear that the Colonel has got home, and hope his health has improved. I have no doubt you had a very pleasant Thanksgiving, and I wished I could have been with you. In consequence of the lack of transportation our Commissary Department has been very poorly supplied, but the Railroad I hear will be done in a week now, and then I suppose we can get enough. We can buy very small loaves of bread in the town at from 12 to 25 cents each, and potatoes at $1.00 a peck. But these are hard to get. The men get little else than hard bread, pork and coffee and fresh meat. They ought to have vegetables, rice, beans etc.

The Rebels are throwing up forts opposite the town and we do not disturb them. I am still on the Court Martial and have a great deal to do, but on the whole it is a pleasant change from the monotony of a camp.

I see no reason to change my former opinion that an advance on Richmond is not contemplated this winter in the face of the enemy. I do not at all expect a great battle. I think we may take Fredericksburg.

I am perfectly well. Weather not excessively cold, and plenty of wood near the Camp.

RIGHT UP INTO THE FIRE

Do you fear at all for your Ships on account of the Alabama?[47] I hope there is no danger for them. As soon as the Express begins to run we shall be very comfortable. If we stay here I shall get up some sort of a log house. My buffalo I find invaluable. I sleep as comfortably as I should at home.

Best love to mother and all

Your affectionate son
Henry.

Enclosed note for J.C.

Camp 20th Regiment near Falmouth Va.,
November 28th 1862.

My dear John.

I have this evening received yours of the 24th November and the 3 packages of paper and the 2 envelopes of envelopes, for all which much obliged. Do you intend to send me for James any receipt (or copy of the receipt) for his $30.00 deposited in the Bank? I think you had better send some proof for him to have. Did you give also $5.00 to his sister?

When do you intend to square up my accounts? I want often *very much* to know how much money I have at home, if any? I am delighted to hear you have succeeded with the tent. Has it a back? Do you remember how wide it is? i.e. the base of the triangle of the back? I want a sponge when you can send one, about as large when swelled as a small Cantaloupe Melon. Perhaps you can send it by mail.

How is Col. Lee really? Does he think of returning to the Regiment?

We are much better off now Abbott and Holmes are back, but still we lack a Commander fearfully. I have almost nothing to say to Shepard now, although we are not openly at sword's point.

I really can do nothing whatever for Mr. Boulnois, although I should be delighted to aid him in any way. Can you not see Col. Revere (our old Major)?

---

[47] The William Ropes & Co. mercantile firm made a tidy profit exporting (among other things) cotton and lighting oil to Russia. The Confederate commerce raider CSS Alabama began in August 1862 to stalk the shipping lanes between the Eastern Atlantic and the coast of New England.

Perhaps he could help him to a Staff either with or under old Sumner. I heard a very good story of him the other day. In one of the late battles, an Aide rode up from one of the Generals with the appalling news that the enemy had got round in his rear! "Then", said old Sumner, "tell the General to face about his rear rank and fight them both ways."

I have no news to tell you. It is cold enough to freeze about every night, and warm enough to melt every day. Roads pretty good here, but bad toward Acquia Creek. Railroad getting on fast.

I envy you Thanksgiving but can only hope that we may all meet again at some future day. Still I believe we shall have another year of war, and the chances are very much against a man's getting through twice what I have escaped.

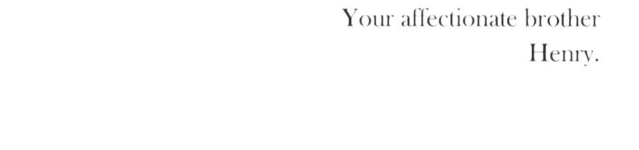

Your affectionate brother
Henry.

December 2nd 1862.
Falmouth, Va.

My dear Mother.

I believe I have no letters to answer, for I have received none for several days, and I am sure I have no news to tell you. I am still on this Court Martial, and it is quite pleasant, for we have got quite well acquainted, and have a comfortable room to sit in, and a very respectable dinner furnished daily by an old negro Benjamin, by name, whom we have fallen in with here. We expect to close tomorrow, but I shall be occupied for several days longer in writing up the proceedings.

All is quiet, and the Army is getting into loghuts [sic]. I am to have a loghut built tomorrow, and hope to be very comfortable indeed. Forts are being built here, and it looks like a long stay. For the last week the weather has been quite pleasant and not very cold.

The Cars run now, and I soon expect the Express will open an Office here and I shall get my boxes, and Sutlers will come up and bring every comfort. Next time you send me anything please send a pair of suspenders. John will get them, and let them be fastened together by a bit of tape, as John's are.

I enclose a letter for Frank which please send when convenient. I expect some more post-paper soon and shall try to write to sisters Mary and Lizzie. I owe them both letters. If I get my log house up, and a good fireplace, I shall be very well off. I saw Phil Mason the other day. He rode over to the Regiment. He is looking very well and hearty.

Your affectionate son
Henry.

Falmouth, Va.
Friday, December 5th 1862.

My dear Father.

I write merely to let you know that I am still here, still hard at work on the Court Martial. I have received no letters from home, but last night one from Henry Jeffries. I have no news about the Army. In our Regiment, however, we have at last had a change. Genl. Howard has ordered Capt. Macy to take command of the Regiment in consequence of Captains Dreher and Sherpards [sic] evident incapacity. Both these Officers are furious, and have resigned, and Dr. Hayward has certified to Capt. Dreher's physical inability to command the Regiment, and indeed for any service.

Capt. Shephards [sic] is very indignant, but his total incapacity and his great ignorance of tactics have of late been so evident, that nobody pities him, and every good Officer is glad that the Regiment is once more in competent hands. Capt. Shephards is a bit of a politician, and has newspaper friends so I think you may see some notice of the matter in the papers.

It is a steady rain now and looks like a long storm. I often hear of the arrival of pontoon trains etc. and the prospects of an advance, but I still think it impossible, or at any rate too dangerous to attempt. I think we shall stay here till Spring. I have begun to put up a log hut and expect to move in in two days. Then I shall be very comfortable.

Best love to mother and all the rest.

Your affectionate son
Henry.

RIGHT UP INTO THE FIRE

Camp 20th Regiment near Falmouth, Va.
Saturday, December 6th 1862.

My dear John.

I have tonight received a letter from Mother of the 2nd, which is the only one I have got for some days. Mother really thinks I sleep in a house at Falmouth, but I really am under only a shelter tent, a miserable protection indeed. My log-hut is getting on, but is delayed by yesterday's severe storm. It is very cold, and 2 or 3 inches of snow on the ground, and we really suffer a great deal. The men will soon get sick unless we get log huts or tents. They get little sleep on account of cold, and are up half the night hanging round fires. Besides, the scurvy has appeared. They get nothing but meat and hard bread, and must have potatoes or onions. I wrote you about sending me some more money. Please do so. We may not be paid till January, although 5 months are now due. Then you know they have reduced Officers' pay, taxed them and raised the prices of meat, sugar, etc. etc. I feel now sure we cannot move on account of the weather and roads, also because the enemy are in strong force and well entrenched, and a great battle would be foolish when, if we won, we could not pursue. So I intend to prepare for winter, and as I have been as a general thing derived of the comforts of life since last Christmas, I want you to get Mother to place me on the widow list and give me a turkey for the celebration of this day. I want you to get up a box containing a *roasted* Turkey, a pot of Cranberry sauce, a plumpudding with sauce and some mince pies. I am not modest you see, as to quantity for *one* Christmas dinner, but you must imagine the fasting of a year. I know all these things will keep and I feel sure, if you send them pretty soon I shall get them in time, as the Express will without doubt run then. If they do not have mince pies at home, order me 4 or 5 at some good confectionery and send them, and if there is room put in a bottle of wine. As soon as I am sure of the Express, I shall order a supply of vegetables etc. etc., but I have determined, if possible, to celebrate Christmas in a home-like manner. If convenient, put in a tongue, a duck, anything you like, a cauliflower, turnips, all are alike rarities here.

We are having great changes in the Regiment, but I will write to you fully when I have a better chance. It is so cold my fingers are difficult to manage, and I fear my writing is rather crooked. Many here desire regards to you. The Court Martial is over, but I shall be 3 or 4 days in writing up the proceedings and shall then hope to have a house of my own, to write and live comfortably in. You may be sure a move is impossible. It would cost thousands of lives. Even here we are about as badly off as the English in the Crimea, and then we would be like the French in the retreat from Russia. However, in two weeks I expect the Army will be hutted, supplies will be abundant, and the men healthy and comfortable.

Abbott has a nice hut. Herbert and Holmes a tent. I am the worst off of the Officers, but thanks to my Buffalo and big Rubber blanket I can sleep warm. I hope you will soon tell me how my account stands. At any rate I shall keep on ordering what I need. I expect to draw a large part of my future supplies from Boston by Express. You can get nothing here. Sometimes butter at $1.00 a lb. and Potatoes $1.00 a peck.

Write soon and tell me what you think of the President and the Administration. I am in much doubt.

Your affectionate brother
Henry.

P.S. You must excuse blots, for the ink freezes as I write. Thermometer (I suppose) about 25° Fahrenheit.

Camp 20th Regiment near Falmouth, Va.
December 10th 1862.

My dear John.

I hardly know how to account for the long silence of you all at home. I have received the newspapers, the account of the campaign by the Prince de Joinville, and the sponge by mail, but no letters. I am now about through with my Court Martial. Today and yesterday are warmer than we have had for nearly a week. My log house is done and I only wait for the Quartermaster to get some shelter tents to draw some to cover it with. We have had 3 days of *awfully* cold weather. I hear that several men have frozen to death, and all but those in log huts have suffered awfully. The Army will be dreadfully reduced by illness if we attempt to move in such weather, or if we longer keep up this state of constant expectation of a move. Only 2 days ago we got quite positive orders to build huts and the Artillery were ordered to build Stables, and this morning I hear from the best authority that we move tomorrow morning across the river. Yet only 10 days or a week ago positive orders came in the same way, rations and 60 rounds ammunition were distributed and the order was to move at 11 P.M.. At 10 ½ however, it was countermanded, and here we are still. I hear and believe that the enemy have fallen back but, unless it is merely a small force to hold the city, I do not see any use of crossing the river. I cannot think a regular advance on Richmond, with the necessary scouting, picketing, reconnaissances etc., is contemplated. The roads are very bad but still quite hard frozen and so passable. A rain storm, however would make them impassable, and we must now expect and calculate upon rain, snow and cold weather the greater part of the time. Still I dare say the Army will advance before you get this, for I hear it today from really undoubted authority. The Regiment is today gone on picket and I stay to write up the Court Martial proceedings. If we do not move my house will be most comfortable winter quarters, and if we do move, I am perfectly sure we must soon stop. The weather may be unusually favorable, but 3 days such as those we had would disable ½ the Army on a march.

I do not despair of getting my boxes by Christmas yet.

As to the Regiment, you know Macy was ordered to take command. Since then we hear that Dreher is made Major. His resignation for physical disability is however now gone up and I dare say accepted. I do not know how it will turn out. Abbott, Tilden and Curtis are Captains, but their commissions have not yet come. Curtis a Captain! I should very much like to see a statement of the principle on which promotions are made. I think it would puzzle anybody to state it. It certainly has no reference to date of commission, length of service, or faithfulness to duty in the Regiment. Shepard keeps to his tent, and is reported sick. I have not seen him for several days.

I cannot get over this moving just after one has got a little comfortable. I am all in uncertainty, and of course feel very uncomfortable, not knowing whether to go on or to stop and pack up. I wish I had the tent.

Your affectionate brother
Henry.

P.S.

12th December 3 P.M.

We had a terrible fight yesterday. I am unhurt. Cabot killed, Wilkins, Shepard, McKay, and Curtis wounded. We occupy the town. Our Brigade stormed it. Desperate fighting in Streets. Our loss heavy. I was bruised very slightly by a spent ball. We are now in rear. Many troops crossed.

In great haste
Affectionately
Henry.

RIGHT UP INTO THE FIRE

Fredericksburg
noon Sunday, December 14th 1862.

Dear Father.

We have had another dreadful battle and I am mercifully preserved without a scratch, though I got 4 or 5 balls through my clothes etc. We were ordered to the assault of the enemy's works and were driven back under the most awful fire I ever stood before. We were entirely unsupported, only the 19th and 20th Mass. could be brought to face the fire at all. The 19th gave way, the 20th stood after advancing close to the enemy and only retired under orders when all was up. Then the enemy opened on us a reserved fire from works and rifle pits with fearful effect. We only fell back to a ditch which we held till night when the Regulars relieved us. Our Brigade is dreadfully cut up. It was a senseless butchery of men. We were all the time under a heavy, flanking fire of Artillery. A new Pennsylvania Brigade brought up to our support broke and ran under this fire alone. Sully's Brigade however came on and staid with us. This after our repulse. Lt. Alley is killed, Capt. Dreher wounded, Lt. Beckwith also, perhaps mortally. Herbert is unhurt, so are Macy and Abbott. We have 5 Company Officers left, the Commanding Officer Macy, and Patten, the Adjutant. Genl. Howard publicly thanked Macy and the Regiment this morning.

We are ordered to the reserve and are now withdrawn to the rear. Only picket firing today. I think the enemy may be retreating, as I hear Franklin was successful on the left. As for us, it was the slaughtering of the best troops before impregnable works. The battle is I fear indecisive and our loss terrible.

Do not be anxious, if there is another battle we shall no doubt be left in reserve. We have but 120 men or so left. 19th Mass. suffered dreadfully. I can only thank God and pray for his protection for the future. Be assured the 20th and the Brigade has gained a name unequalled in the Army. Macy deserves the *very highest* praise.

I shall try to write fully when I can. All quiet now.

In great haste

Your affectionate son
Henry.

Enclosed letter from Herbert to his father.

RIGHT UP INTO THE FIRE

Camp 20th Mass.
near Falmouth
Tuesday, December 16th 1862.

My dear Father.

You see by my date that we are safe back again in our old Camp, having been 4 days across the river, fought two battles, lived under Artillery fire the whole time and lost one half of our men and two thirds of our Officers. I feel I cannot be too thankful to God for my really wonderful preservation, especially as in these actions the Officers were especially singled out. We recrossed at midnight on the 14th without molestation. I received in the first battle a pretty severe blow from a spent ball in the groin and narrowly escaped a very serious injury. For some moments I was stunned, but now nothing remains but a black and blue spot and a little stiffness of the limb. I also got a bullet through my coat, and in the second battle one through my coat collar just twitching my whiskers, one through my hat, one which passed just over my shoulder and through my blanket, which I had strapped on top of that knapsack John sent me, and one on the other side which cut off one of the small straps. Beside these I was several times covered with mud and dirt thrown up by shot and shell. Altogether I do not see how I escaped. The fire was perfectly terrific, every inch of ground seemed to be struck.

On the whole we have met with a tremendous repulse and lost almost 12000 men (I hear) and all wasted. The Army is *completely demoralized*. The new troops behaved shamefully. Hooker's men ran by us like sheep. I saw a whole Brigade of Pennsylvania cowards (Tyler's Brigade) break and run in total disorder when they were brought up to our relief, our men cursing them most heartily. As to our Regiment its praise is in every mouth. Dana's or rather Hall's Brigade is up high enough, but the 42nd and 59th New York and the 127th Pennsylvania (a new Regiment) are not included in the praise. They gave way horribly, and of the 3 good Regiments, 7th Michigan, 19th and 20th Mass., the 20th is far above all. We were repulsed but the 20th got nearer the enemy than any other Regiment, and only retired by orders, and when *every other* Regiment had broken and fallen back. Then we rallied by a ditch and held our own till night.

I shall try to write John a long letter soon. We shall winter here.

Your affectionate son
Henry.

RIGHT UP INTO THE FIRE

December 19th 1862.

Dear John.

I send James who embraces this opportunity of getting home about some money matters of his own. I have no time to write much, am writing a long letter to you. I send by him several books, your pipe and a cup, taken from Fredericksburg, which please give to Mary Ann from me. I will write what to send him back with.
    All well.
    In great haste

Your affectionate brother
Henry.

James takes my watch and some private letters.

Camp 20th Regiment near Falmouth, Va.
December 18th 1862.

My dear John.

I have determined to write you a tremendous letter, giving a full account of our late battles and answering your letter about my expenses, the Estates etc. received by Col. Lee. And first the account of the battles etc.. The Regiment went out on picket, on the 10th and I staid in camp to finish my Court Martial proceedings. I heard of our expected move, but did not in the least anticipate what was to come. The Regiment came in from picket at 4 A.M. on the 11th and we were ordered to march at 5. About that time the firing began at the river, and at 6 A.M. we marched down to a point about opposite the Northern part of the city. It was still very dark, the valley of the river was filled with smoke from our batteries along the bank, and the noise was tremendous. We staid on an open plain which was filled with troops. Our Brigade was to cross first, the 7th *[Michigan]* leading as skirmishers. They put a pontoon bridge half over and then the Rebels in the houses and from the cellars which they had made into Riflepits poured in such a hot fire as to drive our men off. The river here is about as wide as Pemberton Square is long, and the banks high and especially steep on our side. The 7th Michigan and the 19th *[Massachusetts]* were deployed as skirmishers along the banks to protect the laborers on the bridge, but they could not do so, for the smoke and fog were very thick. The weather this day and for the 3 following days was mild. Occasionally the Rebels would throw over a few shells to where we were, but not much damage was done. After a little time the guns were directed to the city to clean out the Rebel sharpshooters, and the bombardment lasted steadily till about 4 P.M. The City was now on fire in 3 places, and this smoke added to the darkness through which our guns incessantly flashed. We were close to the batteries. The sound was tremendous. We had now lain all day here and still nothing was done. Several of the Officers were lounging on a pile of boards, I was rather tired and almost asleep when Col. Hall rode up and said the 7th Michigan had volunteered to cross in pontoon boats. This was indeed a desperate thing, but in a few moments someone said they were crossing, we heard a sharp firing and some cheers, and then that they were across and had occupied the nearest houses. We were ordered to fall in at the same time, and in a few moments marched down the bank and followed the 19th across in pontoon boats. The 19th, as I said, were already at the foot of the bank, deployed. Some of the 7th Michigan wounded were being brought back, among them the Lieut. Colonel shot in the shoulder. The Michigan men made a rush at the nearest houses and took quite a number of prisoners. The orders to the whole Brigade were to bayonet every armed man found firing from a house, this being, I believe, contrary to the rules of war, but it was not of course obeyed. In fact no prisoners were taken but the few the Michigans took, and the wounded who lay about struck by our shells. The 7th Michigan were deployed on the left and a short distance up the street at the foot of which we landed, and the 19th on the right, both holding houses, fences etc. and exchanging shots with the Rebels who were a little farther back. The pontoon bridge was hurriedly finished, and the Rebels then opened on it with shell, doing little damage, but somewhat disturbing the troops crossing. When a good many troops had got over, we were advanced up the street in column of Companies right in front and Macy was ordered to "follow the skirmishers", that is the 7th Michigan, and advance into the town, at the same time the 19th on the right and the 42nd *[New York]* which had been deployed on the extreme left were ordered to advance also. I can explain our position best by a plan.

RIGHT UP INTO THE FIRE

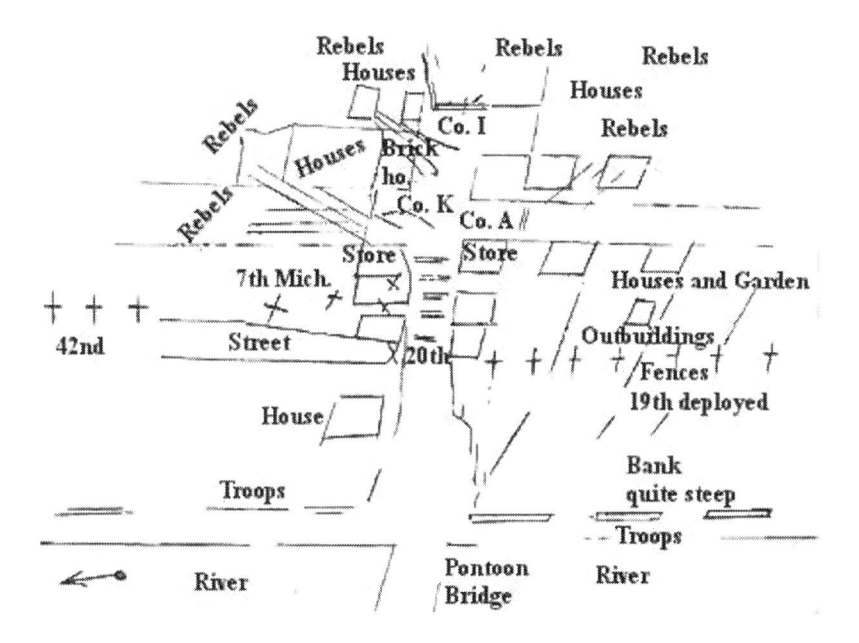

[Map showing positions with labels: Rebels Houses, Rebels, Rebels Houses, Rebels, Co. I, Houses, Brick ho., Co. K, Co. A, 7th Mich., Store, Store, Houses and Garden, 42nd, Street, 20th, Outbuildings, Fences, 19th deployed, House, Bank quite steep, Troops, Troops, River, Pontoon Bridge, River]

The 20th advanced up the street, and when the head of the column got to where the 7th Michigan men were, on the left, in a kind of alley way, and occup/r/ing a house, Macy called to them to go ahead. Capt. Hunt, their commanding Officer was there, and he hesitated and refused. Macy was obliged to halt and urge him to go forward. Capt. Hunt still refused, saying he had no orders, and Macy, much irritated, told him *his* orders, which were very plain, to go forward and *follow* the 7th. Orders came from the rear to press on, Hunt still hung back, saying the Rebels were there in force, and "no man could live round that corner", or some such words. Macy was of course terribly angry, and turned off saying: "Go to hell with your Regiment then", or something like that, and gave the order to advance. All this occupied but 2 or 3 minutes, yet it was very troublesome, as the rear was pressing on. My Company was close to Abbott's, and we entered upon the main street within a moment of each other. That instance a tremendous and deadly fire swept down from the front and left. The Rebels occupied the houses and were behind fences, and could not be seen except by the flash of the guns. It staggered the column, but in a moment they pressed on, led by Abbott in his usual fearless manner. At the same time, my Company was ordered to left wheel, and Capt. Shepard gave the first word, and the Company swung round right across the worst line of fire. Capt. Shepard rolled over, hit in the foot, and shouted to me to take command. 1st Sergeant Campion fell, and 2 or 3 more, and before I could get to my place, they had fallen into a momentary confusion, and it was with no little difficulty I could bring them into line and open fire down the street. The Rebels evidently took good aim. Almost every ball struck, and a very large proportion were killed outright or desperately wounded. The 3rd Company had wheeled to the right but had found the fire coming from the rear and left (to them) and had soon entered the houses on the left and fired to the front. The men were killed and wounded so fast that the rest of the Regiment was immediately called up and supported the Companies first in position. In this way Companies D, G and C came up and filled that part of the street my Company could not cover. The central place was heaped with bodies, and although night was coming on, the Rebels were not silenced, but still fired, and even got into a small house on the left of Company I, from which Abbott vainly tried to dislodge them by entering a house on his left. Our guns were getting clogged, our fire slack, and Macy sent back urgent requests for help, and for the Regiments on our right and left to advance, and altogether to clear the Rebels out. The 59th New York were sent up to relieve us, but as soon as they got under fire, gave way, and ran back, and were only rallied by the efforts of our Officers, and their own Lieut. Colonel who seemed the only decent man they had. Just before they came up, I was struck by a spent ball in the upper part of the groin, a very severe blow which cut completely through my trousers. I fell backwards, and was assisted by soldier. My leg was completely paralysed, and I almost lost my consciousness, and felt sure I was shot through. I left the Company to sergeant Clark and limped to the rear, suffering considerable pain. Just round the Corner I leaned against a fence, and now felt better and found I could move my leg. Just then the 59th gave way and came running back, and I made an effort to stop them, and after a few minutes they were rallied, and I then found I could stand, and got back immediately to my Company which was still as I left it. My leg was pretty stiff for 3 days but is now perfectly well. It was now getting dark, my Company had dwindled down to about 8 men and the rifles were so foul they could hardly be loaded. We had fired about 30 rounds. Macy had sent up other Companies and the left of the street was left open, the men who were left firing from the right partly sheltered by the brick building. The 59th had been got up and were ordered to relieve us, and my few men were allowed to go to the rear with Company D under Perkins. I did not mention that Capt. Dreher had been ordered to support me with his Company and had come up, but he almost immediately withdrew his Company and they fell entirely back. The color-bearer, however, was shot.[48] Abbott had suffered terribly and the 59th were sent to relieve him, and as it was now dark and the firing less deadly, they stood about the corners and kept firing while our Companies were drawn a little back, but only to the head of the street where were two stores. In a few moments, however, they all came running back in terrible confusion and were only stopped by Abbott, Herbert and myself who placed ourselves across the

---

[48] Possibly Corporal Anton Steffens of Company C.

street and fairly forced them to halt. They could not be brought up and so (as we had received orders) we got back our men to the houses and stores at the head of the street and the firing gradually dropped off. We got in our wounded and helped them to the rear as well as we could. Just as the 59th gave way the last time, I went forward to where two men were carrying back a wounded Captain of the 59th and helped him off. His blood was pouring out in a stream which I could hear but not see. He was mortally wounded and was I hear their best Officer.[49] Lieut. McKay was shot just by me, a short distance behind Company I near the corner, just before we fell back for the night. He was one of our very best Officers. We occupied these houses all night. The enemy fell back, and there was no more firing. On the whole it was about as trying a fight as could well be. Abbott says it was far worse than Ball's Bluff.

December 20th.

Dear John.

I was obliged to leave off the other day and have been so busy with necessary Company matters since as to have been unable to continue till now. I heard yesterday of Major Willard's death, and I assure you I feel it most deeply. I saw him for the first time since I came out the day before his death. How dreadful for his wife! Well, I suppose it has been worth 13000 men if the wretched Government at Washington is now convinced that it takes a General to fight a battle. The state of feeling against the Radicals at Washington is tremendous, and they well deserve it. Thirteen thousand men uselessly butchered to satisfy them of their ignorance! We who are out here feel this. It is very easy to cry "forward" at Washington. There is but one thing now that can restore the Army, or rather prevent a *total demoralization* that is the restoration of McClellan with *full, unrestrained* powers, and the *utter* overthrow of Halleck and Stanton. That and that only can give us an Army that can fight, and whether war or peace is to follow, that is the most important thing now. It is all humbug to say that the troops fought well, they never fought worse as far as I saw. The Pennsylvania troops and the new Regiments behaved miserably. There was no head, no definite attacks, a mere slaughter. We were 4 hours without any support. I never saw so many men streaming to the rear in total confusion. Nothing but the old Peninsula troops saved us from rout, and they did so at fearful cost. I hear every General, including old Sumner, opposed the assault. When Sumner wants to hold back, others had better not venture. You see by the lists that Sumner's old Corps, the 2nd, lost 2 or 3 times as many as any other. The papers give generally poor accounts. Howard's

---

[49] Captain Edward Reynolds of Company D died of his wounds on December 24, 1862.

RIGHT UP INTO THE FIRE

Division was held in reserve, except our Brigade which assaulted the works without support. I left off at the end of the fight of the 11th. On the 12th there was no battle, troops constantly crossed the bridges, greatly harrassed by the Rebel shells. We were in the streets and houses all day. Fredericksburg is a fine city. It was evidently hastily evacuated, houses left with everything just as if occupied. As the City was defended against us, of course it was given up to pillage. Everything was ransacked, Clothes, Furniture, Pictures, Silver, glass and China were scattered about everywhere. There was an abundance of flour, meat, salt, poultry etc., wine, pickles, preserves, sauces etc. were brought out and eaten. You would see a Mahogany table brought out with 2 or 3 velvet covered chairs, and soldiers eating off them with silver or fine china ware. Articles of female dress were scattered about; soldiers cleaned their guns with silk dresses and lace veils. Many safes were broken open, and watches, Jewelry and Gold found. Several packages of Gold coin were found. Almost every house was riddled with Cannon shot. In one was found the body of a young Lady shot in the breast by a shell. A few inhabitants remained in the cellars, particularly in the South part of the town, and were unmolested. I saw very little property wantonly destroyed, that is such things as pictures etc. which could be of no use to the men. Many pianos were in the houses, and the men got up concerts and sang and played all day. All this time we were under fire whenever the Rebels chose to throw shell at us, which they did whenever they saw a party together. We kept behind and in the houses. It was like what one reads about to see this sacked city. The men took what they pleased, but of course could not carry much except small articles. Books were carried out by the armful, read a few minutes and thrown down. You would see splendid Copies of Byron or Milton or Scott, kicking about in the mud.

While we were waiting in the streets about noon, Macy came up to me and said: "Here is some one you would like to see, Ropes." I turned round and saw Major Willard, looking the same as ever. I need not say how glad I was to see him. We had a very pleasant talk for some minutes. He took me aside and showed me the portrait of his wife, which he took from his breast. He spoke of her a moment and then we walked back. Soon he said he ought to go back to his Regiment, which was quite near, and I started to walk along with him. There had been no firing for some time, but just as we turned a corner a shell came, and bursting in the house where we were passing, scattered the bricks and dust almost over us. I said we might fall in if there was to be an attack, and therefore bade him good bye to return to the Regiment. We shook hands most cordially and parted with best wishes for each other's safety. I returned across a small rear-garden, being the shortest way, and had hardly left him when another shell burst very close to me, within a few feet, the pieces striking all round, many not 10 inches from me. I never was so nearly hit before, and I think few people have had so narrow an escape as that was. After a short time the Rebels ceased firing. The next

RIGHT UP INTO THE FIRE

day we were kept back till about 12 o'clock, although there was very heavy firing, especially of musketry, and we knew that a battle was going on. Then we fell in and marched to the front, to the outskirts of the town, crossing a small canal on a bridge. Here we came under fire of the Rebel Artillery in direct range. The streets were filled with dead and wounded. A shell burst in my Company and knocked over 2 men, mortally wounding one. Two more I missed from that time but do not think they were wounded. Our Brigade was marching by the left flank, and the 20th the right Regiment last.

I will give you a plan.

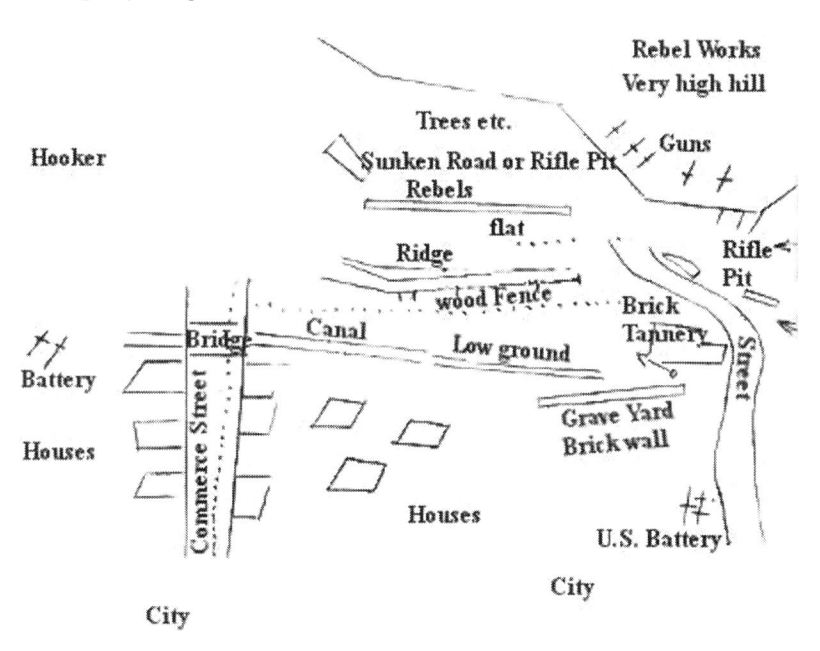

[sketch map showing Hooker, Rebel Works Very high hill, Trees etc., Sunken Road or Rifle Pit, Rebels, Guns, flat, Ridge, wood Fence, Rifle Pit, Battery, Bridge, Canal, Low ground, Brick Tannery, Houses, Commerce Street, Grave Yard Brick wall, Houses, U.S. Battery, City]

The dotted line represents our march. We were under a tremendous Artillery fire when near the bridge, and here my Company lost. Marching by the left flank we formed on the left by files in to line, our Regiment getting last up and forming the extreme right of the Brigade. The order for the Brigade to advance was given before we got up. The 19th had already got up the slope enough to get under fire from the Rebels in the pits, and as we formed were driven back in confusion behind the ridge and fence where we formed. I understand that none of the Generals who ordered the charge knew how great was the Rebel force nor anything in fact about it. Col. Hall commanding Brigade saw what a desperate undertaking it was and protested in the most earnest and solemn manner, but received positive orders to assault, or rather to advance. Just as we formed, the order to advance was given. None knew against what we were going, we only saw the Rebel works towering high above us and felt the shot and shell and musketry

RIGHT UP INTO THE FIRE

almost shake the ground. As we got up the slope, the fire was indeed awful. No man could stand up against it. Only the 19th and 20th advanced at all. The 19th gave way in disorder. We had got ½ way to the pits, the men began to fire and could not be got to advance, and only by the desperate efforts of the Officers could they be made to stand and close up the fearful gaps which were made in the line. Part of Company I was deployed on the right and behind the brick house there, and were not exposed to this fire much. The ridge was completely swept by every gun and musket which could be brought to bear. At last an order came to retire. Macy ordered the Regiment to fall back to the fence. The men fell back hastily, eager to get under the cover of the bank, and the instant the retreat began the enemy suddenly opened a fire which I cannot describe, so tremendous was the storm of bullets. They must have had a second line in reserve, the ground was torn up, and it was like the drops of a heavy shower striking the ground all round you. I distinctly felt the balls strike my coat, hat and knapsack. A ball passed over each shoulder, one just touching my whiskers and cutting my knapsack on either side. We rallied at the fence and expecting an instant attack of the enemy, fixed bayonets and determined to hold the fence and ditch. The men lay down and we advanced a few who lay flat close to the top of the ridge. Those deployed on the right kept the Rebel rifle pits busy on the right. A battery was now sent to the road in rear of our right, and this was the first support we had had. The Rebels still raked us at long range from guns which came from the direction of the arrows I have made, one striking the corner of the brick house. This house was a tannery. All this time we were under a heavy shell fire from the advanced redoubt, but now our battery near the bridge played so accurately as to silence and at last dismount the gun. They, however, got up another. This gun was so near we could distinctly see them load and aim. I should think it was as near as from the State house to Charles street. At about 3 o'clock Sully's Brigade came to our support, and advanced beyond the fence, just under the brow of the ridge, leaving us in the 2nd line. A part also were placed behind the brick tannery. Not long after a very large Brigade, I heard it was Tyler's Brigade of Pennsylvania troops, came up from the road, and formed behind us, filling up the field. I heard they were to assault the same place. The Rebels opened fire on them and killed and wounded a great many and soon the whole Brigade broke and ran in total confusion, the Rebels playing into them all the time. They were finally got off somewhere in the town and we did not see them again. It was now perhaps 5 P.M. and still the fire of musketry raged on our left, swelling and then dying away, and the Artillery continued without interruption. An attack had evidently failed, the bridge and road were covered by a constant stream of fugitives, and the plain in front of us heaped with our own dead and wounded. The cries of the latter for aid were dreadful, but they could not be got at, for the enemy shot at every one who appeared. A very brave fellow, Dugan, of Company F crawled out and brought in

Alley's sword, although he was shot at and narrowly escaped. At last, night came on and we put our vedettes, lying down, just on the crest of the hill. The Rebels did the same. We could hear them talk and sneeze. Having got the range they drew [sic] in shell about every 5 minutes till perhaps 10 P.M., and then all was still. It was pitch dark. We got Alley's body and sent it in, and got off most of our wounded, but some lay so far out we could not get to them, and they groaned all night. At about midnight we were relieved by Sykes' Regulars, in perfect silence we were drawn in to the city and lay down in the streets greatly exhausted. So ended this great slaughter, for not producing which McClellan was removed.

You see that on the whole our Brigade has done a great deal, crossing the first, etc., and that our Regiment has done nobly and exhibited the first quality of a good Regiment, perfect steadiness. The day after the battle Genl. Howard rode up to the Regiment, called for Capt. Macy, and said: "Capt. Macy, I have come to thank you and your Regiment for your noble conduct in the late battles. You have done nobly. The Regiment has done nobly. Massachusetts men always do nobly. Be assured not a life shall be uselessly sacrificed. Today you are in reserve of 2 corps, and will not be called upon but in the last extremity. All I ask for now is constancy, constancy, and that is enough to say to Massachusetts men." These are as nearly the words as I can recollect. Genl. Howard then rode off amid tremendous cheers and half a dozen shells which the Rebels immediately pitched in by way of being on the safe side.

Now, you know, I have told you not ever to publish my letters, but now I want you to do this: Make up a short piece giving an account of this event, and stating that Macy led the Regiment in the noblest manner. Macy did *splendidly*. So we all say, and we say it ought to be known, and we are the ones to tell it. Macy's good judgment, bravery and perfect steadfastness deserve the very highest praise. I want you to write a short article for the Advertiser, just stating how Macy did and what Genl. Howard said. Do not of course use my words, or make any allusion to me, but let it be known for his sake. After Genl. Howard's speech we were taken to the rear near the river, out of the fire of shell, and staid there all day. Col. Lee joined us here, quite sick and perfectly unable to endure the trials of a soldier's life. I received from him a package of silver of Ten Dollars and several letters. Thank you for the shoulder straps, and for your congratulations on my promotion. The next day (Monday) was quiet, not many shell thrown. They began to remove the wounded and we heard we were to be withdrawn and then that we were to throw up earth works and hold the place. About midnight we marched quietly across the pontoon bridge and found troops pouring over in silence. It was dark and cloudy. We marched straight back to our old Camp, and I found my hut in a good state of preservation and 2 sick men of the Company there. They got me something to eat and I then turned in and slept. It rained hard till about noon of the next day, and has been fine and cold since. I am now well housed and look forward to winterquarters here. The day after we got to Camp Genl. Howard made a speech to each Regiment of the Brigade drawn up to receive him. He complimented us in the very highest terms, and said the 20th Mass. would be always near his heart. He spoke well of the 19th but blamed the 42nd because they were driven in from picket on the place where we fought the next day, and he blamed the 126th Pennsylvania, a new Regiment, because they ran away in battle. He praised the Michigan 7th for its gallant exploit in crossing in boats first. On the whole the 20th is on the very highest shelf.

I believe I have now given you a correct though rapid account of the battles, and will now answer your letter. First, my account. I was indeed surprised to see the sum total $630.00, but I have no doubt it is correct. If it is not too much trouble, please send me a list of the articles and the charges. You acknowledge the receipt of $490.00 and you have before acknowledged, I think, some $10.00 from C. B. Porter which I think was from sale of some of my private property at Cambridge. If so, I still am $130.00 in debt. Government will in 10 days owe me about $670.00 of which I can send home $300.00 leaving a balance on hand of $170.00. In all probability, however, we shall be paid for 4 months only now, i.e. $450.00 or so. In that case I shall send home $200.00, more than enough to make me square. I feel that I have ordered nothing I did not need; and with all my expense, I have no doubt been much more comfortable than a day laborer at home; and I suppose the increased cost of everything on account of the taxes has raised prices. When for 9 tenths of the time a man *has* to endure a great deal of hardship, he ought to live well the other one tenth, and if he does not, he will suffer for it. I think perhaps you have spent rather more than necessary for my things not supposing economy was necessary with me. However, I shall need no more clothes this winter, and if the Paymaster would only come, I should be well off. My income is raised $120.00 per annum by my promotion, and the same in addition, as long as I remain in command of the Company. So, knowing I can eventually discharge all obligations, I shall run on Father's kindness to the extent of advances, to pay for whatever I may order (which cannot remain charged till I send the money).

I find that Henry Burckmeyer's expenses in coming out were $22.50, and that Mr. Peirson besides brought $11.50 to me, in all $34.00. I enclose the mess account which you sent me before.

James McGohan went to Boston yesterday with Lieut. McKay wounded. He went at his own urgent request and at his own expense in going and returning, to see about the money and effects of his sister who has died. I allowed him to go, and got a man in his place and advanced him $15.00 which I borrowed from Quartermaster Folsom, giving him a note for the amount on you which he will send to his brother and which you will please honor and charge to me. James promises me to bring back for me as much as he can carry. Please send by him a strong pocket knife. Capt. Cabot lost the one he brought on for me. Also the small things sent by Col. Lee which he did not have here to give me and which I suppose he will take home. Please also send the following things or as much as he can take. 2 boxes yeast powder, 2 cans preserved peaches, and 2 cans Strawberries from Davis & Co. (or some equally good place, that is cheapest and best I think), 2 cans roast turkey, 2 cans green peas, 1 bottle Worcestershire (or Club) sauce from same place, 2 bottles brandy, 3 lbs. Raisins, 1 doz. Lemons, some apples or pears, if convenient. Also please give him $5.00 to buy for me in Washington a turkey or some ducks or chickens, in case he can carry them. It is hard to get meat here, except Government beef. Do not burden him with unnecessary things. Please ask Mother to give him a small pot of her nice Cranberry sauce. He can carry some small things for Quarter Master Folsom, Herbert and Abbott, but, besides this, I think he owes me all the rest of his transporting power. I want him principally to carry food, i.e. something better than beef and bread, almost all we get here. I send by him my watch to be repaired. It keeps miserable time and constantly stops. I send a cup from Fredericksburg, a sample of what was kicking about the streets. Please give it to Mary Ann. I send enclosed for you an address delivered at some Church there. One of my men found several in a house there. Also a little drawing of 2 sirens. Please give it to Louisa. It is of no particular value but as a relic.

    I expected to contribute to the usual Christmas presents, but the alarming state of my finances stares me in the face. As soon, however, as I get paid I will send home enough and wish you and Mary Ann and Louisa each to have a present from me, say $3.00 each, and I wish also to have a share in Father's & Mother's presents. I should be very glad if you could arrange this so that I need not be left out of the list of donors. Perhaps I shall be paid in time yet.

    I believe I have finished this tremendous letter. I expect James back in a week or so. I wish I could pass Christmas with you. I shall remember you all, and think of last Christmas and hope for the next. I also sent by James a flask and note for Mrs. Lee. It is part of the Colonel's property. Reading this over I have not given our loss. The 20th went into action the 1st day with about 320 men and 15 Officers including Macy, commanding, and the Adjutant. They lost altogether in both days 168 men killed and wounded, a very large proportion killed and badly wounded, and the following Officers:

RIGHT UP INTO THE FIRE

1st day (11th)

Killed:
Capt. Cabot

Wounded:
Capt. Shepard (foot)
Lieut. Wilkins (arm, bad)
Lieut. McKay (shoulder)
Lieut. Curtis (slightly)

2nd day (13th)

Killed:
Lieut. Alley

Wounded:
Capt. Dreher
Lieut. Beckwith (very badly)

My Company, K, crossed the river with 23 guns and 2 Officers, and returned with 9 guns and one Officer.

I lost *first day* 1 Officer *wounded*
Killed: 2 privates: Donnelly and Carver
Wounded: 1st Sergeant Campion (right arm amputated), Privates: Blake, Dillon and Morrison [*Morrissey*] (legs amputated) and Dana (in foot slightly).

2nd day

Killed:
Private Hastings

Wounded:
Corporals Crowell and Blankenburg (both mortally, and since dead), Flannigan [*Flanagan*] (leg)

Missing:
Privates Keenan, Wentworth, and Collier, the last may be wounded.[50]

Total both fights: 1 Officer wounded

---

[50] None of the three was listed as missing, so all of them most likely returned to the regiment before the lists were made out.

RIGHT UP INTO THE FIRE

Enlisted men:
Killed: 5 including mortally wounded
Wounded: 6
Missing: 3
Total: 14

Returned: 9 and 1 Officer
Went over: 23 and 2 Officers.

This statement will show you what kind of a fight it was. Write soon and tell me how you feel.
Best love to Mother, Father and all from

Your affectionate brother
Henry.

December 20th 1862.

Dear John.

In my long letter to you which I finished today I entirely forgot to tell you what I think of your plan of the sale of the Estates. I entirely approve of it. It would be indeed very unpleasant to be left with such a little income as $3500.00. I think it would be wrong for us to wish to deprive Mother of the comforts of a liberal income for the sake of a possible future advantage which we children certainly would be the only ones to enjoy. Still we must remember that this state of things was brought about principally by Father, and I do not think we or Mother should be made to suffer, on account of his bad management, more than is absolutely necessary. I should be in favor of selling and discharging every real legal obligation, but hardly like your quick and perhaps too liberal way of passing off obligations *we* did not incur. If the whole question, will and all, should be brought to a settlement on perfectly just principles, then of course meet halfway and allow for every claim, but since we are to suffer by an exceedingly forced and unjust representation of our property and claims, I see no reason why we should give up any claim not legal, or waive any legal right. At all events, I leave it in your hands to act for me. I am decidedly in favor of selling and putting beyond question the certainty of a decent income.

Please let me know what Father thinks of my expenses etc., and how money and business were. I intend to live strictly within my own income, but even if I should draw, to some small extent, on Father, I really think it would not be improper, considering how little expense I am to him compared with the rest and how much I am enduring and how much greater the chances of my death are. Tell me plainly how it is, and whether I had really better *not draw at all* beyond my remittances.

Please let me know what packages are now on the way to me, by Express or otherwise, as far as you know. Please send a little post paper.

Your affectionate brother
Henry.

Falmouth, Va. December 20th 1862.

My dear Mother.

I have written fully to John and to Father about the late battles etc., and these letters must do for you all.

I want to direct your sympathy and charity to the families of my poor men who have fallen. John Donnelly, Private in my Company, killed on the 11th leaves a father and mother in Roxbury at "Mayor Gaston's House", and Thomas Carver has a wife and family in Boston. He worked for many years in Knotts' Ladies' shoe store and they of course know where he lived. He has two sons in my Company, one of whom was in both battles and escaped injury. Corporal Crowell, a most excellent man leaves a family in Braintree. Thomas Flannigan *[Flanagan]* wounded by a shell leaves a family in Pleasant Street near Washington Street, Boston. He was once my servant and a most excellent man and soldier. I do not know how badly he is hurt. Private John Dillon leg amputated, doing well, leaves a wife, Mary Dillon in rear of Pinckney Street. He was a most excellent man. 1st Sergeant Champion *[Campion]* right arm amputated has a family in Boston. If you would visit any of these families, especially Flannigan's and Dillon's I should be very much obliged. As soon as we are paid off I shall send John some money and shall then be glad if you would assist any of these you see fit, for me.

I think we ought to do what we can for these poor people who have risked and endured so much for us. Please say to Mrs. Dillon that I will send her husband's pay to her as soon as I can get it, as he requested. I know Mary Ann would like to visit some of these families. Company I (Abbott) and my Company suffered worst of all. We were the leading Companies.

I am very comfortable in my new house. We shall no doubt winter here. I hope the Express will soon run. James will tell you all about things here and the battles, and I hope he will soon return and bring me many useful things. James is a good meaning fellow and on the whole I like him. He is honest and faithful at any rate.

Your affectionate son
Henry.

20th Regiment
December 24th 1862.

Dear John.

Just received yours of the 19th. Major Willard's death is indeed a great blow to us all. Yet I think out here, though we feel it as keenly, it makes less outward impression, and we go on and laugh and talk just as ever. If ever I get back home I shall then miss my friends more than now. War does not harden one permanently, but makes one less to be influenced for the time by the misfortunes of others and the death of friends. An evil which at home would completely upset a man, does not do so here. I shall never forget my last interview with him.

As to the Christmas box, I dare say James can bring on some things, and if he can only get them as far as Acquia Creek , I can probably send for them from there. It is shameful, after all we have been through, not to allow us to get such little luxuries as we can from home. Officers, especially, should have the privilege, instead of being obliged to pay exorbitant prices here. I believe I have given you a full account of the battle in my long letter. I cannot at all agree with you as to McClellan, or as to the policy of the present movement. I know (from Col. Hall, privately) that McClellan's plans were ripe when he was removed. By his apparent delay in the valley he obliged the enemy to keep a large force under Jackson at or near Winchester. At Warrenton Junction heavy reenforcements met the Army, and McClellan had calculated on this, and intended, having as it were passed Jackson to fall immediately on Lee at Culpepper and overwhelm him by his immensely superior force, then turn on Jackson and then on Richmond. We never before had succeeded in getting our *entire* Army between the *divided* Rebel Army, and never was a plan more certain of success. Just at the moment of completion McClellan is removed. I have no words strong enough to condemn the President, the Government, and the whole Anti-McClellan or radical party. Every day increases my confidence in McClellan, and I think him the noblest patriot and the best General the country has had since Washington. He is the *only* man who can now restore this Army. All the newspaper talk about our still being anxious for a fight is miserable falsehood, and the Government and the Country had better not deceive themselves with it. Do not think I am fainthearted, for I am not. The 20th will fight *always*, whenever ordered, as long as the Officers are alive, but the Army, as an Army, is a thing of the past. They can fight a defensive battle, if attacked, and do well, that is all. It seems to me that we are very near the end, and that a very unpromising one. I can merely wait and see. Peace would be hailed with joy on almost any terms by the country, and the Army feeling a consciousness that it has done its duty, does not care. I still hope, but it is a hope founded on nothing. If I see Halleck superseded by McClellan, I shall have confidence, not till then.

Mr. Boulnois has just arrived, with Charley Whittier, and Genl. Sedgwick. Sedgwick is to have our Corps. Mr. Boulnois has gone up to Brigade Headquarters now, perhaps to dine. I shall do everything I can to make his stay agreeable. His baggage has not yet come. Abbott, Macy, Murphy, and all desire regards.

You may meet Capt. Shepard possibly. Do not be anxious to show him any attention on my account. I believe I wrote to you that he had treated me unhandsomely in a Company matter, and that we were no more of friends than necessary. I have lost about all the very little respect I ever had for him.

I am again out of stamps, and must ask for some. I have quantities of letters, now about killed and wounded men to write. One of my missing men has turned up slightly hurt. That makes me 7 wounded and 5 killed, out of 23, and 2 missing. Do not let James stay too long at home, and do not let him be burdened so as to risk losing all. He cannot of course carry much for others.

Write often.

Your affectionate brother
Henry.

Enclosed letter for Mary Ann.

RIGHT UP INTO THE FIRE

Camp 20th Mass. Volunteers
near Falmouth, Va. December 26th 1862.

My dear Mother.

I have just received yours of the 20th December and for this and the previous two am much obliged. I have now got a great many letters from home. I was amused to see in one of your letters an illusion *[sic]* to my adventure in the woods at Yorktown last Spring, as if it was a very narrow escape for me. I hope I did not give you that impression in my letters. I was not in any danger then, and only escaped a rather uncomfortable night and loss of supper.

We had intended to make as much of Christmas as possible, and Abbott and I were to have had a combined dinner in my hut, but the afternoon before we were detailed for Picket and so spent the day and night there and have just got in. Abbott and I however went to a house and got quite a respectable dinner, and tried to believe we were keeping Christmas. Here we saw the evils of war, for the poor old woman told us that her cows and sheep had all been stolen by the soldiers and her fences torn down and that she hardly knew what to get to eat.

Mr. Boulnois has been here all day yesterday, he had a fine time, dining with the Generals and high Officers. He is a very agreeable man and seems to enjoy his visit very much. Tonight he stays with me, after supping with Holmes. I have today heard that our Corps is to move to Alexandria. I hardly know whether or not to believe it.

I suppose you have seen James McGohan, and I dare say he will bring on the Christmas dinner you were so kind as to prepare for me. Mr. Boulnois brings me Towels, handkerchiefs, soap etc., and Abbott has given me the shirt, for all which much obliged. If you do not send a pair drawers (ribbed woolen) by James, please send them by mail lightly wrapped in brown paper, and with 2 or 3 stamps only. Also a pair woolen socks like the last. These can come easily by mail.

I wrote to you about my wounded men. I should be very glad if you would visit Mrs. Flannigan, Pleasant Street, near Washington, right hand side as you go to Washington St., and tell her that her husband, Thomas Flannigan, is only slightly wounded in the foot, and is at a Hospital near Washington. Flannigan is an excellent man and has done a great deal for me, and I would like to be of service to him in any way I can.

Best love to all. I shall write to Frank and to others abroad when I get some post paper.

Your affectionate son
Henry.

RIGHT UP INTO THE FIRE

Camp 20th Regiment
December 30th 1862.

My dear John.

Yours of the 26th just received. Mr. Boulnois is still here with me. I like him very much and he is a great favorite with everyone. He has seen a great deal of the Army and the Generals. I am deeply *grieved* by what Mr. Boulnois tells me of your Anti-McClellan feeling. Every day I think more of that man. I am now by recent revelations, perfectly convinced that he has twice been on the point of utterly destroying the military power of the Rebellion, and that his plans had been interfered with by Government. Look at the testimony in the McDowell case, it is overwhelming. Burnside has proved himself a weak man and a miserable General. In McClellan the Army has confidence, and certainly the judgment of an Army like ours ought to be of insight. Then he has held his peace although he had only to come out openly and raise a tremendous opposition to the Government. He is a noble patriot, indeed. As to the demoralization of the Army, I am perfectly willing to leave my statement to be proved by events. McClellan alone can restore the Army. We hear it is to be consolidated. The Government altogether appears to me weak and inefficient. I can only hope for better things. As to the Regiment here, however, we are in good spirits as ever, in fact I consider it a duty to keep in good spirits, but my judgment remains the same and my opinion as to the state of the Army. We are going to move, where? I cannot tell yet. I hear that we are to exchange places with Heintzelman's Corps at Alexandria, and that our Corps is reported unfit for service. Also that we are going to Suffolk. I do not know what to believe, but I feel sure we shall march in a day or two. Rations are issued and marching orders have come. If Richmond is ever taken, we must return to McClellan's old base, the James river. The greatest blunder of the war was McClellan's removal from Harrison's Landing. The troops that have since been uselessly slaughtered would have enabled him to take the city and end the war.

I am very glad to get the shirt, handkerchiefs, towels, soap etc. sent by Abbott and Boulnois. Tell Mother the shirt is just the right size. My old ones have become much too small. I want now drawers (ribbed wool) and socks, both which I wrote to Mother can be sent by mail. There are plenty of mine at home. Please send two darning needles by mail, and don't forget post paper. I may not write till we get settled down again. James received $15.00 from me when he started, and he had $30.00 in the Bank at Boston, so there was no need of Father's advancing him the $20.00. I made a special agreement with James that I should not be at any expense for his trip to Boston and back. I have to supply his place while he is gone, and for this he agrees to bring on as much as he can carry for me. I am to pay him his regular wages without deduction for the time he is absent. Do not let him get the whole amount due him, else he might not return. Do not let him come on loaded with a great bag of clothes for himself. I am glad you think I do right in drawing on Father and in my way of living here. I have no doubt you have done for me exceedingly well as to my expenses etc. I hear from Abbott of the tremendous rise in prices for clothing etc.

I am sorry not to be able to contribute to the Christmas gifts, but shall not forget you all when I am paid. Tell Mary Ann to write me *most fully* all about Christmas etc. What do people at home think of the battles? They appear to be thirsting for more blood. You may as well make up your mind that you must wait till spring for an Army. The old Regiments must either be recruited or consolidated. You have no idea what a glorious name the 20th has here.

I am very glad you have determined to sell the Hanover Street Estates, and hope you will do well. Mother's comfort is the *first thing* of course, and anything which would annoy her should be avoided, even at some cost. Thank Louisa for her letter. I shall answer soon. I shall await anxiously your letter on the war, the battles etc.

Your affectionate brother
Henry.

1863

January 3rd 1863
Camp 20th Falmouth.

Dear John.

We have not marched and I hear the orders are countermanded. Weather now cold and clear. Boulnois still here. He has received a letter from you. I am getting somewhat anxious about James. He has not yet come. I hope you have not entrusted him with too much money, nor advanced him much. He ought not to have asked any from Father. I hope you saw to it that he was supplied with some sort of pass or order by which he could get from Washington to the camp. Capt. Putnam or Lieut. Riddle would probably have given transportation for him. I can get him a pass here and send it to him at Washington, if I knew how to find him.

Write and tell me if he has started on and how he expected to get here. No News. All well.

Your affectionate brother
Henry.

P.S. Send any boxes for me on to Washington by Express. I have got a way of getting them from Washington here.

H. R.

Sunday evening January 4th 1863.
Camp 20th Regiment.

My dear Mother.

I have received your letter of the 29th and one from Father with it, and I am indeed very sorry to hear of John McFeely's death. He was a most excellent man, and I am sure he tried always to do his duty and was faithful and honest. He is a great loss to you, for I suppose you will hardly feel as safe with a new man to drive.

Mr. Boulnois is today at Corps Headquarters, but I expect him this evening. He is a most universal favorite, and a man of uncommon social qualities, certainly for an Englishman. He likes the Army and especially the Regiment very much.

At last you will be glad to know that the Express has opened and I have received today my 2 boxes and a bag. The bag contains 2 Blankets - most excellent ones - Coat, trousers, shirts, socks, drawers, etc. So please do not send me by mail the socks and drawers I asked for. I am now abundantly supplied with all kinds of clothes. In one box (that sent by Grafton) was the Cherry cordial, Brandy, Tea, Coffee etc. and in the other the new shelter tent, Books etc. etc. all of which are most acceptable, and will contribute greatly to my comfort and health. I had just got out of Tea, and had been obliged to offer our miserable Coffee to Mr. Boulnois when this opportunely arrived. Our Commissary is now out of everything, and we have eaten our last potato and piece of meat, but expect a supply tomorrow. In fact I began to get tired of offering Boulnois day after day nothing but beef fried or beef stewed for breakfast and dinner all the same, for this, with occasionally flour or potatoes, has been about all I could get. But I am astonished to see how easily he puts up with anything and declares he enjoys Stew above everything and could not be better fed etc. Although when he goes to Headquarters he dines on Canvas back Ducks and Champagne. Now that supplies and Sutlers are allowed the Camps will be more cheerful and the Officers and men healthier. I found tacked to Grafton's box a letter from Father of September 22nd and from Mary Ann of same date, and in the other box one from John of November 19th all which please acknowledge. Herbert's lantern etc. arrived all right. Nothing in any of the boxes or bag was injured in the least. You were very kind to get me up such a nice Christmas box. I dare say I shall get it soon now.

There is every reason to believe we shall winter here. Things are perfectly quiet. Weather pleasant, cool at night, warm in midday. I send a pair of 2nd Lieutenant straps belonging to my dress coat. Please ask John to have a 1st Lieutenant's bars put in, and send them back by mail. A small bit of gold braid might be neatly sewed in by any one. Best love to Father and all.

Your affectionate son
Henry.

RIGHT UP INTO THE FIRE

Camp 20th Reg. Jan. 5 near or in Falmth., Virga.

Dear Father,

I have just received your letter of the 31st Dec. enclosing one from sister Anna of the 26th, and the list of contents of a valise to be sent to me by James. Please thank sister etc. I am indeed very much obliged to you for sending me so much. Surely one of the articles will be most acceptable. We are dreadfully hard up for food now, and today I dine of hasty pudding and molasses for our three courses in one. I am glad that Boulnois dined at Sedgwick's Hd. Qrs. Tomorrow we expect a supply of bread, meat and flour. I am delighted with the contents of the boxes and bag, the receipt of which I acknowledged in my last. You speak of James not coming on the day appointed and I am beginning to fear he may have given you the slip. He ought not to have asked you for any money. He had 80.00 in the bank - I advanced him 15.00 and had previously advanced 10.00 more - in all 55.00 and your 20.00 - making in all 75.00 is 5 mos. pay.

He came to me Aug 4th so he is now paid up to Jan 4th. I agreed to pay him always when I received my own pay - i.e. payday. I fear he may get hold of more money - or of clothes etc. and then never return. I never had any reason to doubt his honesty, but the temptation may be too strong for him. However, I hope it may all turn out right and James come back safely.

Better send my money by mail - small sums at a time. I think this is the safest way. Mr. Boulnois fears that some important letters he sent to Europe never were put in the post, and has been daily expecting letters from England. I told him any letters to him directed to you you would immediately forward to my care.

Today he accompanies Genl. Sedgwick to a review of the 2nd Brigade. I am again detailed, this time as recorder of a Court of Inquiry - a matter of only a couple of days I suppose. I am perfectly well. The men suffering a great deal for lack of fresh food and sufficient variety. Diarrhoea and scurvy almost universal. Most of the officers troubled with diarrhoea also. I do better for I try to get a change of diet as often as possible, and frequently succeed. Capt. Tilden is really very ill. Holmes has gone to Hospital in Washington quite used up. Herbert very well. The men are getting comfortably quartered, and are much more cheerful than they were a few weeks ago.

I want to write several letters abroad when I can get some thin paper.

Your affec. son
Henry

Letter for J.C.
enclosed.
Wm. Ropes Esq.

20th
January 5th 1863.

Dear John.

I have just seen the Advertiser of Friday and the 20th article. I am vexed that there should be 2 errors and cannot think how they got in. 1st it says Macy commanded *because* of absence of Colonel, Lieut. Colonel and *Major* Dreher. Dreher had not then heard of his promotion, and, besides, Macy was placed in command by order of Genl. Howard, over the heads of Captains Dreher and Shepard, his superior Officers, on account of their incompetency. Dreher was in the fight with his Company, on my left across the street, and withdrew without orders behind the shelter of a house. Then, in reporting Howard's words it should be "in reserve of *two* Corps", i.e. the 2nd and 12th Couch's and Wil///cox's, not of the 2nd Corps. Neither of these may be of much importance, but I should be sorry to think I wrote so inaccurately. On the whole the fellows are greatly pleased with the piece. What do you think of the letter to Col. Lee? Holmes wrote it.

I have written to Father what I fear about James. Still I have no particular reason to doubt him. Thank you very much for your selection of the books, blankets, etc. received by Express yesterday.

If you could send a barrel of vegetables etc. to viz.: 1 bushle Apples, 1 bushle Cabbages (or Cauliflower), ½ bushle Turnips, I should be very glad. Also a bag Buckwheat to make Cakes. If the Express is in good running order and not extravagant in price, I should be very glad of a box of meat, say 30 lbs. Mutton and Poultry, all freshly killed. I think it would keep, and it would be cheaper for me than to buy here. *Very much* pleased with tent, have not yet pitched it. Please send a few stamps.

Your affectionate brother
Henry.

Thursday evening January 8th 1863
Camp 20th Mass.

My dear John.

I have had no letters from home for 3 days, but the papers have come regularly, and today I received by mail the bundle of clothes, viz.: 1 pair drawers, 1 pair socks, 1 scarf, and in the socks some post paper and envelopes. Please thank

Mother for sending them. They are very well to have, but as I received drawers etc. by Express in the sack with the blankets the other day, I did not absolutely need these. However, when I wrote I did need them and had no prospect of getting any by the Express. I found I did not need all the blankets I now had, and therefore let Patten have one of the thick yellow plaid ones lately received. Please write me what they cost as he is to pay me the exact price you paid for one. I am now bountifully supplied with warm clothing of every kind.

I am *very anxious* in regard to James. I fear he has absconded. He ought to have been back long ago. I am sorry to lose the valise Father wrote about, and hope nothing else was entrusted to him. But, perhaps he never came to you, and so never started to come on with my things. I feel very sorry he got Twenty Dollars from Father. He protested to me in the most solemn manner that he would certainly return and bring everything. I hope you gave him a proper pass, in case he started really. I am very anxious to hear from you about it. Please tell me what packages are now on the way to me. I think of but one: Mother alluded to sending certain articles of crockery, some time ago, and I suppose they are coming in a box. Then there is James' "Valise", as Father writes, and perhaps a Christmas dinner box. Let me know exactly what has been sent. Sister Anna speaks of 2 jars Brandy Peaches etc. What are they in?

Boulnois has been at Corps Headquarters enjoying himself very much for 3 days, so I have seen little of him. I got one or 2 old letters from you and from Mary Ann in the boxes by Express. By the way, I observe my new tent is sewed as the old one was, and I fear the seams will leak. Have not tried it yet. What did it cost?

No change in matters here. All quiet. Weather colder. Have had some rain.

Your affectionate brother
Henry.

Enclosed letter for Hazeltine.

Camp 20th, January 11th 1863.

My dear John.

I hasten to answer your letter of January 6th enclosing the key to the valise and the Express order. I see by your slight reference to James and by a like reference in Mary Ann's last letter that I never received a letter written on about January 1st by you, telling me of James' sickness and perhaps many other things I should be very sorry to lose. Your letter (6th) does much to relieve us all from extreme anxiety about the new Colonel reported to have been appointed. The appointment of *any man whatever* from outside would be an insult to the Officers of the Regiment which could not be borne and would lead to the resignation of every one of the Officers who have made the 20th what it is. We heard the report several days ago, and the indignation was intense, not only among us but at HeadQuarters [*sic*], as high up as Genl. Sumner. Genl. Howard immediately wrote most earnestly, and advised a "manly and earnest protest" to be sent in by us, saying to pass over Col. Palfrey was most shameful, and even if his health would not allow him to take it, that he could "make half dozen Colonels out of the Officers of the 20th". In case Governor Andrew should appoint a new man and the Officers here take any action, we are assured that such action will be approved at Brigade, Division, Corps and Grand Division Head Quarters publicly. With such backers we are safe. The only reason which Governor Andrew could possibly urge against Palfrey and Macy is their political views. Their ability is too well established to be doubted.

By the way, you sent me 2 second vols. of Dombey and Son. Please send the 3rd before long. The Coffee in the box does not seem to be like that we used to have at home. It is of a very light color and has an herby flavor, and cannot possibly be made strong. I think it must be Mocha (?) not Java. Please, when you send next, put in a little of the old black kind. The tea is most excellent. As I may not be able to get the valise for some days, please send in an envelope 2 or 3 oz. of yeast powder. I use it constantly and am nearly out. You know by a recent order, you must now prepay the entire postage.

I am very sorry to hear of Col. Lee's illness, yet I expected he would be ill after he got home, he seemed so weak when here. I am a little anxious about the coat strapped to the outside of the valise. I am sorry to tell you that Boulnois is quite unwell and thinks of returning soon to Boston for proper medical treatment. He is now at Corps HeadQuarters in a house. I am going down to see him today. In case he returns in say a week and there is no sign of a move, I want you to come on again and spend a month with me. I can get a pass which will bring you from Washington with as much baggage as you like, from my friend Major Mallow, Provost Marshal of the Grand Division. It will do you good and wake you up. Perhaps you can get over with a flag to the city, and at any rate you can see a good deal here and enjoy yourself in the Regiment. I do not consider that little call at Bolivar a visit worthy of the name. You can be very comfortable in my hut, and by the time you will be here, we shall have food enough to satisfy your civilian delicacy. I will let you know when you had better come. When next you send any books, please let me have "Scott's Poetical Works", and some good history of Cromwell or else "Napier's Peninsular War". I want to read upon [*sic*] both of these important eras. I shall be obliged to leave you to pay for my letters until I get some stamps.

5 P.M.

I have been to see Boulnois and found him about, but quite lame. He fears some letters to his bankers in London miscarried, by which I believe his funds are not sent as he expected, and I believe he has sent to you for some notes. I remember about 9 months ago Father sent me 2 drafts of $50.00 each on Washington, one of which I used and the other I accidentally sent back in a parcel of private letters. It seems to me that a draft of this kind would be very convenient for Boulnois, as he could draw the money when he got to Washington. This, I suppose, you could easily send to him in a letter. Everybody here is out of money, owing to the long delay in paying us off. It is really shameful to make the old troops suffer so. Sumner has returned. Col. Hall's report of the late battles praises our Regiment in the very highest terms. I will try to get you a copy.

I hope you received my letter acknowledging the receipt of the blankets etc. Be sure to tell me instantly if a Colonel is appointed. Could not you telegraph in case Palfrey has it? It would call down blessings on your head here.

Your affectionate brother
Henry.

P.S. As to James, he has now been away since 20th December, although he was to return by the 2nd or 3rd January at farthest. I know nothing of his sickness or the cause of it, and as he did not fall sick in my service but in a pleasure trip on his own account, I am not going to keep on paying him wages for time I get no good from, especially as I must pay the man I now have for all this time. I am exceedingly sorry Father gave him $20.00. It was by no order of mine. I wanted to keep him a month behind to ensure his speedy return. Be very sure he gets no more money, certainly from me. The agreement was that on my part I was to give him a furlough as it were, of 10 or 12 days and in return he was to bring on a valise or box for me. The expenses of the journey both ways he expected would be defrayed by the money his sister left. Unless he comes back *immediately* I wish him to understand that I shall stop it from its wages, and if he does not come back at all, that I shall only pay him up to the date of his departure. I do not know anything about his illness as yet. I never was quite satisfied with him and feel under no obligations, as I should to a faithful and tried servant.

H. R.

RIGHT UP INTO THE FIRE

Camp 20th Mass.
Jany. 12th 1863.

My dear Mother.

I have just received your letter of Jany. 7th. You need not be in the least anxious about Picket for there is no enemy anywhere near our line. We picket on the flank towards Warrenton and Culpepper, and have never seen the first sign of an enemy. It is only a necessary precaution to take. An Army is always surrounded by pickets, whether there is an enemy near or not. Our Cavalry go out scouting far beyond the pickets. I am very sorry the Colonel is so poorly. Did you see a letter we all signed to him? I think it was excellent. Holmes wrote it. I shall be delighted to get the Christmas box you speak of, and the valise which I now expect daily. I am very sorry for James, but fear he does not want to come back and so is playing off. Unless he returns immediately I shall be glad to get rid of him. I am very much obliged to you for seeing after the families of my wounded men. I wrote to the nearest relatives of those who were killed, as soon as I could write after the battle, and from some I have received some very thankful letters in reply. I am glad to hear Dr. Frank is getting on so well. I shall write to him very soon. Thank you for the post paper received by mail in the stocking. Mr. Boulnois, as I have written to John is quite unwell, and fears a return of his chest trouble. He expects soon to return to Boston for treatment. We have had a heavy rain here, and now the weather is quite cold again. I am abundantly supplied with clothes now, and am perfectly comfortable. The Regiment goes today on picket, but I do not, as I am again put on a Court, this time however not a very important one. You say nothing of a new Colonel for our Regiment, and this silence with John's remarks in a letter received yesterday sets us all quite at ease. We had heard that a Frenchman was to be sent out here to command us and were of course highly indignant.

I enclose an order for a pair of boots which I wish John would have made by Rice and sent out by Express. Also an order for a cap to be sent out at the same time.

Please tell John to put in a package of tacks (carpet size) and 2 or 3 lbs. Nails in the next box he sends. Nails are very scarce here. I was obliged to pay 75 Cents for 3 lbs. to build my hut with. If they would keep and not break I should be glad to get some eggs in a box.

We hear rumors of McClellan's return, but I place no confidence in them as yet.

Your affectionate son
Henry.

RIGHT UP INTO THE FIRE

Camp 20th Mass. Volunteers, near
Falmouth, Va. January 13th 1863.

My dear John.

I have received this morning your letter of the 10th giving your views of the Peninsular campaign, and am very glad indeed to read it and very much obliged to you for giving yourself so much trouble. In my letters to you I almost never sit down to give anything more than a reasonably clear narrative, and rarely draw any but the most hurried deductions. And indeed it is hard for men to agree calmly about what concerns themselves so very nearly. If your property had been placed in the hands of a firm who had shamefully misused it, you would hardly be yourself an impartial critic of their management, much more so if the firm had power to maim and kill you and had so done to others you know, all by some mistake they never ought to have made. So I feel I must of necessity be a less impartial observer, because the decisions of Generals may any day affect my life and happiness. Still, if I could free myself from these influences, which tend to make me too earnest, and to blind my judgment, I should be a remarkably good observer, because I cannot but feel that out here I have had unusual means of information, and have picked up a good deal of practical knowledge of war and the act of fighting battles, just as any man who goes to sea picks up a good deal of practical seamanship, if he is observing and enquiring. For instance, I saw in a moment, could not help seeing, the tremendous fault of our recent attack on the *left* of the enemy's position here, and just as much expected defeat as I felt sure of victory at Malvern Hill, where I had a very extensive view of the field.

Now I have just read over your letter with Abbott, and we both agree perfectly as to how to answer your objections and to clear (as we think) McClellan from all blame. I have read many strictures on McClellan's Peninsular Campaign, but I think yours altogether the best and fairest I have seen. You do not attempt too much. Only I might observe if McClellan was fool enough to violate all these fundamental rules you speak of without *sufficient reason* (as you imply) he could hardly have been the General he has proved himself to be in his Maryland campaign, and indeed on his great retreat. I have carefully read the Prince's paper and am exceedingly pleased with it, and have made small notes in the margin (wherever I felt perfectly sure I was correct) to explain or alter some statement. I did this for my own advantage at the time, but perhaps I may have noted several small things I have not told you. I will try to send the pamphlet to you as we both take so much interest in the matter. For my part I make a point of enquiring of almost every Officer I meet about the battles and movements we have been through and every day come to a clearer view of the matter. One thing I observe in every book or article against McClellan I ever saw. Many facts are stated positively, some of which I know all about myself, personally, and these I generally find utterly untrue, and therefore conclude that other important facts stated are untrue. The matter of transports for instance. I know there were just enough. I *know* we had to wait days for transports and then were crowded so as to be very unsafe. I *know* that troops could not have been hurried up to Williamsburg, for Phil Mason, who was there, told me of the awful state of the roads which I myself saw a few miles back. Now, when I read an account which says that McClellan wasted time at Washington and Fort Munroe and omitted to hurry up troops (Sumner's Corps) to Williamsburg and such things, I am tempted to disbelieve other equally important statements. It is impossible for me to present more clearly than the Prince does the dreadful consequences of taking McDowell's Corps from McClellan just at the critical moment, but merely to remind you of it and to pass on. One thing I would say, after a General's excellent plans have been thwarted, he cannot begin again and do as well as if he had never been interfered with. His confidence is gone. He must make few plans for the future for he cannot depend upon them. I mean if his plans are to be divided into 2 classes, one certain, the other contingent, he must make few of the latter and these not important, and do as well as he can with the certain plans. Supposing Wellington had received notice a few days before Waterloo that Blücher had been ordered to fall back and protect some large city after he had calculated upon his coming up on Napoleon's right, do you suppose that he or any man could go to work and arrange the army he had left just as well as if Blücher's army never had existed? This was McClellan's case. His advance had already crossed Bottom's Bridge before he was sure that McDowell would not co-operate with him. Now you say he ought to have resigned etc. For himself and his own glory he ought, for the country he ought not (I think). McClellan never showed his patriotism more than in bearing everything, keeping silence and pushing on the work without complaint, though he knew he *could* have resigned, published his grievances (thereby exposing the plans of the campaign to the enemy) thrown himself on the country and instantly raised a howl of indignation against the Government and set himself at the head of a most powerful opposition. But this would have paralyzed the Army and destroyed every hope of success, and this he would not do. Like a real soldier he obeyed orders and held in his just anger, as long as to let it loose would have worked injury to the cause. Besides, even as late as Fair Oaks it was supposed that our force was greatly superior to the enemy, and McClellan probably expected to be able to beat them *in some way* as it was. As to crossing the river, of course it is foolish to suppose that McClellan did not know all about the rules of war you refer to, and therefore the question is not "why did he violate the first principles of war?" but, "were his reasons for violating these principles sufficient?" And I reply that they were. But, first let me correct a mistake of yours. There were more than 2 bridges. Sumner's, the Railroad bridge,

RIGHT UP INTO THE FIRE

Bottom's Bridge, Long Bridge and Alexander's and the New Bridge away up on the right. Besides these, I feel sure there were others. At any rate, when the Army got to the river a part must cross on the heels of the plying enemy to preserve the communication. Had we waited this side, as you suggest, the enemy, recovering from his first fright, might have so fortified the farther bank as to make it impassable, and then we should have been obliged to march round to the North and attack the City on its most defensible side. In spite of any dangers and violations of rules, the river *must* be crossed and no more men could be thrown over than could be fed, and this depended on the state of the roads and bridges. I think McClellan intended to hold the Western side till he could complete the roads and bridges, then bring all over but Porter's Corps, make an attack to allow Porter to cross above, and then attack mainly with his centre and left, leaving Porter to make a feint and to cover the Railroad and communications. I say he was obliged to cross the river at the very first, and that he could not cross all for lack of bridges and roads through the quagmires on either side of the stream. To postpone crossing would have been to relinquish the idea altogether. His intention undoubtedly was to build in a few days plenty of bridges, but the difficulties were tremendous. The troops and engineers were employed the whole time. The rains were tremendous and the mud was so deep that in many places the engineers were obliged to give it up after wasting material and labor enough for a dozen common bridges. Then the enemy attacked at Fair Oaks before he had his bridges done, and although every effort was made to prevent it, almost every bridge was swept away by Sunday night. The freshet was perfectly unexpected. A man who came over Saturday night told me the water was nearly to his chin on *Sumner's bridge* and he only got through by a miracle. Henry Burckmeyer had to come round on *Monday morning* by the Railroad to bring me food, and he said he saw the tops of wagons just above the water in the road near the river. How any bridges could have been thrown across during Saturday night and Sunday, I cannot see. This, to my mind, perfectly accounts for McClellan's failing to pursue after the battle of Fair Oaks. The men were dying for food. As we now know (which we had no reason then to suspect) the enemy were much demoralized for 2 days, and perhaps a bold attack by a small force might have been successful, but it would have been madness to have tried it then. From that time the enemy were constantly receiving re-enforcements which we did not then know of. As to Gaine's Mill he could not have re-enforced Porter safely then, for you know the order to fall back to the James had already been given, and besides it would take one day for troops to march from the centre to Porter, and it was not till the middle of the second day Porter thought himself in much danger. McClellan might certainly have thrown his whole force against Jackson, and attempted to turn the Rebel left, and, if unsuccessful, to fall back on White House, and I could never see any great objections to this course, except that to retreat there would have exposed him more, and put him in a bad place to resume operations. The Pamunkey at White House was small, and few gunboats could operate there, and the roads to White House were awful, much worse than the more sandy roads to the James. I rather think by the time of Porter's battles McClellan had become convinced that the enemy had received re-enforcements which would enable him to successfully resist any direct attack, and that his best course was to get as soon and as safely as possible to the best base from which when re-enforced himself to renew the attack, and that Jackson began the fight early enough to force Porter into doing with loss what he had intended to do quietly and safely. The enemy had certainly made great preparations to resist an attack by us from the right, and expected it, and had it been attempted and been unsuccessful the Army might have been destroyed.

I do not know whether I have succeeded in replying to any of your criticisms, but I feel I am trying to defend a man who has everything against him clean before the world, and whose proper defense is still half hidden. See what splendid testimony comes out in his favor in these Courts Martial! Now we are *sure* he had not the transports he wanted. We are *sure* McDowell was included in his plans. For anything we know he was *ordered* to throw a part of his force across the Chickahominy, and at any rate we are sure his best plans were spoiled, his earnest appeals for more men and for McDowell's cooperation disregarded, and that he could be sure of nothing and was forced to wait in uncertainty and distrust and deprived of that vigor and singleness of purpose without which no General can achieve great success.

Now, I think that a very humble spectator, if he takes pains to observe, can see when things are well managed and when they are badly managed, and I am sure everything went on better under McClellan. He attended to comparatively small things, such as the general cleanliness of the camps and roads, the food of the soldiers etc. Our men actually fed better before Richmond (except when actually on outpost duty) than they do here. Our men are now suffering from scurvy, all for lack of vegetables etc., which certainly could be brought up by this time. I have never seen the least sign of ability in Burnside. As to our crossing and re-crossing, I cannot understand why the enemy allowed it, or allowed us to remain three days in the city. They might have almost destroyed us. The troops were jammed up in the streets and houses, Artillery would have had terrible effect, and the bridges themselves were under the fire of the enemy's guns. A very few shell hitting the bridge would make awful confusion. I cannot see why the enemy did not attack us on Sunday, or at least open fire on the city and destroy it, and with it ½ the Federal Army. Look at Franklin's evidence before the Committee on the war. I think they allowed us to come so as to beat us, and let us go to save the city. Now, their defenses are doubled, and it would be impossible to cross here. As to Burnside showing any particular skill etc. I can't see it. The enemy gave him that day to remove his wounded from the city, and at night he marched back his troops, all without molestation. As to McClellan's violating the rules of war by crossing the Chickahominy, what do you think of Burnside's crossing the Rappahannock with his very bridges under the fire of the enemy's works?

I think no reasonable man can say that we have a better General than McClellan, however low he may reckon him. Add to this that the Army trust McClellan alone, and I think his case and the duty of the Administration is clear. McClellan should be in Halleck's place and someone who would heartily co-operate should be Secretary of war. Perhaps we overrate Lee, Davis, Jackson and the other Rebel leaders, but I certainly think McClellan has gone as far to prove he excels them all, as his limited sphere of action could prove it. Now, instead of one active mind and will to rule the Army, we have a Committee, and even Burnside submits plans to the President. Father tells me I write too freely of my opinions, but I think those whose lives are daily depending on such things, have the right to criticize if any have. I have not been more open than Officers of every grade are here. There is one great universal condemnation, not of Burnside in particular, but of the whole state of things which has brought us to this pass. It is not, as many think, that the Army is sick of fighting, but sick of fighting for nothing. When I think of Cabot and Alley and the others before, Lowell and our many friends, I feel that they were murdered, and I must put the crime at someone's door. In this last battle there was no hope or expectation of success. Now, I have just read Dr. Walker's sermon, and I believe, as he says, that from all this suffering and evil a better state of public virtue will arise, and I am daily looking for some great move on the part of the really patriotic men of the country which will oblige Mr. Lincoln, a very honest and well-meaning man, to turn over a new leaf, turn out his worthless advisers, restore McClellan, give him *full* powers and as it were, begin again and try once more what an Army can accomplish. The people must be content to leave the affairs of the country in the hands of the President and the Generals for at least one year. I do not despair, although I think we have lost 50 chances out of 100 since the spring. We may crush the military power of the South yet. I have written hastily to you, and I think I have shown how I feel. You probably see through all I say a blind faith in McClellan, and I dare say it is so, but I think I have formed it fairly. I do fully believe he is the man for the crisis and no one else is. In short *I believe in* McClellan.

Now for a change of subject. Boulnois is quite sick and wants to get home to Boston for medical advice etc., but lacks the one thing needful with which I cannot supply him. I believe he expects drafts from you. I cannot account for the Paymaster's delay. You know I have overdrawn about $150.00. I have owing to me for pay about $700.00, so you see I am not insolvent by any means. I hope you will send on some money to Boulnois in some way very soon. A draft on Washington is the best way, I suppose. Frank Haven wrote to Boulnois that he forwarded a letter to Boulnois through me, soon after Boulnois left Washington, but I never got it. Did you send it to Boulnois by Haven?

I have sent to Mother an order for a cap. Please see that it is wide across the temples. Those straight vizers are apt to bear too hard there. I shall be delighted to get the boxes etc.

Our anxiety about the new Colonel has about died out. Tell me any news on the subject. I have a plan in my head (which probably is impracticable) but which I sometimes amuse myself by thinking of. In case we settle down a little more steadily here, or in case we should move to the rear, nearer Washington, I intend to apply for a very short leave, say 5 days, which perhaps I could get, not intending to go home, but only at farthest to Baltimore, for a few days relief from camp duty, camp life etc., and to feel free for a day or two. There, at Baltimore, we will say, to meet you, stay at some nice Hotel, eat like a Christian, take a civilized bath, walk, ride, go to some concert, theatre, lecture, panorama, or some such thing in the evenings. Call on Keighler and Grinnell, if they were there, and try to spend a few days in rational amusement and innocent pleasure consistent with the dignified society of an eminent lawyer, and at the same time adapted to the wants of a blood thirsty soldier just returned from scenes of rapine and carnage. I think we could manage 4 or 5 very pleasant days. As to going home that would be out of the question. One or two days at home would be poor satisfaction, and then it would be hard to come back. I do not think it would be much pleasure to Mother and Father and it would be bad about getting away. With you, of course, the thing is quite different. Women folks, you know, can't look so easily at these things, and I am sure it would worry Mother dreadfully to have me make a flying visit and then go back to dangers her anxious mind would magnify to an alarming degree. I would not consent on any account to go home now, but I think this plan about meeting you is very practicable. Of course do not speak of this, certainly not to Mother and Father, for they would want me to come home, I am sure. Only if ever I saw a chance to get away, I want to have it all ready arranged with you. Of course Payday must first come, and then I should have plenty of tin and feel ready for anything. Just tell me what you think of this plan. I have no doubt I could get a leave for 5 or 6 days, stating I was to go only so far as Baltimore, much more easily than one to go home. Perhaps I could only get to Washington, which would be less pleasant, for it is a very crowded place and seems almost like a camp.

I want to know before long what you have decided as to James. One thing I entrusted to him to buy for me in Washington which I so much need that (in case he does not return) I wish you would send by Express. It is a "spider", "skillet" or "oven" so called by the natives here, and is an iron instrument, merely a deep frying pan with short legs and a thick cover with a handle. Thus:

RIGHT UP INTO THE FIRE

The cover has a low rim. Sometimes there is no handle, then I believe it is called a "Dutch Oven". Its uses are these: with it you can boil stew, bake, fry and roast. With it I can have bread baked, instead of flour and water fried in grease, roast beef, instead of fried steak, baked beans, baked potatoes, and many other luxuries I am now without. It should be about 10 or 12 inches in diameter and 4 or 5 in depth. Its only objection is its weight, but as it does instead of a great many small things that makes little matter. Every house has one here, where they cook in open fire places with wood fires, but I understand they are scarce at home. However, I think you can get one. They cost 75 ¢ or $1.00 only. Try to get me one as soon as possible. We are again poorly off for food. I find I get tired of nothing but beef, potatoes and onions. Fried steak for breakfast. Boiled beef for dinner. This has been the bill of fare for so many weeks now, that one gets tired of it. It would be considered great on a march, but in a steady camp I have discovered that it is necessary to live as well as you possibly can. You probably would hardly believe it, but I am sure that a steady diet upon wholesome food produces a steady diarrhoea, one which almost every one now has.

Father wrote some time ago about sending on $50.00 by James, and I wrote to him I thought it better to trust it to the mail a little at a time. I am not now in absolute want, because there is nothing to buy, but should be glad to have a little on hand.

By the way some months ago, June, I think, I took charge of 22 or 23 Dollars for one of the men, Whitman by name, who afterwards died. I gave him a note at the time for the amount, and this Captain Shepard now has and has written to me he would like, if convenient, to draw the amount of Father, now he is at home, and pay Whitman's family. So please ask Father to pay the money on my note and charge the same to me. I have no doubt Whitman's family need the money, and I should have paid it long ago if I had known where to send it to. Write soon.

Your affectionate brother
Henry.

RIGHT UP INTO THE FIRE

January 15th 1863.

Dear John.

I send herewith by Boulnois the Prince's narrative, some private papers, and a pair of old straps I want to keep. Boulnois will tell you everything. Please send at any rate $5.00 by mail without delay, as I borrowed $15.00 to advance to him. $15.00 I owed him, so I really lent him $10.00. Please put the private letters away in the box.

In haste

You affectionate brother
Henry.

Camp 20th Mass. Volunteers, near
Falmouth, Va. January 16th 1863.

My dear John.

I have received your letter of the 12th enclosing one from Curtis. You have probably seen Boulnois by the time you get this, and he will have told you how ill he is and how he stood the journey to Boston. I bade him good bye last night at Corps HeadQuarters, where he has been several days. He expected to start at 6 A.M. today by Railroad to Acquia Creek, thence by Steamer to Washington and right on to Boston. I sent a small package of private letters etc. by him.

By the way, it occurred to me the other day that you once sent me a letter which said that there was an "agreement" inside, and there was none, and so I wrote to you. Was anything of that kind ever lost, or was the document I signed before you at Bolivar the one you omitted to put in? Also was there any money or stamps in the letter to me which I suppose you wrote to me lately and which I never received? I know there must have been some such letter, for the first notice I had of James' illness was an allusion to a fuller account in some other letter. Boulnois was very glad you kept his important letter, as the mail has been irregular lately.

I was very much interested in your account of Major Willard's death. As to the photograph, I leave it with you to choose the best likeness. I should be indeed very glad to have his picture. I never respected any man more than I did him.

293

RIGHT UP INTO THE FIRE

I hope you will see that whatever one you take is framed or carefully put up, so as not to be injured in any way. You say Mr. Mason's son is to send me a *large* picture of Herbert. If it is larger than a common card photograph, better keep it at home against my return. I could not take care of it here. By the way, I am afraid you will be unable soon to get me a full set of Class photographs. Had you not better see Jeffries, and ask him about it, and write to the Artist who took the Class to preserve a full set for me. You know what a loss it would be to get too late. I suppose they will cost say $20.00 in all, but if ever I get back I would not miss having them for anything. No doubt the man will wait for payment till I get paid.

Today we have marching orders, to be ready tomorrow morning with the usual 3 days rations and 60 rounds ammunition. Yesterday the pontoon train moved. I hear it went *up* the river. Last night was very stormy. It blew and rained tremendously. I feel sure neither pontoons, wagons, nor Artillery can move today on account of the roads. Perhaps we are to try it again. On the whole I incline to think some movement is contemplated, but I do *not* think an advance of the whole Army is to be expected. I think that a demonstration on the enemy's left is the extreme to be expected. The enemy have thrown up new fortifications in front of Falmouth and dug more rifle pits, and therefore it is thought they have sent to the South and West a great part of their force. I dare say the rain of last night has put all movements out of the question. Perhaps this is the beginning of a withdrawal of the Army, part (say the right) by way of Warrenton.

If another real attack is to be made, I cannot see what can avert another great disaster. Whatever move may be made, the suffering of the troops will be terrible on account of the cold and wet and lack of food and tents. The roads have been very bad for some weeks and will grow worse and worse till Spring. This morning it has cleared off with a strong West wind and is growing cold. I will write again soon, if I can. It seems to be generally thought that Hooker is to advance, and that at any rate our Corps is not to be put forward. Boulnois says that Sumner rubs his hands and says laughing that his Corps has lost thirteen thousand five hundred men in these two last battles, and seems quite delighted and proud at the thought. I shall be very sorry to lose my nice hut, but after carefully balancing all the chances, have come to the conclusion we (i.e. our Division) are not to move.

I hope to write and tell you how it turned out soon.

Your affectionate brother
Henry.

RIGHT UP INTO THE FIRE

Saturday, 17th January 1863
20th Regiment.

Dear John.

I received today your letter enclosing Twenty Dollars, for which very much obliged. I am sorry I could not have told Boulnois of his drafts and set his mind at rest as to his letters. I suppose he will not go to the Post Office in Washington, but no doubt you can easily get them back for him. I hope soon to hear from him. Please give him my kindest regards.

Our marching orders were countermanded last night, and it was said the march, or attack, or whatever it was was postponed till Monday. I hear only a reconnaissance was intended, and that it will take place Monday, and our Corps is to go. I think the probability is we shall not move.

Today was fine but awfully cold and we had a review by Burnside. I think I never suffered more than I did waiting on a plain over which a strong North West wind swept for 2 or 3 hours this morning. The cold was I suppose not really very intense, say 25° or 20° Fahrenheit, but after a warm spell it seemed very cold. I am sure I was almost frozen. After all this delay Burnside rode by. Here and there a feeble cheer was raised. I really felt sorry for him when he took off his hat as he rode down our front, but there was a dead silence, and he put it on again. When he got through General Howard thought he must get a little enthusiasm out of the poor frozen men, and riding in front called out: "Now 3 cheers for General Burnside! one, two, three!" but not one single shout was raised, not a single voice, and he rode back apparently much vexed. I heard at a late review probably of a less disciplined Corps, the men yelled: "Butcher" at Burnside, as he rode down. I cannot but pity the poor man, for he certainly tries his best to please all parties. Now the men will always cheer old Sumner, in spite of his recklessness, but half of Burnside's unpopularity is because he follows McClellan and because his faults are on the weak side. An army can bear any General but a weak one. I hear rumors of our going back to Washington still, but I cannot think we shall move in this cold weather. Until you see it you cannot imagine what a dreadful thing suffering from cold is, and how quickly it sickens the strongest men. I mean continued cold, no sleep at night and marching all day. I have seen it here, before the log huts were put up, men crowding round a fire all night, with one blanket wrapped round them, and perhaps wet too. We have had a man die here from illness brought on by frozen feet, and another of diarrhoea, both the effects of cold. If we should attempt active operations now, the men would die just as they did at Sebastopol. One day is awfully cold and another pouring rain. Officers might get along with good clothing and servants to carry blankets and food, but for the men the suffering would be dreadful.

No news here. The Twenty Dollars *very* acceptable. Tell me what has been done about James.

Cannot you number your letters and I mine? so as to tell if any miscarry. I think you might devise some plan. I fear the mail is sometimes robbed, but I notice a small, thin, unpretending letter generally comes safely.

Please send stamps.

Your affectionate brother
Henry.

Camp 20th Mass. Volunteers
Sunday, January 18th 1863.

My dear Father.

I have just received your letter of the 14th. I have not yet received the valise, but expect it daily, as the Quartermaster has sent down a man for Express baggage to Aquia Creek. I received duly your letter containing a list of Articles in the valise. As to our moving I hear today that only a reconnaissance was intended, and that we may go tomorrow. I hope it is not so, for of all military duties I dislike these most. You get generally no sleep at night and march all day, and are every moment on the alert, and half the time out skirmishing in front and on the flanks, and when you do rest often can have no fires. As we did not go yesterday however I hardly think we shall go at all. Such things must be done secretly. We have Genl. Couch now, a very careful and able Officer.

I have no doubt I have often written too freely about the Generals etc. and will take care in future not to do so. Opinions are expressed with great freedom here, and often most emphatically even by those of very high rank.

Rosecrans has certainly done very well in the West[51], but I am astonished to see how easily everyone at home draws the conclusion that he is such a great General for a large Army. Burnside was an excellent General for North Carolina, Hooker and Franklin are excellent Commanders of Corps, but to handle 130,000 men is quite another question. Halleck and McClellan are the only Generals, who have tried to manage a large Army, and I am sure the former did not show

---

[51] Battle of Stones River, December 31, 1862 to January 2, 1863.

remarkable ability or alacrity at Corinth. It is hard for anyone who has never been with an Army to understand how long it takes to move and what a vast undertaking it is. You can only compare it to the motions of the planets and stars. To a child for instance, it is hard to teach that the earth takes a whole year to go once round the sun, and yet that the earth goes very rapidly.

Now we must fight with large armies for we are opposed by large armies, and no dashing General of small ability to take in a vast field, however energetic he may be, can accomplish much. Now it seems to me that McClellan is the only man who has ever attempted large movements, such as the advance of 120,000 men via Yorktown and the flank movement of McDowell and 50,000 men from Fredericksburg taking in all this and the vast quantity of lesser things such as the cooperation of the fleet etc. Halleck and Burnside can command large Armies while they lay still but they either fail or accomplish nothing when they attempt to move.

I hope you have carefully followed the cases of McDowell and Porter and read the evidence, especially McClellan's evidence.[52] To me it is conclusive. I think it is fairly shown that, as far as it is possible to speak of certainty in human affairs, that McClellan would certainly have taken Richmond and utterly defeated the whole Rebel Army of the East in June last had he been let alone. I also think from what I learn from Generals and Officers here, that McClellan would have utterly destroyed the Rebel Army at Culpepper in November last, had he not been removed. I feel sure this will all come out by and by. For a long time nobody admitted that McClellan ever was near taking Richmond in June, now few deny it. I feel most fully that McClellan is the man and the only man for us, and I fear that less able men may bring the country to the brink of ruin before the Administration acknowledge their error, and call back the man who has twice saved the Capitol [sic] and twice had his hand on the Capitol of the enemy. If I am right, then the responsibility those took who first interferred with him and then removed him is dreadful indeed.

It almost makes me sick to read the reports of Congress and to read the violent speeches of men about the Army, about abolishing West Point etc. It seems as if the men were mad. To West Point we owe it, that we have an Army at all. I hope for better things from the new Congress.

Weather cold but pleasant. I am perfectly well as usual. I have just heard a sermon at Brigade Head Quarters preached in the open air to a large number of Officers and men by Dr. Childs. I do not know where he was from. Sermon was very good indeed. I hear that Regiments near us are being paid off today and

---

[52] After the debacle at Second Bull Run Generals McDowell and Porter were court-martialed for alleged insubordination and misconduct.

hope our turn will soon come.

Your affectionate son
Henry.

P.S.

January 18th 1863.

Dear Father.

To accommodate Capt. Macy in the present uncertain state of the mails, and for my own convenience in case we are not paid for a long time, I have just drawn on you for Forty Dollars and received the same from him.

Your affectionate son
Henry.

Camp 20th Mass. Volunteers
Falmouth, Va.
January 19th 1863.

My dear Father.

Your letter of the 15th just received. I am much disappointed at not getting my valise last evening, especially as Herbert got his valise and box, the latter of which was only sent on the 13th (I think). I cannot see what detained mine. I shall write immediately to Adams & Co. in Washington to forward it.

Please let me know what other boxes or parcels if any are on the way. I received about 2 weeks ago a bag containing Blankets and Clothes, a box, sent by Lt. Grafton, and a box sent by John containing a new light tent etc. Mother wrote to me that she had sent a small covered Crockery dish, and you do not mention this as being in the valise so I thought there must be another package of some kind.

I wrote to you yesterday and told you I had signed a draft of Forty Dollars on you, payable to order of Capt. Macy. It was a great convenience to him, and I was very glad to receive the money to keep in case of need, although I did not absolutely need it because I had just received $20.00 from John in a letter.

This morning was the day it was said we were to begin our march, but all is quiet and there is no sign of a move. Weather still very cold. Thermometer say [sic] 20° at night, but sun very powerful at midday. Roads of course very bad. Before sunrise today a Regiment passed to the front with Spades, Axes etc. so I suppose at last the exposed state of our flank here has been noticed, and it is to be protected. Our pickets are about one mile out from this camp and several Regiments camped not more than ¼ mile from the pickets. The enemy could cross the river 5 or 6 miles above any night, especially a foggy or rainy night, and drive our feeble pickets back into these advanced Regiments in 20 minutes from the first shot, and in ½ hour they could be upon us all, entirely unawares and unprepared. There is no arrangement for defense in such a case or any preparation at all. Now I hope they are going to fortify. Abbott first called my attention to this exposed condition of the flank some days ago. When we were at Fair Oaks, and even lately, at Bolivar, the pickets were farther out and were strongly supported, and also standing orders were given to the Regiments in Camps where exactly to form, and what to do in case of an attack. I have no doubt if Burnside does fortify, the old cry of spades and mud will be raised as it was against McClellan. You speak of the shameful surprises of our Western Armies. There is no excuse whatever for it. If pickets are properly posted and supported a Camp *cannot* be surprised. But nothing is so good as a few fieldworks. I cannot see why it is not best to make every position as strong as it possibly can be made. We can learn this from our enemies.

Frank's letter was enclosed in yours. I shall answer him without delay.

Your affectionate son
Henry.

Camp 20th Mass. near Falmouth, Va.
January 20th 1863 (1 P.M.)

Dear John.

We have just been drawn up in line and heard an order from Genl. Burnside read, which stated that the Army of the Potomac was again about to meet the enemy etc., and stated that the Rebel forces were weakened by sending men South etc., and hoping for a great success. Then we have orders to be ready to move at an "early hour tomorrow." So I rather think another attack is contemplated. Artillery is now moving by our Camp in a North Western direction, and I heard the other day that pontoons had gone up the river, so, I rather think, it is expected to turn their left, and perhaps Franklin will attack their right at the same time.

As we suffered so much both at Fredericksburg and Antietam, I suppose we shall not be shoved in at first again. I should not at all wonder if our Corps was left here on this side to await the attack on the enemy's left. As to the result I incline to think it will be successful so far as taking these works in front. But the Rebels certainly have had warning enough to get plenty of men, if they can spare them. Perhaps they will evacuate, but I incline to think they will make a good defense until entirely outflanked, and then withdraw, which they easily can do with their Railroad. I do not in the least anticipate a brilliant victory, neither do I think a great defeat at all likely. Perhaps another Williamsburg on a larger scale. If we took these works, we should be little better off, for in such weather and on such roads a quick advance would be impossible. We shall see.

Best love to all.

Your affectionate brother
Henry.

20th Regiment 21st January
Camp near Falmouth. (2 P.M.)

Dear John.

We have not moved yet. No orders have come. Franklin moved up a mile or so beyond us yesterday P.M. and an immense train of Artillery. Yesterday afternoon it began to rain and has rained tremendously all night and is drizzling still. Wind North East, no sign of clearing off. Quite cold. The Pontoon train, entire Artillery and wagons are stuck fast in the mud about one mile from here. Roads awful of course and quite impassable. Troops exposed last night must have suffered dreadfully. I hear they have moved on but are of course without wagons, Artillery or Pontoons. I cannot but think the attempt will be given up. The utmost dissatisfaction, almost insubordination, was shown by Regiments about here at the prospect of an attack. Regiments openly said they would not cross a bridge, the

RIGHT UP INTO THE FIRE

42nd New York of our Brigade hooted at the order, even the 15th Mass. cheered for Jefferson Davis and groaned for President Lincoln. Our men of course were perfectly silent, but almost everyone expects utter defeat, if we cross again now, in such weather and after giving the enemy so long a time to prepare. The state of the Army is shocking. Our Regiment will not disgrace itself, you may be sure, but the Army is more demoralized and dissatisfied than I had ever thought before. They have no confidence whatever in their leader. It is no use to attempt to disguise the fact. And this state of things is not among men only, but it is very well known that the leading Commanders do not work together, and that Burnside is not man enough to command them, and therefore takes principally the advice of Sumner who has more character than the others. You may be sure we are in a bad way enough now, and I only hope the enemy will not take advantage of it. If the move is entirely given up, and the troops are made comfortable, and well understand there is to be no fighting till Spring, they may improve in spirit and be fit for work in the spring, but what with constant fighting, poor food, no pay, innumerable hardships, and defeats in battle, and now no leader, Officers of high rank all squabbling and almost talking treason, and the prospect of worse hardships and more senseless fighting, the Army is completely used up, and I hope it is not treason to say so. At any rate, I must say so, or say nothing. Our Regiment, as I said, is good for anything, but I do not know another like it.

It is colder now than it was, for the wind is more northerly, but while I have been writing the rain has set in heavily. I pity the poor fellows marching.

Received this morning Mary Ann's letter of January 17th enclosing needles.

In haste

Your affectionate brother
Henry.

Camp 20th Reg. near Falmouth
Va. Jan. 23, 1863.

My dear Father.

This morning the troops are all coming back. The whole thing is an utter failure. The troops suffered awfully and when they got up to the place where they expected to cross found the Rebels fully prepared and so strongly entrenched that

RIGHT UP INTO THE FIRE

it would have been madness to have attacked. Our entire pontoons train, and a great part of the artillery is left in the mud. I hope the rebels cannot cross and get possession of it. The men came straggling by this morning. They are half starved, for provisions could not be got up. Dr. Crehore of the 37th Mass. stopped and told us about it. He says he thinks 8000 will hardly cover the number this short march will use up by sickness in his G.D. *[Grand Division]* (Franklin's). Burnside rode along yesterday and was followed by hooting and yells. The troops are in a dreadful state. Our loss in sick and in horses and mules will be very great, but the utter demoralization of the Army is the worst. Our G.D. was held in reserve, so we have been saved this fearful exposure. Everyone expected this result, for there was every sign of a heavy N.E. storm when they started. As far as I have heard every General was opposed to Burnside's plan, and I know that they feel very much disheartened. We cannot be too thankful that the storm prevented another awful sacrifice of human life, although the misery and suffering that this march has already occasioned is immense, and of a kind which the people outside will hear little of.

Burnside has now been in command nearly 3 months. He has marched about 20 miles, sacrificed uselessly about 30,000 men in all and brought the Army to the verge of mutiny and the Country to the worst case it has ever been in. What next the President will do, no one can see, but certainly it will take 2 or 3 weeks to get this Army together and able to do anything. If the President drives the Army to extremities the most dreadful consequences may follow. The hatred to him is universal, and they feel that his ignorant interference has been the cause of all their sufferings and defeats.

This morning it is clearing up and promises fair weather. No letters from home for two days. Sermon about Maj. Willard received today.

Your affec. son
Henry

P.S.

Capt. Holmes arrived in Camp last night, very well.

RIGHT UP INTO THE FIRE

(1)

Camp 20th Mass. near Falmouth
Va. Jan. 24, 1863. Sat.

My dear Father.

I hasten to acknowledge your letter of Jan. 20th and the $10.00 enclosed – all right. I am indeed very much obliged to you for supplying me so fully with money, which I certainly should have needed but for the recent receipt of $20.00 from John, and the draft of 40.00 on Capt. Macy which I wrote to you about. At last however our Paymaster has come, and today pays us up to Nov. 1, 1862 4 months. I get $416.00. The extra pay for 1st Lt. and for command of Co. will come in next time. The Paymaster returns immedl. to Washington to get money for the next 2 months. Then I get $236.00 more. In all $652.00. Besides that, I have about $50.00 here now. I expect to send home of this 4 months pay $200.00 about enough to cover what I have overdrawn. I shall wait for a safe conveyance.

All is quiet here. Weather fair and warm. The more I hear of our late move, the more I see what a desperate thing it would have been. The enemy – unlike our present Commander – are sure to spend every moment of spare time in digging, and although we marched 5 or 6 miles up the river, every available place was fortified and protected by rifle pits which would have been about as difficult to take as the old works were. Generals Lee and McClellan were alike in this thing – whenever they stopped, they fortified. They are not afraid of the cry against spades and mud. I cannot but hope that it is at last proved that this Army *must* rest and recruit. An army cannot fight constantly for 10 months, unless in a constant succession of victories with small loss. Every General has wintered his troops, and unless this Army is rested and supplied with comforts, it will be useless in the spring.

I hope to get a letter from John tomorrow and hear how Mr. Boulnois is. A man has gone down to Aquia Creek today for express baggage, and I hope to get the valise.

I fear many of my letters missing. Cannot you number your letters to me? If it would not be much trouble I should like it, for I then could tell when a letter miscarried. I shall begin to number mine to you, and therefore put a "1" on the first page. Best love to mother.

Your affec. son
Henry.

Wm. Ropes Esq.

RIGHT UP INTO THE FIRE

Falmouth, Va.
January 26th 1863.

My dear Father.

I cannot tell you how glad I was to see Joseph, totally unexpectedly, yesterday morning at a very early hour. Rev. Mr. Means of Roxbury came with him. They breakfasted in my hut, and soon after we got an order to prepare to march immediately and to go to Falmouth to relieve the Regiments now on duty there as Provost Guards to the town. So here we are, and very comfortable in a good room, looking out on the river, with a nice view of the Rebel pickets. Our men are quite well off in houses and we Officers hire very nice rooms. Mason and I have a good upper room together, with Abbott. Willard and the Quartermaster Folsom in the lower room. So we are very comfortably situated indeed, and are no doubt to remain a long time. Joseph is very well. He will stay for 5 or 6 days. Thank you very much indeed for the nice contents of the valise. It is most acceptable. I shall keep Joseph as long as I can.

Today we have the news of Hooker's appointment and the displacement of Burnside, Franklin and Sumner. Thus we lose 3 good *Division* Generals, and gain a doubtful Chief. I dare say Hooker will attempt some grand move. I have little confidence in his honesty of purpose and fear he my risk all to gain a great name. Joseph desires me to say he may be a day in Washington on his return and so not in Philadelphia till the end of the week or beginning of next. Received $10.00 and Stamps from J.C. Have been paid off and shall send home money by Joseph.

Your affectionate son
Henry.

Falmouth, Va. January 29th 1863.

No 1.

Dear John.

Your letter No. 1 of January 23rd received today. Have very little time to answer it now. Will write fully. Joseph is to leave early tomorrow morning. He was to have gone today, but tremendous snow-storm prevented. Received duly all moneys to viz.: $10.00 from Father, $20.00 from you and $10.00 from you.

Have been of course very much engaged with Joseph and in moving camp and on guard duty since I came here. My kindest regards to Boulnois. Shall write to him very soon. Received from Whittier $2.00 to give Smith (servant) from him. I send home $250.00 by Joseph to you. How do I stand then?

Shall write you fully about military matters and Pope and Porter. I sent on a letter for Hazeltine lately, did it go? Glad you favor McClellan etc. Send on anything new. To move is impossible. All well and desire regards.

Your affectionate brother
Henry.

Please ask Mary Ann to visit Flannigan and, if possible, Mrs. Humphrey, and let Mary Ann spend as much as she thinks well from the overplus of my funds for their benefit.

20th Mass. Falmouth Va. Jan 30, 1863.

My dear Father.

Brother Joseph left me this morning by the first train, after a very pleasant visit only too short. I enjoyed his stay exceedingly, and I think he had a pleasant time, and liked the officers here very much. They were all delighted with him, and enjoyed his good spirits and his jokes and conversation exceedingly. He has left behind a character for ability, especially for Finance matters which would be very flattering for him to hear of. Everybody was delighted to hear him talk of business etc. He was to stop at Aquia Creek and see about my valise, and I am happy to say it came on this afternoon, no doubt hastened by his enquiries.

I am sorry to say the bottle of Sherry was broken and lost but did no injury to other things. In the can of fresh peaches there was a small puncture, as if made with a knife point through which some of the juice had run out, but has done no damage. Mr. A's vest soaked it up, and this is to be washed. I was astonished to find this damage, and also to observe that the other tin cans were bent up, but I see that when things are packed in a valise or bag they must be *very* carefully protected. The leather sides probably were jammed together. Bottles etc. are safer in a wooden box. Thousands of bottles and tins containing every kind of liquid are coming on every day, and I never heard of much damage to goods, so do not think it dangerous ever to send liquids, but only let them be packed in a box, not anything that can be squeezed.

Comparing with your list of the contents I find all right, and besides my watch, apparently in perfect order, a quantity of religious tracts, some raisins, fine sugar, a crockery dish, cover, plate, cup and saucer. The saucer was broken, all the rest safe. I am indeed *exceedingly* obliged to you and to mother for these luxuries which I enjoy very much, and which probably add more to my comfort than you imagine, being at home accustomed to regular and good food, and constantly feeling that it is in your power to get almost anything. I never received a package of any kind from home better selected than this and I anticipate a great deal of comfort and enjoyment in its use. The coat came perfectly safe, and is a perfect fit, exactly as I wanted it - could not be better. Please to thank mother especially for her nice gingerbread, and Mr. A. for the vest.

I have no particular news to tell. Jos. will tell you what weather and mud we have, and I think his evidence will satisfy any fair man that to move is impossible. I have heard two excellent things of Genl. Hooker, 1st that he made it a condition that he should be perfectly untrammelled by the President, 2nd that he has given orders to Div. Commanders to grant a reasonable number of leaves of absence and furloughs, thus pretty plainly saying that we are to remain here. I think the prospect of rest and the removal of B. has produced a better feeling already in the Army. Bro. J. will tell you how comfortably off we are here, in good rooms, perfectly sheltered. My window looks right out on the river, the enemy's pickets and rifle pits as near as Cambridge Bridge is from our back windows, but no firing. The river is rising and is already quite a torrent. I forgot to mention the scarf in the valise. Thank you very much for the most excellent paper and envelopes in the valises Jos. brought.

Best love to Mother

Your affec. son
Henry

Wm. Ropes Esq.

RIGHT UP INTO THE FIRE

Camp 20th Mass.
Falmouth, Va.
[January 30, 1863.]

My dear Mother.

I wrote to Father about the arrival of my valise, and now thank you very much for the many delicacies it contained, all of which I shall enjoy exceedingly. I am very sorry the wine was lost, but I see that it is not safe to send bottles in anything which could be easily jammed. The crockery will be very useful. As I must now have most of that old set, I am going to ask you to send when you next have a box or anything coming, 2 or 3 of those little egg cups. They would be very nice not only for their proper use, but for liquors, or for mustard, pepper and salt. I think they would be very convenient. I find myself getting more and more comfortable every day, and have now plenty of everything necessary though of course should greatly enjoy the dinner you sent. Joseph is to get me some poultry in Washington. Herbert and I now room and mess together, and find it very pleasant. Please ask John to call on Mrs. Patrick O'Hara, wife of my pioneer, when he has time, and pay her Ten Dollars from her husband. She lives in No. 80 West Cedar Street. John can take the money from my account, as O'Hara has paid it already to me. Joseph will tell you all about things here better than I can write. All were delighted with his visit.

I received today your letter of January 26th. I have told Joseph everything that I want and he will explain to you about the shirts. I am very glad you have seen Flannigan. I wrote to him to draw on John for $20.00 as a loan from me till he is paid. I send some money home by Joseph. I told him to tell you and Mary Ann to make use of any surplus as you saw best in aiding my poor wounded men and their families. Flannigan is a most excellent man though perhaps rather rough.

I enclose a letter for sister Mary which Father will please send. I did not seal the envelope, thinking they might want to put more in. Herbert has had a bad sore throat, or rather mouth, a sort of swelled face, but is about well now.

Your affectionate son
Henry.

RIGHT UP INTO THE FIRE

20th Mass. Volunteers, Falmouth, Va.
February 2nd 1863.

No. 2.

My dear John.

Your long and interesting letter No. 2 received today. I have not time now to answer you about McClellan, but agree with you heartily as to the trust due to Genl. Hooker, and that he is an able man etc. However, you probably know he is an intemperate man, and a man of low moral character. From his course thus far, I should judge him to be an ambitious man, rather unscrupulous, but sensible and energetic. He has begun by setting us at last at rest and granting furloughs, and has taken steps to get back deserters. He has also set about cleaning up and burying dead horses etc.

 I have read the two articles in the Traveller, the one a letter (I believe from Mr. Raymond) the other Holt's review of the Porter case. I consider the first a shameful libel on the Army. Many of his statements I *know* to be false. For instance, about the pontoons. They were moved 2 or 3 days before, there was no secret of the matter. The day before my servant went to a house in Falmouth where I get bread and the man, a half Union man, whose wife is a bitter Rebel, told him the *exact place* where Burnside would try to cross, to viz.: Bank's Ford. Then as to the pontoons having been got up to within ½ mile of the ford, the rear of the train, 5 or 6 boats, were stuck in the mud not ½ mile from our camp where I saw them, and I hear that they were thus left all along the way. Phil Mason, who was there, says the enemy's works were very strong, equal to Fredericksburg, and to say the attempt was a surprise is mere folly. In such weather and roads a surprise is perfectly impossible.

 As to Generals etc. not doing their duty, and throwing obstacles in the way, I do not believe it, I saw no sign of such a thing, and have not heard of any such conduct. I think everyone felt the thing could not succeed, and felt no confidence in Burnside. From all I can learn, and I have taken some pains to find out the truth, it was a mercy that the storm prevented our crossing, for we could not have been successful. It was only the desire to save the city that saved us at Fredericksburg.

 As to Franklin, I have always considered him one of our first men. The testimony before the Committee which I read shows, I think, that he attacked with as much of his force as was possible, and as well as he knew how. As to the absurd statement that his men drove the enemy and were on the point of success etc., I know it to be all false. I have seen those who were there. Dr. Crehore told me we gained no advantage to speak of, and never once got near the enemy's real works, and that at no time was there any gleam of victory. He also says that they lay under the Rebel guns and only wondered that the enemy did not see fit to destroy them or at any rate inflict great loss.

As to Porter, the first thing that strikes me is the shameful unfairness of Holt's summing up. It seems like the plea of a lawyer of the prosecution. As to Porter's dislike of Pope, that is very natural. Pope had lost all character long before in the regular Army. He was despised by every regular Officer I ever met. Porter felt of course hurt at being put under such a man. Pope had got his Army all mixed up, and did not even know where the different Divisions were. This I learn from Sedgwick who went up with Sumner. Porter knew that Pope was utterly incapable, and that to follow his orders blindly was to risk the safety of his entire Army, and he therefore felt called upon to act on his own discretion. Holt's attempt to rebut such tremendous evidence as Genl. Sykes' and others with Porter, by the foolish evidence of Captain DeKay, for instance, about Porter's sitting under a tree etc., is really disgusting. This DeKay is a man who signs his name in immense letters an inch long at the bottom of Hospital Clothing returns etc. which I get every day. As to Holt's assumption that Pope really had a plan, and only lacked Porter's attack to bring about a glorious victory, I see no proof of it whatever. Still it is very possible that had Porter attacked, we might have gained a victory, also that by great exertions he might have attacked, also that Pope ordered him to attack, but the question yet remains how far is an experienced General bound to obey implicitly the orders of a superior he knows to be a fool when he knows that by thus obeying he may sacrifice thousands of lives? He may have done wrong this time but I am sure I cannot believe he meant wrong. Then there is the most serious matter of all. The Jury was packed. Holt was known as Porter's bitter enemy. Martindale was once arrested and tried by Porter, and only Van Allen was Porter's friend. The evidence was public, everybody read it, and yet the sentence took everyone by surprise. An honorable acquittal was everywhere expected. These are my present views, but I still feel I have not fully enough examined the matter. You speak of the insubordination etc. of the Army. It seems to me the Army is a mighty servant who has been most shamefully abused. Of course disaffection exists. You cannot deprive men of their due and lead them on forever to useless slaughter and expect them to shout out for more. The Army is the most noble and patriotic Army that ever existed, and if it is now disaffected, lay it to the President not on us.

All quiet now. Leaves are being granted and probably during the next 2 weeks I could get a leave of 6 to 10 days. You do not answer my Baltimore plan very fully, but I have spoken to Joseph about it, and he will tell you how it stands. As to the expense, I expect you will be my guest while at Baltimore, and *insist* on this. I want you to come very much, I assure you, and if you do not, I shall probably remain here, although I should like a recess of a few days on any terms.

As to James, I am very glad you have got hold of the $30.00 deposited, and beg you to pay him nothing more without an order from me. I consider his conduct shameful. I have paid him now as follows:

Dr.
From Father 20.00
From You 2.00
From me here 17.00
From me (Boots at Sutler's) 8.00
From Savings Bank 15.00
From his sister 5.00
―――
67.00

Cr.
I owe him wages @ $15.00 from August
4th till December 20th, 4 months
16 days 67.50
―――
67.50

If he wants the balance 0.50 let him ask me for it. Besides these sums, I believe I, at various times, gave him $2.00 or $3.00 more. Considering the poor quality of his services, he is more than paid now. Did you not pay for the Doctor? He left no property here, only a few bad debts from the men, none of which I have collected. I have a very good man from the ranks now, James Smith, and shall keep him at present.

Write me fully about Baltimore etc., after you see Joseph. If I get a favorable answer from you, I shall apply for 6 (to 10) days, and if I get it, will telegraph from Washington to you.

Couch is a most excellent Officer, and very far from being a newspaper man. Smith I have heard *very* highly spoken of. As to McClellan drinking with Wood etc., I do not like it, but attach little importance to it. Public men might be accidentally thrown together in a hotel in a thousand ways.

Thinking over the Baltimore scheme, I hope you will not do what you feel is not best, for my sake. I urge you, but you can judge best, and if you should not come, I should know you decided rightly. You see I cannot judge as to your business, Father's views etc., and I know he is sometimes very set. I should be indeed delighted to meet you, and we could talk over things at our leisure and perhaps arrive at similar opinions on military matters.

I enclose a draft on the State Treasurer for $17.00 payable to order of Jos. H.

Parker which I advanced the money on, to oblige my men here. Please draw the amount and credit it to me. I authorized Flannigan in a letter to borrow of my money in your hands $20.00. I sent home by Joseph $250.00. He was to spend about $10.00 for poultry in Philadelphia, and I suppose my debts at home do not amount to more than $180.00, leaving $60.00 to you with which to pay $10.00 to Mrs. O'Hara (as I wrote to you) and to settle for other things I may order. I wish you would let Mary Ann spend what remains, or as much as she sees fit, for the benefit of my wounded men.

I hope you will write me an early answer.

Your affectionate brother
Henry.

20th Mass. Volunteers, Falmouth
February 5th 1863.

No. 3.

My dear John.

I was sorry not to get letters from you either yesterday or today, especially as I hoped that on receiving my last letters and speaking with Joseph, you would resolve to come on and meet me at Baltimore, in case I go. I now have to tell you that I have applied for "8 days to visit Baltimore", and feel *quite sure* of getting so modest a request. I expect to get the leave and start on Saturday morning or on Monday morning, and expect to be in Baltimore the afternoon of the day I leave. I have lots of Commissions to attend to in Washington about Express matters etc., and must spend some hours there either in going or coming, but shall without fail push on to Baltimore the day I start. Now I do not know what you may have written or decided upon, but I most earnestly hope you will come on and spend the 6 days with me. I had to apply now, before I heard from you, or perhaps lose all chance. The spring campaign will no doubt open by the 1st April or sooner, and then we have the promise of another year of danger and hardship, and, laying aside the chances of battles etc., there is a certainty of my not seeing you or any of you for a long season. I therefore would press you to come on, and if possible, after enjoying 4 or 5 days in Baltimore, return with me to Falmouth and stay with Herbert and me as long as you like. We are very comfortable now in a house, and can get horses easily, and you would see a really big Army. Well, I leave you to decide, but be assured I shall look for you and expect you to come, if you possibly can arrange it.

Already I find enough to do for others and myself to occupy me during a day and a half in making purchases. I shall get a pass to bring on baggage to Falmouth.

I hope you have seen McClellan. I have thought over your last long letter, and talked it over with Abbott, but I feel sure I can answer it perfectly to your satisfaction. I want very much put before your mind all the facts which I know, and I feel sure you will then agree with me. I reserve myself for an after-dinner talk at the Eutaw House, Baltimore. You cannot imagine how I look forward to this short release from the constant duties of camp, and freedom from camp restrictions etc. It is really a great thing not to have to get up by a drumbeat for 8 mornings. I shall telegraph from Washington, if possible, and shall "put up" at the Eutaw House in Baltimore. It is possible I may be delayed several days, but not probable.

Enclosed you will find a document of a legal nature. The facts are as follows: Thomas Carver, widower, enlisted in Company K 20th last September, and was killed December 11th in action. He left issue Chs. Carver, now in Boston, Thomas H. Carver, private now in my Company, and Philip M. Carver, private in my Company, now home sick furlough, and Stephen A. Carver, minor, now at home in Boston. Charles is desirous of obtaining all the money left by his father, pay, bounty etc. and appropriating it to his own use. The next two children, Thomas H. and Philip M., desire to waive their claims to their father's property in favor of their youngest brother Stephen A. (minor). Thomas H. brought me just now the enclosed paper, stated these facts and asked for advice, he not thinking the enclosed paper a good legal one. I told him I would send it to you and ask you what could be done to bring about the distribution of property the heirs desire. Please send to me any paper to be signed and tell me what is to be done. I suppose the 4 children share equally and in accordance with their wish Stephen is to have ¾ and Charles retains only his own fourth. Is not this so?

Hoping soon to see you in Baltimore, I remain

Your affectionate brother
Henry.

RIGHT UP INTO THE FIRE

20th Mass. Falmouth, Va.
February 6th 1863.

No. 4.

Dear John.

Yours No. 3 2nd February just received in regular course. I have written you fully of my probable trip to Baltimore, and will not repeat, but only hope to get it and to meet you in due time there. I dare say I may get it tonight. I am astonished at the size of my account $750.00. It was only $630.00 when you told me before, if I recollect, and I remember nothing but Coat, Shoes and Cap since ordered. However, I have no doubt all is correct. If you come on please bring a list of my expenses. I then now stand as follows:

Dr.
To - sent to Father 490.00
To - Boulnois' debt 10.00
To - Balance from Presents 1.00
To - C. B. Porter's debt 10.75
To - Savings Bank (James) 15.00
To - Sent by Joseph 250.00
To - Sent by draft in last letter 17.00
   to Corporal Parker
_____
$793.75

Cr.
By - Expenses to February 1st 750.70
By - Pay, as requested in last 10.00
   letter to Mrs. O'Hara
Thus you will have on hand for me 33.00
_____
$793.75

I really had no idea my expenses were so large, or I should not have given any orders for new things yet. I suppose in your account you consider Capt. Shepard's note for $23.00 for Private Whitman; Capt. Macy's Note of $40.00 and Mr. Folsom's note of $15.00 as paid. By the way nothing was ever said to me about Macy's Note of $40.00. Was it presented and paid? I have been paid "to include the 31st day of October 1862, and have pay due from that time to the present date", to viz.:

2nd Lieutenant pay to January 1st ... 208.50
1st Lieutenant addition from October 2nd ... 15.00
Command Company from December 12th ... 5.50
This is what I expect to get every day ... $229.00

Then from January 1st I draw at the rate of $119.50 per month, payment due February 28th.

Besides this I have $50.00 or 60 on hand.

Thank you for the vegetables. I will give Holmes ½. Please tell me the total cost of my half as this will be for Herbert's and my mess. Glad you did not send meat. I will get some in Baltimore.

So you have seen McClellan. I want to have a talk with you about him. I do not by any means share in the prejudice against Hooker. He has done well thus far, and he promises well now. But I still believe him to be an unprincipled man. I have heard of his speaking against McClellan in Washington. In this last battle I hear he did really nothing, merely sat on his horse and let his routed troops rush by him. He probably saw his own rise in Burnside's failure. I do not think him anything like so big a man as McClellan, but a very quick and ready man, and a man of experience, education and courage. I think after so many failures he will do well.

There is an intense feeling of disgust at the raising of Negro Regiments. It is foolish to attempt such an unpopular thing with the Army in its present temper. They had better not bring any here. It would create an instant mutiny. Men *will not* fight (and Officers will not) on an equality with the Negro. Right or wrong this is the feeling, and it would be madness to resist it.

I hope the Radicals have had their day, and that wisdom will yet appear in the councils of the nation.

Tell me what boxes or camp chests have come and what is in them? I forget what I left in those boxes at Poolesville.

Your affectionate brother
Henry.

P.S. As to James McCrohan, do not give him one cent more. I find he ran away leaving poor men here of whom he had borrowed money. Also that he told someone he did not intend to return, although he vowed he would to me. He is a swindler, nothing better. Better transfer the $15.00 in Bank to yourself, and do not pay him anything. I never want him to return. My present man, Smith, does very well.

H. R.

RIGHT UP INTO THE FIRE

20th Mass. Falmouth, Va.
Sunday, February 8th 1863.

My dear Father.

I have received no letters from home for several days. My leave of absence of eight days has come, and I expect to start tomorrow morning and hope that John will come on and meet me in Baltimore. Brother Joseph has arrived home I suppose and has told John of my plan.

I feel that I may not be able to see John or anyone for I cannot tell how long, as we are no doubt to begin a new campaign in a month, and so I feel very anxious to see John once more.

Major Macy left for Boston yesterday. I hope you may meet him, for he is a noble fellow and commanded the Regiment finely in the late battles. He is one of my best friends here.

Best love to mother and all. I hope to write next from Baltimore.

Your affectionate son
Henry.

Washington, February 10th 1863.

To John C. Ropes, 21 Barristers Hall, Court Square.

I shall be in Baltimore tonight. Hope to meet you there.

Henry Ropes.

Coleman's Eutaw House, Baltimore, February 16th 1863.
Monday.

My dear Father.

I have just received yours of the 14th. John and I leave this morning for Washington *and I* expect to be in camp tomorrow evening. I am sorry the skillet etc. was not sent on here, as I have arranged to carry on anything to the Camp. Please tell mother I cannot get good shirts here, and ask her to send me 2 like the last. Then the box can come right on by Express. I shall be very much delighted with the contents of the box as John describes it. I have laid in a good stock of Groceries, etc. here.

We have been treated most kindly by Mr. Grinnell my classmate's father, by the Keithlers and by Mr. Jacobson. The Keithlers are Secessionists, as are almost all the first people socially here, but we dined there and had a delightful time. They all were very kind.

Love to mother. We leave in a few moments. Better send on any box to the Camp, direct. Shall write and thank Brother Joseph for his munificent present.

Your affectionate son
Henry.

Flannigan is all right. Dr. Jeffries' certificate is sufficient. I should think it was only necessary to notify the Dr. of the Hospital from which he came. Better be careful to do everything in the regular way.

H. R

20th Mass. Falmouth, Va.
February 22nd 1863.

My dear Father.

I have received your letter of February 18th and the one you sent to the Eutaw House which was sent on. I am sorry you did not send the box on direct to the Camp, or else to me at Baltimore earlier, but I think it is of no consequence, for I have written to have it brought on here by Express and the Express matter is daily expected. I shall be very much obliged for the contents, especially for the skillet. If I had known I was to go to Baltimore, I would not have troubled you with so many things. I got a very large supply of Groceries, canned Vegetables, Wine etc. in Baltimore, not only for myself, but to be divided among the others and found an excellent place there (recommended by Mr. Jacobson) where everything was reasonable in price and good in quality. They packed all up in 2 barrels and I got it safely through, though with a good deal of trouble. Capt. Robinson, Assistant Quartermaster at Washington treated me very kindly and through him I got transportation for all that I had bought, and for a box and barrel for Herbert and a barrel for myself from Adams Express Office. Capt. Robinson knew you and said his father knew you, and that he had been for some years in business on Commercial Wharf, Boston.

The vegetables were all in good order. I gave one half to Capt. Holmes, as John requested. We are now well supplied in every way. Yesterday was a warm pleasant day. Today we have a foot and a half of snow, and it is still snowing hard. It is just like New England weather. As to Mrs. Humphrey and her box, I knew nothing of her coming till I received your letter just now. I have heard indirectly that her husband was discharged, and if so, he has probably gone home. When last I heard from him certainly, he was almost well and able to be about. I do not think his wife has any reason to be anxious about his health.

I have received 3 recruits and 6 or 7 returned sick men, so my Company now makes quite a respectable show. I have now two boxes on the way, Joseph's present of Poultry and your last box. I will let you know as soon as I get them.

Your affectionate son
Henry.

20th Mass. Volunteers
Falmouth, Va. February 23rd 1863.

My dear Father.

I have just received yours of the 19th. I do not think there is any danger that I shall not get the box you sent. I left my address at the Eutaw House and received from there your letter which arrived after I left. I have written to Harnden's Express and expect the box very soon.

Please ask Brother Joseph to thank the Rev. Mr. Means for a copy of a sermon on the death of Lt. Newcomb, 19th Mass. which I found here for me on my return and which I suppose he sent. Cold weather, deep snow. All well.

Your affectionate son
Henry.

Enclosed a letter for Frank and one for my friend Curtis, to be left at No. 4 State St.

H. R.

Falmouth, Va.
February 26th 1863.

My dear Father.

I have just received your letter telling me of another box containing shirts, Sherry wine, Lemons etc. which you have sent by Harnden's Express, and for which I am very much obliged. I hope to get both boxes very soon.

All quiet here. Heavy rains and deep mud. Received letter from Mary Ann with yours. We have had deep snow, but it is now almost gone.

Your affectionate son
Henry.

Falmouth, Va.
February 27th 1863.

My dear John.

I have received no letters from home for a day or two. There is nothing new here. The river has risen very much. Weather cloudy and snow melting fast. Murphy has gone home and took my silver watch which is out of order again. That watch has given me much trouble. Please get it repaired, and send it back, if possible by Murphy. Patten expects to go off very soon and Herbert in a week. All well. Very comfortable. No Express yet. Joseph's present of Poultry is probably spoilt by this time. Captains Robeson and Grafton of the 2nd *[Massachusetts]* spent a day with us this week. Please send me by mail a few sheets of blotting paper. I may act as Adjutant while Patten is away. Have finished the "Pilot". Think it good in nautical matters, but otherwise very silly and ridiculous. Enclosed is a letter for Flannigan which please give him.

Your affectionate brother
Henry.

P.S. February 28th.

Yours 24th with Louisa's 21st, also Mother's 23rd received this morning. Please thank Louisa for the sweet meats in the valise which I did not before know were sent by her. They were very nice. Patten expects soon to leave for home. Murphy you have probably seen.

You must have enjoyed Philadelphia very much. Please send me by mail one of each of my photographs. I will send back the original ones to you soon. You can give them away probably and thus save having more of the new kind. Remember as a general rule when you give away any of my photographs you should get one of the person to whom you gave one in exchange, and these please put in my book. I have just come from muster for January and February so I have now 4 months pay due, and expect soon to send home plenty of money to pay for Class photographs and all other expenses. All quiet as usual. River falling but still very high. The Citizens here all agree that after such an open winter the roads will not be fit for travel till very late in the spring, April at least.

Your affectionate brother
Henry.

RIGHT UP INTO THE FIRE

20th Mass. Falmouth, Va.
March 3rd 1863.

My dear Father.

The Express matter for the Corps has come, and I have received the box of poultry sent by Brother Joseph, and I am sorry to say it was totally unfit for use. Our men said that perhaps the poultry would have kept had the dealer first taken out the entrails of the fowls, which he did not do. I am indeed very sorry to lose such an addition to our fare, but it cannot be helped now. The box you sent to Baltimore has been taken again by Harnden's Express, but was too late for this trip. The last box is probably now at Washington. I do not expect to get either box for some weeks, unless I have some chance of sending privately. I am very sorry these boxes should just have missed, but they are no doubt all safe and will turn up by and by.

Adjutant Patten of our Regiment has just gone home, and has taken several little things for me. He is a most excellent fellow in every way, was the intimate friend of Lt. Lowell both in College and in the Regiment, and I think if you meet him you will like him very much. He has been in all our battles and has once been wounded. I asked him to call at the house. While he is away I am acting as Adjutant. The weather and roads are improving, but still we have frequent rainstorms and deep mud. Herbert Mason expects soon to go home for 10 days. Everything is quiet here and there is nothing new.

Your affectionate son
Henry.

Head Quarters 20th Mass.
March 5th 1863.

Dear John.

I have received your letter enclosing a map of Antietam. So many Officers are going home that you will not lack for constant news from the Regiment. Mrs. O'Hara lives No. 80 West Cedar Street. McDonough money is all right. Please ask Bro. Joseph if he delivered any money for private Ed. O. Graves, drummer of my Company. He tells me Mrs. Graves has not received it.

We had a grand Corps review today. Hooker looked well. He is gaining in the confidence of every one every day. Such a change from Burnside. Men are now well fed, housed and clothed, and discipline is enforced. It seems more like the good old McClellan days again. The Army under Burnside was rapidly going to ruin. Hooker is energetic and acts like a soldier, not like a politician. There was no cheering whatever today, and no attempt to force cheers. Everything is quiet. Herbert goes home in a day or two.

    I read with great interest your business plans. It seems to me that with Mr. Trask's aid, and with the stimulus of self support, you will do as well at law for the next 2 or 3 years in New York as in Boston. Then you can learn every day much about the business, and after becoming well acquainted with it, judge whether and under what conditions you would join the firm. I believe fully with you that you would do better, be more happy and in fact live faster, that is see and do and learn more in New York than in Boston. A home like ours, in fact so good a home like ours, sticks to a man and impedes him. Of course you only can judge whether a year's practise in New York would injure your legal prospects, in case you should conclude after all to practise law and live in Boston. I do not suppose it would. I am decidedly in favor of the New York plan on the whole. But I would explain to Father, or at any rate to Joseph, the exact state of the case. Father would not object long. Let him think it over a few days, and I feel sure he will agree to your plan. One thing, however. You leave Mary Ann, without anybody to put her through and keep her from getting the dumps, and the blues, which are bad things when they get to be chronic. Mary Ann needs you very much. If I was at home, it would not so much matter, but if you go off she will not go anywhere and will get to be an old maid before she is a woman. But then she could come on once in a while and see you and stay at Martha's.

    In spite of these objections (and the scarcely less serious one of leaving Mother) I really think you ought to go and not let slip an opportunity which is now presented to you, or at any rate now particularly brought to your remembrance. In New York you would have your rooms, your friends, your society, and be perfectly independent. You would probably work hard, and play hard, and be better for both. You would find plenty of men and of women too and very likely if business or law prospects brighten you may see your way clear to a pretty little wife, for you have a good pick in New York, and to be a first rate man from Boston is a great thing in spite of all they say and laugh about us. So I think you had better go and set up in New York and leave the final decision as to entering the firm until you have seen a little into the state of things in Mr. Trask's Office. I hope you will write to me your opinions as they come up. I should be delighted to see you in the business for its benefit, for yours and prospectively for mine.

    Tell me if ever you got the Soho sauce in Washington. And whether you took home safely those little things for me?

Best love to Mary Ann. Tell her to write whenever she feels like it. I hope you will see Patten and Herbert of course.

Your affectionate brother
Henry.

20th Mass. March 7th 1863.

My dear John.

I have looked over this map I send enclosed, and find it so entirely incorrect as to positions of troops that I thought you would like to see it somewhat corrected. I have rudely marked our positions. I am not certain as to where exactly we camped on the 16th, nor where we crossed the Antietam, nor where we formed line, but you know this as well as I. The principal absurdity is in putting the Rebel line so far back. My Company picketed on the right, and my right post was the toll house. The enemy were in a cornfield and on a hill ¼ of a mile or less in front.

The celebrated *Cornfield* is put too far to the right. It was almost opposite the Church. The 34th New York was the left Regiment of Gorman's Brigade, and the Church broke them as it did our 42nd New York.

All quiet, no news. No letters.

Your affectionate brother
Henry.

Falmouth, Va. March 10th 1863.

My dear Mother.

I have not received letters from home today, the last I received was from Brother Joseph. I have acknowledged the receipt of the shirts but am very sorry to say they are too small. Abbott however needs some and he took them of me. So if you will tell me what they cost I will get it of him. I wish you would get me 2 more of the same size as the one you sent out about a month ago. All these woolen shirts shrink constantly. Those I now have were made to order, and are now much too small. Please let the new ones be 42 inches round the Chest (that is what they call 21 inches at the Stores) and 17 inches in the neck. Sleeves etc. much longer than you would think it possible for me to wear. Wrists also quite large. If I do not make this allowance for shrinkage, the shirts will be too small before they are worn out. I should also like 2 good *thin* undershirts, for I shall send back my present thick ones soon. I am very sorry for the loss of my new boots, but as I bought a pair in Baltimore, I will not order a second pair. I am exceedingly sorry to lose the nice preserves etc. I am abundantly supplied with all kinds of Clothing. If you can conveniently I should be very glad to have you call on Mrs. Rodgers, No. 2 Board Alley, Boston (leads out of Purchase St., I believe). Her husband was in my Company and was an excellent man. He fell sick at Bolivar and went into Hospital. His wife has written to me twice and both times I have had to tell her that I had heard nothing from him. I have written to the Surgeon in charge of the last Hospital where I know he was, and intend to find out all I can about him. I dare say you could comfort her a good deal by a short call. Perhaps my letters never reached her.

As to Mrs. Humphrey I have not seen or heard of her or her husband. There is due him for work on the Post Bakery $1.50. If you can give it to him and get his receipt for it, I shall be much obliged, for I am Treasurer of the Post Fund and have to pay out all moneys for Regimental purposes.

I have heard that Humphrey is discharged, but I hardly believe it, for he always seemed a stout man and was generally well.[53] Please hand the enclosed little Memorandum to Herbert Mason. John will see him probably quite often. Herbert will bring on the shirts no doubt. If he cannot, the Sergeant Major of the Regiment who is soon going home on furlough will. Please let me know if you shall have anything to send in about 2 weeks, and I will ask the Sergeant Major to call and get it. I have received a letter for Flannigan in John's handwriting. Flannigan is not here and I did not know he was coming on. All well and comfortable, but rather dull without Herbert.

Your affectionate son
Henry.

---

[53] Corporal Charles E. Humphrey was discharged for disability on March 6, 1863.

RIGHT UP INTO THE FIRE

20th Mass. Volunteers
Falmouth, March 14th 1863.

My dear Father.

I have to acknowledge yours of March 9th and one letter from Mother dated March 11th, also one from Lizzy dated Albyns. I am very glad to hear that you have passed so pleasant a week. I am glad to hear that Boulnois is so much better. Your dinner party must have been a very pleasant one. Patten will be back in a few days and will tell me all about it. I am glad you saw him, for he is a most excellent fellow and a very good friend of mine. Dr. Hayward, our Surgeon, has just come home on leave. He is one of our oldest Officers, and has always done well by the Regiment. We all esteem him very highly. I hope you will manage to see him. As to the shirts Mother wrote about, I dare say Patten, Herbert or the Dr. will bring them on with pleasure. I am very sorry to lose so much out of the box that was broken open. I think you had better have any other box you may send well bound round the edges with iron hoop or rattan, and firmly nailed. The Express runs regularly now and we get baggage every 3 or 4 days. As soon however as there is the least prospect of a move, I suppose it will be stopped. There was a rumor that the Rebels were about to make a raid on our right the other day, but it did not come to anything. We had orders to hold ourselves in readiness. Hooker is doing a great deal to improve the Army. Our flank has been fortified. Provisions are plenty and Stores of all kinds are brought up and everything is done to make the troops more comfortable. A Board of examination for incompetent Officers has been established, a thing much needed. The Army will be in excellent condition by the time that the roads are dry enough to travel. Weather is cold again, with frequent snow squalls. Roads hard frozen. All well.

We had a fire night before last, and a house was burnt down, but all the property saved, and all the outbuildings and neighboring houses. Capt. Murphy and Lieutenants Hibbard and Kelliher roomed in this house. If we could have got Ladders we could have put it out, for there were plenty of men to pass water, but it began in an upper room, and the smoke was so dense they could not get at it before it got fairly started, and then we only attempted to save everything we could.

Your affectionate son
Henry.

Enclosed letter for M. A. R.

RIGHT UP INTO THE FIRE

20th Mass. March 15th 1863.
(Sunday)

My dear John.

I have received yours of the 7th No. 6. I find I shall have to give up the numbering of letters and therefore have not numbered this or the previous ones. I wrote you rather a long but hurried letter about your business plans, which I suppose you have now received. I did not know that law practise in New York was so different from that in Boston, and so thought it perhaps better for you to continue law for some time in New York.

Hooker is doing well, as I have written, and has got the confidence of the Army to a great extent. Still, by the time operations commence, the 2 years and 9 months men will be gone and we shall be inferior to the enemy in numbers. I do not believe the conscription will work, and the Negro Regiments are worse than useless. This is the most impolitic step the Government has yet taken. If unsuccessful in raising many men, still the evil effects are done by dividing the North and uniting the South, and if they raise men there will certainly be mutiny in the Old Army. If Hooker fights, he must fight a doubtful battle, and if he wins it will be at the cost of his Army. This Army is all that is left to depend upon now, and if that is sacrificed, we shall be in a bad plight. Therefore I do not expect an active campaign to open soon but rather a policy of threatening delay.

Glad to hear Boulnois is so much better. Macy and Perkins are back. You must have had a very pleasant time at home with the young Ladies. Glad they are all so lively. It is rather dull here, and I like to hear of pleasant times even though I cannot enjoy them. I am *very sorry* to hear that Mary Ann is dull and is not well. Still I see no prospect of a change of life to her. You must get her to go out as much as she can, and visit often.

Steve Weld was here to dine yesterday. He his */sic/* now alone on Genl. Benham's staff. The General soon expects to have a Corps. He was kind enough to ask me to come on General Benham's staff, and he had the General's permission to ask anyone he thought proper. It was very kind of him indeed, and I thanked him for it, but told him of course that I could not think of leaving the old 20th. Please not to mention this. All well. Cold weather now, roads frozen. I miss Herbert very much.

Your affectionate brother
Henry.

Holmes desires his regards.

Dear John. I send "Peveril of the Peak" which perhaps can be bound sometime. Also Mary Ann's vest. The cold weather is about past and I take this opportunity of getting rid of everything I cannot easily carry. Please have it carefully kept.

H. R.

Falmouth, Va. 18th March 1863.
Wednesday.

My dear John.

I rather wonder that I have had no letters from home for 3 or 4 days but suppose you have sent them on by Herbert or Patten. I have received a letter from Flannigan whose wound has broken out afresh and who is now in Hospital at Alexandria. Will you please send him $5.00 in a letter and charge the same to me? Direct to "Private Thomas Flannigan, Company K, 20th Mass. Volunteers" and enclose the envelope thus directed in one directed to "Thomas Flannigan, New Camp of Convalescents, Fort Barnard near Alexandria, Va." Please be very particular about these directions. I would send him some myself, were I not rather short, just now. We expect 4 months pay in a day or two. Please send this to Flannigan as soon as possible, as he is in want of it.

I wish you would order for me at Nason's a very thin light waistcoat, of blue flannel or thin cloth. He has my measure, only tell him that it is a little too large in the waist. Also a thin sack coat, of dark blue Cloth, very thin, or of good flannel, neither to be expensive. The coat to button up to the chin close, and to be cut in to fit the shape of the body, not a loose sack. In coat 2 inside breast pockets. No side pockets at all. Coat quite short, sleeves large at elbow, 5 buttons in front, one at each cuff. You can get a little bit of gild binding and put in a bar to my old 2nd Lieutenant straps, and they will do. Coat should fit neatly so that the belt would not crease it up. I want it *very* thin and light and not expensive. Vest the same. Not too dark a blue. As to the camp-chest etc. sent from Poolesville, did you find there a pair of leather leggings? I should like to have them cleaned and kept for me. Please send on the Coat and Vest as soon as made. No wadding in any part of either, cannot be too thin. Of course they must be made on a smaller measure than thick Clothes.

Be very careful when you send on these things to have them in a strong box, that cannot be easily opened. Put in a couple of boxes yeast powder and a pot of pickles, if there is room. So much for business. All quiet, no prospect of a move. They think at Corps Head Quarters that Hooker will try a great dash before 9 months and 2 years men are gone.

I have had another staff offer. Col. Morgan at Corps Head Quarters sent for me yesterday and wanted me to be Provost Marshal of the Corps in place of Major Mullen, who is to return to his Regiment, the Lieut. Colonel having resigned. I told him I could not leave the Regiment of course. It would have been a very comfortable place there, no doubt permanent. 100 Infantry and 50 Cavalry under my orders, plenty of transportation, several horses, a camp by myself, always close to Corps Head Quarters, and a very easy, independent and rather swelly time generally. On the march the duties would be arduous and in action very tiresome, although not of danger. I suppose there must be somebody to drive up stragglers etc., but I do not like that kind of thing. The great temptation to me is the having one or 2 good horses to ride. I have ridden a good deal lately and like it very much. I enjoy this kind of rough riding across an open country better than a regular ride on a beaten road at home.

I am very glad you saw Patten at the house. Hope you saw the Doctor too. Macy is very sorry to have missed you. He is as well as ever and an exceedingly happy man. He left Maj. Macy in Philadelphia. We are all disgusted here that Lieut. Colonel Baxter of the 7th Michigan is made a Brigadier-General over Col. Hall. Mr. Chandler of Michigan however, I understand, could not consent to have a man of Col. Hall's politics, especially a West Pointer, and as Michigan had not had her fair share of Generals, it was left to this worthy representative, and now Baxter, instead of being a very ordinary Lieut. Colonel, is a miserably inefficient General. One of the most shameful things we have heard of lately is the sending home the 2nd New Hampshire Regiment to carry the election which they did. Their Colonel is a leading Republican Politician. They were nominally sent home to recruit, but as they were about twice as big as the average Regiments of our Corps, this ruse did not take.

Please send me a few postage stamps, and a dozen or two large envelopes, such as Official business comes in.

Love to all. I hope to get letters tomorrow.

Affectionately
Henry.

RIGHT UP INTO THE FIRE

Memorandum of Articles sent to Henry in a Box

March 20th 1863.

3 Mince Pies and 6 Tin Plates (to cover)
1 Can Raspberry Jam 1 Qt.
1 Can Ginger preserved 1 Qt.
3 lbs. crushed Sugar (white)
1 lb. Tea (English Breakfast)
1 box Figs about 3 lbs.
2 cans Milk
1 can Coffee (ground) Java 3 lbs.
1 can 2 Qt. Orange Marmalade
1 lb. dried Ginger (preserved)
1 Bologne Sausage for trial
1 Sugar cured Tongue (cooked)
1 bottle Sherry Wine
1 small do. Cherry Cordial
filled up with Apples and Gingerbread.

Directed to Lt. Henry Ropes,
20th Regiment Mass. Volunteers,
3rd Brigade, 2nd Corps, 2nd Division,
Falmouth, Va.

Falmouth, 21st March 1863.

Dear John.

I have received your letter in which you asked for a horse to be sent to Herbert. Herbert has come all right, and McKay and Murphy and Walker too. The shirts are just the right size. Please ask Mother what the first ones cost, and let me know. Herbert has brought the books, blotting paper, ground ginger, hinges, locks, envelopes and tooth wash. You probably forgot I got a copy of "Nicholas Nickleby" in Washington. Also Herbert brought a very nice pair of slippers which I suppose you got for me. I do not need them, however as I bought a pair in Baltimore. I will not order another pair of shoes yet, for I think my present boots will be enough. I sent home by somebody, I forget whom, a parcel of Company papers. I have got some more papers and some Company Books which I intend soon to send home to you. Please keep them for me. I have written to Capt. Shepard that I shall send these to you and that there may be some private papers of his among them, and that he can get them from you at any time. So please let him have whatever he asks for. As we cannot tell when we may move, and as we certainly shall have but little transportation, I intend to reduce my baggage to the lowest limit, and expect soon to send home a box of things to you, to be kept for me. Please tell me if there was anything I might want in those two boxes I left at Poolesville.

Herbert has had a delightful time and very favorable weather. I envy him his sleigh rides.

I really feel unable to say anything to you about your business plans. I feel unable to come to any very positive opinion, but incline towards the business plan. John Gray's reasons are certainly strong. You would have to give up all hope of a partnership with him, and this is much to lose. Now that you have presented the other side, I feel quite at a loss, but am sure you will decide rightly yourself and shall be glad when the question is settled.

Please send me out 3 or 4 of my own pictures, old ones, just as good as any, for some of the fellows here want them.

Letter for Mary Ann enclosed.

Affectionately
Henry.

Falmouth, Va. March 22nd 1863.
Sunday.

My dear Mother.

I wrote to you some time ago and asked you to call on Mrs. Rodgers, wife of private James Rodgers, of my Company, as she had twice written to me about her husband, and seemed to be much distressed, not having heard from him for a long time. I replied to her letters and have written to the Surgeon of the Hospital where he was sent, that I might be able to tell her all about him. Yesterday I received an answer, telling me that Rodgers died at the Convalescent Hospital,

Alexandria, Va. on November 29th 1862, five days after he was admitted there. Dr. B. Hunt was the Surgeon in charge. This is all I can find out about Rodgers. He was a most faithful man and never shirked any duty and kept up on our long marches before Antietam, although he was pretty well used up then. His pay and Clothing accounts and final Statements have no doubt been sent in to the War Office by the Surgeon, and Mrs. Rodgers can get what money was due by applying to the New England War Protective Claim Association. No papers from me are necessary. I return two letters directed to Rodgers. Now if you would go to see Mrs. Rodgers and break to her the news of her husband's death and tell her all that I have written, I should be much obliged, and it would be a great kindness to her. She lives No. 2 Board Alley (near Purchase Street) Boston. If it is not a proper place for you to go to, I dare say John would go.

The Shirts are most excellent, and the right size. Next time you have an opportunity please send out 2 *very thin* undershirts. Also if convenient 5 or 6 Tapes marked in as large letters as possible "Lt. Ropes, 20th Mass." These are for my blankets etc. Herbert desires his regards etc. to you, and says he was very sorry to find you out when he called. We have now had snow and drizzling rain for 3 days, and plenty of mud. No prospect of active operations for some weeks. Many of our Officers have returned, and it is getting more cheerful every day.

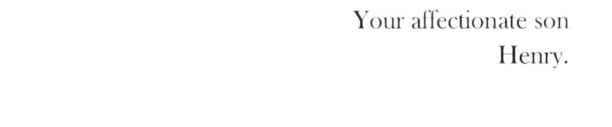

Your affectionate son
Henry.

Falmouth, Va.
Wednesday, March 25th 1863.

My dear Father.

I received last evening your letter dated 20th containing the receipt for the box and the list of contents.

I am indeed very much obliged to you for these nice things. I shall enjoy them all very much, especially the Pies and Marmalade. The Pies made by the people here are horrible things and I shall be delighted to taste a sample of home cookery. They do not know how to cook anything but meat in the South.

Herbert has just been so fortunate as to get a box of Poultry, Vegetables, Butter etc. in perfect condition just a week from Boston. So when my box comes, we shall have a real Christmas dinner.

We all are deeply grieved at the death of Genl. Sumner, our old Commander.[54] He is a great loss to the Army, for there must be some such fearless men to use in an emergency. I do not know anyone who can supply his place.

Lt. Bowditch's death is very sad.[55] I hear it was a desperate hand to hand fight. Bowditch received several sabre cuts and was finally shot in the stomach. Our Cavalry seem to have done well.

Herbert and I are to have the use of an old house on the march and expect to be quite comfortable. We see no signs of a move, but as it is now a month later than "slow" McClellan's advance last year, I suppose we may go very suddenly. They are fortifying Acquia Creek, and this leads me to think that the Army is to move by water, in which case we may be left here or at Acquia Creek.

As I am out of Stamps I shall have to frank this letter.

Your affectionate son
Henry.

Falmouth, Va. March 26th 1863.

My dear John.

I received your letter No. 8 of March 21st last evening. Herbert has paid me for the locks etc. which are excellent. I shall be delighted to get the box. On the whole I feel relieved to think you have determined to stick to law, a lawyer is an eminently respectable person. If I should ever get into the business, I should probably like to have you there, but while things are so unsettled by the war, I am glad you are not to change. Did you ever receive a letter from me about this matter?

As to the Negro Regiments, I never said that was the cause of the divided South /*North*/ etc., but one of the causes, and perhaps the principal. You say "the

---

[54] Edwin Sumner died of a fever on March 21, 1863, aged 66.

[55] Lt. Nathaniel Bowditch of the 1st Massachusetts Cavalry was gravely wounded in the cavalry action at Kelly's Ford on March 17, 1863. He died the following day.

RIGHT UP INTO THE FIRE

Government has no idea of having Negro Officers." Now within a few weeks a number of Maine Officers have been put in arrest for refusing to report to a Negro Captain at New Orleans, and privates arrested for not saluting Negro Officers. The whole scheme is carried on by a party who believe in *forcing* the Negroes to an equality with the whites, and in the bill providing for the employment of Negroes as Soldiers, no prohibition of Negro Officers is made. Gov. Andrew has acted very wisely for the success of his scheme in having white Officers in his new Regiment and has picked these Officers from the choicest Regiments now in the field. I will venture to say no Regiment was *ever raised* officered better than the 54th Mass. The leading Officers are Gentlemen, and besides most of them have seen a great deal of real service, have shown themselves able and brave Officers in battle and are taken from Regiments of especial reputation for strict discipline. Of course with such Officers the Regiment must be at least splendidly disciplined and drilled, and will be splendidly led. But how are Negro Regiments in New Orleans officered by Negroes and common white Officers? Capt. Hooper, Banks' Staff, Herbert's brother, writes that they are a miserable good for nothing mob. I have no more doubt of it than I have that the 54th is a model Regiment. See then what a price we pay for a *good* Negro Regiment! We take away Officers capable of making a *much better* white Regiment. You make a mistake, I think, in saying that "they will do to garrison forts etc.". To hold a fort well attacked requires as soldierly qualities as to attack a fort well defended. If Negroes will not fight in one way, they will not in any way. I never saw the principle stated before, that inferior troops will do for defense. I do not believe this is so. If then the expression means anything, it means that "they will do to hold forts, not attacked". But, then the question is: "What need of any troops" or at any rate a merely nominal number of little consequence? In both cases, if the forts were attacked, we should be obliged to send good white troops to defend them, and what a waste of money and of white Officers it is to keep such useless troops. But it is said that white troops cannot stand the climate. This I doubt, but if so, white Rebels cannot attack in such a climate. Then what is the use of the Negro troops? You reply: "We want men". I say: "We want soldiers, not men". My experience is that poor troops are really worse than useless, and from what I have seen of Negroes, I believe they will make *poor* troops. The great majority of them must be field hands, not Northern free Negroes, half white. I think then (for the sake of argument, throwing prejudice aside) that Negro troops are useless in the same sense that Regiments of boys under 12 years would be useless, or (if it were possible) Regiments of women.

There is another and more important aspect of the question. There exists in our country (right or wrong) a tremendous, deeprooted *[sic]* prejudice against the black race. Not against their *color,* nor against them personally in their own station of life, but against the Negro taking equality with the white. I dare say I do not express myself clearly. I mean that an ordinary American does not hate a Negro servant or laborer, but a negro who tries (or whose friends trie [sic] for him) to raise himself to his (the white's) position in life. This is the result first of the evident inferiority of the Negro race to the white; 2nd to the fact that the one race has held the other so long in slavery. Now nobody objects to an intelligent Negro bettering himself, and filling any position he can, but people object to a party who have for so long striven to *force* the negro into social equality with the white. For this reason the majority of soldiers in our Army would consider it a disgrace to serve under a black Corporal, or Officers, and *would never have enlisted* had they expected so to serve. There is no difficulty in enforcing obedience and respect to a white Officer, however stupid, brutal or ignorant he may be, for there is no reason why he should not be intelligent, kind and wise but the strongest feelings men have are these feelings of nationality and social position. You can no more offend this and avoid an outbreak in our Army than you could abolish caste in India. Now I believe I am as little affected with prejudice against the Negro, as anyone can be, but I think it so plain as to need no proof that the Negro race, as it exists today in the United States is utterly inferior to the white, as inferior as the reptile is to the bird or the animal. Exceptions of course often occur, and were it not for this antagonism of race against race, each Negro, like each white man, would rise or fall to the position in life he was fitted for; but this difference of race is a boundary which cannot be passed. Negroes and white men as naturally are separated as dogs and cats.

Now, in the South, while there is less repugnance to them as individuals, there is more hatred to them as equals. In fact they cannot acknowledge equality and support slavery, and to break up slavery would not only cause a great convulsion but is what to attempt which they have been bred to consider the most horrible of crimes. With them the raising of the Negro to an equality with the white is perfectly insupportable. Thus I say our raising Negro troops has divided the North and united the South. Divided the North by breeding dissatisfaction and insubordination in the Army (New Orleans, Genl. Stephenson etc. etc.) and by offending the strong prejudices of a great part of the people. Uniting the South by making the question of war not a political matter, capable (theoretically at least) of being compromised and arranged, but a question whether or not to stand by the old institutions of the country and oppose the awful horrors of a slave insurrection. A Union man in the South *now* is thought the same as a man who favors a slave insurrection, i.e. worse than a murderer. Of course it is foolish to suppose that I expect the Rebels will actually fight harder in battle now than they did at Williamsburg or Fair Oaks, but now they will not give in until they are reduced far beyond what was the yielding point a year ago. The Americans fought as well at Bunker Hill as at Yorktown but the way of peace and compromise was open until by repeated acts or barbarity not the least of which in the public estimation was the employment of Hessian troops, had driven the Americans to a determination to have Independence at all costs. So I think it is now with the South. If our acts had not been constantly "uniting" them closer and closer, they never would have stood what they have stood and are now standing. The best proof that the South is more united than ever is that they are still united at all. And as to the North. Where is the enthusiasm of this time last year? Where the confidence? Where, I might say, the patriotism? If you think there is the ten thousandth part of it left; if you think that anything but discipline influences this Army, you are very much mistaken. Among the better class of Officers there is patriotism, that is, a determination to stand by the Government and the Country, but I have not yet seen the least enthusiasm anywhere. The Army will fight better than ever, but if it had last year's enthusiasm combined with its present discipline, it would be the best Army the world ever saw.

There is one other view to take of this Negro matter. The Constitution speaks of the soldier as an "able-bodied, free, white citizen, etc.", and I think it was a tacit agreement with every soldier, when he enlisted, that this should be the soldier and nothing else. To use an absurd illustration for the sake of example, suppose the Government should raise a female Regiment. Would not this cause mutiny? Suppose I am ordered to report to a female Captain for duty, suppose a female Colonel is put over me, what am I to do? Or suppose the Government should reduce the pay of the soldier to $1.00 a month? Would there not be mutiny? Yet, as far as I see, they have a technical *right* to do this. I ought to say finally that I do not think we are in such want of men as you imply, and that, if I did, I dare say I would consent to the enlistment of Negroes, under two restrictions. 1st No Negro Officers, 2nd No Negro non-commissioned Officer *ever* to be put over a white soldier. These restrictions would obviate most of these social difficulties.

I think it is not a mere question of raising troops, but that this matter is taken as a means of *forcing* the whites to recognize the Negro as a social equal. The people of America, it seems to me, look on a Negro in much the same way as an English Nobleman looks on a laborer. Both are willing to acknowledge the other in his station, and give him his rights, but to force white men to act under and salute Negro Officers would be like forcing every English Gentleman to invite half a dozen laborers to dine every week, or in some other way to acknowledge equality of social position, which he would not do, of course.

I have written rather a lengthy and disjointed letter, but I dare say you will get from it my reasons for *opposing* Negro *troops*, which I do heartily. I *do* go in for a rigid adherence to the Constitution and obedience to the Government and for enforcing the draft and carrying on the war. But I detest this way of bringing politics into the Army. Men's lives are too valuable to be trifled with so awfully, and I think it is an awful sin to place a miserable and ignorant General in command of men, because he is of this or that political party. Yet, this is done, even in our own Brigade. Probably Lincoln sacrificed hundreds of lifes [*sic*] by detaching Blenker[*'s*] Division a year ago "to satisfy the friends of Genl. Fremont", as he says he did.

While I am sick of this sort of things of which I see so much, and by no means so hopeful of a brilliant and successful Campaign, as you are, I hope I am as really patriotic as ever, and as determined to do what I can to carry out heartily whatever the Government determines on attempting with this Army.

Leaves are stopped from April 1st, so I shall not be able to come home, even if I thought it best.

Your affectionate brother
Henry.

Falmouth, Va.
March 28th 1863.

My dear Father.

I have received your letter of March 24th enclosing a letter from Frank. I received and acknowledged some days ago your letter containing the receipt for the box by Harnden's Express and a list of the contents of the box. I am very sorry to have lost so many letters as you say you have sent, and hope I may get them at last. I always acknowledge letters I receive and will in future note the date of letters I write to you and to the others, and beg you will acknowledge any you receive. Thus I shall know what ones of mine miscarry. I found it very inconvenient to number letters, although it is a good plan, but when one writes so hastily as I often must one is apt to forget to number.

I have heard that Flannigan und Humphrey are discharged, and if so both will probably draw their pay in Washington and repay you your loans. I am glad to hear that we are soon to be paid up to March 1st.

The Christian Commission have now opened a Room in an old Mill here, and have daily prayer meetings and preaching once a week. There is quite a good Minister here, and the meetings are all well attended. Last Sunday the Major and 8 of us Officers went, but usually there are but four Officers. We have greatly improved by our long rest, and the Regiment never was so clean, orderly and healthy. Col. Hall has come back and taken command of our Brigade. Genl.

RIGHT UP INTO THE FIRE

Howard is in command of Siegel's [sic] Corps, and Genl. Gibbon has our Division. Genl. Gibbon is considered a fine Officer.

There are no signs of a move yet. Continual rain for 5 days or so has brought back the deep mud. Herbert and I are to send home our buffalos and a box of baggage which we could not carry. I have directed both to you and will put in the box a list of Herbert's things. I enclose a letter for Mary Ann.

Your affectionate son
Henry.

Falmouth, Va. March 31st 1863.

My dear Father.

I received last evening the box sent last by Harnden's Express. The contents were all right, nothing injured or broken and all most acceptable. I found the tongue very delicious and the pies a greater luxury tha[n] I have enjoyed for a very long time. I never received a box in which everything was better packed nor one which was better filled. I am indeed very much obliged to you and to Mother for it. The preserves I have not opened, but the Marmalade is very nice. The tin cans I shall find very useful after I have used their contents. The Cherry Cordial and Bologna Sausage I shall keep for the march.

Yesterday was so warm and pleasant that we thought summer had really come, but today we have snow and sleet and mud again. We are expecting a move very soon, but it appears likely that our Corps will remain to cover this front and conceal our movement from the enemy, in whatever direction the Army goes. I hear there is to be a strong raid made from our right up the river.

Hooker's army in now very large, fully 130,000 men for duty, and well supplied. It seems to be the general opinion that he will move secretly down the river, cross say 40 miles below under cover of the gunboats and move on the enemy's communications with Richmond. But it is also thought that the enemy are not in strong force opposite us, and are ready to withdraw to Richmond when we move. I cannot but think that the enemy will be obliged to transfer the seat of war to Kentucky before long.

I am a little afraid they will abandon Vicksburg and fall on Rosecranz [sic] with overwhelming forces. I think they will try this sooner than leave Virginia, but if not successful in such a move I think they will abandon Virginia too and stake everything on a campaign in Kentucky. Burnside and his Corps have gone West, I see. There seems to be a good deal of delay about Charleston and Vicksburg, but I suppose we are all waiting for one another, and when dry weather sets in there will be a pretty general waking up.

    I have received no letters since I last wrote, but several papers.

Your affectionate son
Henry.

April 2nd 1863.

Dear John.

    Abbott goes home this morning, and I send a letter by him because it seems as if the mail had completely failed. I have not received letters for a long time. Please say to Mother that the socks she sent by Carver have come all right. Please ask Mary Ann to write again any letters she may have sent during the last week or two.

    I hope you will see a good deal of Abbott, who will settle your McClellan heresies with Jomini and other Authorities.

In haste
H. R.

Falmouth, Va. April 2nd 1863.

My dear Mother.

    I have just received your letter of March 27th, the first from home for a long time.

    Abbott left this morning and by him I sent a hurried note to John. I hope you will see a good deal of Abbott. I know you would like him very much, and I am sure he would like to see you all too. Abbott, you know, has always been with the

Regiment and is one of the very best Officers we have. He and I are very intimate indeed.

The socks by private Carver have come on all right and are very useful. The box was received duly and acknowledged. Its contents were most acceptable. The pies and tongue were capital.

I am very sorry you had so much trouble about Mrs. Rodgers. I did not know where "Board Alley" was myself, but one of the men told me it was close to Purchase Street.

I hope Mary Ann will go to Newport this summer. Such trips are just what she needs, and a very pleasant change from Swampscott. I have received no letters from her for about 2 weeks, but Father says she sent several, and as I fear they are lost I hope she will write again the same letters. We are quite busy now with our quarterly returns, which must go in this week.

Yesterday we had a visit from our old Classmate Temple, Capt. 17th Infantry. He looks remarkably well and has grown a great bit taller.

I sent home by Express a few days ago a box and two Buffalo skins, one mine and one Herbert's. In the box were a number of things belonging to Herbert, and I put in the top a list of these things. Please send them with the box to Mr. Chs. Appleton, Beacon Street. The rest of the contents of the box are mine which please keep. I enclose the receipt of the Express Company.

Flannigan and Corporal Humphrey are discharged and are probably home by this time. Flannigan is a most excellent man and I hope he will get a pension if he is permanently disabled. I dare say he may not know how to go to work but John would show him. All well.

Your affectionate son
Henry.

Falmouth, Va. April 6th 1863
Monday.

My dear John.

I have received your letter of March 31st. Much obliged to you for taking so much trouble about the men of my Company. I have sent 3 Company books and some more Company papers in the box containing my things and Herbert's. Capt.

Shepard will probably not call for the papers, as he expects to be back by May 2nd. The Slippers I do not now need but will send for them perhaps by and by. The Buffalo may be useful for a few weeks at home, and then had better be put away like any other skin and kept for next winter.

In addition to the Sack and Vest, I would like a pair of trousers, light or dark blue (the light preferred provided they are as strong and as cheap.) I wish a light, perhaps coarse cloth serviceable and *not* expensive. A private of my Company, Fitzgerald, has gone home on leave, and returns by the 15th April. He will call at your Office and will bring on anything. If the pants are done soon, I dare say he would take them. I would be much obliged if you would buy 2 balls, suitable for playing "base-ball". I want them for the use of the Company. I am sorry I did not think to tell you of these things before, so that you might have sent all together, but I dare say it will now be in time for Fitzgerald. Lieutenant Willard has left us for a Captaincy in the 54th colored. He owes $60.00 to the Regimental fund of which I am the Treasurer, and I asked him to pay it to you, to be credited to me, and when you notify me of that, I will assume the debt here, and pay it when we are paid, which will be very soon now. I suppose this $60.00 will about half pay my indebtedness to you and Father.

I am now acting as Provost Marshal of Falmouth, while Holmes is away. Do you know whether Joseph has received one or 2 letters from me about the money matters of my Company, and whether it is all right now?

I am glad to hear that Jarvis (24th) has a good appointment. What does Jim Perkins think of Negro Regiments? Pen. Hallowell is, I hear, in favor of Negro Officers. Willard said he opposed them. We do not think Willard has done exactly the right thing in leaving us, for he was strongly opposed to Negro Regiments until he was offered a Captaincy, and then he suddenly changed.

By the way, have you seen a letter from McClellan about the capture of Harpers' [sic] Ferry and the Antietam Campaign? It settles the whole question to me, and again McClellan comes out bright from one of the things he was terribly abused for. The delay in going to the Peninsula, the delay in returning, the evacuation of Harrison's Landing, and the taking of Harpers' Ferry are the things that at *the time* did more to create distrust in McClellan, than any others; yet we now see how perfectly innocent he was and how sure victory would have been, had his advice been followed. As you said in regard to Gov. Andrew, the evil results remain long after their cause has been shown to be false.

As to this Army. I heard from pretty good authority it was to be broken up and sent West and South. I do not believe it, at any rate it seems likely we are to remain some time here. We had a snow storm yesterday, and much mud. Still I think the Roads are as passable as they were when we moved last year. I have heard something about Fair Oaks I never knew before. It seems that by McClellan's orders a vast quantity of logs had been cut and fitted for bridges, and piled up close to the Chickahominy in front of Porter's Corps, and ready to be thrown across immediately, and also logs for Corduroy roads, and it was arranged that these logs should be carried over by Regiments as soon as the bridge should be built. As soon as the enemy attacked, Porter was ordered to throw across these bridges and cross and attack, and attempted to do so, but the flood *swept* all away and in spite of his utmost efforts, and every preparation, he had to give it up. This proves to me that the attack on Casey was foreseen and provided for, and but for circumstances beyond human control, would have resulted in a awful defeat of the Rebels and perhaps the capture of Richmond.

I am glad you have enjoyed John Gray's visit and have taken his advice. On the whole I feel easier to see you as you are, at least for the present. Please send me some stamps. If it would not cost much, say 2 or 3 $, I wish you would have 100 of each of the enclosed blanks printed for me, on ordinary paper, and in perfectly plain style. It is not a matter of very great consequence, however. I think a few stamped envelopes with your and Father's printed direction would be very convenient, and I dare say not expensive. I give examples of the form for passes. The words underlined are *not* to be printed, but room enough left to fill in in writing. I should like 100 of each, if convenient.

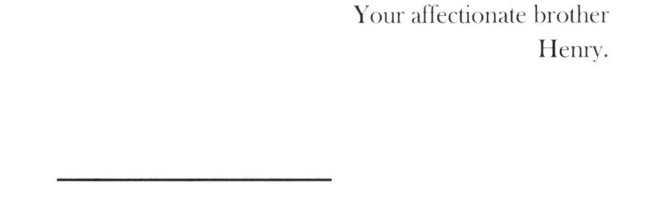

Your affectionate brother
Henry.

Falmouth, Va.
April 9th 1863.

My dear Father.

I received last evening the box containing the Coat, Pickles etc. all in perfect order. I acknowledged some time ago the receipt of the box of Apples, Preserves, Pies, etc.

All is quiet and no signs of a move. Please give the enclosed note to John.

Your affectionate son
Henry.

RIGHT UP INTO THE FIRE

April 9th 1863.

Dear John.

Yours de nigris received and will be answered. Please order for me at Rice's a pair *light* Army shoes like those lost. Same measure as boots, single sole, not heavy. Soles not to protrude, no toe-caps; made to buckle; same as buckle gaiters, Feby. 5th 1863.

Yours in haste
H. R.

Falmouth, 14th April 1863.
Tuesday 9 A.M.

Dear John.

We have every reason to expect an immediate move, but in what direction, no one can tell. I incline to think it merely a demonstration to prevent the Rebels sending more troops South, and perhaps cover the embarkation of re-enforcements for Hunter and Foster. At any rate, as we may not now be able to see the Paymaster for a long time, I wish you would please send me instalments of $5.00 in each letter you write until I get $50.00. I have now nearly $800.00 due, and the Paymaster was to have been here this week; but this move may put him back.

All well. Cavalry and Wagons went towards the right yesterday.
In haste

Affectionately
Henry.

RIGHT UP INTO THE FIRE

Falmouth, Va. April 16th 1863.

My dear John.

I have just sent a box to Washington, to be sent by Express to Boston. It is directed to "Wm. Ropes, 92 Beacon St., Boston, Mass." It contains first 1 pair long heavy leather boots and one pair Rubber boots which belong to Holmes, and he would be much obliged to you to send them to his Father, Charles St. Also one wool blanket, one pair thin boots, (legs cut) a dress-coat, waist coat, pair straps and watch. This is all I think, but I made up the box in a great hurry and may have forgotten all I put in. I wish you would send to me, either by someone coming on or by Express, my *thin* dress coat. It will probably come together with the shoes and trousers I wrote for last. The Straps I returned. I did not want these old ones, but the much nicer pair you sent out to me last June and which I always wore on my best coat. However, no matter now, for I have some. I send back again the Silver watch which is again out of order and will not go. It is no use trying to patch it up any more, it has always been a miserable watch and never went well for a month. Please get some watchmaker to allow you something for it and buy me another. I must have a hunter, and a watch that will keep reasonably good time under all circumstances. I do not in the least care for a handsome watch. No need of a second hand. I dare say this one is too finely made for an Army watch. I see it has a compensation balance-wheel, and perhaps it will do very well for home use. I want a watch that can stand hard usage, go in any position, and will not stop when exposed to cold. I dare say a good Lepine watch would be best. Do not send out the new watch by mail.

I wrote to you for some money as the Paymaster has not yet come. I think it is shameful to leave us thus 6 months without pay. Did I or did I not send $3.00 to Corporal Humphrey in a letter to one of you, I think Mother or Mary Ann?

Abbott and Holmes are back. Abbott brought me some stamps from you. Received a letter from Father yesterday dated 11th. Father alludes to the box of Herbert's and my things, which I suppose came all right. The Apples came all fresh and sound in the box with the Orange Marmalade etc.

We are ready but as far as I know nothing has yet moved but a few Cavalry toward Warrenton. Day before yesterday and yesterday we had *very* heavy rains. The river has risen tremendously, say 12 feet. Roads muddy of course. We do not in the least know what to expect or when we are to go. Extra clothing of the men has been sent to Washington and extra baggage of Officers got rid of.

I am sorry we were unsuccessful at Charleston, but fully expected it, and fully expect repulse at Vicksburg.[56] We shall meet with nothing but disaster till we turn

---

[56] On April 7, 1863, Rear Admiral Du Pont, with nine ironclads, engaged the Confederate forts in

over a new leaf. I hope you read McClellan's reports. Better read again his letter from the Peninsula about the evacuation and about the necessity of forces. This Army may win a victory but certainly cannot follow it up. Our Corps loses 3000 2 years and 9 months men by May 31st.

I am sickened by reading the report of the War Committee, or rather of 2 men, one the great opposer of West Point, the other the vilifier of McClellan. What more can be said in his favor than that he is picked out for constant abuse by such a compound of ignorance and falsehood? I wish I had a chance for a long talk about the recent developments concerning McClellan and the Peninsula. I have read Everett's speech with great pleasure, and hope the Country feels with him.

Hooker seems to be about a great thing now, if the impossible order to carry 8 days rations means anything. If this is often repeated we shall lose half the Army by sickness, but it may be only for a great march and a great strike and then a rest.

Your affectionate brother
Henry.

Falmouth
April 17th 1863.
My dear Father.

I received yesterday yours of the 13th. I think the buffalos must have come safely, for Herbert's family have received his and John alludes to mine. I enclose letters to Mary Ann, Frank and Lizzy, the last two on the thin paper you sent me some time since and which I find most excellent. I am very glad my last boxes came to hand so promptly and was delighted with the contents.

We are quiet yet, and it is said that the recent storm and rise of the river has prevented Hooker from carrying out his plans. The weather is now very cloudy and threatening. The river has gone down some three feet but is still very high.

Capt. Abbott enjoyed his visit to you very much. Holmes is very sorry he was unable to go. I have sent home a second box and have everything ready for a move. We are all to carry eight days rations; I hardly see how it is possible. Our horse will be very useful.

Your affectionate son
Henry.

Charleston harbor and was beaten back without inflicting any significant damage.

RIGHT UP INTO THE FIRE

Falmouth, Va. April 17th 1863.

My dear John.

Yours of the 11th received last night. Am very much obliged for all you have done. Did 2 Buffalos come tied together with the box? Mine is marked distinctly "H. Ropes". I received the base-balls. Have no doubt I shall like the trousers. Rodgers of my Company was *not* wounded at Antietam, nor was he there at all to the best of my recollection. He fell out 3 days before on the march completely used up. He died of diarrhoea.

I am glad you got the $60.00. Does this pay all my bills? If not, how much is still wanting to make me square? Fitzgerald has not yet come, but I expect him daily. I dare say there is difficulty in getting to the Army now. I should think it not worth while to get any printed stamped envelopes. The passes will be very convenient indeed. I am very glad you all liked Abbott so much. He has written you a most excellent letter about McClellan, which I have read. I want to ask you a question. In case you find your arguments against McClellan overthrown, are you ready to come boldly out and stand up for him, and take back all you have said against him? I fear you are not. I fear you have a prejudice which nothing can remove. I fear that when your arguments against McClellan are overthrown, you will content yourself with a silent acquiescence in the fact that he was really a great man and that it was a pity he was removed etc., and will not come out and lift up your voice like a trumpet and show the people their sins and Abraham his transgression. Now I do not look for a blessing on our arms till this tremendous wrong is righted. God has given us great work to perform, and a great and good man to do it, a man *will not* stoop to low truckling politicians, who *will not* make the slightest effort to gain popular favor, who does his duty before God according to his own conscience, regardless of results, and who is therefore unacceptable to the low masses of the people who hate him because he is an educated Soldier and a Gentleman and despises popular applause. McClellan's friends are not among the lowest of the rabble, but among the middle and upper classes. If he had gone home like Butler and made speeches and tickled the vanity of the populace and courted their favor and talked a little violent radicalism, he might have now had the Rebellion under his feet, and have been the idol of the people, and because he would not do this, I like him the more.

Butler and Hooker are the men for the American people now. McClellan is only called in when fear has overpowered everything else and when the enemy is at our gates. Then they rush to him, him whom they had abused, he saves them, they cheer, and kick him out again.

I have nothing to say against Hooker, as you know, but I do not expect to see the Rebellion put down till Genl. McClellan is in Halleck's place and is left with full control for at least 18 months. Perhaps we must wait till he is in Lincoln's place.

Your remaining objections against McClellan are true civilian objections. You have read of Napoleon falling like a thunderbolt etc., and you do not understand the real working of an Army. If McClellan had been let alone, it would have been said 20 years hence that McClellan dashed on Richmond, McDowell hurled his forces on the Rebel left, and you would have had the impression that it was like a boxing match. I really think that no one but a soldier can understand the movement of an Army, its size and the rapidity of motion possible is the great thing that it is impossible to explain to a citizen so that he will really allow for it.

Henry Wilson was here yesterday and came to our Head Quarters and saw Macy. No signs of a move yet. Perhaps the storm has frustrated Hooker's plans. Perhaps it is in consequence of our failure at Charleston.

By the way Col. Hall told me that the bridges in front of Porter were *really put down* and taken up again and piled up after being perfectly fitted. There were 3 or 4 of them, Col. Hall had charge of one. The enemy were constantly sending down flags of truce, merely to observe the bank, and it was not safe to let them know where the bridges were really to be, when the attack was to be made. So the bridges were kept for instant use. On the night of the battle of Fair Oaks, Col. Hall had two entire Regiments in the water up to their necks trying to put down his bridge but could not: Everything was swept away by the flood. By his measure the water rose one foot an hour.

I have read part of the report on the war, and wish to call your attention to one lie, the statement that McClellan was not at the battle of Fair Oaks, June 1st. *I saw him* and his staff ride along and heard the tremendous cheers roll along the lines, and I remember we feared he would be hurt, because the enemy would fire where they heard the loudest cheers. He rode right to the front, some distance to the left of us.

By the way in this last review, *not one* cheer was given for the President or for Hooker. At Bolivar the President was cheered loudly, but the recent trials and reports have opened peoples' eyes. This sending home of Regiments to vote the Republican ticket, when thousands of others have done and suffered more and are left here still, has stirred up terrible indignation in the Army. I hope to live to see the day when Abraham Lincoln is brought to an account for all this, but at present we must do all we can to bring Jefferson Davis to an account.

Your affectionate brother
Henry.

RIGHT UP INTO THE FIRE

Falmouth, Va. Saturday April 18th 1863.

My dear John.

I have just received yours of the 15th enclosing one from Tom Curtis. Very much obliged for all you have done and very glad I still have some money on hand. I suppose Willard's $60.00 paid off everything. Do you mean I still have $10.50 after paying for my last suit, shoes, passes etc. etc., and my class photographs? I think you must not have paid for the photographs yet. I am very glad to tell you that the Paymaster arrived today, and will pay me about $500.00 in a day or two. So you need not send me any money in a letter. If you see Willard, please tell him I have destroyed his note for $50.00 and Cowgill's (for him) of $10.00 and charged the $60.00 to myself in the fund accounts. I do not know what to make of Fitzgerald's absence. I cannot think he has deserted. Of late he has done remarkably well. If you see Riddle you might mention to him that Fitzgerald has been absent without leave for four days now. Perhaps he may have heard of him, or may know of some else coming on. However, if he does not come, you might send on the thin dress coat, trousers and shoes by Express. I hear really nothing. I incline to think the movement is for the present given up, or at any rate is to be altered. The Rebels know all about it now and are shouting to our pickets in a derisive manner about the 8 days rations they are to carry, just as they shouted to Burnside about being stuck in the mud. It would be strange if Hooker also has been stopped by a storm. The river has now resumed its usual size. I hear that Heintzelman has moved down to Dumfries with 50,000 men, also that 40 loaded transports have gone down the river. I can get no positive news. I feel sure the move *was to have been made* last Monday or Tuesday. Some say the news from the South has changed matters. I have read the Committee Report with feelings of the deepest indignation. It is indeed a tissue of lies. I *know* about some things, the state of the Army at Antietam, Harrison's Landing etc., and I know the statements of the Committee are false. The misrepresentations are too numerous to mention. You observe they often say: "a number of" or "several" Generals testified in a certain way, and rarely mention who. One of the few they do name has come out and publicly stated that their report of his evidence is false (Corcoran John), so what may we conclude of the evidence of unnamed Generals? Then note the absurdity of saying the Army at Harrison's Landing could not march "three miles", when a day or two after it began a march to Antietam. Also see the silly implication that the "heights" of Harrison's Landing were not occupied till the day after the arrival of the Army (and works thrown up) and that the enemy came down and shelled us, and might have destroyed us. There were no "heights" there. Not a hill 25 feet high anywhere, the idea of digging on the day we arrived was absurd, and, besides, where were the tools? What greater activity could there be than beginning the works the *next* day? Our troops were in position by the time that shelling took place, and the Committee seem to have forgotten the best proof of it, namely that McClellan attacked and *took* the entire Rebel battery which did shell us. The day of the arrival there was indeed great confusion, for we had marched all night in the rain, and in 3 columns abreast, through mud and darkness, and McClellan truly says there were not probably more than 50,000 men *then* with the colors, but 2 days after there were probably 75,000. That very morning of our arrival McClellan rode among the men and was received with cheers. It was that morning, you remember, he asked me about the ration of whisky. This was July 2nd and we had a grand review July 4th. The more I read and the more I think, the more I believe in McClellan as the greatest General we have yet found, and a man of very great ability, and able to handle well a large Army. I do not claim for him the genius of Napoleon, I merely say he is the best man we have, and he has been shamefully treated, and that he deserves the post of Commander in Chief. I think Halleck has proved himself a most miserable General. I want to see McClellan in Halleck's place, and a Secretary of War who will carry out *fully* the wishes of the commander in chief. That report will do great harm to McClellan among people at home, but it will do him good among military men, especially those who have been with him. If he is not now embittered against the President and the Government he is not a mortal man. He must hate and despise them from the bottom of his heart.

We are still ready with our 8 days rations. Our horse will be very useful. Herbert desires to be remembered. So have Patten, Abbott and others very often. Today warm and pleasant, roads quite passable. Phil Mason and Captains Robeson and Grafton (2nd) were over here today.

Our Corps is the only one that is not supplied with pack-mules. This *may* mean we are not to want them. But, on the contrary, I have heard that the old 2nd Corps is to be shoved ahead again, as of old. Couch is Senior Major General, as Sumner was.

I hope you have read "Halleck's report reviewed in the light of facts" also Peterson's pamphlet "Military Review of Campaigns" in Virginia, Maryland, etc. The first I have read and like very much. The 2nd Herbert says is excellent. I intend to read it.

I believe I have nothing more to tell you.

Your affectionate brother
Henry.

Glad you are Clerk of Trinity Church.

RIGHT UP INTO THE FIRE

Falmouth, Va. April 22nd 1863.

My dear John.

I have no letters to answer from you. I received a most patriotic letter from Charley Grinnell yesterday. He is to visit Boston soon. I am sure you will look out for him. You remember how kind his father was to us. I intend to answer his letter very soon.

We have been paid off and I shall send home but $50.00 to you, because I have not many debts at home. I shall also send to you $80.00 to be put in the Savings Bank for Theophilus *[also listed as Theodore]* Chase, private of my Company. Please send me back the receipt to give to him. The whole Regiment has subscribed largely to the relief of the Irish. As we have seen by the papers that Joseph is on a committee to collect funds, several of the Companies have brought me their subscriptions and asked me to send it to him. I enclose a letter to Joseph about the matter.

I fear Fitzgerald has deserted. Quartermaster's Sergeant, Baker, has gone home on furlough, and is to bring out several things for Mr. Folsom, and his brother (your class-mate) will call on you to take any small parcel for me, which he will give to Baker. You might thus send out the trousers and herhaps *[sic]* the boots or coat. Some of the passes might be sent by mail as newspapers. I enclose a draft on you for $107.00, $80.00 for Chase, $27.00 for me. I enclose to Joseph an order for $33.00 of which he will pay you $23.00 which with your $27.00 makes ($23 + 27 = $50.00) Fifty.

No more. All the same.

[Your] affectionate brother
Henry.

Falmouth, Va. Wednesday
April 23rd 1863.

Dear John.

I enclose another draft for $30.00 for Mrs. Patrick O'Hara. It did not come in time for the first lot. Mr. John L. Roberts will call at your Office and get it for her. I have no letters to answer. Pouring rain today. We hear reports than *[sic]*

348

RIGHT UP INTO THE FIRE

General Hooker has had a fall from his horse and is out of his mind. No signs of a move yet. Cowgill has gone home on leave. All well. I hope you will manage to send out my coat, shoes, etc. soon.

Please send me 3 or 4 of my photographs; old ones will do as well as any. Capt. Murphy wants one of you.

Your affectionate brother
Henry.

Falmouth, Va. April 24th 1863.

My dear Mother.

I have just received yours of the 22nd. I entirely forgot to mention that in the box I sent home, was an old coat belonging to my servant Smith which he did not want to throw away and I took it to fill up. If you could keep it till next autumn I dare say it can be sent out to him again when he needs it. I am very glad all the other things came safely. I have since sent home another box, containing an extra blanket, some boots etc. about which I have written to John. It contains also that silver watch which has given me so much trouble. I have asked John to get me another and dispose of that one.

I am very sorry to hear that Dr. Mercer is to leave Trinity, and glad to know you will still have him this summer at Newport. No doubt the change from Swampscott will be a benefit to you, and especially to Mary Ann, who I suppose must be rather tired of Swampscott. We are all quiet, and the move seems either to be given up, or to have been merely a hoax to distract the enemy. We have had a great deal of rain, and the river is very high still.

I have got a very nice letter from my old friend Charlie Grinnell, of Baltimore, who you know is studying for the Ministry at New Haven. He is soon to visit Boston and I hope you will see him often, for he is a most excellent fellow, and one of my best friends. His parents treated John and me very kindly in Baltimore. I have no news whatever to tell you.

Your affectionate son
Henry.

RIGHT UP INTO THE FIRE

Falmouth, Va. April 25th 1863.
Saturday.

My dear John.

I enclose a letter which I should be much obliged to you to forward to Tom Curtis.

I hear from undoubted authority something which I tell you and do not wish to have go farther at present, viz.: that it was and probably still is Hooker's plan to attack Fredericksburg again *in front*, to accomplish what Burnside failed to do. The recent storm stopped it but a few days ago, the bridges were actually moved down and ready to be thrown across in the same places again. In addition to this, movements were to be made on the right and left. All this I know to be true, whether or not the plan is now given up, I cannot say, but think not. Another thing: Macy has been asked if he will volunteer his Regiment to lead in a desperate assault and has of course accepted. So you may hear of another Fredericksburg any day and the 20th will probably be ahead. Do not of course speak of this, for it must not get round. Nothing would so demoralize the Army and destroy the little confidence they feel in Hooker, as to know that he intended to repeat Burnside's move. I certainly hope he will attempt no such mad plan; if he does, it will probably be unsuccessful and certainly barren of important results, and desperately bloody without doubt. Yet at this thought Hooker will attempt it and redeem his boast that he "could take Fredericksburg in 2 days". John Gray is here and dines with us, with him Capt. Wheaton. He looks very well. I shall keep this open till tomorrow, for today's mail has gone.

Sunday 26th.

I received last evening yours of the 22nd No. 13. If you have not yet sent the box of clothes etc., please put in a quire or two of medium sized ruled writing-paper, and a tooth wash. The latter might be sent by mail, and if the box has gone, but not the paper, as I dislike to write on paper that has been rolled up, I have enough for some time yet.

I heard from a Staff Officer last night that the projected move across the river here is given up. Couch told them so. Also that Wilcox's Corps moves tomorrow, and that some troops move today, supposed down the river, also that we occupy Warrenton and that Railroad and telegraphic communication from Washington there is in working order. Halleck and the President had a consultation with Hooker at the Creek, a few days ago. It is thought that our Corps will not be pushed ahead unless we cross right here, and as that plan is given up, I suppose we may wait.

I see in the papers accounts of the scarcity of beef in the Rebel Army. I do not think this is so in regard to the Army in front of us, for a large number of Cattle are grazing in the fields close to the river, and have been there all winter, sometimes more and sometimes less. If the men were on ¼ lb. meat a day, these cattle would not be safe right on the picket line. I do not place much faith in newspaper accounts of Rebel starvation. There was plenty of food in Fredericksburg of every kind, except tea and Coffee, which was scarce. Salt was plenty. The Rebels appear to be fitting up their works and increasing them. The river has now gone down to about its usual size. Weather fine.

I perfectly agree with you in regard to the principle of placing the safety of the Country far above the regard for any one man etc., but you see, in my opinion, the *first step* to be taken to put down the Rebellion and thus end the war, is to displace Genl. Halleck who has almost ruined the Country, and call back McClellan who has twice saved the Country. Of course it is supposed that the President does not interfere with the Commander in Chief again. Now, if the Government put in any man, not known to be incapable (as Fremont for instance) in place of Halleck, I must of course support him, but now, as Halleck has proved himself a miserable General, and McClellan proved himself the best we have got, why, I think the louder we call for McClellan the sooner we shall get him, and the sooner we shall beat the Rebels, and besides if we get him soon we shall save many lives, which (judging from the past) the Government and Genl. Halleck intend to waste this summer.

I think one can support the Government faithfully and yet see the faults which have been committed and call for their remedy. I would pay my tax cheerfully, lend money, enforce the draft, and in short *do* everything a thorough Abolitionist would do, but all the time I would vote and speak and do all I could to bring back McClellan to the *supreme* command. I rather think you will agree with me in this following statement.

If Genl. Hooker should meet with an overwhelming defeat and the Rebels should take Washington, and Congress and the President escape to Philadelphia and the whole country be thrown into panic, then every eye would turn to McClellan, the President and Halleck would fall on their knees and beg him to save them. I feel sure of this, judging from the past. A great many people do not want McClellan back because they think it a "back-down" on the part of the Government. For my part, when we have made a fearful mistake, I say let us remedy it as soon as we can. If we have taken the wrong road, go back to the fork and take the other; do not try to shove through blindly, for the sake of saying you never turned back.

I hope these views will meet your approval.

Abbott's letter I thought was excellent. It seems to me that your objections to the Peninsular Campaign are about answered now.

Your affectionate brother
Henry.

RIGHT UP INTO THE FIRE

Falmouth, Va. April 28th 1863.

My dear John.

Many happy returns of your birthday. I send with this a pipe I had made for you out of Laurel wood which grew on the bank of the river, on our side and under our batteries. It was not exactly on the battle field, but it was where the shells were falling, and I thought you would like it as a sort of relic of Fredericksburg. The trefoil in front is the new distinguishing mark of our corps. Please accept it as a birthday present. It was carved by a man of the 19th Regiment, and he says the top will be apt to be burnt in lighting it, unless you have a little metal rim put inside. You need not send me any writing paper as I have got a supply.

The great movement has commenced, and our Division is, I hear, to be left to cover this front for the present. We are under marching orders. I also hear that the real attack is to be made in front here, and that the movements up the river are feints. I can hardly believe this; it seems like stark madness. You may hear exciting news very soon. I sometimes think the entire thing may be a great feint, but it is generally thought that we are on the eve of a great battle. Today it is cloudy and looks like a storm tomorrow. Shall perhaps be unable to write again for some days.

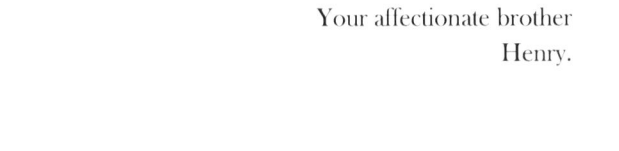

Your affectionate brother
Henry.

Falmouth, Va. April 29th 1863.

My dear John.

We are still here, and as yet there has been no great battle. I heard there was some firing far on the right yesterday. 2 deserters came over this morning; they say they want to avoid the fighting. The Rebels know we are up to something. As far as I can make it out, the whole of the Army, except the 2nd Corps, has gone down to make a grand attack on the enemy's right, and of our Corps 2 Divisions are sent to our right to make a diversion, and one Division, ours, kept here to picket the front. So we stand a chance of not being in this time. Some firing was heard far on the left at about 8.30 o'cl. this morning, and it is rumored that Sedgwick has crossed there. The enemy have increased their pickets in front.

Deserters came over this morning, I hear. I understand the troops are in good spirits, and I am sure I hope for success, but I do not see how it can be decisive, for the enemy have a perfect line of retreat, unless Hooker crosses so far below as to be able to get between them and Richmond, while the bulk of their force is gathered to resist the feigned attack on their left. However this would be to give battle with a river in the rear, a dangerous thing. The utmost I expect is that Hooker will force the enemy to retire from this line. This morning is foggy, very favorable for us to hide movements.

I have had no letters for three days. I hope you will get a little birthday present I sent you yesterday by mail. Do not leave off writing.

By the way, have you read Col. Green's (14th) letter? Washington was safer than Wadsworth thought, and McClellan was right after all. Truth is great etc. Every day something turns up to prove that McClellan was right and everybody who differed from him wrong.

Your affectionate brother
Henry.

Falmouth, Va. April 30th 1863.

My dear John.

All is quiet this morning, which we hardly know how to explain. Sedgwick lay all day yesterday with 3 bridges across, and one or 2 Divisions over. He has 3 Corps there and Reynolds has bridges below him. The enemy are moving up fast, and still there is no attack. We hear 3 Corps and some Cavalry are moving on the right. We cannot explain these movements. No appearance of our moving. The enemy are occupying the rifle pits in front of us in considerable force.

We have just heard that John Putnam is striving hard for the Colonelcy of the Regiment, and Riddle has written a most insulting letter to Macy because Macy has nominated Patten for the next Captaincy, instead of him. Macy has been most strongly recommended for Colonel by Col. Hall, Genl. Gibbon, Genl. Couch and Genl. Hooker, and how Putnam can have the face to try for it, I cannot see. Putnam is utterly incapable of taking the Regiment, physically, mentally and morally. He is a notorious drunkard, and has been living on the Government for 18 months doing no duty, taking a much larger pay than any Officer in the field, and keeping down his betters, and those who have fairly won promotion. And this has been tolerated because everyone pitied Putnam for the loss of his arm. Putnam has frequently promised to resign and has eluded dismissal, by getting nominally on the Recruiting service, but now that recruiting is over he sees this must stop, and to save himself from the expulsion he deserves, he is now trying to get promoted over his superior Officer Macy. Remember Putnam has seen no service whatever, having been wounded in the skirmishing shortly before the battle of Ball's Bluff, and for the last 18 months has done nothing but loaf about bar-rooms and brothels and spend the money he has no honorable right to. It is an insult to the Regiment to promote Dreher, but as he is reported to be on the verge of the grave this will probably be of little moment. We must not let compassion for a wounded man blind our eyes to the real rights of a Regiment. Dreher is an utterly incompetent Officer. When he commanded the Regiment in face of the enemy on the march from Harper's Ferry when we were actually in line of battle and loaded and primed and expecting a battle, he got drunk and was incapable of using the small brain he possessed, and when we got to Falmouth he and Capt. Shepard were superseded by Macy, by order of Genl. Howard (commanding Division) on the ground that they were utterly incompetent. Dreher then resigned on Surgeon's Certificate of *mental disability*. We then went into the battle of Fredericksburg, Macy commanding over the heads of his two incompetent superiors, and there Macy showed that he was fully equal to his post, and received the public thanks of Col. Hall and Genl. Howard. Shepard and Dreher were both wounded. Dreher's resignation was in the meantime accepted and he was honorably discharged the service. The Governor immediately promoted him to Major and subsequently to Lieut. Colonel, and now, I understand, to Colonel. There is nothing to excuse this. Gov. Andrew was most fully informed of Dreher's incapacity. I myself saw the medical letter Dr. Hayward wrote to him, and the Governor knew that before he was last wounded he was incompetent in the opinion of his superiors in rank here. He was promoted then, when both physically and mentally incompetent, and judged so by the highest medical and military authorities. You probably know that he was promoted in accordance with a promise given to the German Abolition Club of which he was a member, who appealed publicly to the Governor.

However, I say no more about him because he can hardly be held responsible, being half crazy and lying at death's door. The Governor, however, has small excuse after his promises to Macy.

But for Putnam I have no words strong enough. It is no matter whether he succeeds or not, he has lost all claim to be considered a man of honor or a Gentleman (in the lowest meaning of the word) and will be cut by *every Officer* here. He will not be spoken to or written to except as his military rank requires and will be treated henceforward as a dishonorable mean scoundrel.

RIGHT UP INTO THE FIRE

As to poor weak Riddle, he can be led by anyone and we feel more pity than anything else for him. He wrote a most insulting letter to Macy. He has seen more service than Putnam for he was at Fair Oaks, and he has done a great deal of recruiting, but he is a most miserable Officer, utterly incapable of commanding a Company, and physically unable to bear the privations of a soldier's life. According to strict rules both these men should have been dismissed long ago. If either dare to come out, they will be court-martialled, no doubt, but they probably will do no such thing. They only want to ensure a longer period of lazy ease and debauchery at the expense of the brave Officers who endure the hardships and face the danger, on whose pay they live.

I have written thus fully that you may see the exact state of the case. There is a time when men must speak for themselves.

I beg you will spread abroad these opinions as widely as you can, and by every means, not as my opinions, but as the opinions of every Officer here. Let the matter be shown up as it is.

Please tell Father how it stands, and ask everyone if they want to see the old 20th disgraced by an ignorant sot or a crazy Dutchman for its Colonel.

Please write to me what you hear of the matter and what the general opinion is. You may think I speak too strongly, but I assure you all is true and we feel strongly about such things out here, where we are powerless to help ourselves, and depend on our friends at home. Remember, a Regiment is not a Chelsea Hospital for broken down Soldiers, but that men's lives and the fate of battles are too important to be trusted to incompetent hands, and besides, that there is such a thing as earning promotion in battle.

I earnestly hope that no injustice will be done and that the Governor will fully attend to the matter and do the right thing; and I want all to know what is the opinion of the Officers of the 20th Regiment now in the field, a body of men whose reputation for courage and honor is high enough to demand that their opinions be respected.

All quiet now. No letters from home for 4 days.

Your affectionate brother
Henry.

RIGHT UP INTO THE FIRE

Falmouth, Va. May 1st 1863
9 A.M.

My dear John.

Orders to be ready to march at daylight this morning, came last night, and we are all ready, wagons loaded and are waiting orders. The enemy's pickets still occupy the front, and I suppose we shall be relieved before starting. Our Regiment goes on guard and picket here today. Genl. Howard sent down a very encouraging order yesterday. He evidently thinks they may evacuate. We go to join our Corps which has crossed above. Sedgwick with 3 Corps is below, and has (I hear) 5 bridges over, evidently for a diversion. Yesterday P.M. there was a good deal of Artillery firing, there we could see the Rebel guns flash from the hills here. We none of us know anything of the movements contemplated, but look forward to a rather quick march, to gain up with our Corps.

I have received no letters from home. I send a poem which which [sic] was sent across by the Rebel pickets here, a few weeks ago. I thought you might like to see it.

All well.

Your affectionate brother
Henry.

May 2nd 1863 9 A.M.
Falmouth.

Dear John.

We have not moved yet. Some firing on right and left this morning. All quiet now. It seems likely that we shall remain here, but we are ready to march at a moment's notice. Rebels still in front. It is thought there must be a great battle today, perhaps the Rebels will evacuate.

I have received safely the coat, pants and shoes. Shoes fit perfectly. I sent you with the other money $80.00 to put in the Boston Savings Bank for private Theophilus Chase of my Company. Please put in $20.00 more making $100.00, for he has given me the other $20.00. Then please send me some kind of certificate to give him, to show that he has $100.00 there. I have received no letters yet. I am a little anxious to hear of the money sent home. I sent Joseph $26.00 in a letter for the Irish Fund.

As to our movements, I merely hear that we are almost in the enemy's rear, and that they must leave or come out and fight with the danger of of [sic] Sedgwick's 75,000 men[37] breaking through and coming in on the rear. I hear we hold Culpepper and probably Gordonsville. Also that Sedgwick lost 2 guns yesterday. We shall no doubt stay here, and perhaps come up at the decisive moment. All well. We took a lot of prisoners yesterday. There is a story about a telegraph under the river having been discovered here near the Brick Church in the papers. It is all untrue, not the slightest foundation for it. The Church is close to my Quarters and is inhabited by the 7th Michigan. All quiet now, beautiful weather.

Your affectionate brother
Henry.

Fredericksburg.
Sunday evening, May 3rd 1863.

My dear Father.

We have won a great victory and taken the heights by storm. I was not much exposed and am unhurt. Holmes probably loses his leg, and Murphy is wounded in the arm. Total loss of the Regiment 17 killed and wounded. We were exposed only to Artillery fire. After charging the enemy 2 or 3 miles we returned here. All quiet. We have taken Guns etc. and quantities of provisions. Our Division, Sedgwick's old one, did the business. Loss not very heavy, enemy in small force. Have heard of no Injuries to friends. Herbert all right. Have heard nothing of the severe battle on the right.

In haste
Your affectionate son
Henry.

---

[57] Ropes most likely meant to write "15,000". At the time, the VI. Corps numbered about 24,000 men present for duty.

RIGHT UP INTO THE FIRE

Falmouth, Va. Tuesday,
May 5th 1863. 10 ½ A.M.

My dear Father.

We are back at our old quarters again, safe and well. After crossing the river on Sunday we assisted in taking the works here, and advanced 2 miles beyond Fredericksburg, driving the enemy. Sedgwick pushed on and our Brigade with a few of the 6th Corps went back to the City supposing all was well and the great battle won. To our infinite surprise the enemy rushed in from the left and retook the entire lines on Monday morning. The pickets rushed in, and for a few moments we had a wild time of it, but our Regiment moved out and held the town and repulsed the enemy. I never passed so anxious and trying a time: our line was weak and the men scattered. There was a most desperate assault from the farther side in the afternoon, and again the Rebels were driven out and their Centre pierced by Sedgwick, but they held the heights on their right and Sedgwick was at last repulsed. This morning at daybreak we withdrew from the town, our Regiment covering the retreat and crossing last. Altogether we have lost only 2 Officers and 17 men, but the experience of these whole 3 days has been far more trying than in any battle we were ever in before. Holmes and Murphy are wounded, not dangerously, I hear. On the right I hear the fighting has been awful beyond description, and the number of killed and wounded on both sides perfectly terrific. I can learn no particulars. I fear we are retreating, and have been outgeneraled, but our men fought splendidly and we have probably given the enemy a terrible loss. We have taken Guns etc. and, I fear, lost some.

You will probably learn particulars sooner than I. I fear we have met with an awful repulse and that the Army is almost cut to pieces. However the enemy are as badly off. I cannot well see how our Regiment suffered so little. Our escapes were wonderful. We have done most trying duty which nothing but Veteran troops could have done, and if we have not been so badly cut up as others, we have that to be thankful for. Herbert all well. *None* of my Company hurt.

Your affectionate son
Henry.

RIGHT UP INTO THE FIRE

Falmouth, Va. May 6th 1863
1 P.M.

My dear John.

I have written 2 or 3 letters to Father telling him of my safety and that of the Regiment. The grand Army of the Potomac is now back again on its old ground (I hear) utterly worn out, dreadfully cut up and much disheartened, with a great loss of guns, small arms, accoutrements, and leaving most of the dead and wounded in the hands of the enemy. I do not expect the enemy will follow us up, and think we can hold on here against all they can do. I will not say more about the general operations, but tell you what we have done, merely asking you what you think of "Fighting Joe", and whether the "people" are yet so far sated with blood that they will be willing to recall McClellan and save the Country yet.

We were ordered to march at midnight of Saturday, and we halted at the "Lacy House", the same old place, while they attempted to put down the bridge. The Engineers were however driven off by the enemy, and we lay there till about 6 A.M. of Sunday, when Genl. Sedgwick penetrated the town from the other side (he had crossed below 3 or 4 days before) and came out opposite our bridge and drove off the very small body of Rebels. Genl. Sedgwick himself rode through and crossed to this side in a boat. We then finished the bridge and marched over passing up the very same street. After some time we were moved far to the right of the town and engaged the attention of the enemy while Sedgwick assaulted on the left. We were here brought under a heavy shell fire and Holmes and Murphy were wounded. I, with Company E, went out as skirmishers in advance and finally lay close to the canal. We could then see everything and hear the Rebels talking. We witnessed the assault and it was a very exciting scene. At first our men were forced back and the Rebels howled with joy, and began to blackguard us, but in a few moments the line of bayonets moved straight up the slope and carried the heights, and the Rebels fell back making still a strong resistance. We were drawn in and all the troops on the right of the town rushed forward and advanced on the enemy who now opened fire from the 2nd line, but were driven off and pursued by Sedgwick. We were then ordered back to the town, thinking the day was won and that we had gained the greatest victory of the war. We staid that night on the left of the city, and part of the Regiment picketed on the left, where the Rebels appeared to have some force. It seems that Sedgwick drive right on and united with Hooker and that these heights were left unguarded. At any rate, at about 7 o'clock next morning the pickets on the Railroad on the left suddenly rushed in with the enemy's bullets flying after them, and at the same time they poured on to the heights from the left and we were carried out instantly as skirmishers on the left. My Company was ordered to hold the Railroad, and before long we had

RIGHT UP INTO THE FIRE

covered the city and had begun to prepare rifle pits. Only our Brigade of about 1500 men (500 of whom were Pennsylvania Dutch Cowards and sure to run) held the city from end to end, a line of 5 miles, a mere thin line of skirmishers. The enemy having filled the entire works, advanced a line of skirmishers on us and we repulsed them and they ran back and did not attack again. However, knowing our own weakness we had an *exceedingly* anxious time and made every preparation to repulse the enemy should they come on again. In the afternoon Sedgwick attacked them from the other side, and after a terrible fight forced their centre, and they began to run away from the works, and our guns opened on them from our side of the river, and it seemed as if we were again to be victorious, but it was not so, and the sun went down with terrible firing on Sedgwick's left where he was driven back a long way. Early on the morning of the next day, in a thick fog we withdrew, and passed over the same bridge, our Regiment covering the passage and crossing last. After a short delay we returned to our old Quarters, where we are now. Last night there was very heavy rain, and the river rose several feet and is still very high with a prospect of more rain.

Trains and Artillery have been passing all day. I hear the Army has all crossed safely above, where there was heavy firing this morning. It is said the Rebels are to cross above us, but the freshet will no doubt hinder them. I do not know what to expect now, for I do not know how badly we are defeated, but it looks *something* like a retreat from this line. Perhaps Washington is endangered.

I will not attempt any remarks, but I think the lesson is a plain one to the whole country.

Everywhere we hear of the shameful cowardice of the 11th Corps. I never had any opinion of them. I am fully convinced that it takes Anglo-Saxons to fight these Anglo-Saxon Rebels. Dutchmen and Negroes will not do.

As to the oft repeated statement of Rebel starvation etc., I know from the prisoners that their rations are short, especially forage, but they look generally well and strong, and are comfortably clad and well armed. I dare say we shall fall back on Aquia Creek and Washington.

I hear the other two Divisions of our Corps behaved well. Can learn nothing about friends. Whittier all right. Howard lost his other arm.[58] Berry killed. Couch slightly wounded.

Shall write again as soon as I can.

Your affectionate brother
Henry.

---

[58] The General merely scratched his hand when his horse reared up.

RIGHT UP INTO THE FIRE

Falmouth, Va. May 6th 1863.
6 P.M.

Dear John.

I wrote you a long account of our doings this morning. I have just heard that Temple is killed. He fell shot through the breast in an advance over the ground lost by the cowardly 11th Corps.

I hear we are not so badly repulsed as I had thought. The 1st Corps hardly lost anybody. Fitzgerald has just come, and I have the watch, socks, passes and Herbert's things all right. I have just received your letter acknowledging the receipt of the pipe. I am very glad it pleases you. The Coat etc. by Sergeant Baker came all right.

I do not remember whether I ever acknowledged the receipt of Father's letter of the 28th about the watch, yours of the 29th and Mary Ann's of the 27th. Please thank all. I also received seven of my photographs, and one of yours for Murphy, for which he is much obliged. I have not yet heard of the safe arrival of the box containing my old watch etc., nor of the letter to Joseph containing $26.00 in money for the Irish fund, in addition to that sent by draft. I hope all has gone safely.

All quiet now. I hear we may move early tomorrow, probably to take the picket or guard duty off some tired Regiment. I can learn nothing of our intended movements. The Army is, I believe, considered "safe". The Regiment has been again outraged by the promotion of Lieut. Colonel Revere, Capt. Shepard and Riddle. If ever a man deserved the Colonelcy that man is Macy. Col. Revere really left the Regiment, was with it but 4 months in the field and is of course not to be mentioned in opposition to Macy who has done so nobly and commanded us so well in 3 battles. Besides, Macy was recommended by every superior Officer including Hooker. It is really fearfully discouraging to go on doing one's duty and risking one's life and see this all disregarded and such incapables as Shepard and Riddle promoted, instead of us who have done the work and born/e/ the hardship. Revere, I know, to be such an honorable man that I feel sure, when he understands the thing, he will not stand in Macy's way. Riddle is a miserably low fellow and by rights should have been dismissed under the 60 days order. Gov. Andrew gave Macy the very fairest promises, and now see how he treats him and the Regiment.

You can hardly conceive of a more ignorant and self-conceited man than Shepard, a man who has been actually superseded in the field for total incapacity, and he being an Anti-McClellan man and a violent Radical is made Major!

I wish a pair of boots from Rice's and I enclose a description therefore, which I shall be much obliged to you to give to Rice and see that they are made properly and sent on, when convenient. *[Description missing.]*
In haste

Affectionately
Henry.

Falmouth, Va. May 8th 1863.
9 A.M.

My dear John.

I received last night yours of the 4th. I have only sent two boxes, one (which arrived safely) contained some things for Herbert and was accompanied by our Buffalos; and the others containing my silver watch and some boots for Holmes. I suppose both these boxes have come. If so please tell me. Please tell me if the drafts are all right, if O'Hara's money has been paid to Mr. Roberts and the (in all) $100.00 put in the bank for Theophilus Chase. Theophilus was wounded at Fair Oaks May 31st but is now here, and well. I hope Joseph's Irish money came safely. Besides the draft, I sent him $26.00 in a letter. I also sent him a draft from Corporal White from which he was to pay you $23.00. Do not forget to send me some kind of receipt to give to Chase. Peter Wilkins owes $30.00 to the Regimental Fund of which I am Treasurer. I have asked him to pay it to you, and if he does, please keep it to my credit, and let me know, and I will pay the $30.00 to the fund here.

As soon as all these money matters are settled and my bills paid, and it is perfectly convenient to you, please let me know how much I still have in your hands, if any.

It was indeed very kind and generous of Father to send me such a splendid watch. I am greatly obliged to him. I have no doubt that the watch I sent home will keep excellent time when not exposed to the hardships of war. If worn on the person or hung up in a room I think it will go perfectly well.

As to the Regiment, Shepard's and Riddle's promotions are infamous. Riddle has made quantities of money by his enlisting and receiving private money from Towns anxious to get his men for their quota, and besides this his full pay and a large commutation for quarters, food etc. etc. Abbott has written him a letter, which will, I think, shame him, if he has any sense of shame.

I am also *very much* astonished at the way you look upon Lieut. Colonel Revere's appointment. He left the Regiment in August, as he and everyone else supposed forever, and Dreher was soon after made Major in his place. He never commanded the Regiment and has only been with it from its formation till October 21st 1861 (Ball's Bluff) and from May till August in all about 5 months. And now he has discovered that by his omitting to have himself mustered out (as he should have done) he has been technically Major all the time, and therefore Dreher and Macy *never were* Majors. And, since Macy was regularly mustered out as Captain and mustered in as Major, and since this mustering in was invalid, Macy is now a Citizen, holds no Office, but through his (Revere's) gracious intercession Governor Andrew has kindly made Macy Lieut. Colonel. Now I say and the whole Regiment says that all this is dishonorable, and therefore we believe Revere was unacquainted with the facts, or blinded, or he never would have done it. Yet, he has written a letter to Macy explaining the matter as above and assuring Macy he shall "retain his position" etc. It seems to us all that Revere left the Regiment and forfeited all claims to his place in it, by accepting a higher rank and pay out of it. Since then Macy has commanded us in 3 terrible battles and done most nobly and received the praise of his superiors and has fairly earned and fought up to the position of Colonel. Is an Officer to be allowed to leave a Regiment and take higher pay and rank and have an easy time on a staff, and 6 months afterwards come back and take promotion over those who have stuck by through hardship and danger and risked their lives, and lost more than one half their number by wounds and death? I consider it outrageous, and feel sure Col. Revere has not known what he did. Besides, Macy is recommended in the highest terms by Col. Hall, Genl. Gibbon, Couch and Hooker, and what higher reference can there be?

It is high time that the principle is recognized that the men who *really do the work*, who brave the danger and suffer the hardships should receive the promotion. Had Revere stuck by the Regiment, we should have rejoiced to see him Colonel, although I do not think he would ever have made a first-rate Officer, because he had had no experience as a Company Officer. But now Macy fairly deserves it, and to take advantage of a legal technicality to oust out an Officer who has fairly won his position is a thing I cannot think Col. Revere capable of.

As to movements, we hear that another attack is to be made! But I do not believe it in the least. My opinion is that, covered by one or two feints of crossing, the Army will fall back part to Aquia Creek and part to Warrenton, Centreville and Washington, and there remain till our ranks are filled by conscripts, or until a disgraceful peace is made. Lincoln, they say, is here, but does not show himself much. We are yet to find out how much of this we owe to him.

RIGHT UP INTO THE FIRE

Have you read Franklin's splendid defense? What do you now think of poor, old, weak Burnside? What of the Committee's Report? What of the Government, which puts aside such men as Franklin, Smith and Porter?

The cry now for McClellan is irresistible; without him there is nothing but disaster ahead. The Army won't bear useless slaughtering much longer, and unless a change is soon made, I solemnly assure you that we are hastening fast to a military despotism, and that the outraged Army will be forced to it. I can only hope for the best.

Your affectionate brother
Henry.

P.S. Genl. Gibbon commands our Division now.

Falmouth, Va.
May 9, 1863.

My dear Mother.

I received last night your letter of the 4th and father's of the 5th. I am sorry to find that you share in the prejudice against McClellan. Remember that documents have since come to light which show that he was not only not responsible for his ill success, but that if his advice had been followed, success would have been sure. Thus we know that if McDowell had advanced Richmond would have fallen, and if McClellan's advice had been taken Harper's Ferry would have held out, and Antietam been a complete victory. As is often the case, the prejudices against the man remain long after the causes of it have been removed. I fully believe that McClellan will yet occupy the first place in the Country, and if not left till too late, will save us all yet and crush the rebellion. McClellan saw from the outset what people at home cannot see yet, that this rebellion is a great and powerful one, and that the rebel army is not a rout of starved and half clothed savages, but a regular army conducted by experienced & educated Generals, and an army which will keep on repulsing all insane and desperate attempts to set the rules of war at defiance and rush blindly on.

The time of a large part of our troops is nearly up, and the old Regiments are very much reduced in numbers, and if this rebellion is to be put down we must now have a long rest and raise a new army and drill and discipline it, and bring back every good officer, and then with our best and purest Officer at the head, we may reasonably hope for success.

I am very glad you are going to Newport, which I have no doubt will agree with M. A. Glad the boxes came safely – as did your things, (watch etc.) for me. I am abundantly supplied with clothing of every kind, but would be much obliged to you to send when convenient 2 pair linen drawers for the approaching hot weather. Only 2 pair. The 6 pair socks I have distributed to the men except 2 pairs for Herbert Mason and me. They were unusually nice ones. I am very glad that Brother Joseph received the money for the Irish Fund safely.

Today it has cleared off finely. I can learn nothing about future movements, but my own opinion is that this Army will be withdrawn to the vicinity of Washington, and perhaps broken up to reinforce the West and South. Very likely a show of crossing below will be made to draw off the enemy from above.

We hear from those who were engaged on the right that it was a terrible battle, and a very disorderly one – that there appeared to be no head, no particular plan, and that the men were massed and shoved forward and fell back again, and this seemed to be all. The Cavalry raid was a brilliant thing, and had it been done a few days before might have prevented the arrival of Longstreet, but as it was Longstreet whom we thought to be at Suffolk was the first to fight us.

Hooker appears to have done his best, and to have acted most bravely, but I think he has shown his inability to take on so vast a field, and thus the enemy beat him by degrees. I should not be at all surprised if the Administration, willing to appease the great McClellan party, should put in Franklin as Commander of this Army. This would be a step in the right direction, but we want the abilities of Hooker, Franklin, Porter, Smith and *all* the good generals we have, and them all directed to right ends by the mastermind of McClellan.

Your affec. son
Henry.

Mrs. Wm. Ropes.

RIGHT UP INTO THE FIRE

Falmouth, Va. Sunday.
May 10th 1863 9 A.M.

My dear John.

I received last night yours of the 6th. I am very glad all the boxes and drafts I sent home have arrived safely. I hope you will see a great deal of Charley Grinnell. I wrote to him not long ago and directed to Boston.

I have read some of the newspaper accounts, and find them wrong as usual, especially in two things: they think the heights of Fredericksburg were retaken from Sedgwick after a fight, when in fact there was no force there and the enemy merely walked in. The only firing was a very little musketry with the pickets just to the left of the town. We had seen the enemy in the works 20 minutes before we could believe it was anything but a part of our force. They wore our uniforms as far as I could see. The other mistake is that the first Corps was with Hooker. They came too late for his great battle, and left too soon to be of use in holding the heights Sedgwick had taken.

I have seen Phil Mason who was in the 3rd Corps. He tells me the fighting was awful and most bloody. His commanding Officer was killed, and his battery lost about 30 men and 40 horses. Cely's *[Seeley's]* regular battery lost 60 men and 70 horses, yet both saved all their guns. The battle was dreadfully confused. To show you this: Phil's battery captured 2 of Genl. Jackson's aides both of whom rode up thinking it was a confederate battery and began to give directions. This shows how surrounded our men were. Phil says the 11th Corps' panic was terrible. Our Corps has lost 3000 men, and this almost all from two Divisions! The entire loss is now estimated at 18,000 men! Genl. Lee told one of our Officers that he considered it the greatest victory of the war, and there is no use of denying our total repulse. You know Hooker was reported wounded. He was stunned by a shell and was insensible for some time, and Couch commanded. I now hear that Couch was bringing order out of confusion and had brought two Corps almost into action, and in fact seemed on the point of repulsing the Rebels finely, when Hooker recovered and took command, and being still a little flustered, ordered our whole line ½ mile back. They say Couch was doing splendidly. I give the story for what it is worth. There is no doubt that we have met with an awful defeat, and that it was caused principally by the superior Generalship of Lee. Our loss is awful and the Army is disheartened and have lost all confidence in Hooker. There is one vast groan from one end of the Army to the other. There is but one cry: "McClellan and an end to useless butchery".

I hear it reported that Hooker intends to attack again! But as I do not believe he is a madman, I place not the slightest confidence in the report.

The 9 months and 2 years men are going out fast. I do not believe many will re-enlist. The old veteran Regiments are reduced to skeletons. God grant that this [sic] additional 18,000 maimed and murdered men will open the eyes of the President and his counsellors and yet save us while there is anyone to save. I hear no cries for peace, no desire to give it up, only a cry for a General who can lead us to victory, for the *only* General who can and ought.

I don't know that success is possible now. I am not sure that even under McClellan Armies could be raised large enough and good enough to crush the Rebellion, but I want to see the experiment tried. No signs of a move.

Your affectionate brother
Henry.

Falmouth, Va.
May 12th 1863.

My dear John.

I have received no letters for the last 2 days. All is quiet here; everything just as before; weather very hot. I hear no news whatever. Col. Revere has come out and taken command. You know how we all felt about his coming over Macy. Abbott wrote to him and explained exactly the state of the case, but he did not receive the letter and came out not expecting anything of the kind. He was shown a copy of the letter here, and gave the subject his fullest consideration and took advice of Genl. Sedgwick and Couch. In the meantime it was of course talked over by the Officers, and the question of the *probable* action of the Governor in case of Reveres resigning etc. taken up, and the fact of Revere being *ordered* to this Regiment etc., and it was generally thought that in case Revere should resign, Governor Andrew would be made angry against the Regiment and would probably not promote Macy, but Shepard or Putnam, or some such man, and that then we should be worse off. Besides this, we all know what a man Revere is, a man of the noblest character, and an honor to any Regiment. Thinking this all over then, and while Col. Revere was considering the matter, Macy determined to waive all claim and accept the Lieutenant-Colonelcy under Revere, and so the matter is arranged.

Still I am sorry to say that Col. Revere's own opinion is that he has a *right* to the place, which we all think really belongs to Macy. As Macy, however, has waived his claim, it is not for us to differ about it and I am glad all is settled harmoniously. But I cannot but be impressed with the injustice of allowing an Officer to leave a Regiment for promotion and an easy time, and let other men fight through and raise the Regiment to a high state of discipline, etc., and then for him to come back and reap the advantages he did not sow. Why should not Tremlett come back when his 9 months are gone and take promotion over Abbott and Holmes? There is not a decent Officer here who has not had offers (like my Provost Marshalship) of situations of ease and safety, and these we have refused, and now the principle is to be established that a man *can* leave the Regiment, shirk all battles and dangers, and then come back to promotion.

Col. Revere is a noble man, actuated by the highest motives, but the *principle* is the same, and as far as I see, nothing can prevent Tremlett, Bartlett, Putnam, Schmidt and Peirson from returning to the Regiment and taking promotion over all of us who have fought the battles and really made the Regiment what it is. I am very sorry that Col. Revere ever left us, but am also *very* sorry that so bad a principle should be established by means of a man of such high character. It is enough to disgust any Officer to see such ignorance and partiality at home, and so much indifference toward the men who are laying down their lives out here.

As to the state of the Army etc., I have nothing to say. I see no signs of a change, no hope for anything. Nothing but ignorance and party prejudice everywhere. I think things never looked worse than they do know [sic].

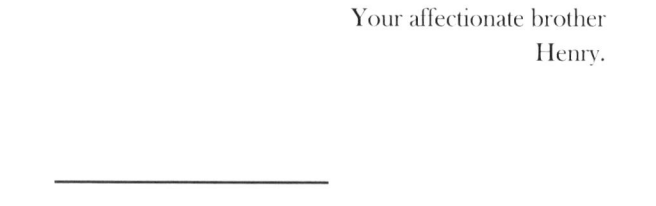

Your affectionate brother
Henry.

Falmouth, Va. May 30th 1863.

My dear Mother.

I received just now your letter of the 26th and Father's of same date enclosing the receipt for the box. As you know I arrived here in safety, and am comfortably established in my old quarters. I enjoyed my visit home very much. It is very pleasant to look back on so much kindness from everyone at home. I shall not forget it at all.

The weather has been very pleasant here, and not very hot, but it is rather dusty. Day before yesterday we had a grand Division Review. Genls. Sykes,

RIGHT UP INTO THE FIRE

Hancock & Gibbon were there, and after the display I went by invitation to Head Quarters where all the Generals and a great many Officers were collected, all of course in full dress, and a Band was playing. It was quite a pleasant meeting. There were three Ladies from Genl. Hooker's Head Quarters there to see the review, one of them a daughter of the late Secretary Cameron. A large tub of iced Punch was served under the shade of a tree, and handed round by negro servants. Altogether it was quite a display.

I passed a very pleasant Sunday with Mr. Trask and was glad to find Martha and the children so well. At church we saw Mrs. Genl. McClellan and Genl. Stoneman.

I am very sorry to hear today that Genl. Couch is relieved from Command. Thus we lay aside in succession our best Officers.

I do not believe Vicksburg is taken and did not when I read the reports. They were so unlikely and absurd. To talk of taking 59 guns from 20,000 men after losing 2500 is simply nonsense.

I think on the contrary that Grant is in the very greatest danger of being utterly defeated by Johnston. It seems to me the Rebels will re-enforce Johnston with Bragg, overwhelm Grant and then turn on Rosecranz who by that time will have left his present strong position and defeat him with superior numbers. However we must hope for the best, but I myself do not look for a successful Campaign in the West.

Love to all.

Your affectionate son
Henry.

Please give the enclosed Photograph of Lt. Cowgill of our Regiment to Mary Ann to put in my book.

Falmouth, Va. May 30th 1863.

My dear John.

I enclose a draft for $35.00; the order for the other $15.00 I sent before and wrote to you about it. I have received yours of the 27th. Will send Macy's photograph as soon as I can get it. I send you that of Temple and others which please have put among my other military photographs. Please thank Henry

Jeffries for it, if you see him.
All quiet, no signs of a move. Very dusty, signs of rain. We had a Division review yesterday.

Your affectionate brother
Henry.

Falmouth, Va. June 4th 1863.

My dear John.

I have no letters from home to answer. Will you please look over the Company papers I sent to you some months ago, and see if there are any relating to "Company savings", that is: Lists of different amounts of pork, beef, rice, bread etc. saved by the Company and certified to by the Company Commander and the Quartermaster or Commissary. Also any papers relating to prisoners of war confined in Richmond in July 1862. If you find any of either of these, please send them on to me, by mail, if there are but few, and, if many, by Express. I would also like you to send on my brown linen riding-pants (at stable) and 3 pairs nice white cotton (or some kind of thread) gloves, size Gentleman's 8. Also one pair leather gauntlets, dark color, not very thick and with cuffs not stiff, and of best quality. I find our horse much improved, and I ride quite often. Herbert and I think of selling him and getting quite a good horse, in case we can make good arrangements for keeping him.
There is no news.

Your affectionate brother
Henry.

RIGHT UP INTO THE FIRE

Falmouth, Va. June 5th 1863.

My dear John.

I received your letter of the 1st last evening. I am very sorry that your business plans should be interfered with by Joseph's great ignorance of his own character, or rather of his own business manners.

    I had quite a talk with Mr. Trask when I was in New York, and he seemed to think the firm was badly organized to conduct the business it did. He thinks William does little good in London, and ought to be in Saint Petersburg, and that the headquarters of the firm should be *by all means* in New York. He thinks the power is too scattered now. He would be glad to have you with him, but thinks Boston a poor place to learn a large business in. I should like to have you talk with him very much. But, as you say, it would be foolish for you to try to enter the firm in opposition to Joseph. So, for aught I see, the matter must be indefinitely postponed. I am very glad the business promises so well for the future. I have no news to tell you of importance. A large part of the Army has moved to the right, including the Artillery reserves. There seems to be some apprehension of an attack. I do not expect it, but expect soon to hear of Burnside's defeat and Rosecranz being forced to fall back. As to our position, I think it is a bad one, useless for offence and not sufficiently covering Washington and Maryland. However, although we should be prepared for every event, I do not anticipate another invasion of Maryland. We hear rumors of Couch's removal, but nothing definite. I send you a piece which Abbott cut from the Herald especially for you. Also an autograph of the famous DeKay who witnessed against Genl. Porter. The absurdity and vanity of the man is shown as well by his writing as by erasing the words: "obedient servant". His testimony is probably better than Genl. Sykes' on a question of Government trousers, but only Holt would think it important in military matters.

    I left off here to take a ride with Abbott, and on returning find orders have come to be ready to move at very short notice, rations, ammunition etc. to be ready. I rather think it is only a precaution, but possibly we may move up a little on the right. I hardly think we intend to abandon this position, though I think it would be better to do so. I also find I am appointed Recorder of a Board to examine Officers of the Corps.

    I have received a letter from Henry Burckmeyer, which I shall answer before long. It is of course rather a curious letter. I am expecting the boxes by Express today, and hope they will not come if we are to make a hasty move.

    In my humble opinion the enemy are scaring Hooker to keep him quiet while they concentrate on Burnside. I have little else to tell you. Col. Revere makes a very poor Officer, is dreadfully ignorant, and yet thinks he knows everything.

RIGHT UP INTO THE FIRE

He makes a laughing stock of himself before everyone in his attempts at drill, and thinks it is the fault of the Regiment. I hope he will have nothing to do if we go into action, for he has no idea at all of military movements, and nothing breaks up a Regiment like mistakes in movements under fire.

All well. Weather beautiful and roads dusty.

Your affectionate brother
Henry.

Falmouth, Va.
June 6th 1863.
Saturday 8 A.M.

My dear Father.

Both the boxes came safely yesterday, and I enjoy their contents very much. Everything was in good order. Yesterday P.M. we put bridges across below the city, and Sedgwick opened artillery and sent a small body of men over, who dislodged a few rebel pickets. We were ordered to be ready to march at daylight today, but the order was countermanded. There has been an occasional gun this morning. The Rebels are moving troops to their right. I rather think this move is to draw them off from our right, where they had concentrated a large force. They now occupy the heights in force. All quiet here. All well. Herbert's things all came safely.

Your affectionate son,
Henry.

RIGHT UP INTO THE FIRE

Falmouth, Va. June 7th 1863.

My dear John.

Yours June 2nd received. Sorry the $15.00 draft missed. Will send another soon. It was signed by Corporal White of my Company.

All quiet here. Sedgwick is over below the city. All quiet here. Have no doubt this is only a demonstration.

Boxes all right. Boots excellent fit. Orange Marmalade a little touched. Everything else in good order.

In haste

Affectionately
Henry.

Enclosed letter for Mary Ann.

June 8th 1863.

Dear John.

I enclose a second order from White for Fifteen Dollars. If you draw this you will have $100.00 from me, enough, I suppose, to pay off everything, which please do. All quiet today. Sedgwick has about 8000 men over, and is, I hear, fortifying himself. Rebels in strong force in front of him, but they keep close. I feel sure this is only a feint, and I dare say it is to cover a move back of our Army. Couch has returned all well. Weather remarkably cool for the season. I have asked Mr. Trask to get some Ale etc. for our mess, and he will send the bill to you. Please pay it and tell me how much it is. Hooker came down to see Sedgwick the other day, and on being told that the Rebels were in force on the heights and might open on our forces at any moment, replied that they were too "damned cowards" to do it. Sedgwick told him he supposed that if they had been cowards they would not have given him so severe a defeat, few weeks ago. Hooker is as much of a boaster as ever, and more despised than ever.

On the whole I think this Army will fall back this month.

Your affectionate brother
Henry.

RIGHT UP INTO THE FIRE

Falmouth, Va. June 11th 1863.

My dear John.

Among the papers I sent home about one month ago, is a parcel marked "Papers relating to the Regimental Fund". Among these is an envelope (probably marked: "Receipts to Voucher 5.", but perhaps it may be on some other voucher) which contains the Regimental Bakery Roll for October 1862 where you will find a sum of money is due to private Bruno Tiesler, Company B, for extra-work connected with the Bakery. This is to the best of my recollection not paid, and therefore not receipted for on the Roll, and if so I wish you would pay the amount to the said Tiesler or whoever may act for him who will call at your Office, and get his receipt for the same on the said Bakery Roll, and charge the amount to me, and let me know, when you have done this, and how much the amount is. Also, to oblige Mr. Folsom, I have given him an order on you for $7.00 payable to this Bruno Tiesler, for which he has paid me $7.00. I shall be much obliged to you to attend to this matter, and it will be a great kindness to Tiesler, who is home sick.

I have little news. Sedgwick is still across and has slightly entrenched himself. There is occasional shelling. Couch is relieved and ordered to report to Pennsylvania. Another of our best men gone to join McClellan, Franklin, Smith, McDowell and the rest of our able soldiers. Sedgwick and Meade being both able men will probably soon follow. Then the Hookers and the Sickleses will have full swing and the destruction of the Army of the Potomac will be near.

I am glad to see a gleam of sense in the revocation of Burnside's order.[59] What a miserable, low tool of an arbitrary Government he is, and covers it all over with pious conscientiousness. What complete humbugs such men are!

I often ask myself how much farther we are going before a crash comes, and how much longer the people and the Army are going to stand the continuance of insult and violation of their rights? Do not think I am getting traiterous *[sic]*. I believe it to be our duty to bear everything in the Army, and if we are led to destruction by ignorant and incompetent men, why, we must go and take our chances, but there is a fearful responsibility somewhere.

The weather here is not very hot, but very dry. We need rain very much. The river is very low. Have received no letters for two days. Please send me in a letter a pair of dark colored thread gloves.

---

[59] In May and June 1863 General Burnside had Congressman Clement Vallandigham arrested for treason, and the offices of the Chicago Times closed for printing antiwar editorials. President Lincoln reversed both decisions.

RIGHT UP INTO THE FIRE

All well. No prospect of a move. Macy will send his photograph very soon. Send yours for him.

Your affectionate brother
Henry.

Letter for Mother enclosed.

June 11th 1863.

My dear Mother.

I have really nothing to write to you about except to say that all is quiet and that we are very comfortable. We have had no rain for some weeks and the roads are very dusty indeed, but the weather has not been oppressively hot. I hope soon to hear that you are enjoying the summer at Newport.

I had the Orange Marmalade boiled, and this process took away all the taste of fermentation, and it is very nice now.

Genl. Couch is relieved, so we shall lose our friend, Captain Potter, of whom I spoke to you. He rode over this morning to say good bye.

I find our horse very much improved and ride constantly. The farms near the town are beginning to look nicely again.

All well.

Affectionately
Henry.

RIGHT UP INTO THE FIRE

Sunday June 14th 1863
7 A.M.

My dear John.

We are certainly falling back from this position. Sedgwick was to have returned last night and we expect to leave tonight and cover the movement. All sick and baggage have gone to the rear.

Yesterday afternoon and evening there was a very heavy shower, and the troublesome dust is at last laid; now it is cloudy and looks like more rain.

I hear the Rebels are fast moving up toward Bull Run.

All well.

Affectionately
Henry.

Near Fairfax Station, Va.
June 18th 1863.
10 A.M.

My dear Father.

We left Falmouth on Monday last at 5 A.M., our Brigade covering the retreat and camped that evening 7 miles South of Dumfries. We marched through the heat of the day and lost a great many men by sunstroke. The Thermometer was about 100° Fahrenheit, and the dust terrible. Twelve men of our Division fell dead by the roadside, and hundreds are disabled. Tuesday was a cooler day and we marched from 3 A.M. till 6 P.M. and camped for the night at Ocoquan [sic] Creek. Yesterday we marched here and are on the Railroad about 3 miles farther West than Fairfax Station. Sedgwick is 2 ½ miles East of us. We have seen nothing of the enemy. The weather is awfully hot, and we have been marched so far and so recklessly that about one fifth of our men are disabled. We hear the Rebels are making a raid to Pennsylvania, but I do not believe they intend another real invasion, or that they intend to attack us here. I expect all will be quiet in a week. Both Herbert and myself are perfectly well and are uninjured by the heat. Dr. Terry has met with a severe accident and is going home. His horse kicked him and broke his leg. We are very sorry for him, and very sorry to lose him.

RIGHT UP INTO THE FIRE

I think we may stay here some time. The Surgeons have made such representations to Headquarters that I think we shall not be again marched between 11 and 4 o'clock in such Indian heat. All is quiet. All friends well. Col. Revere was used up for a time but is well now.

Please ask John to send me by mail one of the little cork hat cushions I saw in Boston, to be put in the hat to prevent Sunstroke. I have received no letters from home yet, since we left Falmouth.

Your affectionate son
Henry.

Centreville, Va.
Saturday, June 20th 1863.
9 A.M.

My dear Father.

We marched here yesterday afternoon from the point near Fairfax Station, or rather between Fairfax Station and Saxe Station, from which place I wrote to you on the 18th. All is quiet. We occupy the earthworks here. Most of the Army has marched on towards Leesburg, I hear. All well. Have had much rain. Weather cloudy and cool. We cannot tell how long we are to be here.

Love to all.

Your affectionate son
Henry.

RIGHT UP INTO THE FIRE

Thoroughfare Gap.
Sunday, June 21st 1863.
8 A.M.

My dear Father.

I wrote you last from Centreville. We left there yesterday at 1 P.M. and marched over the old Bull Run battlefield through the little villages of Gainsville and Haymarket, and halted for the night a mile beyond the latter place. This morning we marched on to the Gap, and are halted here and about to breakfast. I know nothing of our future movements. All well. No signs of the enemy.

Your affectionate son
Henry.

Monday 22nd 6 P.M.

Still here at the Gap and in position. All quiet.

Affectionate
Henry.

Thoroughfare Gap, Va. Tuesday
June 23rd 1863 8 A.M.

My dear John.

We have been perfectly quiet here and seen nothing of the enemy. Our Cavalry pickets were however driven in by Rebel Cavalry day before yesterday on the new Baltimore road, but I now hear we occupy Manassas Gap and our communications are open with Centreville. We have been completely isolated, our pickets being in a circle and no communication whatever. I cannot see the object of pushing out this Corps so far and in such an exposed way. No one knows anything of our movements or intentions, or of that of the enemy. I find the light tent you had made for me is much too weak to stand the campaign, and would be very much obliged to you to get me another one made of strong linen. White is the best color but if brown linen is stronger better get it. Of course it must be of the strongest and coarsest material but light. I would like the tent to be *longer* but no higher than the last, of the following dimensions. Each side to be 7 feet by 5 ft. 6 inches, the ends to be 6 feet wide at bottom, thus:

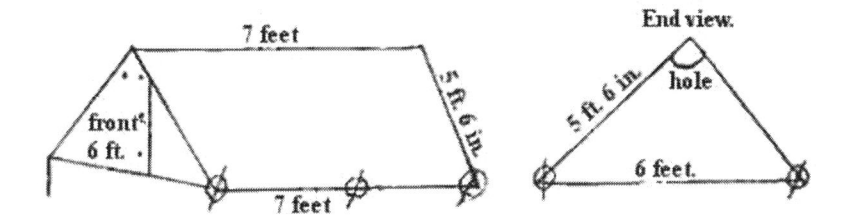

[Diagram: side view showing tent 7 feet long, front 6 ft., side 5 ft. 6 in.; End view showing triangular end 6 feet wide, 5 ft. 6 in. sides, with hole at top]

I should like the back to be whole, one piece with the sides, and the front to be divided like the back of the other tent. The front to *button* not *tie* and to flap over like a double-breasted coat, and both sets of buttons to button through. There must be a small hole for the ridge pole. Cords at ends of course, and loops all like the last tent. If the linen is strong (as it should be) there is no need of a strip under the ridge pole. Three loops on each side and one at each end, as in the drawing. The principal use of the tent is to shed rain, so the material must be capable of being stretched quite tight. I should also like a piece of light and strong bamboo cane for a ridge pole, 8 feet long. I can carry it easily on the horse. You had better roll the tent round the pole and do it up with bagging or stout brown paper, and send it by Express, "Lieut. Ropes, 20th Mass." to be painted on the tent.

I think this last trial will succeed, and shall be much obliged to you to see to it for me. Whenever you send anything by Express, please send 5 lbs. best coffee and 2 lbs. tea. No Sugar. The Commissary Coffee is very bad.

Weather fine and cool.

Your affectionate brother
Henry.

Have received no mail for 3 days.

Edwards' Ferry near Poolesville, Va.
June 26th Friday 2 P.M.

My dear John.

Our pickets at Thoroughfare Gap were attacked by a force of Rebel Cavalry supported by a small body of Infantry at an early hour yesterday morning, and I am sorry to say our Cavalry was driven in in confusion, and I hear 2 squadrons captured. We (our Regiment) were not engaged but we were under arms and loaded. At about 9 o'clock the enemy were repulsed and we received orders to move and at 9.30 marched out of the Gap, and our Division remained to cover the retreat and our very large train. We had quite a skirmish at Haymarket with the enemy's light Artillery and Cavalry, and had 2 caissons smashed and 1 man killed and 9 wounded, all of the 19th Maine, close behind us. Our Artillery went into position and drove them off. We then continued our march without molestation, and after a very tiresome tramp in a pouring rain we arrived at Gum Springs, 18 miles, at about 9 P.M. Here we rested for the night and this morning marched here, 12 miles also in a heavy rain, which has now ceased, however. We are now resting on the banks of the Potomac, right opposite our old camp Benton, and waiting for the teams to pass the Pontoon Bridge. I hear the HeadQuarters of the Army are at Poolesville, that we are the rearmost Corps and that Sedgwick is just before us. From all I can learn, I think the Rebels are not in full force in Maryland, and that Lee is near Winchester, and that after drawing us all up here, he will leave Ewell or somebody to draw off safely from Maryland with large quantities of supplies and will make a demonstration on Centreville and Alexandria, and thus keep us running about while 40 or 50,000 men fall on Burnside or succor Johnston. However, this is all conjecture, and I earnestly hope he may scare the President enough to make him recall the old deliverer of Maryland.

All well. Please get two linen tents, one for Herbert, both alike and as I described in my last. Please get for me another Rubber Coat, the strongest and best and lightest possible. I hear that the English Silk ones are best, but it must be strong enough to wear through brambles and woods, and as waterproof as possible. Please excuse this rough letter. It has just begun to rain again, and I am sitting on the ground and writing on my knee. Besides my ink has given out.

All well.

Affectionately
Henry.

We expect to cross to the Maryland side tonight. Herbert all right. Have had no mail yet for a week.

H. R.

Saturday 27th 9 A.M.

We crossed last night on Pontoon Bridge, and are now about 3 miles from Poolesville. All quiet. Most of the Army is here.

H. R.

RIGHT UP INTO THE FIRE

Near Frederick Md.
Mond. June 29, 1863. 8 A.M.

My dear Father.

I wrote last from Edwards ferry to John. We marched thence on Sat. at 5 P.M. and at midnight reached a spot 2 miles beyond Barnestown [*Barnesville*], where we slept till 5 A.M. and then marched here arriving at 4 o'clock yesterday afternoon.

We expect to march from here very soon toward Baltimore. The march has been miserably conducted thus far - roads blocked with trains and we detained for hours, and moving at a snail's pace, and thus using up time we much need for sleep. Genl. Hancock is utterly regardless of the comfort of the men, and orders us to fall in, hours before it is time, and then attempts to keep up so close to the trains that our march is like people coming out of a crowded church aisle. It has rained almost constantly for 4 days. We were awakened this morning for instance and ordered to be ready to move at daylight, and now it is past 8 there is no sign of a start. The men are deprived of their much needed sleep, and time to wash, all by this carelessness.

We were all delighted yesterday afternoon to hear of Hooker's removal and hope well for Meade and at the same time cannot but think that this presages better things yet. I hear the rebel cavalry have been to Tenallytown 6 miles from Washington.

I cannot but hope that all this mismanagement will yet be put right and a General put in the supreme command who knows something more than how to "move on the enemy's works." The rejoicing at Hooker's removal is very general and all are hoping for McClellan before long.

In haste
Yr. affec. Son
Henry.

Tuesday, 30th June 1863.
9 A.M.
near Uniontown, Md.

My dear Father.

I wrote last from our Camp of yesterday morning near Frederick at the Monocacy bridge. We marched thence yesterday at 8.30 A.M., and after a perfectly tremendous forced march of 30 miles we got here at 8.30 P.M. last evening.

RIGHT UP INTO THE FIRE

We had a few halts of not more than 10 minutes each. This was all, and we marched very fast, and the weather was rainy and very hot. I believe it was absolutely necessary to hold this place. No signs of the enemy. All well. We passed through the towns of Liberty, Johnsville and Uniontown.

Affectionately,
Henry.

Head-Quarters, 3d Brigade, 2d Division, 2d Corps,
Gettysburg, Pa., July 5, 1863.

My dear Sir,

The painful duty of recording the death of your son has been imposed upon me. He died at his post in battle.

We have become so familiar with scenes of blood and death, that our comrades fall besides us, barely claiming the most ordinary rights of burial; but I speak of this brigade at least, when I say that an unusual bereavement has befallen us in the death of your most noble son, and shrouded in deep gloom even the hearts that would leap with joy and thanksgiving for the great victory accorded our arms and the holy cause to which they are devoted.

The living example of that true nobility which it is possible for a man to attain has indeed passed from us; but we must ever remember with pride that we have been honored by association with a heart so pure, a spirit so brave, with a man who would not hesitate to give his life cheerfully for his and his country's honor.

I cannot give expression to the admiration and love which your son, above others, claimed of us, still less speak in fitting terms of the profound grief that fills our hearts. While we live, his memory will be sacredly cherished, and we will always point to Lieutenant Ropes as an heroic man, worthy of a life-long effort to imitate in every particular.

Colonel Norman J. Hall.

```
           Red Brick House   Cluster of small trees
           Barn
                        Elm
one large tree              Tree
 mason.    Rail-fence
                  ditch               4 small maple
                H.R. died here.         Trees


                          Elm Tree

 apple tree    Gettysburg:
  ×
 with shell in it  Sketched in pencil by
                J.C.R., accompanied by Macy, in October, 1863.
```

———

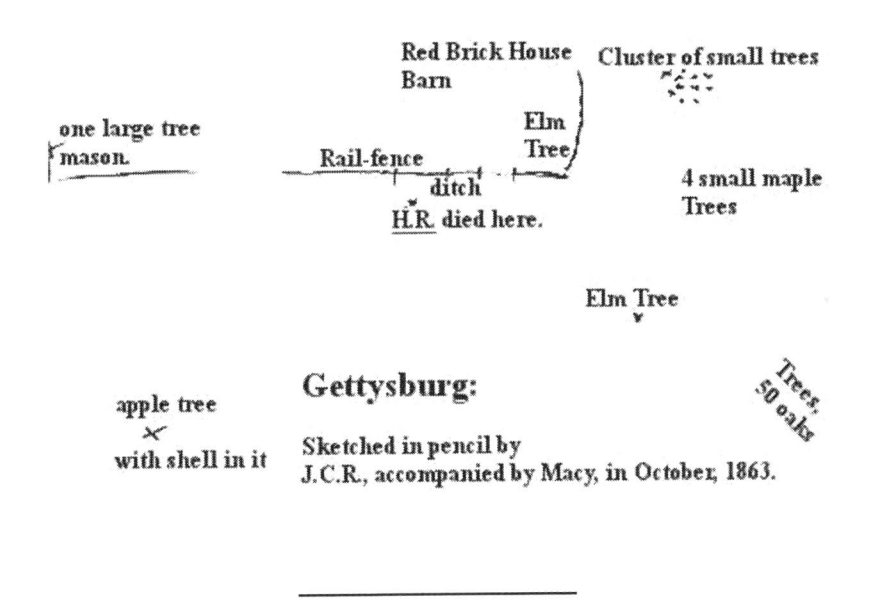

Head Quarters 3rd Brig. 2nd Division
Nov. 5, 1863.

John C. Ropes Esq.
Dear Sir

I intended long before this to have written you a few lines in accordance with the expressed wish of your late Brother Lt. Ropes with whom I was servant as perhaps you are aware, but knowing that the Officers of the 20th must have written you full particulars of the event, and our late rapid movements, I was prevented from fulfilling my desire, and altho' I may have nothing new or of any additional interest to communicate, yet I think it my duty to write in accordance with the wishes of your late Brother. When he died from his wounds at the battle of Gettysburg, Capt. Abbott found in his pocket $128.00 notes and one dollar in silver and his watch and chain which he handed to me and I afterwards returned him for the purpose of being restored to you. It will be satisfactory to me to learn that you received the property all in proper order.

When Lt. Ropes sent home his superfluous clothing last spring from Falmouth, Va. there was also a blue cloth military overcoat belonging to me sent with the rest, if it is not putting you to too much trouble I should feel obliged by your sending it to be expressed to me here as I require it much, and do not fancy the idea of drawing a new one for only one winter's wear, as they cost considerable $9.56.

The envelope covering this was one written by your late Brother and found in his valise, together with one directed to his Father, which if you wish to have I shall send.

I need not here assure you of my sympathy in the loss sustained by your family in the death of Lt. Ropes, he was also my best friend in the army, and on many accounts I deplore his death.

With much respect
I remain
Your very obedt. Servt.
James Smith
Head Qrs.
3rd Brig.
2nd Divn.
2nd Corps
A. P.

Camp near Brandy Station
Nov. 19, 1863.

John Ropes Esq.
Dear Sir

Your kind letter of the 10th I received on the 16th and now have pleasure in replying. On the 17th Qr. Mr. Folsom handed me $21.00 for which I beg you to accept my best thanks, and also for the assurances you give of the interest you express in my future welfare. I enclose the Envelope addressed by your late Brother as you request. The overcoat has not yet arrived but no doubt I will receive it when the Express matter comes up. You ask me a question "of my own *personal knowledge*" relating to your late Brother which I am happy in having it in my power to answer. Your Brother was reading one of Dickens' Novels in a sitting posture slightly reclining and it is my opinion he could not have possibly received the wound he did unless in that position.

The photograph of your late Brother I am truly glad to have in my possession, nothing you have sent me is so valuable in my estimation, and I shall treasure it as a memento of one whom I not only greatly respected, but to whom I was much

attached. Should it be my good fortune to reach Boston after the conclusion of my period of service, I shall feel it not only a privilege and a pleasure but also a duty to call for you and have the pleasure of your acquaintance, with much respect
 I remain

Yours very truly
James Smith.

[Private James Smith was killed in the Battle of Cold Harbor on June 9, 1864.]

APPENDICES

Appendix A: Biographical sketch of Henry Ropes.

Second Lieutenant 20th Mass. Vols. (Infantry), November 25, 1861; First Lieutenant, October 2, 1862; killed at Gettysburg, Pa., July 3, 1863.

(Source: "Harvard Memorial Biographies." Sever and Francis, 1867.)

Henry Ropes, the youngest son of William and Mary Anne (Codman) Ropes, was born in London, May 16, 1839. His parents at that time and for the three years following resided in England. Soon after their return to the United States Henry was placed at the Chauncy-Hall School in Boston, where he remained more or less steadily till 1852 or 1853. At this time his eyes began to show disease, and for the succeeding six or eight years they were a constant source of trial. As he had a very vigorous constitution and an active, inquiring mind, this infirmity hindered and annoyed him beyond measure. He was obliged to leave school and was for a short time under the instruction of Mr. William W. Goodwin, now Professor of Greek in Harvard College. On the departure of Mr. Goodwin for Europe in the summer of 1853, Henry was placed under the care of George D. Porter, and afterwards of Sidney Willard, who fell at Fredericksburg as Major of the Thirty-fifth Massachusetts Volunteers. Mr. Willard was of the greatest service to Henry in developing his physical powers by gymnastic exercises, boxing, rowing, walking, and fencing. Under his tuition he passed four happy years, during the last of which his eyes became sensibly better. Having completed his preparatory studies in July, 1858, he obtained admission to the Freshman Class of Harvard College, passing a satisfactory examination and entering without conditions.

He was at once recognized as a leader by his classmates, and took an active and prominent position among them. Hardly had he begun, however, the duties of his first term in College, before the old weakness of the eyes returned, and increased to such an extent that, at last, much against his will, he was compelled to yield to the command of his medical advisers and give up college life for several months, and when he came back to study with the aid of a reader.

Interested in everything relating to physical development, Henry Ropes from the first football match to the last boat-race was ever prominent. As a man of great strength and uncommon powers of endurance, he was known to all the College;

while his position as president of one of the earliest boat-clubs and as member of the victorious University crew gave him especial influence. His college life was eminently happy. From the first a great favorite, his personal popularity never declined. His high sense of honor, straightforward honesty and integrity of character, and sound common-sense, secured him the confidence and respect of his classmates, while his genial temper, his hearty frankness, his kind and loving nature, won their esteem and affection. He pursued the regular course of study with his Class through the Sophomore, the Junior, and part of the Senior years, his life being only disturbed by the war of the Rebellion, which had now begun to absorb the attention of the students, and which gave rise to the warmest debates between the representatives of the different sections of the country. In all these controversies Henry felt a deep interest, and took a manly and consistent stand against the advocates of secession.

His impatience to be with the army in the field became more and more marked. His attention was directed almost exclusively to the study of military tactics and drilling, and during the summer of 1861 he obtained an appointment as Second Lieutenant in the Twentieth Massachusetts Volunteers, then organizing under Colonel William Raymond Lee. His parents were unwilling that he should give up his course in College, and, yielding to their wishes, he declined the proffered commission. But when the news of the unfortunate disaster at Ball's Bluff reached the North, in October, 1861, he again determined to enter the service, and now obtaining the approval of his parents, he accepted the offer, and was commissioned a Second Lieutenant in the Twentieth Massachusetts Volunteers on the 25th of November, 1861. On the 1st of the following January, 1862, he joined his regiment at Camp Benton, near Poolesville, Maryland, and with characteristic energy entered at once upon the duties of his new career. The winter at Camp Benton was spent in pursuing the usual round of camp duties, and the only active service in which the regiment was engaged was in picketing the Potomac from Edward's Ferry to Seneca Mills. Lieutenant Ropes soon gave evidence of a fitness for military life which fulfilled the expectations of his friends, and proved to them that he had not mistaken his calling. Particular in the discharge of the minutest details of duty, he became known to his superiors as an efficient and trustworthy officer. In a letter written soon after he joined his regiment he says: "My little experience has taught me that business ability, fairness of judgment, consistency of character, and a spirit of disregard of personal comfort are necessary to a good officer. Above all, he must be prompt, and not make mistakes."

Another letter, written by him some time after, illustrates some traits in his character. He says: "You speak of discouragement. I have never for an instant felt discouraged or looked wistfully towards home. When I lay abed sick, I was, of course, very uncomfortable and in pain; but I have never once wanted to go home, and shall not, until the regiment returns, if my life is spared to return with it. Of course we have all sorts of discomforts, and perhaps I am not quite so cheerful as I used to be in Cambridge, and do not see enough of the fellows, &c., but I am not in the slightest degree discouraged or disappointed with my profession; and although I long to see the war over for the sake of the country and humanity, and would very well like to come back as one member, however humble, of a conquering army, and lay aside the sword, yet personally I am willing to stay for any length of time. I find here an opportunity to do as much good as I shall find in any profession. My time is occupied very fully, my pay is sufficient, my trade honorable, and one which calls out all the ability a man may possess. I have enough of pleasant companions, and I can see nothing better to look forward to in life. As to the danger, somebody must endure it, and why not I? Above all, I feel now it is my duty. If I live till the war is over I shall probably find some other path open. So do not think I am discouraged, or longing for home, for comforts, and for society. I do want to see you all, though, very much; and being away from you, and mother, and all, is the greatest trial I have. But this is not discouraging, only an evil every young man must bear."

On the 25th of February the Twentieth Massachusetts broke camp, preparatory to entering upon an active campaign. The regiment at this time belonged to the Third Brigade (Dana's), Second Division (Sedgwick's), of the Second Corps (Sumner's). The division crossed the Potomac near Harper's Ferry in the early part of March, to render assistance to General Banks in his advance down the Valley of the Shenandoah. Here Lieutenant Ropes received his initiation into active military life. On the 27th of March the Twentieth embarked on board the transport Catskill, on the 28th started for the Peninsula, and on the 31st landed at Hampton, Virginia. Sumner's corps marched towards Yorktown on the 5th of April, over a country utterly desolate, and through the recently abandoned fortifications of the enemy. In a letter dated Big Bethel, Virginia, April 6, 1862, when an engagement was expected to take place immediately, Lieutenant Ropes wrote as follows: "I expect before this reaches you I shall have been in the greatest battle which ever took place on this continent. I do not like to write much, but of course I know what may happen, and I feel perfectly prepared for any result to myself, and feel only anxious to do my duty in battle. God grant I may. I do not feel much concerned for my own life, and am glad to rest the result in higher hands."

Before Yorktown the Twentieth performed its share in arduous and perilous picket duty, besides much fatigue service. It was among the first to plant its flag upon the abandoned fortifications of the enemy; and Lieutenant Ropes, temporarily in command of Company K, had the honor of leading it first within the works. From Yorktown the regiment went to West Point, and on the 7th of May were engaged with the enemy there. Of Fair Oaks Lieutenant Ropes writes:

"Our regiment was opposed to the famous Hampton Legion of South Carolina. They fought well, and rallied in the open field just at the last, and we drove them there at the point of the bayonet, which was no doubt the last charge of the day. General Pettigru [sic] was found on this field. So you see we have done our part."

As to his own feelings during the battle, he says: "I think no man of sense would act differently in a battle from the way he before determined and expected to act. I really do not remember that I had any particular feelings to describe, except, perhaps, a sort of eagerness, and a strong desire to beat the enemy, the latter feeling one I had not before expected to have particularly ... I do not suppose it was at all a trying battle, but I certainly felt perfectly collected, and do not think my conduct was at all influenced by the knowledge of the danger."

The Twentieth immediately after the battle was placed on picket, where it remained nearly twelve days. During these twelve days it rained almost ceaselessly, and for a part of the time the' men were without blankets or tents. From this state of things Ropes draws certain conclusions: "I really suffered a good deal. I did not remove my clothes from Saturday, May 31st, till Wednesday evening, June 11th, and was soaked with water a great part of the time So you see there are some inconveniences of campaigning not down in the books. In fact one has to get over one's old ideas of necessaries, and comforts, and finds out how little is really needed for a man to live with."

On the 28th of June the army began its retreat towards the James, and in the terrible scenes of the seven days' battles the Twentieth Regiment took a prominent part. At Peach Orchard, Allen's Farm, Savage's Station, White Oak Swamp, Nelson's Farm, and Malvern Hill it was either actively engaged or constantly exposed. How it suffered, the lists of killed and wounded will show. At Nelson's Farm alone, seven officers and sixty-three enlisted men were killed or wounded. Half the men in Ropes' company were hit, and two of his sergeants were instantly killed.

His hopeful temper and unconquerable spirit never, perhaps, showed to greater advantage than after these reverses. The North was disheartened, stunned by the succession of disasters to the Army of the Potomac. A letter dated at Harrison's Landing, August 10th, has the following passage: "I am astonished at the fears of the people at home. We have none here. Our army is in splendid fighting trim and ready for anything. We have no idea of giving up, and if the people at home could only come out and see the army, they would hurry to enlist so as to be in time to see the last struggles of the Rebellion ... Our army is healthy, well fed, and confident. I fully believe we shall utterly crush the Rebellion before cold weather."

In August, 1862, the Twentieth left the Peninsula and was sent from Newport News to Alexandria. After crossing the Potomac with the rest of Dana's brigade, and advancing a few miles beyond Fairfax Court-House, it took position there, and allowing Pope's army, then in retreat, to pass by, covered the rear.

At Antietam the division under the immediate direction of General Sumner was in the thickest of the fight. The Twentieth lost one hundred and thirty-seven enlisted men in killed, wounded, and missing. Lieutenant Ropes was struck twice, once by a spent ball, and once by a round solid shot. The former, he says, "made a hole in my coat, scraped up the skin a little, and made me lame for a day. The cannon-ball I saw distinctly. It first hit the branch of a tree, glanced, passed between my legs, slightly bruising my knee, and leaving a black mark on my pants." A comrade writes of this circumstance, "He (Ropes) took it so coolly, I laughed outright."

On the 2d of October, 1862, Ropes was promoted to the rank of First Lieutenant. His conduct through the Peninsular campaign and in the battle of Antietam had not been unnoticed. He was offered positions on the staff, which he resolutely declined. His own words on this subject were, "I intend to stand by the Twentieth as long as we both last."

At Fredericksburg the Third Brigade, then under Colonel N. J. Hall of the Seventh Michigan, a captain in the Regular Army, crossed the Rappahannock in pontoons on the afternoon of Thursday, December 11, 1862, and after a fierce and obstinate contest, which lasted till evening, occupied most of the town of Fredericksburg. It was the difficult task of the Twentieth, then under command of Major (later Brevet Major-General) Macy, to march up the main street, exposed to the cross-fire from the houses and from behind walls and fences. Early in the engagement Lieutenant Ropes was left to command his company, his captain having been wounded. How well he discharged his duty may be inferred from a letter of a brother officer: "We were under a most terrific fire. Poor Ropes was almost alone when I arrived; scarcely three files of his company were left. I formed my fresh company on his left, and opened fire. We stayed there till we were relieved by two other companies. Once, during the fire, we stopped to speak to each other. That instant he was struck by a spent ball. The blow was so violent that he would have fallen if I had not caught him. It nearly took away his breath, and we both supposed he was badly wounded, and I helped him a step or two to the rear; but in less than a minute he was back in his place, saying: 'It was only a spent ball! I've got my breath again!'"

The same writer, speaking of the fight of the next day, in which again the Twentieth was terribly exposed, says: "I showed him (Ropes) a hole in my coat made by a bullet, and he showed three or four places where his coat and knapsack had been struck, and, laughing, said, in answer to my question, how it felt, 'Like fishes nibbling.'"

On the morning of Thursday, July 2, 1863, the Twentieth, after a series of rapid marches, reached the battle-field of Gettysburg. On the evening of that terrible day, when the firing ceased, nothing remained in the Regiment's front save the dead and wounded. Throughout that whole night, Lieutenant Ropes, unmindful of previous fatigue, forgetful of his own anxiety, and regardless of his own comfort, was engaged, with a detachment of men, in bringing the sufferers within the Union lines, cheering them with words of encouragement, and ministering to their wants from his own canteen. "It was his last night on earth, and it was all spent in labors of love." On Friday morning, while the Twentieth, partially sheltered by a slight and hastily constructed breastwork, was awaiting the attack of the enemy, a New York battery, hardly fifteen feet in the rear of the line, was shelling the works of the Rebels, firing over the regiment. Henry was sitting with his back to this battery, reading a book. A fragment of a shell which exploded at the moment of leaving the gun struck him as he sat there, and, uttering only the words "I am killed," he fell back and expired instantly.

"Corporal Jones, of his company," writes a brother officer, "suddenly cried out to me that Lieutenant Ropes was killed. I ran over to him, and grasping his hand, spoke to him. Though his fingers closed on mine and seemed to return the pressure, he never spoke again. His eyes were just fixing, with the most placid expression on his face I ever saw. It was purified of everything earthly."

"Few tears," writes another, "are shed by soldiers over their comrades killed in action; but even while the battle of Gettysburg was still raging, officers and men alike wept over Lieutenant Ropes."

His remains were sent to Boston, and on the 8th of July, 1863, all that was earthly of Henry Ropes found a resting place in Forest Hill Cemetery. A family monument was later erected, on which is a simple inscription commemorative of his life and death.

Appendix B: Historical sketch of the Twentieth Regiment Massachusetts Volunteer Infantry.

(Source: "Massachusetts Soldiers, Sailors, and Marines in the Civil War." Norwood Press, 1931.)

The 20th Regiment Massachusetts Volunteer Infantry was recruited at Camp Massasoit, Readville, in July and August, 1861. The main part of the regiment was mustered in August 28. Its colonel, William Raymond Lee, had once been a cadet at West Point. The regiment left Camp Massasoit September 4, and on the 7th reached Washington. Assigned to General Lander's Brigade, General Stone's Corps of Observation, it was stationed near Poolesville and was occupied in picketing the Potomac. October 21 it was engaged at Ball's Bluff, where it lost 194 officers and men, of whom 38 were killed or mortally wounded. The regiment also lost Col. Lee as a prisoner. Now under Lieut. Col. F. W. Palfrey it remained at Camp Benton, near Poolesville, during the rest of the fall and winter picketing the Potomac from Edward's Ferry to Seneca Mills.

In March, 1862, the 20th, forming a part of Dana's Brigade, Sedgwick's Division, was sent to the Shenandoah Valley, but before the end of the month it was ordered to the Peninsula, becoming a part of Sumner's (2d) Corps. It participated in the siege of Yorktown in April, the battles of Fair Oaks, May 31, Allen's Farm, June 29, Glendale or Nelson's Farm, June 30, and was slightly engaged at Malvern Hill, July 1. After a six weeks stay at Harrison's Landing the regiment was brought back to Alexandria and early in September joined the advance toward Frederick, Md. At Antietam, September 17, it was severely engaged in the West Wood, losing 141 officers and men, 20, including Assistant Surgeon Revere, being killed or mortally wounded. At Fredericksburg it was one of the regiments of Hall's Brigade, Howard's Division that crossed the river in boats on the 11th of December and fought in the streets of the city. Here its losses were very severe. In the assault on Marye's Heights on the 13th it again suffered severely, its total casualties on both days amounting to 200, of whom 48 were killed or mortally wounded. The winter of 1862-63 was spent at Falmouth.

During the Chancellorsville campaign in May, 1863, Gibbon's Division, including the 20th Regiment, remained in Fredericksburg in cooperation with Sedgwick's (6th) Corps, and suffered small loss. At Gettysburg, July 3, it was heavily engaged near the Union left center, losing Colonel Revere and 43 officers and men killed or mortally wounded. On October 14, the 20th was in action at

Bristoe Station, and was in the Mine Run campaign in late November. The winter was spent near Stevensburg. Here during December, 1863, 173 of the original members of the regiment re-enlisted.

At the Wilderness, May 6, 1864, as a part of Webb's Brigade, Gibbon's Division, Hancock's (2d) Corps, the 20th was heavily engaged on the Plank road losing Major Abbott and 35 officers and men killed or mortally wounded. At Spotsylvania it was in action near Laurel Hill, May 10, in the assault on the Bloody Angle, May 12, and in the general assault, May 18. In this last assault Capt. John Kelliher was most severely wounded, but survived, returned to the regiment, and served many years after the war in the Regular Army.

The 20th was engaged at North Anna, May 23, lost heavily at Cold Harbor, June 3, and moved on to the front of Petersburg. Here on the 22d of June, when the 2d Corps was outflanked and the men of the 15th and 19th regiments were largely made prisoners, the 20th changed front to the left and stopped the enemy's progress. About July 18 the men, present and absent, about 60 in number, whose time was about to expire were sent to Boston to be mustered out.

After being engaged in both movements to Deep Bottom in July and August, at Reams' Station, August 25, the regiment suffered great disaster, being outflanked and all but one officer and ten men made prisoners. This fragment, increased by recruits and returned convalescents to a battalion of three companies, was engaged at Boydton Road, after which it went into winter quarters near Fort Emory. February 5, 1865, it was in action at Hatcher's Run, and April 2, in the assault on Petersburg, then joined in the pursuit toward Appomattox.

Returning to Washington it received 223 men from the 37th Regiment, and on July 15 was mustered out of the service. On the 17th it left for Massachusetts and was assembled for the last time at Readville, July 28, when the men were paid off and discharged.

Appendix C: Detailed combat losses of the 20th Massachusetts Volunteer Infantry.

(Source, except where otherwise noted: "The Twentieth Regiment of Massachusetts Volunteer Infantry 1861 - 1865." Houghton, Mifflin and Company, 1906.)

October 21, 1861 - Battle of Ball's Bluff:

FIELD AND STAFF.
Captured: Colonel William R. Lee; Major Paul J. Revere (wounded in leg); Assistant-Surgeon Edward H. R. Revere; Adjutant Charles L. Peirson.

COMPANY A.
Killed: Sergeant John Merchant; Corporal George W. Waters; Privates George F. Kelly, Patrick McDermott (died January 4, 1862), William Welch, Charles Wright.
Wounded: First Lieutenant Oliver W. Holmes, Jr. (chest); Sergeant Otis L. Battles (slightly); Corporals William Babcock (slightly), Thomas Dwyer (thigh); Privates Thomas Chapin, William A. Edson, Alphonso K. Graves, Leander Hanscom, Benjamin F. Heath, Charles N. Homer (back), William O'Grady (finger amputated).
Captured: Third Sergeant Robert H. Weston; Privates Abraham Brown, Alexander Brown, Gilbert W. Dresser, Jeremiah C. Haley, Thomas Hartford, Henry R. Heath, Thomas Kelly, Daniel Murphy, Valentine P. Rollins, James R. Russell, Herman H. Shaw, William H. Smith, Timothy T. Torsey.

COMPANY C.
Killed: Second Lieutenant Reinhold Wesselhoeft (drowned); Private Joseph Meyer (drowned).
Wounded: Captain Ferdinand Dreher (severely in head); Sergeant Gustave Magnitzky (leg); Privates Philip P. Joseff, Alois Kraft.
Captured: Sergeant Frederick Will; Corporals James T. Goulding, David Griffin, Albert Reiss, Henry Vogel; Privates Charles Christely, William Fuchs, John B. Hayes, Joseph Heim, Franz Minuty, Christian Moegle, John Quimbly, Herman Rank, John Rohm, Frederick Ruppert, Jacob Schlicher, George Schuster, Jacob Wipfler, Franz Zeuner.

COMPANY D.

Killed: Corporal Frank Sampson (died November 3, 1861); Privates Warren F. Eames, James Galligan, Patrick McCullough, Daniel O'Brien, Calvin Porter, Joseph Wire.

Wounded: Privates Josiah Proctor (in body), Albert Sherman (leg amputated), James G. Warren (front right shoulder, left side, and right thigh).

Captured: First Lieutenant George B. Perry; First Sergeant Richard H. L. Talcott; Sergeants James M. Cogans, Horace A. Derry; Corporals Charles J. Curtis, Richard Hawkins, Seeley P. Reeves; Privates Alexander Aiken, John Baxter, John Dag, Richard Duffin, Job W. Dupee, Francis Giesler, William Graham, William Irving, George Lucas, Clinton McQuestion, John Murphy, John J. O'Connell, Hugh O'Harren, Amos H. Partridge (wounded, died in Richmond, January 16, 1862), Henry Place, Jr., Willard O. Reed, John Rumble, William H. Simester, James Smith, James Tettler.

COMPANY E.

Killed: Second Lieutenant W. L. Putnam (gut-shot, died October 22, 1861); Privates William Augustus Leonard, Michael Murphy.

Wounded: Captain G. A. Schmitt (three wounds in leg, one in small of back; never rejoined regiment). First Lieutenant J. J. Lowell (leg); First Sergeant Horace Moses Warren (fractured left forearm, flesh wound left side and right thigh); Corporal Edward Seymour Stockwell; Privates Joseph F. Bent (groin), Timothy Dinahy, Samuel Hamilton, Cilenius Mason Pierce, James Riley (shoulder), Uriah James Streeter, Michael S. Sullivan, William Tootell.

Captured: Sergeant Bernhardt L. Eckenstein, David W. Johnson; Privates George Britton, Patrick Doherty, Arthur Johnson, Cornelius Leary (wounded in right thigh), Cornelius O'Neil, Andrew Regan (wounded), John William G. Smith, William Thompson.

COMPANY G.

Killed: Captain Alois Babo; Sergeant John P. McKay; Corporals George E. Simpson, Ebenezer Tripp; Privates Patrick L. Burke (died November 18, 1861), Patrick McDonough, John McGoldrick, George H. Meader, Daniel J. Roach, Dennis Shine.

Wounded: Privates Patrick Crowley, John Dolan (left arm), Joseph Yeager (left side near base of lung).

Captured: Sergeant Emery A. Mellen; Corporals Reuben Harlow, John Powers; Privates Frederick S. Allen, Edward Barry, John Chapman, Ezra D. Chase, Thomas Glacken, Lawrence Griffin, John Noonan, Patrick Quinlan.

COMPANY H.
Killed: Privates Henry W. Brewer, James H. Collyer (died November 25, 1861), Edward P. Dunn, John Dwyer, William R. Hathaway (died November 27, 1861), Joseph Snell.
Wounded: Captain John C. Putnam (right arm amputated at the shoulder joint); Corporal Charles Cowgill (side); Private Thomas Lew (lost right arm).
Captured: Sergeants Thomas Armstrong, Thomas J. Pousland, William H. R. Reid; Corporal Thomas E. Ireson; Privates Henry Allbright, Jacob H. Alley, Nathaniel Q. Alley, James Clark, John Corbett, Thomas Donovan, William Duffie, Henry A. Fairbanks, John Flynn, Daniel Foley, James Folsom, Charles A. Foster, Richard L. Gardner, Thomas F. Mack, Charles O. Newell (wounded twice in body), William Powers, Tolman C. Richards, Joseph F. Rumney, William Woodward.
Missing: Private Timothy Hart.

COMPANY I.
Killed: Privates Alexander M. Barber (died November 21, 1861), Benjamin Davis, Peter McKenna, Albert Stackpole (died October 26, 1861), George E. Worth.
Wounded: First Sergeant William R. Riddle (right arm amputated above elbow); Corporals Thomas Hollis, James Seddon (ankle); Privates Thomas Dolan, Orlando N. Gammons (lost first joint forefinger of right hand), George C. Pratt (head and hip), Julius Strieck, John W. Summerhayes.
Captured: Privates Isaac S. Barker, Lewis Dunn, William F. Hill, Albert Kelley, Martin V. Kempton, Samuel Lowell, Edward V. Skinner.

Unknown date between October 22, 1861 and August 1, 1864:

COMPANY D.
Wounded: Corporal Lot Tripp.

April 18, 1862 – Picket firing near Yorktown:

COMPANY H.
Wounded: Private Samuel Kershaw (chest).

April 23, 1862 – Picket firing near Yorktown:

COMPANY I.
Wounded: Captain William F. Bartlett (leg amputated above the knee).

May 31 - June 1, 1862 – Battle of Fair Oaks:

COMPANY A.
Killed: Private Alvin Tower (died June 8, 1862).
Wounded: Private Jeremiah C. Haley (slightly).

COMPANY B.
Wounded: Corporal William Wanders (severely in head); Private Joseph Pabst (slightly).

COMPANY C.
Wounded: Sergeant Philip P. Joseff (slightly); Private John S. Betz.

COMPANY D.
Wounded: Private John Lyon.

COMPANY E.
Killed: Corporal Thomas Dwyer (died June 2, 1862).
Wounded: Corporal Uriah J. Streeter (thigh).

COMPANY F.
Wounded: Privates John Daly (slightly), Levi Gilman (finger), Thomas B. Love (slightly), Eugene McLaughlin (slightly), Michael O'Connor (toe).

COMPANY H.
Killed: Privates Alexander Devlin (died June 2, 1862), Charles A. Foster.
Wounded: Privates Patrick Foley (slightly), Christian Spicer (in side).

COMPANY I.
Killed: Private Abraham C. Rush.
Wounded: Second Lieutenant William R. Riddle (injured by horse); Corporal William Kelley (slightly); Private George R. Bailey (slightly).

COMPANY K.
Wounded: Privates Henry Bowman (slightly), Theophilus Chase (slightly),

Michael Donnelly (in chest), Martin Foley (slightly), John F. McQuade (thigh), Adam Morton (slightly).

June 25 - July 1, 1862 – Seven Days Battles:

FIELD AND STAFF.
Wounded: Colonel William R. Lee; Lieutenant Colonel Francis W. Palfrey (slightly).

BAND.
Killed: George S. Reiser.

COMPANY A.
Wounded: Sergeant James Ford; Privates Alfred L. Bishop, George F. Cate, Daniel C. Lane, James H. Noble, William Ryder.

COMPANY B.
Wounded: Sergeant Balthazar Wagner; Corporal Christian Buettinger; Privates Christian Wagner, Charles Arnold, Joseph Pabst, Julius Boehme, William Frank, Charles Haas, John Hanifer, Gustave Kawell, Frederick Kleeberg, Conrad Seibel.
Captured: Privates Adolph Asher, Philip Gilbert.

COMPANY C.
Killed: Sergeant Joseph Wolf.
Wounded: Privates Werner Hahn, Gottfried C. Speiser, Henry Vogel.

COMPANY D.
Killed: Private James Buckley (died July 26, 1862).
Wounded: Captain Norwood P. Hallowell (slightly); Corporal Charles J. Curtis; Privates John J. O'Connell, Richard Duffin.
Missing: Privates Alexander McKinley, Francis A. Wheeler.

COMPANY E.
Killed: First Lieutenant James J. Lowell (gut-shot, died July 6, 1862); Privates Edward C. Gleason, John McGowan.
Wounded: Second Lieutenant Henry L. Patten (leg); Privates Joseph F. Bent, John McIntire, John W. G. Smith.

COMPANY F.
Wounded: First Lieutenant August Müller; Sergeant Bernard McGuire; Corporal John Powers; Privates James DeForrest, Patrick McCarty.

COMPANY G.
Killed: Private David Root.
Wounded: Sergeant Thomas M. McKay; Corporals Fred S. Allen, William A. Johnston; Privates William Casey, Ezra D. Chase, John Goodman, George Lawson, James Madigan; Drummer Joseph Lovejoy.
Captured: Private Hiram Whiting.

COMPANY H.
Killed: Privates Robert Grieve, James Lynch.
Wounded: Privates Josiah Armington, George Babcock, John C. Ford, Samuel H. Gordon, John R. Johnson, Neal McCafferty, James McKenna, Cornelius Monahan, John M. Stearns; Drummer John Stevens.
Missing: Sergeant George White; Private George H. Carroll.

COMPANY I.
Killed: Privates Richard Brooks, Jared M. Hunter.
Wounded: First Lieutenant Henry L. Abbott (arm); Sergeant Andrew J. Bate; Corporals E. G. W. Cartwright, John W. Summerhayes; Privates John Daisy, Charles F. Goodwin, James A. Bucknam, Francis McNamara.

COMPANY K.
Killed: First Sergeant Alfred L. Holmes (head); Sergeant Theodore Compass (breast); Corporal Isaac M. Sampson (leg torn off); Private Patrick Cronan.
Wounded: Sergeant Patrick J. Campion (slightly); Privates Charles W. Bartlett, James W. Bryant, George A. Hastings, John Hinds, George W. Kehr, Chester A. Leonard, Joseph H. Parker, Samuel Tucker.
Missing: Private Lansford Bowman.

September 1, 1862 - Picket firing near Germantown:

COMPANY C.
Wounded: Private Andrew Beska.

Unknown date after September 1, 1862 (most likely early 1864):

COMPANY B.
Captured: Private Thomas J. Richards (died September 2, 1864, in Camp Sumter, GA).

September 17, 1862 – Battle of Antietam:
[The following incomplete list was compiled from the regimental roster contained in Volume II of "Massachusetts Soldiers, Sailors, and Marines in the Civil War" (1931) and accounts for 114 of the regiment's 124-141 (sources disagree) losses.]

FIELD AND STAFF.
Killed: Assistant-Surgeon Edward H. R. Revere.
Wounded: Lieutenant Colonel Francis W. Palfrey (shoulder); Major Paul J. Revere (arm).

COMPANY A.
Wounded: First Lieutenant Oliver W. Holmes, Jr. (neck); Corporal Edwin B. Mead; Privates Abraham Brown, Hollis H. Chase, John M. Edson, John D. Grose, Thomas Kelly, Thomas C. Tiernan.

COMPANY B.
Killed: Privates Frederick Gutermuth, Ludwig Rabenan, John Shilling (died September 20, 1862).
Wounded: Corporal George Joeckel; Privates Lorenz Hartleb, Louis Reffel.
Captured: Privates George Greim, Johann Kast (wounded).

COMPANY C.
Killed: Private Jacob Schneider.
Wounded: Sergeant Philip P. Joseff; Private Otto Stoll.

COMPANY D.
Killed: Private Clinton McQuestion.
Wounded: Sergeant George Wilson; Privates William M. Butler, John E. Coffin, George Davis, William Denningham, Hiram B. Howard, Eli Merrill *[uncertain but probable]*, John Slattery.

COMPANY E.
Killed: Privates Horatio N. Faxon (died October 2, 1862), Lucius E. Griffith, Ezra O. Harwood.

Wounded: Captain George A. Schmitt; 1st Sergeant Edmund D. Wetherbee; Sergeant Edward S. Stockwell; Corporal James Corcoran; Privates Joseph Devlin, Cornelius Kallaher, Cornelius J. Kelly, Donald McGilvary, Philip McGuire, Morris Wilson.
Captured: Private Lawrence Kehoe.
Missing: Private James C. Somerville *[later returned]*.
Deserted: Private Cilenus M. Pierce.

COMPANY F.
Killed: Privates John Brown, John McDonough.
Wounded: Sergeant James H. Spencer; Corporal Mathew Clune; Privates Michael Bresney, Dennis Collins, Thomas Downey, Patrick Drumney, Levi Gilman, Bernard McGuire, Martin Mulroy, John J. Schoeffle.
Missing: Privates Timothy Buckley *[later returned]*, Eugene Connelly *[later returned]*, David Leonard *[later returned]*.

COMPANY G.
Wounded: 1st Lieutenant William F. Milton (slightly); Sergeant William H. Walker; Corporal Frederick S. Allen; Privates Ezra D. Chase, Patrick Crowley, Lawrence Griffin, James Howe, Lambertus W. Krook, Samuel K. Paulin *[uncertain but probable]*, Patrick Quinlan, Hiram L. Whiting.
Captured: Private Felix Owens.

COMPANY H.
Killed: Sergeant Friend H. Keith; Privates Leonard Cressey, George H. McDonald.
Wounded: 1st Lieutenant Norwood P. Hallowell (arm); Corporal William H. Warren; Privates Hugh Blain, Maurice Clancy, Smith W. Cofran, Stephen Collins, Charles Cowgill, Thomas Daily, Thomas Donovan, William S. Douglas, John Doyle, Edward Early, George C. Flanders, Leander D. Hamblin, James Kirk, Frederick A. Lucas, John W. Quimby, John M. Stearns.
Missing: Private Tolman C. Richards *[later returned]*.

COMPANY I.
Killed: Privates Edward Alexander (died January 14, 1863), William E. Buck (died September 28, 1862), John Mather.
Wounded: Sergeant Thomas Hollis; Corporal Patrick Lanergan; Privates Thomas Davis, William B. Low, Charles H. Raymond, Elisha M. Smith.

COMPANY K.
Killed: Corporal George W. Kehr; Private John Riley.

Wounded: Sergeant Hannibal A. Faunce; Corporal Edward J. Campion (shoulder); Privates Henry Bowman, Patrick J. Campion, John Hinds, Peter Keenan, John Kenny.

December 11 & 13, 1862 – Fighting in the streets of Fredericksburg & Battle of Fredericksburg:

COMPANY A.
Killed: Privates Benjamin F. Bumpus, James Cauraugh, Benjamin D. Clifton, Jonathan Francis.
Wounded: Privates Oliver S. Bates, Benjamin B. Besse, Joshua Besse, 2d, David G. Chapman, George H. Curtis, Thomas W. Green, Thomas C. Tiernan, Lyman P. Tilton.

COMPANY B.
Killed: Private Andreas Wilhelm.
Wounded: Second Lieutenant Henry E. Wilkins (arm); Sergeant Frederick A. Schoof; Privates Samuel Elliott, Jacob Getz, Pankratz Herbst, Frederick Karcher, Herman O. Schieferdecker.

COMPANY C.
Killed: Lieutenant Colonel Ferdinand Dreher (died May 1, 1863); Corporal Anton Steffens; Privates Frederick W. Bushe, James Meghan.
Wounded: Sergeant Albert Reiss; Corporal Charles Light; Privates Leopold Bender, Joseph Heim, William Leiblein, Franz Minuty, Patrick Murphy.

COMPANY D.
Killed: Corporal Richard Hawkins; Privates Daniel W. Borden, William Calon, Charles Cero (died January 1, 1863), James Donahue, Junius J. Johnson, Josiah Proctor.
Wounded: First Lieutenant Arthur R. Curtis (slightly); Sergeant Horace A. Derry; Corporals Charles J. Curtis, Alden H. Holbrook, Robert Hart; Privates John Dag, John Devine, James Dow, Job W. Dupee, Francis Giesler, Joseph H. Jordan, John Leyson, James P. McVey, David Murphy, Andrew Phillips.

COMPANY E.
Killed: Corporal John McIntire; Private William Tootell.
Wounded: Sergeant Martin F. Davis; Corporal James Corcoran; Privates Eugene Conners, Thomas Conway, John Fenton, Owen Hirl, Edward S. Stockwell, Michael S. Sullivan.

COMPANY F.
Killed: Captain Charles F. Cabot; Privates Thomas Downey, Nathaniel F. Hooper, Daniel O'Brien, James Sullivan, Thomas Kelly.
Wounded: Corporal John Cummings; Privates James Carroll, Simon Cass, Dennis Collins, Daniel Daley, Timothy Hartnett, James Long, James McGregor, James McGuire, Thomas McGuire, John McLean, Patrick O'Hearn, Patrick O'Leary, Patrick Quinlan, Felix Riley, Morris Rowland.

COMPANY G.
Wounded: Second Lieutenant Thomas M. McKay (shoulder); Color Corporal Charles H. Hunt; Corporal John Powers; Privates Frank A. Bernenher, Daniel Casey, William Casey, Ezra .D Chase, John Driscoll, Mathias H. Krook, James McGinnis, Michael Pentonay, Morgan Sweeney.

COMPANY H.
Killed: Second Lieutenant Robert S. Beckwith (died December 31, 1862); Privates Thomas Donnelly, William Tasker.
Wounded: Sergeant William Powers; Corporal Joseph P. Powers; Privates Edwin F. Briggs, William Duffie, Richard S. Gardner, Gardner Goodwin, Bernard Harkins, Peter Kelty, Andrew Kervick, Stephen Longfellow, Donald McPhee, Tolman C. Richards, John C. Sloeman, James A. Smith.

COMPANY I.
Killed: Second Lieutenant Leander F. Alley; Corporal Peleg B. Davenport; Privates Alonzo Arling, Isaac S. Barker, Joseph Berry, James Briordy, John Dacy, Charles F. Ellis, Martin V. Kempton, Peter McEnany, Charles A. Morris, George E. Snow, Jacob G. Swain, William H. Swain, William H. Welcome, William H. Winslow, Ezekiel L. Woodward.
Wounded: Privates Frederick W. Barnard, James H. Bartlett, Daniel B. Chase, George H. Coffin, Edward P. Greene, James Kearns, Benjamin N. Luce, Miles Muldoon, Josiah F. Murphy, Owen Murphy, John O'Connor, Edward P. Orpins, Albert C. Parker, Thomas J. Russell, John Ryan, Gottlieb Sessler, Charles F. Swain, Patrick Waters, John Wells, Alexander Winthrop.

COMPANY K.
Killed: Corporals George Blankenburg, Thomas J. Crowell; Privates Thomas Carver, John Donnelly, Charles S. Hastings.
Wounded: Captain Allen Shepard (foot), Sergeant Patrick J. Campion (right arm amputated); Privates James Blake, Henry F. Dana (foot), John Dillon (leg amputated), Thomas Flanagan (leg), Patrick Morrissey (legs amputated).

May 3, 1863 – Second Battle of Fredericksburg:

COMPANY D.
Killed: Sergeant Charles H. Bixby.
Wounded: Privates John Lynch, Hugh O'Harron.

COMPANY F.
Wounded: Captain James Murphy (arm); First Sergeant John Ronan; Privates William Meaney, Terrence Wade.

COMPANY G.
Wounded: Captain Oliver W. Holmes, Jr. (leg); Privates James Hayes, George Lawson, Alonzo L. Stetson.

COMPANY H.
Killed: Private William J. Smith.

COMPANY I.
Wounded: Corporal Samuel C. Crocker; Privates Thomas Ahearn, Barzilla Crowell.

July 1 - 3, 1863 – Battle of Gettysburg:

FIELD AND STAFF.
Killed: Colonel Paul J. Revere (died July 5, 1863).
Wounded: Lieutenant Colonel George N. Macy; Adjutant William H. Walker.

COMPANY A.
Killed: First Sergeant George F. Cate; Privates Thomas Kelley, George L. Plant.
Wounded: Second Lieutenant Lansing E. Hibbard; Corporals Joshua Besse, 2d, John C. Orcutt, James Sullivan; Privates Oliver S. Bates, Bradford W. Beal, Martin Coon, Michael Gleason, James R. Hamilton, Leonard Harrington, Levi Lamson, Jr., Michael Hearty, James K. Morse, Daniel Murphy, James R. Russell, Stephen B. Stewart, Thomas C. Tiernan, Lyman F. Tilton, George E. Wood.

COMPANY B.
Killed: First Sergeant George Joeckel; Privates Clemens Weisensee, John Dippolt.
Wounded: Corporal Jacob Pfeiffer; Private Christian Wagner.

COMPANY C.
Killed: Corporal Jacob Schlicker; Privates August Duttling, Alois Kraft.
Wounded: First Sergeant James T. Goulding; Sergeant Patrick Huitt; Privates Franz Huhn, Adolph Kernberger.

COMPANY D.
Killed: Privates Alexander Aiken, William Inch, John Lovering, George Lucas, John Neary.
Wounded: Captain Henry L. Patten; Sergeants J. Proctor, Charles J. Curtis; Privates John Brown, Hiram V. Howard, Edward Kestin, Marcus J. Long, Patrick Manning, John E. Murphy, Albert W. Stetson, James G. Warren.

COMPANY E.
Killed: Corporal James C. Somerville; Privates Thomas Downing, Jonathan F. Lucas.
Wounded: First Sergeant William H. Carroll; Sergeant Charles F. Carpenter; Corporals Patrick Gorman, Arthur Johnson, Philip McGuire; Privates Malachi Garrity, Benjamin F. Hanaford, Moses H. Gale.

COMPANY F.
Killed: Corporal Eugene McLaughlin; Privates Thomas R. Gallivan, Peter Keefe, James Lane, John McLean, Patrick Quinlan, Felix Riley.
Wounded: Second Lieutenant John Kelliher; Corporals Arthur Hughes, David Leonard, John Powers; Privates Timothy Buckley, Patrick Fee, Thomas A. King, Edward McGrath, Thomas Woodman.

COMPANY G.
Killed: Privates Edward Barry, James O'Brien, Morgan Sweeney.
Wounded: Second Lieutenant Charles Cowgill; First Sergeant Gustave Magnitsky; Sergeant Luke Miller; Corporal Patrick Coughlin; Private Thomas Glacken.

COMPANY H.
Killed: Privates Michael Kinnark, Hugh Blain.
Wounded: Captain Herbert C. Mason; First Sergeant Edward Wilton; Privates Thomas Donovan, Daniel Foley, Stephen Longfellow, Timothy Wiley.

COMPANY I.
Killed: Second Lieutenant Sumner Paine; Corporal Elisha M. Smith; Privates Horace P. Burrill, Horatio L. Fay, William F. Hill, Henry Jones.

Wounded: Sergeants Benjamin B. Pease, Patrick Lanergan; Corporal William B. Low; Privates James Barry, Samuel Christian, Daniel B. Chase, Daniel McAdams, William B. Parker, Peter Williams, Arthur M. Rivers.
Missing: Private William H. Barrett *[later returned]*.

COMPANY K.
Killed: First Lieutenant Henry Ropes; Privates Charles Hearney, George S. Sawtell, John I. Burke.
Wounded: First Sergeant Joseph H. Parker; Corporal Lusher G. White; Privates Thomas Broinham, Peter Kennan, Benjamin Jones, Chester A. Leonard, Marcus T. C. Miles, Edward Murphy.

October 10, 1863 - Near Culpeper Court House:

COMPANY A.
Captured: Private John Russell.

October 14, 1863 - Battle of Bristoe Station:

COMPANY A.
Captured: Private Joseph Smith (wounded, died September 1, 1864, in Camp Sumter, GA).

COMPANY B.
Killed: Private Gebhart Raubs.
Wounded: Private Michael Kessler.
Captured: Private Miles McHugh (died January 27, 1864, in Richmond, VA).

COMPANY C.
Deserted: Private Philip Hoffman.

COMPANY E.
Wounded: Corporal Joseph Smitts.
Captured: Private Charles Stanwood (died March 11, 1865, in Richmond, VA).

COMPANY F.
Wounded: Private Terrence McGuire.

COMPANY H.
Wounded: Sergeant John Doyle; Private John Maguire.

COMPANY I.
Captured: Private Robert Baker.

COMPANY K.
Wounded: Private Thomas Brown.

November 27, 1863 - Picket firing near Mine Run:

COMPANY B.
Killed: Corporal James Marsh (died November 29, 1863).

COMPANY E.
Captured: Private Henry Barge (died April 20, 1864, in Camp Sumter, GA).

Unknown date before December 8, 1863:

COMPANY B.
Wounded: Private John Hanifen.

Unknown date in 1864:

COMPANY E.
Captured: Private John Cahalan.

COMPANY F.
Wounded: Private Patrick O'Connor.

COMPANY G.
Wounded: Private Andrew Radicke.

COMPANY K.
Captured: Private William Carney (died September 18, 1864, in Camp Sumter, GA).

April 26, 1864 - Near Stevensburg:

COMPANY I.
Wounded: Private Frederick Coffman.

May 5 - 7, 1864 - Battle of the Wilderness:
[Since separate reports of casualties during the Overland Campaign were not made on account of the frequency of battles, some of the regiment's casualties in the Battle of Spotsylvania Court House are likely erroneously listed under the Wilderness.]

FIELD AND STAFF.
Killed: Major Henry L. Abbott; Adjutant Henry M. Bond (died May 14, 1864).
Wounded: Colonel George N. Macy.

COMPANY A.
Killed: Privates William Armstrong, Bradford Beal (died May 28, 1864), Charles Goodwin, Tyler Richardson.
Wounded: Captain Albert B. Holmes; Privates August Brown, James R. Hamilton, Michael Hearty, Benjamin F. Heath, Thomas D. Leines, Abraham Moss, Heinrich Riensberg, Albert Steiber, James Sullivan, James T. Thompson.
Missing: Private August Brice.

COMPANY B.
Killed: Privates Henry Bode, Carl J. W. Einhorn, James Harrington, Thomas C. Mack, Thomas Mack.
Wounded: Corporal Ferdinand Decker; Privates Henry Beddigs, Julius Boehme, Louis Bres, Edward Dillon, Otto Ecker, Frederick Gluer, Theodore Kessler, Louis Gurlitz, __ Hortsheiner *[name only appears on one casualty list and does not seem to be on the regiment's roster]*, Jacob Leib, Joseph Mannsmann, John McDonald, James Mealey, Edward Natter, John Reardon, Charles Schulze.
Captured: Privates Henry C. A. Bornemann, Carl Carcher (died August 8, 1864, in Richmond, VA), Jacob Miller (wounded), John Schamer (died September 27, 1864, in Camp Sumter, GA), Henry W. Schultz (wounded, died January 31, 1865, in Salisbury, NC), Frederick Tent (died November 25, 1864, in Camp Sumter, GA).
Missing: Drummer John Tuttle *[later returned]*; Privates Franz Bauer, Michael Bauer *[later returned]*, J. Bihard, Hugh McDonald *[later returned]*, Carl Miller (wounded).

COMPANY C.
Killed: Privates Frederick Hunck, Carsten Jacobsen, Patrick McGovern, Theodore Moehle, John Quimbly, Edward Reymers, Edward Tepfer (died August 29, 1864).

Wounded: Sergeant William Fuchs; Privates Ernst Bierlig, Lyman R. Blood, Alois Boehmer, William Brandtberg, Carl Buser, William Finn, Charles Freeman, George Garment, Werner Hahn, William Hammell, Albert Hausch, Samuel Hodges, Martin Koch, Simon Otto, Herman Reidel, Peter Rooney, Henry Schmidt, John Schroeder, Henry Schwabe.
Captured: Sergeant Albert Smoke (wounded); Privates Franz Boehme (wounded), Leon Fevier, William Ohlenschlager (wounded); Hospital Steward Henry Deck (died October 25, 1864, at Salisbury, NC).
Deserted: Private August Proehl.

COMPANY D.
Killed: Sergeant Robert Blackburn, Jr.; Private John Fischer (died July 1, 1864).
Wounded: Captains Henry L. Patten, William F. Perkins; Sergeant Alden H. Holbrook; Corporal James Donnelly; Privates Hugh Armstrong, John M. Cheeney, William Davis, Herman Humpke, William F. Keefer, Lewis Kempton, Nathan P. Kendrick, John Lynch, John McDonald, Patrick O'Neil, William D. Perry, Julius Pommersche.
Captured: Privates Thomas Bryson (wounded, died November 7, 1864, at Salisbury, NC), Robert Clare, John B. Kernachan, David Scanlin (wounded), James O. Sherman.
Missing: Privates Thomas A. Dow *[later returned]*, Hugo Grah (wounded).

COMPANY E.
Killed: Privates Noah L. Cummings (died May 26, 1864), James B. Wilson (died June 1, 1864).
Wounded: Sergeant Henry Borden; Privates Karl A. J. Albers, Theodore Bostell, Eugene Connelly, Josiah M. Darrell, John Ehles, Edward F. Fisher, Nathan H. Gray, Frank Heill, William H. Ingalls, Heinrich Jäger, Carl Jordan, Charles E. Leslie, John McCaul, John Murphy, John Neuer, Patrick O'Leary, William Ponnaz, Henry Rakke, Henry Thorn.
Captured: Corporal Henry Kelly (wounded, died August 23, 1864, in Camp Sumter, GA), Private Edward Kippler (died of wounds May 22, 1864).
Missing: Privates Senrin Bender *[later returned]*, William Detmer *[later returned]*, Ludwig Miller, Harry Schmidt.

COMPANY F.
Killed: Privates John Amende, Charles Myatt.
Wounded: Privates Frank Bartley, Adam Bolmer, Julius Caesar, Felix Chaplin, Jean B. Dalpe, Heinrich Hagedon, George Haines, Julius Hillse, William Huffman, Thomas Joy, John Keefe, William Langhinrichs, Levi Lock, Charles McCarthy, Patrick McManus, Emil Pinkan, Charles Rosenau, George W. Russell,

Peter Scherer, William Schriever, Eugene Sullivan, Henry Urban, George Warren.
Captured: Privates Francis Constant (wounded), Christian Diercks (wounded), Albert Henry, John B. Rinaldo.

COMPANY G.
Killed: Corporal Charles E. Jones; Privates Robert Kelly, Owen Kough.
Wounded: Corporals John Chapman, Patrick Coughlin; Privates John Brunt, Robert Derner, James Duker, James French, Daniel Kenney, Christian Leckbaud, Charles Lynch, Christian Mennich, Albert Miller, Julius Moeller, Joseph Potter, Henry F. Sternberg, Martin Sturm, Jeremiah Sullivan.
Captured: Privates Luke Miller (died October 1, 1864, in Camp Sumter, GA), William Metro (died August 7, 1864, in Camp Sumter, GA), Philip Morton.
Missing: Privates James Lynch *[later returned]*, John Jackson, John Palm.

COMPANY H.
Killed: Corporal Henry A. Fairbanks; Privates Carl Gieppe, Charles Harris, John H. Merrill, Charles A. Mohr, Albert Paffrath, William Platte, William Schiller, Darby Tucker.
Wounded: Second Lieutenant Benjamin B. Pease; First Sergeant Edward Wilton; Sergeant Stephen Longfellow; Privates John Hehl, Peter Kennedy, Charles Ricketson, James Rourke, August Schubert, James A. Smith, Carl Unrein, John Wheeling, Timothy Wiley.
Captured: Privates James Dunn (died October 22, 1864, in Camp Sumter, GA), Henry Epp (wounded), Richard Evans, Hermann Rahe, Fritz Schwerin (wounded).
Missing: Privates Frederick Cortez, John Lowry.

COMPANY I.
Wounded: First Lieutenant Henry W. T. Mali, Jr.; Sergeant Patrick Lanergan; Corporals Edward P. Green, William E. Manning; Privates Paul Bixler, Samuel Crocker, Barzilla Crowell, Jonas Zeis, Julius Zeir.
Captured: Private Charles H. Raymond (died June 12, 1864, in Camp Sumter, GA).
Deserted: Private George L. Temple.

COMPANY K.
Killed: Privates William Dorchesky, Frederick Messerschmidt.

Wounded: First Lieutenant Nathaniel B. Ellis; Corporal David A. Smith; Privates John Anderson, John Boyd, Frederick Buck, Thomas Corbett, John Hinds, Fritz Katz, Peter Keenan, Herman J. Lorenz, Edward Murphy, Augustus Nesi, George E. Wentworth.
Captured: Privates John Cott (wounded; died August 12, 1864, in Camp Sumter, GA), Samuel Sloan (died October 19, 1864, in Camp Sumter, GA).
Missing: Privates Michael Donnelly, Julius Krass, August Sohm *[name only appears on one casualty list and does not seem to be on the regiment's roster]*.

UNASSIGNED.
Missing: Private John H. F. Schmidt.

May 8 - 20, 1864 - Battle of Spotsylvania Court House:
[Since separate reports of casualties during the Overland Campaign were not made on account of the frequency of battles, some of the regiment's casualties in the Battle of Spotsylvania Court House are likely erroneously listed under the Wilderness.]

NON-COMMISSIONED STAFF.
Wounded: Sergeant Major George W. Leach.

COMPANY A.
Killed: Private Albert A. Manley, Frederick Rodnitzky.
Wounded: Sergeant Peter Newkirk; Corporal John C. Orcutt; Privates Thomas C. Haskins, James T. Nickerson, John Smith.
Captured: Privates George H. Loring (wounded, died December 10, 1864, in Camp Sumter, GA), William Ryder (wounded).

COMPANY B.
Wounded: Sergeants Gustave Otto, Charles Rost; Privates Emil Breitfeld, Michael Burke, Francis Belwer, Carl Clare, John Frank.
Missing: Private Jacob Seip.

COMPANY C.
Wounded: Captain John Kelliher; Privates Oswald Durant, Patrick Hogan, August Krug, Frederick W. Miller, Hermann Seifert.
Captured: Private James Fowler.
Missing: Private Ludwig Damp.

COMPANY D.
Killed: Corporal Dennis Dugan.
Wounded: Sergeant Charles J. Curtis; Privates Frederick Hampe, George C. Kendrick, Samuel Tullar.
Missing: Private Henry Heescher.

COMPANY E.
Killed: First Lieutenant Edward Sturgis.
Wounded: Privates Moses H. Gale, Thomas Kehoe, Samuel Torrance, Thomas Waters.
Captured: Private William Volker (died September 4, 1864, in Camp Sumter, GA).
Missing: Privates William Picher, Rudolph Seeberg *[later returned]*.

COMPANY F.
Killed: Sergeant Charles Cane; Private Rudolph Alpen (died June 14, 1864).
Wounded: Captain John W. Summerhayes; Privates Carl Gesper, Albert Meyer, John Staum, Herman Zeitz.

COMPANY G.
Killed: First Sergeant William A. Johnson; Private James Horne.
Wounded: First Lieutenant James W. R. Holland; Sergeant Patrick Crowley; Corporals John Flynn, Edward Long; Privates __ Ackard *[name only appears on one casualty list and does not seem to be on the regiment's roster]*, August Huhn, Mathias H. Krook, John Little, Jeremiah Lucius, Michael Nelligan.
Captured: Privates Charles C. Lewis, Henry C. A. L. Peitz.
Missing: Private Thomas Moeller.

COMPANY H.
Killed: First Lieutenant Lansing E. Hibbard; Private Charles A. Warren.
Wounded: Sergeant John Doyle; Corporal Charles O. Newell; Privates Carl Biewald, William Haessner, William H. Homer, John T. Horan, William Wilson.

COMPANY I.
Wounded: Captain Arthur R. Curtis; Privates Frank Andrews, William O. Day, William B. Low, George B. Starbuck.
Captured: First Sergeant William P. Kelly.
Missing: Privates Samuel H. Bailey, William Hartenstein, Theodore Laidsch.

COMPANY K.
Wounded: First Sergeant Joseph H. Parker; Privates John Anderson, William Fordham, Sylvester Slow, Edward Wettberg.
Missing: Privates George Arlein (wounded), Ernst Kyd.

May 23 - 26, 1864 - Battle of North Anna:
[Since separate reports of casualties during the Overland Campaign were not made on account of the frequency of battles, the majority of the regiment's casualties in the Battle of North Anna is most likely erroneously listed under the Wilderness, Spotsylvania Court House, and Cold Harbor.]

COMPANY A.
Captured: Private Heinrich Riensberg.

COMPANY B.
Captured: Private John Veillard.

COMPANY C.
Wounded: Private Henry Connor.

COMPANY D.
Killed: Private August Steinhofer (died May 30, 1864).

COMPANY G.
Captured: Private Henry P. Louis.

COMPANY H.
Captured: Private Otto Heldt.

COMPANY K.
Captured: Private John W. Baxter.

May 28 - 30, 1864 - Battle of Totopotomy Creek:
[Since separate reports of casualties during the Overland Campaign were not made on account of the frequency of battles, the majority of the regiment's casualties in the Battle of Totopotomy Creek is most likely erroneously listed under the Wilderness, Spotsylvania Court House, and Cold Harbor.]

COMPANY B.
Missing: Private Hugh McDonald.

COMPANY E.
Wounded: Private John Smith

May 31 - June 12, 1864 – Battle of Cold Harbor:
[Since separate reports of casualties during the Overland Campaign were not made on account of the frequency of battles, some of the regiment's casualties in the Battle of Cold Harbor are likely erroneously listed under the Wilderness and Spotsylvania Court House.]

COMPANY A.
Killed: Privates Nehemiah F. Ball, Julian W. Swift (died November 15, 1864).
Wounded: Privates Benjamin B. Besse, William Gartland, Patrick O'Connor.
Captured: Drummers William Baker, Charles H. Hall; Private Charles Milton (died September 22, 1864, in Camp Sumter, GA).
Missing: Private George Marshall.

COMPANY B.
Killed: Private Adolph Wolfram (died June 20, 1864).
Wounded: Privates Henry Eggers, Constantin Elsner, Edmund G. Lippert.
Captured: Private Michael Bauer (died September 17, 1864, in Camp Sumter, GA).
Missing: Privates Philip Carey *[later returned]*, Frederick Schrader *[later returned]*.

COMPANY C.
Killed: Private Michael Wolf.
Captured: Private Albert Hausch (died November 11, 1864, in Salisbury, NC).

COMPANY D.
Killed: Privates John Dagg, Charles Monroe.
Wounded: Privates John Devine, Frederick Dreckmann.
Captured: Private John Stamp (died September 27, 1864, in Camp Sumter, GA).

COMPANY E.
Captured: Privates John H. F. Schmitz, Joseph Chapman.

COMPANY F.
Wounded: Private Martin Mulroy.

COMPANY G.
Killed: Private Ezra D. Chase.
Wounded: Private Michael Hassett.
Missing: Privates John Brunt, James Franklin.

COMPANY I.
Killed: Private Albert C. Bean.

COMPANY K.
Killed: Private James Smith.
Wounded: Private Michael F. Hogan.
Missing: Private Eugene Albanis *[later returned]*.

June 15 - 24, 1864 – Battles around Petersburg:

COMPANY A.
Killed: Private Oliver S. Bates (died August 18, 1864).
Wounded: First Sergeant George E. Tower; Privates Edward E. Dresser, Albert F. Hathaway.
Captured: Private John Liford (wounded).

COMPANY B.
Wounded: Privates Thomas Molter, Henry Beddigs.

COMPANY C.
Killed: Private Nathan Freidenburg.
Wounded: Privates George Fritsch, Joseph Heim.
Captured: Private Patrick Huitt.

COMPANY D.
Wounded: Sergeant Charles J. Curtis; Corporal Peter Dudley; Privates Robert Hart, Charles Matthews.

COMPANY E.
Wounded: Sergeant Cornelius Kallaher; Privates Elisha M. Lord, Samuel Torrance.

COMPANY F.
Killed: Sergeant John Powers; Privates William Albert, John Cronin, William E. Talbirt.
Wounded: Sergeant Dennis Shea; Privates Charles McCarthy, Levi Lock.

COMPANY G.
Killed: Private Thomas McFaul.
Wounded: Privates John Lauriche, William Mitchell.
Captured: Private Heinrich Grotte (died September 13, 1864, in Camp Sumter, GA).

COMPANY H.
Wounded: Privates Robert McKenney, Louis Rose, Timothy Wiley.

COMPANY I.
Killed: Private Isaiah A. Burgess.
Wounded: Private William Dean.

COMPANY K.
Killed: Sergeant John T. Burke; Private Henry Bowman.
Wounded: Sergeant Orrin Day.

July 20, 1864 – Near Petersburg:

COMPANY I.
Captured: Private John Junghantz.

July 21, 1864 – Near Petersburg:

COMPANY C.
Captured: Private Heinrich Strassig.

July 27 - 29, 1864 – First Battle of Deep Bottom:
[The following list was compiled from the regimental roster contained in Volume II of "Massachusetts Soldiers, Sailors, and Marines in the Civil War" (1931).]

COMPANY D.
Captured: First Lieutenant Arthur G. Sedgwick; Privates Charles H. Denton, Samuel McFarland, Ashbury M. Woods, Franz Wurbs.

COMPANY F.
Captured: Privates Horace P. Hammond, William Langhinrichs (died October 26, 1864, at Salisbury, NC).

COMPANY G.
Captured: Privates Daniel Guilfoyle (died December 15, 1864, at Salisbury, NC), Julius Voight.

COMPANY K.
Captured: Corporal Charles McFarland; Privates Charles Greenwood, James E. Sheppard.

August 14 - 20, 1864 - Second Battle of Deep Bottom:
[The following list was compiled from the regimental roster contained in Volume II of "Massachusetts Soldiers, Sailors, and Marines in the Civil War" (1931).]

FIELD AND STAFF.
Killed: Major Henry L. Patten (died September 10, 1864).
Wounded: Colonel George N. Macy.

COMPANY A.
Killed: Sergeant Leander Hanscom.
Wounded: Private James Smith.
Captured: Private Manton A. Wood.

COMPANY B.
Wounded: Privates George Gramberg, Frederick W. Hauer.
Captured: Private Frederick Wirth.

COMPANY C.
Killed: Private Ludwig Friedrichsen.
Wounded: Privates George Gatzens, Dominick McTague.

COMPANY D.
Wounded: Private Charles DeCourcey.

COMPANY F.
Captured: Private Dennis O'Connor.

COMPANY G.
Wounded: Private James Lynch.
Captured: Privates Herman F. Fathaurn, August Frieman, Max Kuhfus (wounded).

COMPANY H.
Wounded: Privates August Schubert, Edward Witte.

COMPANY I.
Killed: Private Thomas Higgins (died October 6, 1864).
Wounded: Corporal William E. Manning; Privates August Beckmann, Conrad Beckmann, Charles Brualt.

COMPANY K.
Wounded: Privates Thomas H. Carver, John Collins, Thomas Depau, Ira M. Richardson, Patrick Ryan.

August 25, 1864 – Second Battle of Ream's Station:
[The following list was compiled from the regimental roster contained in Volume II of "Massachusetts Soldiers, Sailors, and Marines in the Civil War" (1931).]

FIELD AND STAFF.
Captured: Lieutenant Colonel Arthur R. Curtis.

COMPANY A.
Captured: Sergeant Joshua Besse; Privates Abraham Brown, James A. Harlow, Levi Lamson, Jr., August Marzaht, James R. Russell (died December 18, 1864, in Salisbury, NC), Lyman P. Tilton.

COMPANY B.
Captured: First Lieutenant Charles Rost; Sergeant Louis Bitzer; Corporals Ferdinand Fleig (died January 29, 1865, in Salisbury, NC), Michael Kessler; Privates Henry F. Bartlett, William Bauer, Henry Beddings, Julius Boehme, John Brown, John Flood (died October 29, 1864, in Salisbury, NC), Louis Heidelberg, Joseph Herz, Frederick W. Hubner (died November 9, 1864, in Salisbury, NC), Carl Lohrmann, Alexander McLean (died December, 1864, in Salisbury, NC), Frank Moekle, Edward Natter (died January 8, 1865, in Florence, SC), John Reichman, Fritz Rohrbech (died January 16, 1865, in Salisbury, NC), Herman Warnecke, Henry Weber, Herman Wirth, Julius Wolf (died February 28, 1865, in Salisbury, NC), Adolph Wortmann.

COMPANY C.
Captured: Orderly Sergeant Frederick Will; Privates Alois Bohmer, Robert Derner, Charles Freeman, William Gibbons, William Hammell, David Holland, Frederick Kuhn (died February 11, 1865, in Salisbury, NC), Henry Schmidt, John Summers.

COMPANY D.
Captured: Privates William Irving, John Jost, Charles Matthews, Gustavus Schoenherr, Levi Whitcomb *[uncertain but probable]*.

COMPANY E.
Captured: Sergeants Edward Cudworth, Cornelius Kallaher; Privates Elbridge Acker, Karl A. J. Albers, James V. Barrett (died February 3, 1865, in Salisbury, NC), Charles Clark (died December 22, 1864, in Salisbury, NC), George Fish, Orrin A. French (died January 2, 1865, in Salisbury, NC), Henry Rakke, Henry Thorn, Martin Welch.

COMPANY F.
Captured: Captain James H. Spencer; First Lieutenant Dennis Shea; Sergeant Bernard McGuire; Privates Adam Bolmer, Michael Desmond (died December 12, 1864, in Salisbury, NC), Heinrich Hagedon, Michael Hennesey (died February 22, 1865, in Salisbury, NC), Christian Riess, Daniel Shanahan.

COMPANY G.
Captured: Captain Henry T. Dudley; First Lieutenant George O. Wilder; Corporals John Chapman, Charles H. Hunt, Charles McCarty; Privates John Goodman, Louis Heller (died September 23, 1864, in Richmond, VA), John Kelly, Edward Long, Robert Mallory, Jeremiah Sullivan, Thomas P. W. Welch.

COMPANY H.
Killed: Private Simon Seeberg (died September 18, 1864)
Captured: Sergeant Major George W. Leach; Sergeant Edward Wilton (died in Salisbury, NC); Corporals James Barrows, Charles O. Newell; Drummer John Stevens (died in Florence, SC); Privates Carl Bertha, Francis Devine, Samuel H. Gordon, Heinrich Helmbrecht, John W. Lyons (wounded), Charles McAlevey, Lewis Martzotte, Louis Mattner (died September 10, 1864, in Camp Sumter, GA), John Neary, Michael Nelligan, Thomas Oliver (died February 14, 1865, in Salisbury NC).

COMPANY I.
Captured: First Lieutenant Benjamin B. Pease; First Sergeant Henry Borden; Sergeant John F. Barnard; Corporals Samuel C. Crocker (died June 5, 1865, in Salisbury, NC), Edward W. Randall (died March 2, 1865, in Richmond, VA), Peter Williams (died December 25, 1864, in Salisbury, NC); Privates Hugo Bochet, Henry Bolminster, Anton Decker, Henry A. Fuller (died June 5, 1865, in Salisbury, NC), Martin Grady, Christopher McRae, John O'Connor, August Ries, Arthur M. Rivers (died June 5, 1865, in Salisbury, NC).

COMPANY K.
Captured: First Sergeant Joseph H. Parker; Corporal George A. Hastings (died January 15, 1865, in Salisbury, NC); Privates David Fitzgerald (died December 29, 1864, in Salisbury, NC), Edward Fitzgerald, Philip Hunt, Henry Lysholm, Louis Rauch, Josiah Stone, Robert Swain.

Unknown date in September, 1864 – Near Petersburg:

COMPANY K.
Wounded: Private Joseph N. Sampson.

October 18, 1864 – Near Petersburg:

COMPANY C.
Killed: Private Lyman R. Blood.

October 27 – 28, 1864 – Battle of the Boydton Plank Road:
[The following list was compiled from the regimental roster contained in Volume II of "Massachusetts Soldiers, Sailors, and Marines in the Civil War" (1931).]

COMPANY A.
Killed: Sergeant Peter Newkirk (died October 29, 1864).

COMPANY B.
Captured: Drummer John Tuttle; Private George Metzger.

COMPANY D.
Wounded: Private Thomas A. Dow.

COMPANY F.
Wounded: Privates Edwin H. Eames, Patrick McManus.

COMPANY G.
Wounded: Corporal George A. Hawley; Private Joseph Mason.
Captured: Private William Lawler.

COMPANY I.
Captured: Private William Mayo.

COMPANY K.
Captured: Private Patrick Ryan.

November 5, 1864 - Near Petersburg:

COMPANY B.
Wounded: Private August Andres.

November 9, 1864 - Near Petersburg:

COMPANY C.
Wounded: Private Michael Fuhrman.

November 11, 1864 - Near Petersburg:

COMPANY E.
Killed: Private Charles Ackerman.

November 15, 1864 - Near Petersburg:

COMPANY E.
Wounded: Musician Elias B. Ellis.

COMPANY I.
Killed: Private Thomas Doody (died December 1, 1864).

February 5 - 7, 1865 - Battle of Hatcher's Run:
[The following list was compiled from the regimental roster contained in Volume II of "Massachusetts Soldiers, Sailors, and Marines in the Civil War" (1931).]

COMPANY A.
Captured: Private William H. Raymond.

COMPANY B.
Captured: Private August Baumann.

COMPANY D.
Captured: Privates Joseph Fitzgerald, Nathan P. Kendrick.

COMPANY E.
Wounded: Private Carl Jordan.
Captured: Privates Wallace W. Crawford, Henry R. Dawson (wounded).

COMPANY G.
Wounded: Private Oliver W. Newton.
Captured: Private Daniel Kenney.

COMPANY I.
Wounded: Private Henry Bolminster.

COMPANY K.
Killed: Private Harrison W. Stone.
Wounded: Corporal Edson C. Bemis, David A. Smith.